Peacekeeping and the International System

This volume explores the development of international peacekeeping as a tool of international relations from the 1920s to the first decade of the twenty-first century. It is concerned with the use of multinational forces to regulate the structure of the international system and to contain local conflicts. The key historical phases identified and explored are:

- the 'plebiscite peacekeeping' of the 1920s, which contributed to setting 'acceptable' boundaries in the new European system;
- the evolution of peacekeeping as a more modest – but more practical – alternative to the ambitious plans for collective security proposed in the UN Charter;
- the subsequent use of peacekeeping by the United Nations in the 1950s and 1960s to ease the process of decolonization and seal off its associated tensions from the cold war;
- the great surge of peacekeeping activity – by the UN and other agencies – after the cold war;
- the possible future trajectories of peacekeeping in the twenty-first century.

Peacekeeping and the International System emphasizes the essential continuity of purpose in the peacekeeping narrative and provides concise but pertinent accounts of the history of the conflicts that have given rise to peacekeeping.

Norrie MacQueen is senior lecturer in International Relations in the Department of Politics at the University of Dundee. His previous publications include: *The Decolonization of Portuguese Africa* (1997); *The United Nations since 1945: Peacekeeping and the Cold War* (1999); and *United Nations Peacekeeping in Africa since 1960* (2002).

Peacekeeping and the International System

Norrie MacQueen

Routledge
Taylor & Francis Group
LONDON AND NEW YORK

First published 2006
by Routledge
2 Park Square, Milton Park, Abingdon, Oxon OX14 4RN

Simultaneously published in the USA and Canada
by Routledge
711 Third Ave, New York, NY 10017

Routledge is an imprint of the Taylor & Francis Group, an informa business

Typeset in Baskerville by
Florence Production Ltd, Stoodleigh, Devon

British Library Cataloguing in Publication Data
A catalogue record for this book is available from the British Library

Library of Congress Cataloging in Publication Data
A catalog record for this book has been requested

ISBN10: 0–415–35354–8 (pbk)
ISBN10: 0–415–35353–X (hbk)

ISBN13: 978–0–415–35354–0 (pbk)
ISBN13: 978–0–415–35353–3 (hbk)

For Betsy and Catriona – as always

Contents

Preface

This book is about peacekeeping as an instrument of relations between states. It is concerned with the role of multilateral military intervention in managing conflict both between and within states. It is therefore a book about international politics rather than the operational tactics, administration, psychology or sociology of peacekeeping, important though these aspects of the activity undoubtedly are. At its most basic, the underlying argument that we will pursue here is that peacekeeping is a tool of international relations with a longer history and continuity of political purpose than has usually been acknowledged in the post-cold war era.

The use of peacekeeping missions by the institutions of the international system can be traced back at least eight decades, during which missions have served the same basic function. In other words, peacekeeping in Liberia or in Georgia in the first half of the twenty-first century serves essentially the same purpose for the international system as peacekeeping on Germany's borders did in the first half of the twentieth century. Immediate aims may differ and military tactics assuredly will be different, but the essential purposes remain the same. In both periods peacekeeping was a self-interested response by the international system designed to contain conflicts that might otherwise threaten the fabric of the system as a whole. In a sense, then, the purpose of the book is to 'reclaim' peacekeeping's proper history after a period in which it has tended to be seen largely as an artefact of the post-cold war era.

The major part of the book is concerned with peacekeeping undertaken by the United Nations (UN) since the end of the Second World War. This is simply a reflection of the UN's dominance of multilateral intervention over the past six decades rather than any sort of statement about what 'real' peacekeeping is or is not. This should, I hope, be clear from the attention given to peacekeeping operations mounted before the United Nations was ever thought about, and to non-UN operations that have been fielded subsequently. Peacekeeping as presented in the book is not, therefore, synonymous with the UN, but it would be wrong to suggest that since its creation the UN has not been the dominant peacekeeper. There have been real obstacles to effective peacekeeping by agencies other than the UN. These difficulties, and the possibilities of overcoming them with and without an associated role for the UN, are discussed in some detail in the later chapters of the book.

One of the main objectives of the book is to present as comprehensive an account as possible of peacekeeping in the twentieth century and beyond. To this end an effort has been made to include some analysis of every mission of any significance. The risk in this approach is that the narrative becomes laboured and mechanical. While it is for others to judge if this danger has been avoided or not, it has not been a cause of any great concern during the writing of the book. It has not been difficult to assign a meaningful place in the book's interpretation of peacekeeping to even some of the smallest and previously overlooked operations.

There have, though, been some difficult judgements required over the relative prominence given to different undertakings. As a general principle the historical significance of operations has been given precedence over their size and duration. There is no doubt, for example, that special attention should be paid to the UN operation in the Congo in the early 1960s. It marked a key stage in the development of peacekeeping and it was also unprecedented at the time in its scale and its demand for resources. But the judgement is more difficult when it comes to the prominence given to, say, the observation group in Lebanon in 1958, which was relatively small and short-lived in comparison to any one of the much larger and longer operations mounted by the UN in Angola in the 1990s. Judgement here, however, comes down on the side of the Lebanon mission because, limited in scale though it was, it provided an illustration of much that was significant in the role of peacekeeping at a critical juncture in the cold war.

Although the book is concerned with exploring the 'long narrative' of peacekeeping, its structure is only partly chronological. Chapters 2 to 6 do track the peacekeeping story stage by stage from the end of the First World War to the end of the cold war. The first chapter, though, is primarily a discussion of peacekeeping as a concept and of its place in international politics. Chapters 7 to 10 then deal with peacekeeping since the end of the cold war on the basis of geographical location and type of mission. This provides a more satisfactory basis for understanding the particularly intense phase of peacekeeping during the 1990s than a straightforwardly chronological one. Chronology reasserts itself in the final chapter, which views, from the historical platform already constructed, the prospects for peacekeeping in the new century.

Throughout the book I have made a deliberate effort to provide as extensive as possible an account of the historical origins and underlying dynamics of conflicts that have led to peacekeeping operations. Again, this has sometimes been a matter for difficult judgements. Oversimplified history lessons can be both useless in themselves and a distraction from the primary focus of the book. But it is just not possible to understand either the political conditions in which a particular operation is undertaken or its significance to the longer narrative of peacekeeping in the international system without a thorough awareness of the local setting. More often than not it is this, rather than anything done or left undone by the peacekeepers themselves, that determines the success or failure of a peacekeeping operation. To an extent, therefore, the book provides a general history of regional conflict as well as an account of the peacekeeping response to it. This historical and geographical narrative sweep raises questions about the proper place of references and citations. Endnotes as such have been kept to an absolute minimum. They are used only to identify the sources of direct quotations and to indicate key primary documents. However, an extensive list of suggested further reading is provided in the bibliography at the end of the book.

The interpretation of peacekeeping presented here is essentially a historical one. It is not concerned primarily with the place of peacekeeping in contemporary international relations theory and therefore does not engage closely with one side or other of these debates. Nevertheless, the persistent focus of the book is on peacekeeping as an activity undertaken in a 'system of states' composed of competing centres of power in pursuit of their own interests. Inevitably, this approach points to a particular theoretical perspective. In giving such prominence to 'power' and 'state-centricity', and by asserting the existence of an international system with a self-generated sense of purpose, the book approaches a 'realist', or more precisely, a 'neo-realist' view of international relations. From a personal perspective I do not necessarily find this a comfortable stand to adopt. It is certainly not one that represents my own view of an ideal international community. But while the neo-realist perspective might be far distant from my *prescription* for international relations, it is, unavoidably, a reasonable *description* of world politics over the past century.

For all this, the actual contribution of the peacekeeping 'project' to the greater humanitarian good, despite manifold failures and inadequacies, has in all but a few cases been a positive one. In providing a means of sustaining the international state system it has mitigated the human impact of colliding national interests and disintegrating structures of governance. While it may have done little to bring change to the basic organization of international relations – its role has instead been to preserve this – peacekeeping has, nevertheless, in many places and over a considerable period reduced the worst effects of the interplay of power in international relations for the most vulnerable local populations. In short, the good that peacekeeping has done has been very far from negligible, whatever the underlying political forces that have driven it.

Norrie MacQueen
Perth, Scotland
September 2005

Abbreviations and acronyms

AMIB	African Mission in Burundi
AMIS	African Mission in Sudan
ANC	Congolese National Army (Armée Nationale Congolese) or African National Congress (South Africa)
ASEAN	Association of Southeast Asian Nations
AU	African Union
CAR	Central African Republic
CIS	Commonwealth of Independent States (former Soviet Union)
CNN	Cable News Network
CSCE	Conference on Security and Cooperation in Europe
DDR	demobilization; disarmament; reintegration
DITF	Darfur Integrated Taskforce
DRC	Democratic Republic of Congo
DTA	Democratic Turnhalle Alliance (Namibia)
ECOMOG	Economic Community of West African States Military Observation Group
ECOWAS	Economic Community of West African States
EO	Executive Outcomes
EOKA	National Organization of Cypriot Struggle
ERRF	European Rapid Reaction Force
FMLN	Farabundo Martí National Liberation Front (Frente Farabundo Martí para la Liberación Nacional) (El Salvador)
Frelimo	Front for the Liberation of Mozambique (Frente para a Libertação de Moçambique)
Fretilin	Revolutionary Front for an Independent East Timor (Frente Revolucionária de Timor-Leste Independente)
FYROM	Former Yugoslav Republic of Macedonia
GPA	General Peace Agreement (Mozambique)
IAPF	Inter-American Peacekeeping Force (Dominican Republic)
ICJ	International Court of Justice

IFOR	Implementation Force (Bosnia)
INTERFET	International Force in East Timor
ISAF	International Security Assistance Force (Afghanistan)
JNA	Yugoslavian National Army
KLA	Kosovo Liberation Army
MFO	Multinational Force and Observers (Sinai)
MINUGUA	United Nations Verification Mission in Guatemala (Misión de las Naciones Unidas en Guatemala)
MINURCA	United Nations Mission in the Central African Republic (Mission des Nations Unies en République Centrafricaine)
MINURSO	United Nations Mission for the Referendum in Western Sahara (Mission des Nations Unies pour l'Organisation d'un Référendum au Sahara Occidental)
MISAB	Inter-African Mission for the Supervision of the Bangui Accords (Mission Interafricaine de Surveillance des Accords de Bangui)
MNF (I-II)	Multinational Force (Lebanon)
MONUA	United Nations Observer Mission in Angola (Missão de Observação das Nações Unidas em Angola)
MONUC	United Nations Organization Mission to the Congo (Mission de l'Organisation des Nations Unies en République Démocratique du Congo)
MPLA	Popular Movement for the Liberation of Angola (Movimento Popular de Libertação de Angola)
MSC	Military Staff Committee (UN Charter)
NATO	North Atlantic Treaty Organisation
NFZ	No-Fly Zone (Bosnia)
OAU	Organization of African Unity
ONUB	United Nations Operation in Burundi (Opération des Nations Unies au Burundi)
ONUC	United Nations Operation in Congo (Opération des Nations Unies au Congo)
ONUCA	United Nations Observer Group in Central America (Observadores de las Naciones Unidas en Centroamerica)
ONUMOZ	United Nations Operation in Mozambique (Operação das Nações Unidas em Moçambique)
ONUSAL	United Nations Observer Mission in El Salvador (Observadores de las Naciones Unidas en El Salvador)
OSCE	Organization for Security and Cooperation in Europe
PDD25	(US) Presidential Decision Directive No.25
PLO	Palestine Liberation Organization

Polisario	Popular Front for the Liberation of Saguia el Hamra and Rio de Oro (Frente Popular para a Liberación de Saguia el-Hamra y Río de Oro) (Western Sahara)
Renamo	Mozambican National Resistance Movement (Resistência Nacional Moçambicana)
RPF	Rwandan Patriotic Front
RUF	Revolutionary United Front (Sierra Leone)
SADC	Southern African Development Community
SADF	South African Defence Forces
SADR	Saharan Arab Democratic Republic (Western Sahara)
SLA	Sierra Leone Army
SNA	Somali National Alliance
SNC	Supreme National Council (Cambodia)
SWAPO	South West African People's Organization (Namibia)
TSZ	Temporary Security Zone (Ethiopia–Eritrea)
UAR	United Arab Republic (Egypt and Syria)
UN	United Nations
UNAMET	United Nations Mission in East Timor
UNAMIC	United Nations Advance Mission in Cambodia
UNAMIR	United Nations Assistance Mission for Rwanda
UNAMSIL	United Nations Mission in Sierra Leone
UNASOG	United Nations Aouzou Strip Observer Group (Chad)
UNAVEM (I–III)	United Nations Angola Verification Mission
UNCIP	United Nations Commission for India and Pakistan
UNCRO	United Nations Confidence Creation Operation (Croatia)
UNDOF	United Nations Disengagement Observer Force (Golan Heights)
UNEF (I-II)	United Nations Emergency Force (Suez-Sinai)
UNFICYP	United Nations Force in Cyprus
UNGOMAP	United Nations Good Offices Mission in Afghanistan and Pakistan
UNIFIL	United Nations Interim Force in Lebanon
UNIIMOG	United Nations Iran–Iraq Military Observer Group
UNIKOM	United Nations Iraq–Kuwait Observation Mission
UNIPOM	United Nations India–Pakistan Observation Mission
UNITA	National Union for the Total Independence of Angola (União Nacional para a Independência Total de Angola)
UNITAF	Unified Task Force (Somalia)
UNMEE	United Nations Mission in Ethiopia and Eritrea
UNMIBH	United Nations Mission in Bosnia and Herzegovina
UNMIH	United Nations Mission in Haiti
UNMIK	United Nations Interim Administration Mission in Kosovo
UNMIL	United Nations Mission in Liberia

UNMIS	United Nations Mission in Sudan
UNMISET	United Nations Mission of Support in East Timor
UNMOGIP	United Nations Military Observer Group in India and Pakistan
UNMOP	United Nations Mission of Observers in Prevlaka (Croatia)
UNMOT	United Nations Mission of Observers in Tajikistan
UNOCI	United Nations Operation in Côte d'Ivoire
UNOGIL	United Nations Observation Group in Lebanon
UNOMIG	United Nations Observer Mission in Georgia
UNOMIL	United Nations Observer Mission in Liberia
UNOMSIL	United Nations Observer Mission in Sierra Leone
UNOMUR	United Nations Observer Mission Uganda–Rwanda
UNOSOM (I-II)	United Nations Operation in Somalia
UNPA	United Nations Protected Area (Croatia)
UNPREDEP	United Nations Preventive Deployment Force (Macedonia)
UNPROFOR	United Nations Protection Force (former Yugoslavia)
UNSF	United Nations Security Force (West New Guinea)
UNSMIH	United Nations Support Mission in Haiti
UNTAC	United Nations Transitional Authority in Cambodia
UNTAES	United Nations Transitional Authority in Eastern Slavonia, Baranja and Western Sirmium (Croatia)
UNTAET	United Nations Transitional Administration in East Timor
UNTAG	United Nations Transition Assistance Group (Namibia)
UNTEA	United Nations Temporary Executive Authority (West New Guinea)
UNTSO	United Nations Truce Supervision Organization (Middle East)
UNYOM	United Nations Yemen Observation Mission

1 The dimensions of international peacekeeping

Few processes in contemporary international relations have been as imperfectly defined as that of 'peacekeeping'. This is not primarily the result of intellectual laziness on the part of practitioners and commentators. Virtually everyone has a personal sense of what peacekeeping is – but it is usually perceived as an activity with extremely flexible boundaries. Defining peacekeeping is complicated still further by the frequent use of the term for political purposes. The word peacekeeping has been employed to describe a huge range of military and quasi-military activities, often in an attempt to legitimize undertakings with less than laudable motivations using less than pacific methods. As one author has put it:

> scholars try to use definitions and categories with precision, states are under no such professional obligation . . . The term 'peacekeeping' has a very favourable resonance, so that states are glad to use it in their statements and rhetoric in circumstances where, at least superficially, it will look appropriate. It is a way of trying to engender positive feelings, and hence support, for their policies.[1]

Russia's military action in Chechnya, for example, has been described as peacekeeping by those favouring Moscow's interests, though many others would see it simply as an attempt, using extreme force, to prevent the secession of part of the national territory. The term has been used even more recently to describe the activities of the American-led coalition in Iraq since 2003. Here, too, its use has been fiercely contested by those with fundamentally different views on the motives and activities of the occupying forces. In short, using the description peacekeeping as a way of making respectable any military action, however well or ill-intentioned, has become a feature of international propaganda. More scholarly, less politically motivated observers, of course, have tried to impose narrow limits on what peacekeeping is and what it is not. But the problem with this approach is that these various definitions rarely coincide with each other and often just further confuse the picture.

Interrogating 'peacekeeping': characteristics and definitions

One approach towards a working definition of what peacekeeping is – and what it is not – is to subject the term to a process of interrogation. There are a number of key questions around the activity that tend to be answered in different ways depending on different points of political perspective and interest:

- Must peacekeeping be a collective activity – or could one state undertake a 'peacekeeping operation'?
- Must peacekeeping be undertaken by an established international organization – or can it be an informal activity among any group of participants?
- Must it be 'international' in the sense of involving only conflicts between sovereign states – or can it be an internal, 'intra-state' activity?
- Can peacekeeping be 'imposed' on a situation – or must it always be embraced by all parties to a conflict?
- Can it involve the use of force other than in self-defence or the immediate defence of non-combatants? In other words, can peacekeeping embrace the enforcement of outcomes?

By exploring some of these questions we can perhaps move towards a fuller understanding of the difficulties of definition – if not a definition as such.

Can one state acting alone – or in a dominating position of leadership – be a genuine peacekeeper?

There have been a number of military interventions carried out either by a single state or by a small group of states in which one participant has dominated the coalition. This is a question that has relevance to the situations of Russia in Chechnya and the Americans in Iraq that we have just touched on. But it is perhaps better put in relation to conditions that are less obviously ones of open warfare or police actions within the national territory. Does France's frequent intervention in crises in its former colonies in Africa constitute peacekeeping? Here, the issue of motive becomes crucial. If France's concern is simply to stabilize dangerous situations to prevent their escalation – if it is driven by essentially humanitarian motives – then most observers would concede that it is involved in something that could be described as peacekeeping. If, however, France is merely pursuing its national interests and supporting governments friendly to it against challenges that it (France) regards as threatening, then the term peacekeeping is clearly inappropriate. In Chad in the 1980s and in the Central African Republic (CAR) in the 1990s, for example, the French intervened, at least initially, to support regimes it perceived as pro-French. Later, in Côte d'Ivoire, though, the French military intervention was regarded with suspicion and at times with outright hostility by the regime in power. It was not clear even here, however, whether Paris was prepared to confront the Ivorian government in the interest of keeping the peace or in support of an opposition movement that it regarded as more friendly to its own policies in the region. Similar questions about motives surrounded France's intervention in Rwanda in the end of the genocide there in 1994. Although the action was formally welcomed and legitimized by the United Nations Security Council, France's so-called 'Operation Turquoise' was regarded with deep suspicion by the Tutsi-dominated rebel movement, which was poised to oust the regime of the Hutu *génocidaires* in Rwanda. In the view of the mainly Tutsi Rwanda Patriotic Front, France was merely acting to protect its long-standing clients in the defeated Hutu leadership – a leadership that had orchestrated the genocide and that was now in headlong retreat.

More problematic, perhaps, was the Australian intervention in East Timor in 1999. This was also endorsed by the Security Council (and the operation was later replaced by a fully 'UN' one). The Australian force was deployed to end a systematic assault on one section of the territory's population by another. Pro-Indonesian militias, plainly supported by the Indonesian military in the territory, were seeking to thwart by violence the clearly expressed aspirations of the majority for independence. Here, initially at any rate, there was very little scepticism of Australian motives. Australia was, after all, a major regional power on the Asia-Pacific interface and under the government then in power had shown itself keen to take an activist role in the security of the region. But here, too, as the extent of Australia's economic interests and aspirations around the marine resources between Timor and its own northern maritime border gradually became clear, doubts were expressed about Canberra's initial motives (not least by the government of the now independent East Timor itself).

A similar set of considerations might also apply to Britain in Northern Ireland from the late 1960s. Was the British army in Ulster a peacekeeping force? For many observers in Britain and beyond the motives and methods were essentially those of peacekeeping. In this view the British army was 'interposed' between two factions in violent confrontation with each other. But the prevailing view in both of the communities in conflict in Ulster was that the British presence was not a peacekeeping one. Each, however, had a very different conception of what it actually was. On the unionist side the British army was seen as acting 'in aid of the civil power' by ensuring the British state's legitimate capacity to maintain law and order within its own territory. On the republican side the British presence was seen quite differently. It was, from this perspective, essentially an occupation force deployed by a foreign power. While peacekeeping dominated by a single state might not therefore be wholly a contradiction in terms, questions of underlying motive and the national interest of the intervening power will usually be raised by one party or another to the conflict in which the intervention is taking place.

Must peacekeeping be an institutional activity?

It is, therefore, difficult to conceive of peacekeeping as a unilateral activity. Yet does multilateralism – intervention by more than one actor – by necessity have to involve an established international organization? In other words, can groups of states acting together in an ad hoc relationship constitute a peacekeeping force? Certainly, various peacekeeping ventures have been formed by 'coalitions of the willing', without formal reference to existing international institutions. But the various examples of these suggest that this is an activity that lacks diplomatic self-confidence and that tends to be regarded – not least by those involved – as a kind of second best peacekeeping effort.

Non-institutionally based peacekeeping often comes about after the failure of attempts to establish forces within an organizational framework. For example, following the Camp David agreement between Egypt and Israel in 1978, a peacekeeping presence was required to oversee the disengagement of the two countries' forces in the Sinai desert. Initially, the western states – led by the United States, which had sponsored the peace process – had hoped to extend the mandate of the existing United Nations force in the region – the second United Nations Emergency Force – which had been deployed since the 1973 war. The Soviet Union, however, anxious to remain on good terms with the Arab states that had denounced Egypt's peace deal with the Israeli enemy, rejected this. With no possibility of Security Council approval, therefore, the west had to act alone. It did so by creating the Multinational Force and Observers (MFO), which was composed of units from different western states brought together outside any formal institutional structure. Very similar circumstances led to the creation of multinational forces in Lebanon in the early 1980s when Security Council approval for the extension of the mandate of the UN Interim Force in Lebanon could not be secured. In all of these cases the resulting international missions were widely seen as peacekeeping forces, despite their lack of 'validation' by an established international organization.

In other situations groups of states have overstated the role of institutions in their military interventions in their attempts to bestow international respectability on them. In 1998, for example, the various recognized neighbours of the Democratic Republic of Congo (DRC) who had intervened to prop up the beleaguered regime of President Laurent Kabila, claimed to be acting as a Southern African Development Community (SADC) operation. Although the states intervening in the conflict were all members of the SADC, the Community had given them no mandate to send forces and it was questionable whether its constitution would have permitted it to do so. In a similar situation around the same time further north and west in Africa, Senegal and Guinea-Conakry tried after the event to have their intervention in the civil conflict in their neighbour Guinea-Bissau legitimized as an action by the Economic Community of West African States (ECOWAS).

As with the unilateral interventions we discussed previously, collective but non-institutional ones might not necessarily differ in intentions and operational objectives from formal organizational ones. But motives will always be more closely examined in these circumstances, and the general acceptance of the ventures as genuine peacekeeping will be harder to achieve.

Can peacekeeping only take place in conflicts between states?

Another key question about the nature of 'true' peacekeeping – one of the most important in any attempt to define it as a political activity – relates to the terms of the conflicts it engages with. In its first manifestations in the United Nations, and indeed earlier, in the inter-war years, peacekeeping was strictly an *inter-state* activity. It had to do with the management of stressed or fractured relations between sovereign states in the international system. The United Nations Emergency Force sent to Suez in 1956 (which is often misleadingly described as the first peacekeeping operation) was interposed between Egypt and the states that had attacked it (Britain, France and Israel) following its nationalization of the Suez Canal. After Suez the essential principles of peacekeeping employed there were seen to apply as well to previous UN undertakings that had not, at the time they were established, been given the name peacekeeping. The military observer missions set up to oversee ceasefires in Palestine between Israel and its Arab neighbours, and then in Kashmir between India and Pakistan, were now recognized as peacekeeping operations too. These ventures were concerned with the management of international relations in a very direct way. So, too, as we have suggested, were the various 'plebiscite operations' undertaken by the post-war allies and by the League of Nations in the 1920s and 1930s, when the finer points of the new post-war map of Europe were being settled.

But the next major peacekeeping operation after Suez, that in the Congo between 1960 and 1964, presented a much more complex picture in terms of its international purposes. And it was a picture that would now become more typical of the peacekeeping experience than the relative simplicities of the 1920s to the 1950s. Although the UN's role in the Congo appeared at the beginning to be concerned with a conflict between two sovereign state members of the international system (the former colonial power, Belgium, and the newly independent Republic of Congo) it very soon developed into an immensely complex arena of competing ethnic and regional interests that were internal to the Congo itself. Later, the UN operation in Cyprus – which began almost simultaneously with the end of the Congo intervention in 1964 – was likewise primarily a conflict of intra-state ethnicity.

By the time the peacekeeping 'project' moved beyond the cold war at the beginning of the 1990s, 'straightforward' inter-state peacekeeping had become almost a nostalgic memory. The large operation in Cambodia that began in 1992 was designed to reconstruct the Cambodian state itself. Simultaneously, operations throughout the African continent – in Angola, Mozambique, Somalia, Rwanda, Sierra Leone and Liberia, and then, completing the circle, the Congo once again – were designed primarily to engage with the problem of failing or even, in extremis, 'collapsed' states rather than with international confrontations between states. Similar problems faced UN peacekeepers in Central America and the Caribbean and, in an especially complex way, in the former Yugoslavia. Post-cold war peacekeeping, therefore, appeared to confirm that the pure model of interposition between states in conflict, which had been dominant in interventions up to the 1960s, was becoming the exception rather than the rule. Peacekeeping had become predominantly an *intra*-state rather than an *inter*-state activity.

But while a simple count of United Nations operations points to peacekeeping having become mainly concerned with internal conflicts, it would be misleading to assume that its purpose was solely the management of domestic crises. The issue was not as simple as this arithmetic might suggest. The conflicts that have given rise to peacekeeping operations have all, without exception, had a significant inter-state/international dimension as well, however intra-state/domestic they might first appear. Peacekeeping in the Congo in the early 1960s had to deal with a tangle of internal problems, but its larger purpose concerned the process of decolonization in Africa, which was building momentum at that time, and how the transformation it was bringing to the international system could be absorbed without creating serious international instabilities. Similarly, the large and varied operations in sub-Saharan Africa in the 1990s may have seemed to be directed at problems of ethnic and regional conflict within states in crisis. But in reality each had a distinct external dimension that, arguably, was the overriding motive for intervention by peacekeeping forces. The conflicts in Angola and Mozambique threatened the stability of the entire southern African region at a time of great change following the end of the cold war and the collapse of apartheid in South Africa. The bloody disintegration of the DRC in the late 1990s was, above all, a regional crisis for the whole of central Africa rather than a domestic crisis for the DRC. Similarly, the civil wars in Liberia and Sierra Leone were seen from the peacekeepers' perspective as interconnected and capable of infecting the larger west African region. Chaos in Cambodia at the end of the cold war threatened to undermine the security and burgeoning prosperity of the south-east Asian region as a whole. And, in Europe, Bosnia was as central – both geographically and politically – to the stability of the entire continent at the end of the twentieth century as it had been at the beginning when the murder of Archduke Franz Ferdinand in a Sarajevo street helped trigger the First World War. In short, whatever the apparent local bases of conflicts that have led to peacekeeping interventions, the response of the international system in undertaking these interventions has been as much about 'systemic self-preservation' as it has been about concern with violence within states.

Of course, this is not to say that genuine international altruism and humanitarian concern were not important factors in the deployment of peacekeepers. The hitherto unquestioned concept of sovereignty as the organizing principle of international relationships has undergone significant change since the cold war. This has been driven by a number of factors. First, the end of cold war rivalry has reduced the use of sovereignty as a defence against political interference by 'the other side'. Criticism of state behaviour within its own territory and concern with the domestic conflicts that this can generate could no longer be dismissed as anti-western or anti-Soviet posturing by the opposing camp. Evident abuses could be denounced without automatic claims of ulterior motives on the part of those doing the denouncing. The liberal conscience was thus liberated. Second – and simultaneously – the passage of time since the decolonization of the European empires in the global south had reduced the colonial guilt complex that had sometimes muted criticism of newly independent states and their shortcomings. The sensitivity of new states about their newly won sovereignty no longer conferred the same immunity to foreign censure. Finally, technology, in the form of instantaneous and continuous news flows, created the social and political phenomenon that has been called the 'CNN effect'. Governments in states with the diplomatic power and the military capability to intervene in foreign conflicts (which were usually also the states with widest access to this type of news delivery) came under increasing pressure from public opinion to act. This has been offered as an explanation for the American intervention in Somalia in 1992. Images of mass starvation, which could, it seemed, be ended with the application of a very little western power, set the interventionist agenda. Paradoxically, of course, it is likely that a year or two later images of the death and humiliation of western peacekeepers were responsible for the end of the intervention in Somalia and had a knock-on effect on responses to other crises. This general weakening of sovereign independence as the organizing principle of the international system brings us to another of our key questions.

Can peacekeeping be imposed on a situation – or must it be accepted by all parties to a conflict?

This question goes to the heart of contemporary international relations and the basis on which they are conducted. The increasingly conditional status of sovereign independence has led to claims that we have entered a 'post-Westphalian' phase in international relations. The Treaty of Westphalia, which came at the end of the Thirty Years War in Europe in 1648, laid down the central importance of state sovereignty in international relations. The long destructive war, which had been fought across much of continental Europe, had in part been a conflict between the old politics of feudalism and the new politics of the nation state. Westphalia asserted the victory of the latter, placing the power of the territorial state above all other actors. In doing so, it created a 'system' of states whose relations were, in principle, based on mutual respect for the sovereign equality of each. Henceforward neither religion nor ancient dynastic claims was to take precedence over the sovereign power of states. States, in other words, were the fundamental building blocks of the emerging system. As the twentieth century drew to a close this characterization of international relations came under challenge. The 'post-Westphalian' argument is based on the 'globalizing' impact of technology and economic interdependence. Large economic and cultural forces, it was argued, were gradually eroding the power of the state.

The debate is important to the discussion of peacekeeping, particularly in relation to its fundamental purposes. If we are in a post-Westphalian system, then peacekeeping, as a systemic activity, must also have entered a post-Westphalian phase. The idea that peacekeeping is developing beyond the constraints of a sovereign state-based system is an interesting one. It is connected with the debates about the economic and social processes of globalization and their impact on the state and its role in 'traditional' international politics. Those who retain a view of peacekeeping as Westphalian in its purposes can be described as 'pluralist' or 'cosmopolitan' in their perspective. In this view different states are rooted in their own national cultures. This plurality of cultures combines to make a cosmopolitan world. In this world different cultures and national viewpoints cannot be ranked according to their acceptability to outsiders. This would involve inappropriate value judgements. In terms of justification for military intervention, such judgements by the strong and dominant in the system (for example, the permanent members of the UN Security Council) would be the ones that would prevail. In that situation any multilateral military actions would better be described as imperialism rather than peacekeeping. Continued respect for sovereignty therefore guarantees global equity. Peacekeeping may not always be an activity that takes place between states, as we have seen, because internal conflicts frequently have consequences for the international system. But external intervention in these crises must nevertheless be a 'voluntary' process that the state or states involved at least acquiesced to.

However, while this might be a sound position to take on the majority of conflicts that seem to require a peacekeeping response, can it ever be a hard and fast rule? What of situations where respect for state sovereignty means remaining inactive in the face of genocide, as in Rwanda in 1994, for example, or 'ethnic cleansing' in the former Yugoslavia? Surely here the response cannot be guided by a live-and-let-live pluralism? Genocide and the violent expulsion of populations are clearly unacceptable on a universal level; they are not legitimate local customs to be respected by outsiders who may not share them but who nevertheless accept their 'validity'. In such circumstances Westphalian sovereignty must become subordinate to global values. The external response should surely be one of solidarity within a world community. That is to say, pluralist cosmopolitanism should give way to 'communitarian solidarism'. By definition, this is not a voluntary process as far as the states that are party to a particular crisis are concerned.

Can peacekeeping involve the use of force other than in self-defence?

Closely allied to the question of voluntarism in peacekeeping is that concerning the use of force by peacekeepers. The model of 'interpositionary' peacekeeping is one in which the peacekeeping force, simply by its presence, creates a kind of moral barrier to the continuation or resumption of conflict. In this way the peacekeeper creates the necessary conditions to permit the peacemaker (a quite separate animal) to begin to facilitate a long-term resolution of the conflict. Peacekeeping in this sense has nothing to do with enforcement, and any use of force by the peacekeeper should only be in self-defence or the defence of vulnerable non-combatants.

We will discuss the relationship between peacekeeping and enforcement when we explore the early development of military intervention by the United Nations. But in the meantime we should note that the issue of the use of force on one hand and that of peacekeeping as an intra-state as opposed to inter-state activity on the other are closely related, both historically and operationally. We have already noted that the first UN military units to be deployed in the 1940s and 1950s – in Palestine, Kashmir and Suez – were involved in inter-state operations. Things became more complex in this respect in the Congo in 1960 where the UN quickly became embroiled in internal conflicts. In the early inter-state undertakings, UN soldiers had no difficulty in keeping their own fingers off the trigger. They were interposed between responsive and responsible states that were unwilling to jeopardize their own international standing by fighting the UN. The confused and contested objectives of the UN in the Congo, however, often brought UN personnel into violent confrontation with local factions. Moreover, the force's frequently shifting mandate meant that it came to be tasked with the accomplishment of ends beyond the possibilities of simple interposition – ends that could often be achieved only by the use of aggressive force.

Subsequently, the extent to which peacekeeping might involve the use of force and whether a clear border can be drawn between peacekeeping and enforcement have been keenly debated by practitioners and commentators. Since the end of the cold war the trend of these debates has been towards a greater acceptance of the use of force. This has been driven in part by a number of high profile supposed failures of peacekeeping, notably in Rwanda and Bosnia. But it is also connected with the broader issue we have just discussed: the changing status of sovereignty in international relations. If a state's permission for a multilateral intervention is no longer a fundamental prerequisite for the deployment of a force, then the presence of the force is more likely to be physically contested. It will also be required to impose outcomes on uncooperative parties by force. Some formal recognition of this came early in the post-cold war period in 1992 when the then secretary-general of the UN, Boutros Boutros-Ghali, produced an influential report, *An Agenda for Peace* (for a fuller discussion of *An Agenda for Peace* see Chapter 7). In this he noted the difficulty of drawing a clear line between peacekeeping and enforcement and proposed the creation of so-called 'peace enforcement units' to be deployed in particular circumstances. Since then – and the subsequent experiences of peacekeeping on the ground, particularly in Africa – there has been less theological debate on the use of force in UN operations. A generally more permissive approach to the use of force has, however, been limited by the attitudes of the governments who contribute UN contingents. Probably rightly, they have seen any radical departure from the principle of moral rather than physical force as posing a threat to the safety of their own soldiers.

These, then, are some of the questions that must be explored in any serious attempt to determine what peacekeeping in the international system is and what it is not. The exercise has perhaps served to highlight the difficulties in reaching a concrete definition of peacekeeping rather than to provide one. All we can say with confidence is that peacekeeping need not be a multilateral activity, and need not be one carried out by an established international organization. But when it is not, the motives and intentions of those involved will always be subject to critical scrutiny, justified or not. Similarly, the agreement of the parties in a conflict is not necessarily a requirement for peacekeeping, but when it is withheld or withdrawn – in other words when there is no longer a peace to keep – then the peacekeepers themselves may be drawn in as parties to the conflict. This in itself does not necessarily mean that this type of intervention cannot be described as peacekeeping. If the operation remains broadly 'legitimate' in terms of international and/or institutional support, and if the motives are not determined by the narrow national interests of those involved, then it can still reasonably be described as peacekeeping. But in such situations peacekeeping comes dangerously close to enforcement, which, in legal and in operational terms, is a significantly different activity.

In the account of peacekeeping in the international system that follows, we will aim to add substance to this tentative description. But before we do so, we need to return to the question of the fundamental function of the activity. What is peacekeeping for? What purpose does it serve in the international system – and how far has that purpose changed since the beginning of the twentieth century and more recently since the end of the cold war?

The 'Westphalian purposes' of peacekeeping: sustaining the state system

We have already touched on the current debate about the nature of peacekeeping in relation to the Westphalian state system. The argument that peacekeeping since the end of the cold war has embarked on new communitarian and solidarist directions in which the old currency of state sovereignty has been devalued is an important and a refreshing one. It has reinvigorated broader debates about the potential of the United Nations and other international organizations for improving human well-being and punishing international criminality. Yet whatever the future trajectory of multilateral military intervention, for the moment the principal international purposes of peacekeeping remain largely Westphalian. The particular objectives of different operations may vary widely, and it is almost certain that the twenty-first century will see these objectives widening even further. But the general proposition of this book is that the fundamental role of peacekeeping remains that of regulator of the state-based international system. There is, in other words, a line of continuity in the use of peacekeeping as a political implement that can be traced from the beginning of the twentieth century into the first decade of the twenty-first.

The existence of this continuity is not always acknowledged even by those who would accept the 'systemic' objectives of peacekeeping. The end of the cold war has given rise to a certain tendency to see peacekeeping as a largely contemporary phenomenon. In 2000 the United Nations produced a major study of peacekeeping that assessed its achievements, sought to clarify the debate about its direction and proposed specific policies for the future. The Brahimi report defined peacekeeping as:

> a 50-year-old enterprise that has evolved rapidly in the past decade from a traditional, primarily military model of observing ceasefires and force separations after inter-state wars, to incorporate a complex model of many elements, military and civilian, working together to build peace in the dangerous aftermath of civil wars.[2]

While this would more or less cover the key characteristics that we have explored thus far – particularly in its emphasis on the growing importance on intra- rather than inter-state engagement – its suggestion that peacekeeping was a post-Second World War invention is misleading. Certainly, peacekeeping tended to become synonymous with the United Nations in the 1950s and 1960s. But the deployment of international military personnel in critical situations and at critical junctures for the international system pre-dated the establishment of the UN in 1945.

We will explore this earlier history of peacekeeping in more detail in the next chapter. But there are a number of reasons why peacekeeping has become so closely identified with the United Nations and why, therefore, it is often seen as a more recent phenomenon than it actually is. One of these is the fraught history of the UN's role in international conflict and the evident failure of the very ambitious scheme for enforcement-based collective security outlined in its Charter. Viewed from a certain perspective, peacekeeping appeared to emerge in the early years of the United Nations to fill the embarrassing gap left when the more robust forms of intervention proved inapplicable to the polarized international system of the cold war. This is something we will return to in Chapter 3. Beyond this, though, other factors have played a role in this failure to fully acknowledge the longer history of peacekeeping. One of these is rooted in what might be described as the collective memory of the years between the two world wars. For decades after the creation of the United Nations the common perception of international relations in the 1920s and 1930s in general – and the performance of the League of Nations in particular – was of generalized failure. In this climate it was important for the United Nations and its supporters to emphasize change rather than continuity with what had gone before. The UN was to represent a fresh start for the international system and the mechanisms established to regulate it. As we will see, this was a misleading representation of the relationship between the League and the UN. The general construction of the two organizations and their peacekeeping activities displayed strong similarities, but the wish to create a structural and operational distance between the two institutions was understandable. The 'failure' of the League had, after all, 'led to' the Second World War, and the United Nations had been formed in the aftermath of this to offer a new beginning to the international system.

Another factor in the disregard of the pre-1939 origins of peacekeeping perhaps lies in the fact that much of the early analysis of and comment on UN operations came from American rather than European academics and writers. America had not participated in the League of Nations despite providing the main impetus for its creation. Instead the United States had spent most of the 1920s and 1930s pursuing a policy if not of total diplomatic isolationism then at least one more focused on the Asian-Pacific side of its international relations than on the European one. It was in Europe that the League and the other structures of the international system of the time had been most active in developing and experimenting with multilateral military operations. Understandably, the perspectives of the generation of American commentators writing in the post-1945 years was shaped by this background.[3] There was a further historical factor that helped engender the perception of peacekeeping as a post-1945 activity. The character and objectives of peacekeeping operations from the 1950s to the 1980s seemed to be determined by two interrelated processes: the cold war and decolonization. The aim of peacekeeping, it appeared, was to 'immunize' peripheral conflicts against the larger 'infection' of the cold war. Frequently these conflicts emerged from the stresses of decolonization and the rapid expansion of the state system caused by the appearance of a wave of newly independent states. In other words, peacekeeping seemed designed to reduce the magnetic pull of the two dominant poles of the bipolar system on new emerging regional sub-systems that might otherwise be dragged helter-skelter into the competition between the superpowers. In this view peacekeeping to all intents and purposes was an artefact of the historical processes of the post-1945 period.

Whatever the various elements that fed the impression that peacekeeping was a new, post-1945 activity, it was a fundamentally flawed perception. It disregarded the long-standing, though dynamic, role of peacekeeping as a tool of the international system. Yes, it did perform a primarily preventive function during the period of superpower competition and the dissolution of the European empires in Africa and Asia. But that merely represented one episode in a larger narrative. When the requirements of the international system were different, both before and after the cold war and the main wave of decolonization, peacekeeping merely performed different roles. In the 1920s and 1930s the plebiscite operations addressed the stresses imposed on the post-World War One system by the break-up of the 'internal' European empires of Germany, Austria-Hungary and Turkey, and the consequent construction of new, potentially unstable states. On the other side of the cold war and decolonization, since the end of the 1980s, peacekeeping has had to meet yet other systemic needs. Here the focus has largely been on the challenges to the stability of the system posed by the disintegration or threatened disintegration of failing states. This latest phase is essentially that described in Brahimi's definition, which we considered earlier. The key point, though, is that this is a phase of peacekeeping and not the entire phenomenon. While the problems in the international system that have elicited peacekeeping responses have changed with historical circumstances, the essential purpose of peacekeeping has not. This has been to manage change in a stressed and fragile system regardless of the nature and form of this change at any one time.

The key Westphalian function of peacekeeping, therefore, is a simple one: to help preserve, by providing a stabilizing mechanism, the state-based international system. This need not necessarily involve the preservation of all states or any particular state. On occasion stability is better served by the reformulation of sovereignties. Peacekeeping has been instrumental in serving this end, from smoothing the adjustment of new national frontiers in inter-war Europe to managing the transfer of power and the creation of new states throughout the world in the cold war and post-cold war periods. Indonesia provides an interesting multiple case study of this. In 1962 its national territory expanded when West New Guinea was added following an act of decolonization by the Netherlands. In 2000 the Indonesian territorial state contracted – and the Westphalian system expanded – with the independence of East Timor. UN peacekeepers were instrumental in both of these processes, as we will see. Most commonly, however, peacekeeping has served to sustain sovereignties under threat either from outside or from disintegration from within.

After 1945 this function was evident, first, in the Middle East, where the system was under strain from the irruption of the new state of Israel into the already unstable complex of newly independent Arab states. It also underlay UN involvement in Kashmir on the contested border of another two new sovereignties, India and Pakistan. Later, in the 1960s, attention shifted to Africa, the next area of post-colonial instability with implications for the bipolar international system. Here the huge Congo operation came to occupy much of the UN's attention and had a major impact on its institutional politics. Next, the peculiarly fragile sovereignty of another new state, Cyprus, became the object of an extended peacekeeping operation. In the 1970s the focus shifted back to the Middle East, where the unresolved conflict between Israel and its neighbours again had to be prevented from destabilizing the system as a whole. Now, though, the superpowers themselves, who were newly conscious of their shared self-interest in the era of nuclear 'mutually assured destruction', were driving the multilateral response through the United Nations.

Then, after a period of dormancy in multilateral peacekeeping when the superpowers abandoned their détente and hardened their spheres of interest, came the multiple shocks to the international state system generated by the sudden end of bipolarity. As these spheres of interest dissolved, so did the superpowers' role in the unilateral management of the tensions within them. With the removal of this external control those tensions frequently spilled over into violence. These situations then required multilateral management – in other words, peacekeeping – in place of the order previously guaranteed by superpower patrons if (Westphalian) international order was to be maintained. This peacekeeping response was required throughout the world now, including, uniquely in the post-1945 period, continental Europe, where the re-ordering of borders that had engaged international military operations in the 1920s and 1930s was resumed.

The beginning of the new century brought yet another set of Westphalian imperatives. The events of 11 September 2001 in the United States and the subsequent 'war on terror' provided a sharp illustration of the practical importance of maintaining an international system based on mutually accountable sovereign units. A vacant space where the state should be creates a vacuum that can be filled by other, less controllable entities, such as international terrorist networks. Afghanistan had been allowed to slip to the periphery of statehood under the Taliban, and the result had been the creation of an unregulated breeding ground for terrorism. After the 2001 attacks, for example, Washington rediscovered its concern about the absence of a coherent state in Somalia – a concern that had faded after the American losses in the failed peacekeeping efforts there in the early 1990s.

The peacekeeper as 'good citizen'

Preservation of the international system by the maintenance, or where necessary the replacement, of its basic state building blocks is the principal Westphalian function of peacekeeping. But it is not the only one. There are other 'services' that peacekeeping can provide to the state system.

Public support for multilateral peacekeeping, either as general activity or for particular operations, provides large and powerful states with a useful means of advertising their acceptance of the rules and norms of the collective. For a time at the end of the cold war – roughly measured between the fall of the Berlin Wall in 1989 and the disintegration of the Soviet Union in 1992 – the United States and the Soviet Union appeared almost to compete with each other in their rhetorical commitment to multilateralism. The United Nations was central to the first President Bush's conception of the post-cold war 'new world order', and Security Council authorization was a central moral prop for the first Gulf War in 1991. On the other side of the by then defunct bipolar divide, Mikhail Gorbachev, in his search for a new foreign policy approach for the Soviet Union, seemed to envision the USSR as active 'world citizen', closely engaged with the conflict resolution activities of the United Nations.

More recently, the policies of the second President Bush are interesting in this regard. At the end of 2002 and the beginning of 2003 considerable effort was spent in an attempt to engage the United Nations in his project of 'regime change' in Iraq. Just as his father had sought UN legitimization for his war to expel Iraq from Kuwait twelve years previously, George W. Bush regarded it as important that the use of America's overwhelming military power be legitimized by the stamp of international approval. He was ultimately unsuccessful in this and the undertaking was therefore pursued unilaterally, but predictions that the UN's 'snub' to the world's hyper-power would prove fatal for the organization proved to be grossly overstated. While considerable ideological hostility towards multilateralism in general and the United Nations in particular clung to the Bush administration, identification with the organization's basic purposes remained an important part of Washington's rhetoric. This provided a necessary balance to an image of unrestrained unilateralism that Washington, with a view to its broader interests in the world, did not wish to foster. Therefore, high-profile American support has been given to UN peacekeeping in Liberia (with which the United States has a special historical interest), and Washington was prominent in threatening robust action through the UN against the government of Sudan over its behaviour in the Darfur region.

The international respectability that can be conferred by support for peacekeeping by big powers can extend to two other groups of states as well. First, there are those states that are subject to peacekeeping – those who are parties to a conflict. These face pressure to volunteer their acceptance of an operation; they risk loss of international standing and sympathy if they do not. But they can also enhance their prestige as states within the international system by demonstrating a high level of compliance with the peacekeeping process. Egypt's prompt acceptance of and cooperation with the United Nations Emergency Force in 1956 was an important propaganda gain for the regime there. By the same token, Israel's lack of cooperation at this time marked the beginning of something of a national tradition of hostility to UN involvement in the region that has done little to improve Israel's standing internationally. Similarly, Morocco's lack of cooperation with the UN's political and military efforts in Western Sahara has tended to undermine international support for its claim to the territory and contrasts unfavourably with the more amenable position of its enemies of the Polisario front (the Popular Front for the Liberation of Saguia el Hamra and Rio de Oro). To positively embrace the role of being the object of a peacekeeping operation rather than to be seen to resent it, therefore, can garner sympathy within the system (though, of course, acceptance or rejection of the role will frequently be driven by the likely outcomes of a particular peacekeeping intervention rather than by any broader calculations).

The other group of states whose position within the international system can be enhanced by peacekeeping are the peacekeepers themselves, the countries who contribute contingents. By the 1960s regular participation in peacekeeping had come to define a particular type of state. These were often described as 'middle powers', with the term having a dual connotation. They were middle-ranking states in terms of military capability. This had to be sufficient to ensure operational efficiency but not so great as to unnerve the parties to the conflict they were despatched to. The term had another sense, though, which related to their place in cold war politics. The ideal peacekeeper should not be too close to either of the ideological poles of the system, east or west. In reality only a few of these middle powers – such as Sweden and Ireland – were formally neutral. Others, such as Canada, the Netherlands and Norway, were actually members of the western alliance; but they projected an impartial and responsible international image. For many of these states the peacekeeping role went far beyond mere participation in particular operations, and came to form part of their essential international identity. Extensive participation in peacekeeping, for example, helped assert Canada's 'difference' from its superpower neighbour and bloc leader, the United States. Similarly, Ireland's peacekeeping role formed the basis of its independent foreign policy in the 1960s and 1970s, which replaced an approach to foreign relations that had been defined by the uncomfortable and unresolved post-imperial relationship with Britain. More recently, micro-states such as Fiji and Nepal have managed to exploit their traditional military cultures to greatly enhance their international recognition and standing. The peacekeeping role, paid for by the United Nations at a relatively generous rate, has also come to have a significant place in these small national economies. The rewards of peacekeeping, therefore, while not entirely tangible, can go far beyond the satisfaction of altruism.

Surveying the peacekeeping century

The central theme of this book is that the peacekeeping project has long been, and continues to be, primarily a means of regulating the international state system. In the chapters that follow, we will pursue this argument by examining key phases and areas of peacekeeping activity since early in the twentieth century.

We will begin by looking at the 1920s and 1930s when the League of Nations and other mechanisms of international regulation employed forces to help deal with the perturbations in the international system in the aftermath of the First World War. Here we will measure the gap between the new aspiration for a collective approach to world security and the reality of inter-war diplomacy. But we will also record the considerable – and subsequently neglected – experimentation with this multilateral military activity, which contributed to the territorial and political adjustments of the international system brought about by the post-1918 settlements. Next, we will look at how the United Nations after 1945 sought to succeed where the League had evidently failed in supplanting state-based, unilateral approaches to security with multilateral, collective ones. Chapter VII of the United Nations Charter placed deep and far-reaching obligations on member states that were designed to regulate the maintenance of international peace and security. Virtually from the outset, however, this revolutionary scheme of collective security became irrelevant. It proved to be profoundly unsuited to the bipolar structure that rapidly imposed itself on the post-1945 international system. The litmus test of this collective security came with the Korean War in which the United Nations was required to play a legitimizing role that was ultimately self-destructive for the organization's aspirations to revolutionize the management of international conflict. Korea sharply underlined the misfit between post-world war ambition and cold war reality.

In the mid-1950s, in the wake of the Korean War, it was evident that the idealism of the original security objectives of the UN had become distorted and their associated mechanisms moribund. But the organization proved flexible enough to recover a meaningful military role in 1956 in the wake of the Suez crisis. Many saw this undertaking as inaugurating a new, productive period of United Nations management of international conflict. In Chapter 4 we will examine the particular characteristics of the Suez conflict, characteristics that made the crisis there a peculiarly appropriate case for multilateral intervention through the agency of the UN even in the face of the rigidities of the cold war. Here we will also consider the UN's earlier deployments of multinational military units in Palestine and Kashmir. These operations, which were established in the late 1940s, raise some important caveats in the description of the Suez force as the UN's first peacekeeping operation. We will also track some interesting and overlooked points of continuity between the UN's first steps towards the creation of what was to become known as peacekeeping and their pre-1939 antecedents. Finally in this chapter, we will examine the process of institutionalization of peacekeeping as a UN activity post-Suez as the secretariat, and particularly the UN's second secretary-general Dag Hammarskjöld, set about conceptualizing the activity and assigning rules to the new approach of interposition by international forces.

The early experience with this model in the later 1950s appeared positive, as we will see in Chapter 5. The UN Emergency Force in Suez was almost wholly successful in carrying out its mandate to supervise the mutual withdrawal of hostile forces and to provide security in the zone around the Suez Canal. Then, in 1958, another UN operation seemed to confirm the value of the peacekeeping approach in fencing off local conflicts from larger cold war ones and thus defusing tensions in the international state system. In Lebanon (which at the time was located in the most fragile sub-system of the larger international system) a military observer mission was established as a direct – and ultimately successful – alternative to a potentially dangerous deployment of American forces. Similar, relatively modestly configured operations in Yemen and (once more) between India and Pakistan in the mid-1960s appeared to confirm the value of this immunizing role of peacekeeping.

At the beginning of the 1960s, however, early optimism about the possibilities of peacekeeping had been dispelled by the quite different experiences in other parts of what had been the imperial world, where decolonization was imposing new stresses on the system. Following a rapid breakdown in order and state authority after the transfer of power in the former Belgian Congo in 1960, the UN deployed by far its largest and most ambitious operation to date. And here the 'Hammarskjöldian' model of peacekeeping as interposition between responsive states quickly fell apart. One by one the key components of Hammarskjöld's post-Suez model were tested to destruction. Interposition was to prove meaningless in a conflict without fixed sides and positions. The line between peacekeeping and enforcement became impossibly blurred. And, perhaps most crucially for the larger world and peacekeeping's supposed contribution to its stability, the UN intervention in the Congo at times appeared actively to provoke superpower conflict rather than suppress it. Meanwhile, in the midst of the Congo operation, the UN for the first time took on the role of substitute state. This was in the former Dutch territory of West New Guinea, which was the subject of a violent campaign for control by Indonesia. Here, too, the high moral tone of peacekeeping that was central to the original vision was placed in question as a UN operation oversaw the transfer of the territory to Indonesia in a process that did not show much evidence of local self-determination. Undoubtedly, though, the operation, however questionable in its local outcome, served the stability of international relations in the Asia-Pacific sub-system. Finally in this chapter, we will look at the creation of the force that would have the longest duration of any of the UN's more substantial operations, the presence in Cyprus. This appeared to revivify the classic interpositionary function of peacekeeping – though between internal ethnic groups rather than the forces of sovereign states. Cyprus, as we will see, provided an object lesson on the difference between peacekeeping and peacemaking, and the importance of the two processes working in parallel. The UN has provided Cyprus with what in most respects has been a model peacekeeping operation – while simultaneously failing to 'make peace'.

In Chapter 6 we move on to a distinct period for peacekeeping (and indeed for other international processes): the years of détente between the superpowers in the late 1960s and the 1970s. The interlude of détente (for such it proved to be) derived from the growing awareness on the part of the superpowers that unconstrained competition pointed towards eventual physical confrontation that now, as a result of technological change, would end in mutually assured destruction. Détente represented a change in the terms of the cold war rather than a cessation of it, however. Its main diplomatic consequence was a tendency by both superpowers to seek agreed means of avoiding confrontations rather than winning them. The co-option of United Nations peacekeeping by Washington and Moscow was one part of this strategy of system management. As might be expected, the dominant arena for this was the Middle East. The Arab-Israeli war of October 1973 came at the high tide of détente and, after some initial wary circling, the United States and the Soviet Union cooperated in exploiting the peacekeeping option through the UN in a way that enabled them to protect their own relationship while still allowing them to exert considerable influence on the situation in the Middle East. The tangible form of this cooperation came with the establishment of the second United Nations Emergency Force between Egypt and Israel in Sinai and, some months later, the Disengagement Observer Force on the Golan Heights between Syria and Israel.

Détente did not bring a fundamental shift away from global bipolarity, however, and its gradual unravelling in the late 1970s was reflected in the fortunes of peacekeeping. By 1978 détente still had sufficient momentum to ensure superpower cooperation in the establishment of another Middle East operation, the UN Interim Force in Lebanon. But pressures elsewhere in the system were now eroding the foundations of détente. As a result, the necessary cooperative will to ensure the success of the Lebanon operation was not available. And, as we have already noted, there was insufficient mutual trust and goodwill by the early 1980s to permit the expansion of the mandate of the Emergency Force in Sinai to oversee the implementation of the Camp David agreement. Instead, the western states had to form their own multilateral force for this purpose – as they did later in Lebanon as well.

The reversion to cold war and the consequent hardening of bipolarity at the end of the 1970s appeared to relegate United Nations peacekeeping to a lesser role in the international system. There was no return even to the status quo ante détente. Established operations were maintained in the Middle East and elsewhere. But in a range of conflicts in Africa and Asia that in other times would have appeared absolutely right for a peacekeeping response, the fundamental divide in the UN Security Council ensured that none was forthcoming. The space lying beyond what the superpowers regarded as their core and exclusive areas of interest, space that had been open to multilateral peacekeeping in the years of détente, now contracted dramatically. Not a single operation was established by the UN between the Lebanon venture in 1978 and the organization's involvement in the process of Namibian independence in 1989 at the end of the cold war.

In the next chapter we look at that operation and the many others that constituted the upsurge in peacekeeping ushered in by the end of the cold war. With the passing of bipolarity, the position of peacekeeping in the international system was transformed. For one thing, it was no longer relevant to speak in terms of the space for peacekeeping between the interests of the superpowers. In principle, nowhere was off-limits to multilateral intervention now. But at the same time, the withdrawal of previously firm superpower control of their client states' behaviour led, as we have already observed, to a rapid expansion in the *requirement* for this multilateral intervention as new conflicts broke out throughout the system. New UN missions became possible in former cold war battlegrounds such as Afghanistan and Central America. More dramatically, in the euphoria of the immediate post-cold war period attention returned to the UN's original larger ambitions for collective security. These were still present in the United Nations Charter but had lain dormant amid the fundamental divisions of the previous decades. Could it be that not only peacekeeping but the much grander scheme (for which it had in part emerged as a weak substitute) might now be realized? In reality, the failure of full-blooded collective security was due to characteristics of international relations that lay much deeper than the transitory bipolarity of the cold war. States remained preoccupied with the sanctity of their own sovereignty regardless of the condition of superpower relations and the configuration of power in the international system at any one time. The millenarian objectives of the UN's post-1945 ambitions simply remained unachievable. The unprecedented warmth of relations between Washington and Moscow in 1990 and 1991 did not change this fundamental position (and did not last beyond the break-up of the Soviet Union anyway).

Beyond question, peacekeeping, if not the feasibility of 'real' collective security, had changed. Whether this amounted to a fundamental transformation and the emergence of a truly 'new peacekeeping', as has been suggested, is questionable, however. Undoubtedly, peacekeeping was now undertaken on an unprecedented scale. In the forty years of cold war between 1948 and the end of 1987 twelve UN peacekeeping forces and military observation missions were established. In the next six years alone, eighteen such operations were established. But the argument that this peacekeeping was different *in kind* rather than just in quantity is more difficult to sustain and will also be explored in Chapter 7. Arguably, the intra-state character of operations and their 'multifunctionality', which are sometimes pointed up as new roles, were already established aspects of the peacekeeping experience and had been at least since the Congo operation in the early 1960s. Similarly, the transfer of local political authority to UN peacekeeping operations did not begin in Cambodia or East Timor in the 1990s, but in West New Guinea in the 1960s. Unquestionably, though, the United Nations as an institution was keenly aware of the changing position of peacekeeping in the post-cold war system. This was reflected in considerable new formal thinking about peacekeeping within the UN. One of the most important examples of this was the 1992 report by secretary-general Boutros Boutros-Ghali, *An Agenda for Peace*, which we will also consider in this chapter.

One undoubted innovation in post-cold war peacekeeping was its extension to continental Europe and its periphery. Previously, of course, these areas did not constitute part of the inter-superpower space open to peacekeeping. But, as we have said, after the end of bipolarity nowhere was off-limits. Simultaneously, the multiple shocks delivered to the European sub-system by the disintegration of the eastern bloc in general and the Soviet Union in particular, generated new nationalist challenges to existing state structures. Consequently pressure grew for the re-drawing of sovereign frontiers – an undertaking that frequently provoked conflict. In this way, peacekeeping operations were undertaken throughout the territory of the former Yugoslavia and on the new borders of Russia and other successor states of the former Soviet Union. This new geographical dimension to peacekeeping and its particular complexities are examined in Chapter 8.

Africa, where the UN's stamina for sustained and costly peacekeeping was first tested in the 1960s, became a major location for its efforts in the

1990s. By that time the mounting political, economic and social challenges faced by post-colonial Africa had reached a point where several states appeared to have ceased to exist as actors in the international system altogether or were on the point of doing so. From Sierra Leone to Somalia and from Western Sahara to Mozambique this crisis of the African state posed a threat to the conventional fabric of international relations. The totality of the UN's engagement with Africa has been enormous as has the range of its success and failure. Africa has also seen important new experiments in the provision of peacekeeping, involving both the legitimization by the UN of operations mounted by non-UN forces and 'inter-agency' peacekeeping undertaken by the UN with other organizations. We therefore devote two chapters to African peacekeeping. Chapter 9 is concerned with peacekeeping as a response to problems of decolonization and post-independence challenges to the African state. Among the operations examined here is that in Namibia, as well as those in Angola, Mozambique and Western Sahara. So too is the traumatic UN engagement with Rwanda and, by contrast, the traditional inter-state operation between Ethiopia and Eritrea. The second African chapter looks at the problems of peacekeeping where the state has effectively ceased to exist. Here we examine among others the operations in Liberia and Sierra Leone. Here we also explore another highly traumatic engagement; that in Somalia between 1992 and 1994.

In the final chapter we turn to the future, or at least the current trends that suggest its possible contours. Is the United Nations likely to remain the predominant peacekeeping agency in the twenty-first century? How strong are the signs, for example, that regional organizations such as the African Union (AU), or indeed the European Union, will supplant it? Is a middle-range adjustment more likely, one in which the United Nations will provide legitimization for peacekeeping ventures by other organizations or by ad hoc groups of states – or even by individual states? Or will joint, inter-agency peacekeeping become more common? Pointers in all of these directions are already present in the international system. Finally, how will new security challenges, whether from transnational terrorism or from environmental conflicts affect the nature of peacekeeping?

Whatever the answers to these questions about the *character* of future peacekeeping responses, the *requirement* for such responses seems set to remain. The international system – still at the beginning of the twenty-first century an essentially Westphalian, state-based one – will continue to require regulation. And, in a world wary of the threat, real or merely perceived, of the unipolar ambition of the remaining hyper-power, this regulation will still be best performed multilaterally and on the basis of consensus: the founding principles of modern peacekeeping.

2 Peacekeeping before the UN

The inter-war years

The problem, even the impossibility, that we have just explored – that of arriving at a firm definition of peacekeeping – creates obvious difficulties when we try to put a date to its beginnings. Collective military intervention arranged between the forces of different nations – multilateralism – is as old as armed conflict itself. These interventions, whatever their underlying motives, have frequently been justified as contributions to the greater good and the security of the international community. Claims of good international citizenship that are designed to distract attention from what is really the pursuit of national interests are not a recent invention. While examples of military interventions that could conceivably be called peacekeeping can be found over the centuries since the Treaty of Westphalia set the terms of the contemporary state system, it is probably reasonable to begin our excavation of the 'archaeology' of peacekeeping in the nineteenth century as leaders became increasingly conscious of the broader implications of conflict in one part of the system for the security of the system as a whole. The modern history of peacekeeping grew out of these beginnings and is associated with the unprecedented attempts to impose mechanisms of regulation on the international system after the shock of the First World War.

The nineteenth century

In 1815 at the end of the French Revolutionary and Napoleonic Wars, the conservative powers of Europe – Britain, Prussia, Austria-Hungary, Russia – had in their own estimation defeated more than just France. They had suppressed a transnational revolutionary challenge and were now determined to manage the post-war system in a way that would prevent any repetition of the threat. The 'concert of Europe' that emerged at the Vienna Congress in 1815 was hardly an 'inter-governmental organization' in the sense that became current a century later, but in many ways it was a precursor to twentieth-century developments. The concert system looked back as well as forward in international relations. The Treaty of Westphalia, which we discussed in the last chapter, came at the end of the Thirty Years War. It was an attempt to regulate international relations following the previous system-wide conflict a century and a half before the defeat of Napoleon. Developments after 1815 can be seen as the next phase in a long historical process of ever more ambitious attempts at international regulation. Westphalia had asserted the centrality of the state; now a new dimension of collective activism among states was introduced. Henceforward positive cooperation was seen as an adjunct to mutual respect for sovereign independence. The next phase of this cycle would follow the next catastrophic breakdown of the system between 1914 and 1918 and would involve the creation of formally constituted, permanent international institutions.

In the meantime the nineteenth-century system was regulated with some success (if success is judged on the absence of serious conflict) under the concert system. It would be quite inappropriate to apply the term peacekeeping to the various military activities undertaken to preserve order in the system. Not all of them were multilateral, and few if any were unequivocally altruistic. Some of them, such as Austria's presence in pre-unified Italy, had more to do with imperial pacification than conflict resolution. Others, such as the involvement of west European states on the rebellious periphery of the Ottoman world (in Crete, Bosnia, Lebanon and Cyprus) were designed to weaken an imperial rival as much as to support the rights of repressed peoples and stabilize the system. But others, such as naval operations against the Atlantic slave trade and Sweden's intervention between Prussia and Denmark in the disputed area of Schleswig-Holstein did, in their different ways, prefigure the peacekeeping of the twentieth century.

An interesting historical echo of the concert system and its approach to international order was heard in the second half of the twentieth century. For Henry Kissinger, the American national security adviser and secretary of state in the Nixon and Ford administrations, the post-1815 period provided a model for the interlude of so-called détente between the superpowers in the late 1960s and 1970s. Although Kissinger viewed the international system from a robustly 'realist' perspective, he considered big powers to be tied to one another by mutual systemic interests. These, he argued, transcended ideological differences between their respective national politics. Like the victorious powers after 1815, the nuclear states of the second half of the twentieth century occupied privileged positions within their international system. Maintaining stability in the system was therefore of pressing importance to all of them, and security should not be jeopardized by self-defeating antagonisms. In the 1970s, as we will see, the United Nations and its peacekeeping capacities became instruments of détente, actively exploited by Kissinger himself in the Middle East (see Chapter 6).[1]

The institutional peacekeeping mechanisms co-opted in this way by Kissinger in the 1970s had emerged over the previous half century, long pre-dating the United Nations itself. The historical cycle we have pointed up – of ever more elaborate regulation after violent breakdowns in the international system – reached a crucial stage after the end of the First World War. If we have the Thirty Years War to thank for the principle of sovereignty, and the Napoleonic Wars for active cooperation in controlling the international environment, the First World War gave us the first formally constituted institution for the management of international security in the form of the League of Nations.

Establishing the League of Nations

That a new international organization like the League of Nations would be established in the aftermath of the First World War was hardly unexpected. In Europe the idea of managing international relations through the creation of new institutions had been germinating since before the war began. It emerged from a broader intellectual milieu in which the new social sciences were developing at the beginning of the twentieth century. Advances in science in the eighteenth and nineteenth century had brought new understanding and new solutions to age-old problems in the physical world, and now there was an optimistic expectation that the ills of the social and human realms could also be remedied employing similar 'scientific' approaches. Karl Marx and Sigmund Freud in their different ways represented this new intellectual paradigm. And if it was possible to diagnose and prescribe for the ailments of the psyche and the economy, why should it not also be possible to solve the problem of war? Hitherto the age of improvement had failed here. In fact, technological 'improvements' had greatly worsened the effects of armed conflict as the horrors of the First World War would demonstrate. But it was part of the spirit of the modernist age that no problem was beyond solution.

In France in the immediate pre-war years the radical politician and social theorist Léon Bourgeois was a powerful advocate of a new approach to international relations. Essentially, Bourgeois advocated the extension of the idea of the social contract to the international from the domestic setting.[2] Meantime, across the Atlantic in the United States, a parallel intellectual movement urged the creation of a new institutional approach to international security. As might be expected in the highly constitutionalist American political culture, the emphasis here was on enforceable legal structures as the bases of international cooperation. In 1915 (before the United States entered the war), a campaign was mounted for the creation of a League to Enforce Peace. Its leader was the former Republican president, William Howard Taft, whose blueprint was for a permanent assembly of states with a world court and mandatory international conciliation.

In the event it was Taft's Democratic successor in the White House, Woodrow Wilson, who would preside over the formation of the League of Nations. Wilson, who became president in 1913 brought a particular moral and intellectual sensibility to the office. He was the son of a Presbyterian minister, and he had pursued an academic career before entering politics. Against considerable opposition he led the United States into the First World War in 1917 'to make the world safe for democracy'. As the leader of the strongest and, by 1918, the most buoyant of the victorious allies, Wilson's influence on the peace settlement would obviously be considerable. That influence was put firmly behind the idea of a new institution that would be an agent of fundamental change in international relations. In January 1918 Wilson had outlined to Congress the fundamental war aims of the United States. These were summed up in the famous 'Fourteen Points'. The last of these insisted that a: 'general association of nations must be formed under specific covenants for the purpose of affording mutual guarantees of political independence and territorial integrity to great and small states alike'.[3] This was the first formal statement of what would become known as 'collective security', a concept closely related to – though, as we will see, not synonymous with – peacekeeping. In its purest form, collective security was to involve replacing national defence with arrangements that would guarantee the safety and independence of states by the international system as a whole. The League of Nations was intended to be the institutional vehicle for this.

The truly radical character of the League as it was originally conceived is easily missed in retrospect. In part this is due to the perception of its failure. The simple fact of the Second World War, which came after a culmination of crises in Europe and beyond that the League proved incapable of resolving, is normally taken as proof of this. But in part the really innovative nature of the League is under-appreciated simply because it established a basic model for international institutions that became almost the standard for later organizations. Yet in 1919 when it began its work, the League was the first international entity of its type. It was established as a permanent institution and it was equipped with a basic 'constitution' (the Covenant), which set out its structure and objectives. The League was to consist of what could be described as quasi-national organs. It had a Council composed of the big powers (initially the allied victors), which corresponded loosely to a national executive. Its Assembly consisted of all the League's members, constituting a parliamentary-type assembly. In addition, the League would be the first international institution with a permanent bureaucracy or civil service: the Secretariat. It would also have a fixed physical location with its headquarters in the Swiss city of Geneva. Any one of these attributes would have been highly novel in 1919; together they were nothing short of revolutionary.

The principles of collective security were embedded in the Covenant, which itself was a component part of the Versailles treaty that ended the war. The preamble to the Covenant required its signatories to accept 'obligations not to resort to war'. Article 8 recognized 'that the maintenance of peace requires the reduction of national armaments to the lowest point consistent with national safety and the enforcement by common action of international obligations'. In other words, there was an implicit recognition of the state's right to defend itself; but beyond this, physical action to ensure the rule of law in international relations was to be collective. The legal basis of this collective security was set out in Article 10 of the Covenant. This committed all members of the League 'to respect and preserve as against external aggression the territorial integrity and existing political independence' of all other members. The League Council was to 'advise upon the means by which this obligation will be fulfilled'. Any 'war or threat of war whether immediately affecting any of the Members of the League or not' was, Article 11 declared, 'a matter of concern to the whole League' which would 'take any action that may be deemed wise and effectual to safeguard the peace of nations'.[4]

The language of the Covenant was certainly impressive. But, ultimately, the rhetoric veiled some considerable limitations on what seemed to be promised. The League's conception of collective security, though radical in the context of the time, was in key senses a conservative one when compared with late twentieth-century thinking. The Covenant took a highly 'statist' approach, which saw security essentially in terms of respect for sovereignty and borders. The possibility that threats to international security might be generated by conflict within rather than between states was not acknowledged. To a great extent, of course, this simply reflected the diplomatic culture of the time, and it would be 'ahistorical' to project later preoccupations back to the 1920s and 1930s. But there was a sense in which the League's state-centric approach presented more immediate difficulties. Its construction of 'security' was an inflexible one that was focused on the defence of a territorial status quo imposed on the international system by the victorious allies at Versailles. Moreover, its workings would be dictated by a Council composed of those same victorious allies. Seen in these terms this collective security was perhaps not as revolutionary as it first appeared. In a certain light it appeared to be a relatively small advance on the post-1815 concert system.

It was not only the objectives of the collective security model of the League that raised questions about its novelty. Its techniques as outlined in the Covenant were also less than radical when closely examined. Great expectations were placed in the potential of international 'arbitration' referred to in Article 13. Again, this may have been reasonable in the exhausted aftermath of the war. The institutional arrangements made to facilitate international mediation and settlement were admirable as far as they went. Article 14 of the Covenant, for example, produced another historical innovation in the form of a Permanent Court of International Justice (later the International Court of Justice under the UN). But events in the following years sharply illustrated the limitations of these procedures. They proved unable to live up to initial expectations when the international system came under severe stress. What was to happen in the event of states not submitting disputes to arbitration? Article 16 of the Covenant pronounced that any state going to war in defiance of the League would 'be deemed to have committed an act of war against all other Members of the League'. But the punishment for this offence was restricted to economic and diplomatic sanctions. The League Council could 'recommend' military action to members and advise on it, but there was no obligation on League states to respond to any such recommendation. As we will see, this was one of the key differences between the League Covenant and the United Nations Charter that succeeded it after the Second World War.

The effectiveness of the League's collective response to security threats was affected not only by the looseness of Covenant obligations but also by a limited and unstable membership. Most significantly, despite the fact that Woodrow Wilson had provided the main impetus for the new organization, the United States declined to join. The enthusiasm of the president for a continuing American diplomatic and moral presence in Europe after the war was not shared by the American Congress. There was a general wariness in the United States about the burdens – political and economic – that this commitment would bring. Whether it is correct to describe this position as isolationism can be debated, but it was certainly true that after the trauma and sacrifices of the war, engagement with Europe and its old antagonisms was unattractive to many Americans. In the absence of the United States, leadership of the organization passed by default to the European victors, principally Britain and France. Neither had fully shared Wilson's new world vision of a re-ordered international system. There was a certain cultural resistance to the novelty of an approach based on collective institutional responsibility for peace and security. And, crucially, the League was not a universalist organization in the sense of having an open, system-wide membership. Germany was excluded initially, as was the Soviet Union, which had withdrawn from the war after the Bolshevik revolution in 1917. The nature of the League's membership, therefore, fed a growing impression that, notwithstanding its innovative structure and rhetorical ambition, it was as much an evolution of the nineteenth-century concert system as a revolutionary alternative to it.

'Plebiscite peacekeeping'

Whatever the League's shortcomings, the world political environment into which it was born was in many ways a favourable one for new experiments in international cooperation. War weariness and the all-consuming demands of domestic reconstruction created an environment in which there was little appetite and few resources for new inter-state conflict. However temporary it was to prove, there was readiness among states to compromise on conflicting interests, and therefore there was a place for multilateral mechanisms that could assist this. The League had a role in this generalized climate of diplomatic accommodation, though it did not dominate it to the extent that its supporters might have hoped and expected. Frequently, the contribution of the League as an institution was combined with, or parallel to, that of other international actors. Much of the adjustment in the international relations of the 1920s took place within what might be called the spirit of the League as we have described it, rather than being directly managed by the League.

This is well illustrated by the sequence of plebiscites held in various parts of Europe as new post-war frontiers were drawn. The war had brought the end of four once-great empires: Hohenzollern Germany, Hapsburg Austria-Hungary, Romanov Russia and Ottoman Turkey. Their subject peoples and territories, following the new international morality, would not simply be transferred to become the possessions of the victors. The doctrine of national self-determination was now pervasive. At the geographical perimeter – in Germany's African and Pacific colonies, and in Turkey's Middle Eastern possessions – this involved another League innovation. The mandate system meant that these territories were assigned as responsibilities to appropriate (war victor) powers who would prepare them for eventual independence. The possessions of the defeated therefore were not distributed as spoils of war as they would have been in the past.[5] (Many of the mandated territories in the Middle East and in Africa would in the future account for a significant part of the overall peacekeeping effort of the United Nations.) Within Europe the peoples of former imperial possessions and other disputed areas removed from the control of the defeated powers were, in principle, to determine their own statehood. The obvious mechanism for this was the plebiscite. Inevitably, with competing ethnic and political interests at odds with each other and neighbouring states in competition for the prize of new territory, the management of these referendums frequently brought security challenges. A standard international response emerged: policing by multinational force drawn from disinterested states, or at least states whose interests lay in the broader stability of the post-war system. A re-ordering of the borders within the international system was for the first time subject to what, by all key criteria, can be described as peacekeeping. Both the League of Nations and other ad hoc collectives were involved in this.

It is interesting to note that although these undertakings have been largely excluded from contemporary explorations of peacekeeping, they formed part of the institutional memory inherited by the United Nations. In a rarely cited General Assembly document of January 1948, the UN Palestine Commission, then considering the likely consequences of Britain's withdrawal from its mandate there and the possibility of generalized conflict in the region, reviewed 'Precedents Concerning the Creation of an International Force'.[6] Evidently anxious to forestall speculation about the UN's response to the Palestine crisis, the document emphasized that its intention was:

> merely to show that immediately after the First World War and again in 1935 it was possible to create international forces with a view toward assisting international commissions to fulfil the functions assigned to them (in each case the holding of plebiscites in disputed regions).

As we will see, a few months after the document was issued, the declaration of the state of Israel and the ensuing war led to a multinational UN peacekeeping operation in Palestine: the Truce Supervision Organization. Whether the form and functions of this were consciously shaped by the precedents laid out in the Commission's document is unknown, but the UN's awareness of the significance of these earlier operations suggests a continuity in the peacekeeping narrative that has not been fully acknowledged.

The Schleswig plebiscite

The first territorial plebiscite to be policed by a multinational force took place in Schleswig (which we have already mentioned as the subject of a nineteenth-century 'peacekeeping' intervention). The Schleswig problem in 1920 was essentially the same as it had been in 1848 when Sweden intervened in an attempt to stabilize the situation there. Located between north Germany and southern Denmark, Schleswig was claimed by both states. It had been annexed by Prussia in 1864, and after Germany's defeat in 1918 it was inevitable that a territory acquired under such circumstances would come under scrutiny. The Treaty of Versailles therefore provided for a plebiscite of the population of Schleswig to determine the territory's future, with an international force to be established to police the venture.

The treaty pronounced that the 'frontier between Germany and Denmark shall be fixed in conformity with the wishes of the population' and in the interim the power vacuum created by the collapse of German authority would be filled by a five-strong International Commission. This was to be formed by three members of the Principal Allied and Associated Powers (that is, the victorious states) along with a representative of both the Norwegian and Swedish governments. The Commission was to be 'assisted in case of need by the necessary forces'.[7] The United States, in line with its general disengagement from Europe and its failure to ratify the Versailles Treaty, chose not to appoint its Commissioner, leaving it to Britain, France and the two Scandinavian states. The Commission began its work in January 1920 supported by a 3,000-strong Anglo-French force under the command of a British admiral. The force was composed of a naval flotilla and a battalion of troops from each of the contributing states (a third planned battalion from the United States did not materialize). A small local police force was also recruited by the Commission. The result of the plebiscite, which was carried out without any significant incident, was a majority for a division of the ancient duchy of Schleswig between

Denmark and Germany. This outcome was implemented by the Allied Powers and has endured since.

The Allenstein and Marienwerder plebiscites

The flurry of post-war adjustments saw other plebiscites policed by international military missions during 1920. Two of these were linked, covering the East Prussian territories of Allenstein and Marienwerder on the radically altered borders between Germany and Poland. The task here, set by the Treaty of Versailles, was to fix the line of the new frontier. An international force was established to support a Commission composed of representatives of Britain, France, Italy and Japan (once again without the planned participation of the United States). This Commission was to 'have general powers of administration and in particular will be charged with the duty of arranging for the vote and of taking such measures as it may deem necessary to ensure its freedom, fairness, and secrecy'. The 800-strong Allenstein component of the force was wholly British, while that covering Marienwerder was composed of contingents from Italy and France. The plebiscite was held in July 1920 and resulted in an overwhelming vote (of 97 per cent) in favour of the territories remaining within Germany.

The Klagenfurt Basin plebiscite

The year 1920 also saw a plebiscite take place in the Klagenfurt Basin area between (defeated) Austria and part of its former imperial possession, the new state of Yugoslavia or the 'Serb-Croat-Slovene state' as it was provisionally known at this stage. Here the international Commission was composed of representatives of Britain, France and Italy but also included members from Austria and Yugoslavia, the interested parties. The Klagenfurt arrangement had been put in place under the terms not of Versailles but of the associated Treaty of St Germain, which codified the settlement between the victorious allies and Austria-Hungary. [8] The process was generally similar to those dealing with Germany's post-war borders but in Klagenfurt the forces on the ground were provided by the local powers. The area was divided into two zones, with Austria and Yugoslavia policing one each. There was, however, an international group of British, French and Italian officers attached to the commission who observed the voting process at local level. Here, as in East Prussia, the popular vote was for the status quo, and the Klagenfurt Basin remained part of Austria.

Upper Silesia

A more formidable task by far was undertaken the following year in Upper Silesia on another part of the German-Polish borderland. The politics and economics of this part of the post-war settlement were so complex that a clear-cut and generally acceptable outcome would be difficult to achieve. In the event the international force deployed to supervise the vote remained in place for more than a year after the plebiscite was held. The region – which had a population of more than two million – contained extensive coalfields and industrial areas that would be a considerable economic (and potentially military) asset for whoever controlled it. In these circumstances the rhetoric of self-determination was always likely to take second place to the realities of international politics. The international Commission for Upper Silesia established under the terms of the Versailles Treaty was composed of British, French and Italian representatives. There were differences within the Commission from the outset. France was strongly opposed to the retention of Upper Silesia by Germany. At the root of this lay a general French partiality towards Poland along with a fundamental apprehension about the long-term consequences of German industrial and military reconstruction. The French therefore were disinclined to accept the outcome of the popular vote that here, as elsewhere, was for the status quo (in other words the continuation of Upper Silesia within Germany). Britain's sympathies were closer to Germany, but it was anxious to avoid embroilment in any wrangle over the issue and had initially been reluctant to provide its proportionate contribution to the very large international force planned for the territory. As a result, the French military presence of ten battalions (about 11,500 troops) was dominant. Italy, which was wary of French support for Polish interests, provided a force of 2,000. Britain eventually deployed a similar contingent, but only on the eve of the referendum in March 1921.

During two phases of the operation, immediately before the referendum and then during politically motivated delays in implementing the pro-German outcome, the international force faced widespread disorder in the territory that involved considerable loss of life. The situation was aggravated by local suspicions over the role and intentions of the international force. Although each contingent had its own national commander, the force as a whole was under the overall command of a French general who did little to disguise his country's sympathies. Specifically, he sought to obstruct the completion of a process that favoured Germany against perceived French interests. This was an early example of participant bias, one of the most corrosive flaws that can afflict the peacekeeping process and one that would later lead to problems across a range of multinational operations at various times and in various places from the Congo in the 1960s to Somalia in the 1990s.

The differences between the allies over Upper Silesia proved to be the League of Nations' opportunity. The deadlock between France on one side and Britain and Italy on the other led to the issue being passed to the League Council for resolution. The impact of this on the morale of the institution was considerable. According to F. P. Walters, a former deputy secretary-general of the League and author of the definitive history of the organization:

> (t)his event was a red letter day in League history. The Council, suddenly invested with authority over [the Allied Powers] by whose proceedings its own had hitherto been completely eclipsed, found its prestige raised . . . to the highest point it had yet reached.[9]

The transfer of the issue to a public multilateral forum allowed a compromise to be reached. The territory was partitioned in a way that minimized the resentment of the population, which had opted for German nationality, while addressing French concerns. For the new post-war Poland, which was already acquiring a reputation for over-assertiveness, it was a timely lesson in diplomatic realities. And for the League of Nations, the affair provided an important opportunity, after an uncertain and confused start, to mark out a role in the management of the post-war international system.

Vilna

This assertion of League authority in the question of Upper Silesia was consolidated in another major plebiscite undertaking in 1921. This related to the status of the city and region of Vilna, present-day Vilnius, the capital of Lithuania. The multi-sided conflict after the First World War over Lithuania, and indeed the larger Baltic region, was highly complex. Lithuania had deep historical and cultural links with all three of its larger neighbours, Germany, Poland and Russia. In the nineteenth century, as the forces of nationalism grew across Europe, Lithuania was part of the Russian Tsarist empire and many in its national movement looked to Poland as an example and inspiration. In 1915, however, the Russians were expelled, not by nationalist uprising but by German forces advancing on the eastern front. This occupation ended with the armistice in 1918, following which Russia returned, now in the form of the Red Army. With the new Soviet regime under pressure within Russia and marginalized abroad, however, Moscow had no real enthusiasm for a reversion to the pre-war status quo and was sympathetic to Lithuania's claims for independent statehood. A Soviet-Lithuanian treaty in 1920 accordingly confirmed the independence of the territory. Poland, however, had different ideas. Sensing expansionist opportunities with the defeat of Germany and the weakness of revolutionary Russia, the Polish government had designs on Lithuania and in particular Vilna, which had long been seen by Warsaw as culturally Polish. As a result, Polish forces had moved in to replace the Red Army when it withdrew as arranged in 1919. Then, after bowing to international pressure to withdraw their own army, the Poles connived at the occupation of Vilna by pro-Polish irregular forces. Although Lithuania was admitted to League membership in 1921 as a fully independent state, its government remained excluded from what it regarded as the national capital.

The League Council attempted to resolve the issue by setting up a five-power Military Commission composed of officers from Britain, France, Spain, Italy and Japan. A plan was developed for a plebiscite in the city that would be policed by an 1,800-strong international force. This was to consist of contingents from the members of the Military Commission (other than Japan) and contributions from Belgium, Denmark, Greece, the Netherlands, Norway and Sweden. The plan was formally adopted by resolutions of the League Council in the autumn of 1920. Had it been implemented this would have been by far the most ambitious multinational operation undertaken by the League, at least in terms of breadth of participation.

In the event, however, it faced an accretion of difficulties that soon caused the entire project to unravel. The likely reaction of Poland to a defeat in the planned plebiscite was uncertain and this was a destabilizing element in the mediation effort. Lithuania too, which had initially welcomed the plan, seemed to have second thoughts as events progressed. There were doubts in the Lithuanian government about the League's ability to dislodge Poland from the areas it occupied whatever the outcome of the referendum. There was also concern in Lithuania over the intention to place the multinational force under a French commander. France's friendliness towards Poland was now well known and had been confirmed by the League's recent engagement with Upper Silesia where French command of the international force had exacerbated an already difficult situation. Soviet Russia meanwhile expressed unhappiness at the prospect of forces from 'capitalist' countries being deployed so close to its own borders. This was more than just an ideological gesture by Moscow; western states were already intervening in the civil war then being fought out in Russia between the Bolsheviks and counter-revolutionary forces. Finally, Switzerland, whose agreement to provide rights of passage to the international force on its way to Vilna was essential, was concerned at the implications for its traditionally narrow view of its international neutrality. The League plebiscite scheme was therefore quietly dropped.

In its place the League established a lower-profile mediation effort that effectively left Vilna in Polish hands. Lithuanian anger at the outcome, and its suspicions of France, found an outlet in its expulsion of the French military administration from the port of Memel in 1923. Although within Lithuanian territory, Memel's population was largely German, and no decision had been taken either by the allies or the League as to its long-term status. The following year the League accepted the Lithuanian fait accompli. Vilna, however, remained beyond the reach of the Lithuanian government. In 1939 the situation changed dramatically following Germany's defeat of Poland and the annexation of the Baltic republics. Vilna was returned to Lithuania only after Germany's defeat – and then to a Lithuania that had been repossessed by Russia. It was not until 1991, on the eve of the collapse of the Soviet Union, that the city finally became the capital of a truly independent Lithuanian state.

The problems that beset and eventually defeated the League's attempts at peacekeeping over Vilna would have strong resonances in later ventures by the United Nations. The destabilizing uncertainty over the reaction of a protagonist to defeat in a peace process based on a popular vote afflicted UN operations in Angola and Mozambique in the 1990s. Suspicions about the neutrality of American forces in Somalia and the French (once again) in Bosnia would lead to problems for UN efforts in these countries seven decades after Lithuanian objections to the prominence of France in the proposed Vilna force. Later peacekeeping operations would also be affected by the concerns of third parties about the possible impact of international forces just as the Vilna plan was by the worries of the Soviet Union and Switzerland. The League's retreat in the face of these challenges, however, lost it some of the credibility it had gained earlier when it had assumed control of the Upper Silesia question.

The Saar administration and plebiscite

A much more successful and substantial venture into plebiscite peacekeeping came several years later, not in east-central Europe, but in the west. The Saar territory lies on the border of western Germany and northern France to the east of Luxembourg. At the end of the First World War its population of three-quarters of a million was overwhelmingly German in language and culture. But it exercised a powerful attraction for war-desolated France in 1918 because of its extensive coal and iron resources. After previous wars the annexation of the territory as a legitimate spoil of war would have been quite usual, but in the new world order of international relations proclaimed by President Wilson at Versailles, this was no longer the case. Moreover, French aspirations were opposed on pragmatic grounds by Britain, which feared the likely reaction in the territory itself and Germany as a whole if the Saar was simply taken over by France.

Attempting to reconcile as many interests as possible, the Versailles Treaty worked out a means by which France's post-war reconstruction could benefit from the Saar's resources without outraging either Wilsonian morality or British diplomatic pragmatism. Germany was to renounce political control of the territory 'in favour of the League of Nations in the capacity of trustee . . .' for a period of fifteen years after which 'the inhabitants . . . shall be called upon to indicate the sovereignty under which they desire to be placed'.[10] During this fifteen years of trusteeship the Saar was to be administered by an international commission appointed by the League Council. This would in effect be the Saar's government, with tax-raising powers and control of the legal system. The Commission was required to present regular reports to the League Council – a practice later followed by the UN Security Council in relation to its peacekeeping missions. A separate Plebiscite Commission was created with responsibility for the organization of the vote at the end of the period of international control. This would offer the inhabitants of the territory a choice between three options: return to Germany; transfer to French sovereignty; or continuation of international administration. Law and order in the territory during League administration was to be overseen by a 2,000-strong French military force. The nationality of this security force was, of course, significant. The French military presence had a dual role. It represented an assertion and guarantee of French interests in the territory, but it was also an 'international' force charged with maintaining the authority of the League administration. In fact, the French force was withdrawn in 1927, and responsibility for law and order was entrusted to the local police, though an Anglo-French-Belgian force remained, with responsibility for the territory's strategic railways.

The political and social calm in the Saar during the period of international administration led one well-placed observer to describe it as 'one of the quietest and most prosperous places in Europe'.[11] But this began to fray in the early 1930s as a consequence of the rise of the Nazis in Germany and the raising of nationalist temperature throughout German-speaking Europe that went with it. Tension was particularly high in the Saar because of the approach of the referendum in 1935. The situation was not helped by Germany's theatrical withdrawal from the League of Nations after Hitler came to power in 1933. It became clear to the League Council that special arrangements would have to be made for the management of the plebiscite campaign and the policing of the vote itself. While the overwhelming German majority in the territory should have made the outcome safely predictable, there was considerable nervousness in Germany, which further destabilized the situation in the territory. The Nazis were concerned that the strong industrial base of the Saar could produce an anti-Nazi backlash among a traditionally socialist-oriented electorate, German or not. Another worry was the nature of the political right in the territory, which was closely tied to conservative Catholicism rather than radical nationalism. The Nazis feared, therefore, that while support for transfer to France would remain minuscule, there was perhaps just a possibility of a vote for continued international administration.

The Council pressed ahead with its plans for an international force at the end of 1934 in the face of fierce opposition from Germany which wished to have maximum freedom of action in the territory during the campaign. There was also reluctance from Britain, which was concerned at the extent of costs and commitments. But the alternative to the international force would have been a unilateral French intervention. The Governing Commission had the right to request this and its (British) chairman had indicated that he would follow this route if necessary in the absence of an international force. Rumours about French preparations for military intervention swirled around press and diplomatic circles in Europe throughout the latter part of 1934, building tensions in the territory still further. In these circumstances Britain had little option but to comply with League plans and, though late in the process, the British government confirmed to the League Council in December 1934 that it would provide a contingent if both France and Germany assented. With its Fascist ally Italy now also offering a contingent, and faced with the alternative of a French military intervention, Germany reluctantly agreed to the arrangement. France meanwhile accepted that if Germany raised no objections to the deployment of this force there would be no question of French intervention. While continuing to dispute the requirement for an international force, Germany acquiesced in the arrangements.

The force eventually assembled was 3,300-strong, composed mainly of British and Italian contributions and under the command of a British general. Units were also provided by Sweden and the Netherlands, 'each the very embodiment of neutrality and respectability', as Walters later put it.[12] Their participation was an intimation of the central role that middle powers would later have in peacekeeping after the Second World War. The deployment proved effective and was well received by the local population. Berlin's nervousness about the outcome of the vote, which was held in January 1935, proved misplaced as 90 per cent of voters on virtually a 100-per-cent turnout opted for a return to Germany. The Saar territory was duly reincorporated in March 1935.

The Saar operation was the largest of the League's peacekeeping undertakings and, potentially, its most dangerous. In hindsight the risks it faced might appear to have been more notional than real – Germany was always destined to regain the territory in the plebiscite and France was ready to accept this. At the time, however, the situation, at least locally, was highly volatile, and the international force was required to navigate some difficult operational waters. The Saar operation highlighted the importance of a particular aspect of peacekeeping planning: contributor selection. The composition of the force – British, Italian, Dutch and Swedish – was designed to match the diplomatic requirements of a highly sensitive situation. Yet it is a measure of the fragility of the international relations of the time that before the end of the year one of these supposedly ideal peacekeepers would itself challenge the capacity of the League to meet its fundamental responsibilities. The Italian invasion of Abyssinia in 1935 and the League's inadequate response to it was a major stage in the organization's march towards oblivion. As for the Saar itself, the fate of the territory was put in question again at the end of the Second World War. Once more France saw access to its mineral wealth and industrial capacity as due restitution for Germany's invasion and occupation. History appeared to repeat itself when the Saar was again given a special international identity. After yet another plebiscite in 1957 it returned finally to the German

Federal Republic, though on this occasion without the necessity of a peace-keeping operation.

Territorial management: Danzig and Leticia

Beyond the management and policing of territorial plebiscites, the post-First World War powers and the League were involved in peacekeeping and policing roles in other crisis points in the system. Two of these had particular significance for the subsequent development of peacekeeping later in the twentieth century. One was concerned with the city of Danzig, where the familiar post-war problem of tension between ethnic identity and national sovereignty could not, as elsewhere, be resolved by plebiscite. The other – less familiar from a Eurocentric perspective but of some importance in the precedents it set – was in a remote part of South America on the jungle border between Peru and Colombia.

The port of Danzig (the modern-day Polish city of Gdansk) sat on the Baltic Sea at the end of the so-called Polish Corridor. This was established by the Treaty of Versailles to provide Poland with an outlet to the sea. It was a highly controversial arrangement as the Corridor was carved out of German territory leaving the province of East Prussia physically separated from the rest of the nation. It was this 'humiliation' that provided Hitler with the pretext for the invasion of Poland in September 1939 that precipitated the Second World War. While the Corridor itself had a mainly Polish population (and the territory had been Polish until the partition of the country in the eighteenth century) there was a large German majority among the 200,000 residents of the city of Danzig. In order to limit German resentment – and to remain faithful as far as feasible to the allies' expressed commitment to the principle of self-determination – Danzig was not transferred to Polish sovereignty with the rest of the Corridor. Instead, it was declared a 'Free City' under the 'guarantee' of the League of Nations. Its status differed from that of the Saar in that there was no long-term commitment to a final resolution of its identity by plebiscite.

The arrangement was a bold and innovative one, but in the fraught circumstances of the time and place it became a focus of conflict, resented in equal degree by the two states concerned. Germany felt abused by the amputation of the Polish Corridor, and the special arrangement made for Danzig could not disguise the fact that a 'German' city had been removed from the nation. For its part, Poland saw the same special arrangement as denying it a natural right to sovereignty over the entire Corridor. International peacekeeping in the territory, although relatively short-lived, was nevertheless successfully undertaken. For most of 1920, in the period prior to the establishment of the Free City, Danzig was administered by a British official supported by an Anglo-French security force. This consisted of a battalion of troops from each country under the command of a British general. The period of international policing passed peacefully and at the end of it responsibility for the city's security passed to a locally recruited (and therefore largely German) force. After the Nazi invasion of Poland in 1939 Danzig and the Corridor were fully reintegrated into Germany. The city and the Corridor were lost to Germany after the end of the Second World War when the entire province of East Prussia was transferred permanently to Poland. The port of Gdansk subsequently became one of the most economically significant cities in the country.

Thirteen years after the bi-national force in Danzig and several thousand miles away in a remote part of the Amazon rainforest, the League became engaged in another novel exercise in international security. Although carried out on a small scale, this undertaking provided significant markers for peacekeeping operations later in the century. The international system of the first half of the twentieth century still radiated from Europe, its original Westphalian centre. Despite the growth of US power and Washington's obvious interests in Latin America, the western hemisphere remained somewhat peripheral to the perceptions of European policy makers who still saw the central balance of the system to be located in the 'old world'. It was this mindset that lay behind much of the wariness of American politicians towards engagement with post-war Europe and that contributed to their rejection of Wilson's plans for an American role at the head of the League. In turn, of course, the absence of a strong American presence in the League had the effect of entrenching the Eurocentrism that opinion in the United States had objected to in the first place. The reality was, however, that the Latin American sub-system was as unstable, dangerous and potentially self-destructive as the European one. Since the emergence of the independent republics after the dissolution of the Spanish and Portuguese empires in the nineteenth century, tensions over disputed territories and borders had been endemic.

The League's lack of engagement with the region was sharply illustrated during the so-called Chaco War of 1932–35 between Bolivia and Paraguay. The Chaco Boreal, over which the war was fought, was a vast unpopulated wilderness whose national status was ill-defined but in which both Paraguay and Bolivia maintained a military presence. Control over it was particularly coveted by land-locked Bolivia, which saw it as part of a geopolitical strategy that would eventually secure it an outlet to the Atlantic. The protracted war was hugely damaging to both antagonists. As well as the loss of about 100,000 troops, the economic and social impact on Paraguay and Bolivia was very severe. Yet, despite the fact that the Chaco War was at one stage the most destructive conflict taking place in the world, the League proved incapable of making any significant intervention. An early attempt at mediation was blocked by the combatants who sought, instead, intervention by regional states outside the League context. Although the League remained on the periphery of the conflict, it did not subsequently succeed in finding a significant role, and the war dragged on to an inconclusive end.

In the course of the Chaco War another border clash took place in Latin America in which the League, chastened by its failure to intervene effectively in the Bolivia–Paraguay conflict, was determined to find a mediating role. A long-standing conflict between Colombia and Peru over their Amazonian frontier had been resolved in principle in 1922 by a general border agreement. Part of this involved the transfer from Peru of the area around the river town of Leticia. This was to provide Colombia with access to the Amazon, which was as important in that part of South America as an outlet to the sea was for Bolivia. Although the treaty was ratified by both states in 1928, local resentment at the transfer of nationality led to disturbances in the region that ended with the expulsion of Colombian government officials by an armed mob in September 1932. A situation of local disorder threatened to spiral into a major confrontation between the two countries when Colombia sought to retake the town by force. Nationalist *amour propre*, which was particularly high in Latin America at this time, meant that the Peruvian government felt it had no option but to support its citizens in the face of Colombian military threats, regardless of the apparently clear-cut legal rights and wrongs of the situation. For its part, the Colombian government could not be seen to have been forced from a portion of its national territory by a local mob. While the dispute over Leticia was relatively trivial in itself, it was capable of escalating into a major international war.

Brazil, which was the dominant local power, made an early attempt at mediation, putting forward a plan by which it would occupy Leticia prior to its orderly return to Colombia. This would remove the provocation of a Colombian military action from the equation. While acceptable to Colombia, the plan was rejected by Peru, whose government had now become trapped by its own nationalist rhetoric into resisting Colombia's attempts to resume control of Leticia. In a rapidly deteriorating situation, with the Peruvian air force attacking Colombian navy vessels on the Amazon, Brazil announced that it was withdrawing its good offices. This provided the League of Nations with an opportunity to intervene in the crisis. The League Council produced a plan that would, in effect, see it take over the role that was to have been played by Brazil in the earlier scheme. The League would administer the territory for a period of one year, supported by an 'international force' that would in practice consist of Colombian troops under League of Nations command. Once again, this was acceptable to Colombia but not to Peru. In an unusually strong response to this, the League Council invoked Article 15 of the Covenant, which gave it the authority, in the event of an intractable conflict between members, to 'make and publish a report containing a statement of the facts of the dispute and the recommendations which are deemed just and proper in regard thereto'. Its determination, adopted unanimously, was that Peru should withdraw from Leticia to permit further negotiations.

For some time it appeared that the crisis would escalate into all-out war as both countries were mobilizing their naval forces. The situation was recovered by a peculiarly Latin American *deus ex machina*, however. In April 1933 the Peruvian president was assassinated (for reasons unconnected with the Leticia dispute) and his radical nationalist government replaced by one that proved more amenable to international pressure. The plan was now implemented and a League of Nations governing Commission arrived in June 1933. This was composed of Brazilian, Spanish and United States representatives, the last by virtue of America's obvious hemispheric interests despite its not being a League member. The 'international' force of Colombian troops was now deployed. In line with the League plan, talks between the conflicting parties led to the return of Leticia to full Colombian sovereignty in 1934. In a foretaste of future United Nations operations, international emblems were employed for the first time in a peacekeeping operation. The force wore League of Nations armbands and was deployed under the League of Nations flag. This was more than merely symbolism; it was designed to reduce resentment against the force, which otherwise would have been identified as a Colombian army of occupation.

Assessment: 'proto-peacekeeping'?

Despite the League's successes in the 1930s from the Saar to Leticia, the larger fabric of the organization's collective security function was rapidly unravelling. The post-war phase of political and military exhaustion in the 1920s, which had provided a favourable environment for the peacekeeping role of the League and other actors, soon passed. By the end of the decade the international system had become bifurcated between two types of power. States such as Britain and France sought to maintain their positions in the international hierarchy by pursuing policies designed to secure stability in the system. Against them were ranged powers such as Nazi Germany, Fascist Italy and militarist Japan, whose foreign and military policies were aimed at re-ordering the system to their own advantage. For the states committed to the maintenance of stability the League was a useful instrument in the right circumstances. The management of the Saar situation was a particularly good illustration of this. However, when the League's more Wilsonian aspirations were tested, these states tended to retreat behind traditional and familiar nineteenth-century concepts of national interest. The League therefore failed to confront – or was prevented from confronting – in any meaningful way the aggressions of other states that sought to overturn the prevailing order. Thus Japan's attack on Manchuria in China in 1931 went largely unpunished, as did Italy's invasion of Abyssinia in 1935. Neither London nor Paris saw any pressing national interest in attempting to thwart Japanese claims against a weak and chaotic China. Later, neither trusted the other to maintain solidarity against Italy over what was, after all, 'just' an African imperial adventure. Subsequently there was little surprise at the League's irrelevance in the face of Germany's redrawing of the map of Europe in the second half of the 1930s.

As we will see, the even more ambitious collective security plans of the United Nations met with no more success at the end of the Second World War, which the League's 'failure' had helped precipitate. In the UN, however, peacekeeping became part of the organization's fabric in a way that proved impossible in the League. The ideological bipolarity of the post-1945 system, built around the politics of nuclear weapons, excluded any possibility of the big-power consensus that is a prerequisite for effective collective security. But bipolarity itself created conditions that allowed peacekeeping to develop into a routine international activity. As the rules of nuclear deterrence were gradually elaborated, means of controlling and containing geographically and politically peripheral conflicts became crucial if the superpower relationship was to be effectively managed. Moreover, such conflicts were particularly frequent after 1945 because of another historical feature of the system: the dissolution of the colonial empires. Post-imperial adjustment after the First World War was managed in many places by what we have characterized as plebiscite peacekeeping. After 1945 there were larger and more enduring issues involved than the location of border populations, and the peacekeeping efforts involved were consequently much larger. Overall, therefore, peacekeeping in the age of the League occupied a political environment that offered less of an opportunity for its institutionalization.

As we have pointed out, in its first years the United Nations secretariat was aware of the antecedents of peacekeeping when the Palestine Commission explored the international military projects of the 1920s and 1930s in pursuit of a response to its own post-1945 challenges. Subsequently, peacekeeping may have been presented as a UN invention and the product of distinct features of the post-Second World War system. But in reality it had a longer institutional pedigree and its fundamental functions remained consistent. Its role was to provide one means of managing an international system in which enforcement-based collective security was unachievable because of the persistence of traditional conceptions of national interest.

3 Collective security revived

The formation of the United Nations

Whatever the fate of the League as an institution, the *idea* of a global international organization with responsibility for the regulation of international security had become firmly lodged in political and popular consciousness by the time of the Second World War. Even as the League of Nations disintegrated in the later 1930s and another world war loomed, there was a general expectation that the experiment would be rerun, though in different terms, when conditions in the international system allowed.

The Second World War and the origins of the United Nations

Two years after the outbreak of the Second World War in Europe and just months before the United States was drawn in to it after the Japanese attack on Pearl Harbor, an Anglo-American commitment was made to the construction of a new organization when the war was finished. The Atlantic Charter was signed in August 1941 during a meeting between the British prime minister Winston Churchill and the American president, Franklin D. Roosevelt held on a warship off the Canadian coast. Collective security was back on the agenda, despite the experience of the League. After the war the signatories intended 'to see established a peace which (would) afford to all nations the means of dwelling in safety within their own boundaries'. To this end, all nations 'for realistic as well as spiritual reasons must come to the abandonment of the use of force'. This would involve the establishment of 'a . . . permanent system of general security', and pending this, 'nations which threaten, or may threaten aggression outside of their frontiers' would be disarmed.[1] The first use of the term 'United Nations' came the following year when it was adopted by the twenty-six states fighting the Axis powers.

American state department officials had, in fact, been working on an outline of a new organization as early as 1940. After the United States entered the war, however, plans for the permanent 'general security' system envisaged in the Atlantic Charter began to take firmer shape. The process accelerated as an allied victory looked increasingly likely. In 1943 the American secretary of state, Cordell Hull, signed up his Soviet and British counterparts – commissar for foreign affairs Vyacheslav Molotov and foreign secretary Anthony Eden – to a declaration committing them to the creation of 'a general international organization based on the principles of the sovereign equality of all peace loving states and open to membership by all such states, large and small for the maintenance of international peace and security'.[2]

Detailed planning of the new organization was, of course, constrained by the overarching priority of winning the war. Human and material resources for this were in short supply and perhaps, too, at some level of consciousness, excessive planning of the post-war system was felt to invite hubris. For President Roosevelt, who among the major wartime leaders was the most enthusiastic for a post-war security organization, there was a particular concern. He was keenly aware of the fate of the American relationship with the League. For all the moral energy of Woodrow Wilson, his fellow Democrat predecessor, the reaction in Congress had still been against continued leadership of the post-war system. It was necessary, therefore, to move ahead cautiously and to design a system in which American power would be enhanced and preserved rather than dissipated and diminished.

The tripartite commitment to a new organization secured by Cordell Hull was made public during the Tehran Conference of allied leaders in November 1943. In the run-up to this, some fundamental differences in national preferences had been revealed. The American view favoured the regulation of international security collectively by the major powers in the system. In real terms, following an allied victory in the war, this would mean the United States itself, the Soviet Union and Britain. The key decision-making processes around the maintenance of international security would be controlled by the big powers. To this end, the American planners argued, there could be no return to the requirement for unanimity that the League had imposed on its members. The burdens and dangers of this big-power role, it was proposed, should be eased by a stage-by-stage process of disarmament among the other states in the international system.

The British view was less radical, and in some respects still informed by the old nineteenth-century concert system. Churchill's view, in other words, was more 'realist' than Roosevelt's in that he did not share American confidence in the transforming power of collective security. States would still look first and last to their own capacities to guarantee their security, Churchill believed. For Britain, the lesson of the League was that the construct of sovereignty would continue to dominate the behaviour of states and could not be negotiated away simply by the creation of a new institution with a new constitution. The participation or otherwise of the United States in the new organization would not alter that fundamental fact. Small and medium-sized powers would not willingly subordinate themselves to the control of big powers, however well intentioned. And, from the other side of the power spectrum, the commitment of the big powers to a consistent effort across all parts of the system was questionable in the British view. With the League's experience over Manchuria and Abyssinia in mind, Britain was sceptical about the extent of big-power commitment to expensive and burdensome involvement in areas of the world that they did not regard as vital to their own national interests. Security cooperation would be best pursued on a regional rather than a global basis, which would focus collective concerns on areas and issues of direct national interest. Britain therefore would be concerned with western Europe, while the United States would be responsible for the western hemisphere. Constructed in this way the United Nations would provide an organizational umbrella with little direct responsibility for security on the ground. The new organization should therefore have a 'council of Europe', a 'council of Asia' and so on. Above these regional bodies there would be a 'high court', which would be a development on the existing Permanent Court of International Justice, which was established under the League.

The Soviet leader Joseph Stalin was initially suspicious of the American plan for the concentration of power in so few – and predominantly capitalist – hands. To begin with he seemed to favour the British position, which in some respects would have legitimized Soviet domination of eastern Europe, at least in terms of the control of regional security. Eventually, however, the American model came to be more favoured in Moscow when the possibility of US rejection of any system other than Roosevelt's was made clear. A repeat of America's rejection of the League could not be contemplated. From Stalin's perspective the most important thing was that any system should be dominated by the major powers and that the USSR should be at the centre of it. The Soviet Union had been excluded from the League until 1934, by which time the institution's authority was already fatally undermined, and Stalin was determined that this history would not be repeated.

Roosevelt's vision of the United Nations prevailed, therefore, just as Wilson's had for the League. In both cases this was no more than a reflection of the 'realist reality' of the international system at each historical juncture. The United States had emerged from both world wars not only as a victor but as the one most able, by virtue of its resilient national power, to dictate the terms of the post-war disposition.

The new organization emerges: from Dumbarton Oaks to San Francisco

Concrete planning for the new organization began the year following the commitment by the powers at Tehran. A crucial sequence of meetings took place in August 1944 at Dumbarton Oaks, an estate outside Washington. Here the Soviet and British ambassadors to the United States, Andrei Gromyko (who was later to be Soviet foreign minister during much of the cold war era) and Sir Alexander Cadogan, were closeted with the American assistant secretary of state, Edward Stettinius. China, at this time still nominally under the control of Chiang Kai-shek's nationalists, was also represented. These states were to comprise Roosevelt's 'four policemen', who would preside at the centre of the new security organization. The purpose of the Dumbarton Oaks meeting was to convert the general thinking already undertaken by the leading allies into a solid set of proposals that could then be presented to the broader anti-Axis alliance now close to winning the war. There was little disagreement about the general architecture the United Nations should be built upon. This was dictated by much the same logic involved in the design of League of Nations, which, as we saw, had resulted in something analogous to a modern state.

Where the League had a Council composed of the major powers, the United Nations would have a Security Council, which again corresponded roughly to a national executive or cabinet. The Security Council would have eleven members (increased in 1966 to fifteen). There would be two classes of Security Council membership. The permanent members comprised the four states represented at Dumbarton Oaks (the US, USSR, Britain and China) and later France, which was still under German occupation at the time of the meeting and did not participate. The biggest of the victorious war allies therefore would be Roosevelt's 'policemen', who would take the lead responsibility for the management of collective security. The legal basis of this role, which we will explore in due course, would eventually be laid out in Chapter VII of the United Nations Charter, the organization's constitution and descendant of the League Covenant.

The special role of the permanent members brought with it the power of veto over actions proposed by other members of the Security Council. In this way, the traditional national interests and prerogatives of the biggest powers in the system would be preserved while decisive action would not, in theory, be constrained by the need for unanimity as it was in the League. While many have criticized the whole principle of the veto, it was designed as a means of acknowledging the reality of power in, and the special national interests of, the biggest states in the system, while still permitting the possibility of workable collective security. While the League required all of the states on the Council to give their positive support to a decision, in the new organization a permanent member might abstain or absent itself from a vote on a resolution without nullifying it.

The six (later ten) non-permanent members of the Security Council would serve for two-year periods. To ensure continuity, half of them would be elected to the Security Council each year by their regional groupings in the General Assembly. This General Assembly was the successor to the League Assembly. Like its predecessor it could be seen as in some senses corresponding to a national parliament. All UN members would have a seat and a vote in the General Assembly. The approach to UN membership agreed at Dumbarton Oaks was essentially a universalist one; admission would, in principle, be open to all. As we have seen, the effectiveness and authority of the League had been vitiated not only by the non-participation of the United States but by the initial exclusion of Germany and the Soviet Union. This had two negative effects. First, it created an impression of the League as an alliance of First World War victors. Second, it fostered a culture in which membership and non-membership were equally valid foreign policy options for states. This became evident when the future Axis powers, Germany, Italy and Japan, withdrew from the organization one by one in the 1930s. This was a fatal flaw in an institution charged with the management of collective security in the international system as a whole. It was agreed at Dumbarton Oaks therefore (and later embodied in the Charter itself) that membership of the United Nations would be open to all 'peace-loving states'. There were difficulties in applying this formula in the first decade of the United Nations when the Soviet Union used its veto on membership applications to control the growth of the then western majority in the General Assembly. But from the mid-1950s, with a very few significant qualifications that we will discuss in due course, the United Nations General Assembly was a genuinely universalist body.

Unexpectedly, perhaps, the first serious signs of east–west division emerged at Dumbarton Oaks over the arrangements for the General Assembly rather than the Security Council. While the Soviet Union's interests seemed to be guaranteed in the Council by its right of veto, the weakness of communist power in the system as a whole was sharply exposed in the more 'democratic' forum of the General Assembly. While playing a crucial part in the allies' final war effort, in a sense the USSR still stood alone in 1944. It remained the only communist state in the system. As the negotiators sat down at Dumbarton Oaks the future of what would become the satellite states of the eastern bloc was still far from certain, though there was an assumption that liberation from German occupation would lead to democratic self-determination. Although the nationalists in China were gradually falling before Mao Zedong's apparently unstoppable communist advance, they still represented Chinese interests at Dumbarton Oaks. They would also, controversially, represent China in the United Nations until 1971. Moscow therefore felt vulnerable in the new forum.

The issue also went beyond the nascent ideological division between east and west. The idea of sovereign equality among members on which the General Assembly was built was a venerable Westphalian principle. It also had a certain emotional appeal in a system that was in the final phase of a war fought against large powers that had trampled on the rights of small ones. But none of this could quite disguise the anomaly that saw a state such as the Soviet Union, with its huge population, given precisely the same power in the General Assembly as, say, a small Latin American country representing perhaps less than a million people. The Soviet attempt to redress this situation involved an inventive piece of multiple counting. Gromyko proposed that all sixteen republics of the Soviet Union should have separate membership of the General Assembly. The other delegates, aware that whatever the rhetoric of the Soviet constitution the USSR was in reality a ruthlessly centralized state, dismissed the proposal out of hand and the matter remained unresolved at Dumbarton Oaks.

Despite this and a number of other issues such as arguments over limitations on the use of the veto being left pending after Dumbarton Oaks, the meeting had been successful overall in reaching agreement on the framework for the new organization. The next phase in its development took place during the conference of allied leaders at Yalta on the Russian Black Sea in February 1945. Here the precise terms of the Security Council veto were agreed, with the Soviet Union accepting that it should not apply to attempts at 'peaceful settlement' of disputes. The issue of General Assembly representation was also settled – though to no one's real satisfaction – when the USSR accepted two further seats for Ukraine and Byelorussia.[3] The squabble was an early portent of emerging cold war divisions within the organization.

The formal establishment of the United Nations took place in San Francisco in April 1945 on the eve of allied victory in Europe but still several months from the end of the war in Asia. The meeting took place less than two weeks after the death of President Roosevelt, who had been succeeded by his vice president, Harry Truman. The new president, although from a different, less patrician, Democrat tradition, nevertheless shared his predecessor's commitment to the new organization. Early fears that there might be a repeat of the League experience, with America (despite its leading role in the construction of the organization) rejecting membership of it, proved misplaced. Roosevelt had been careful to build a bipartisan consensus and Republican support for the new body had been carefully secured. The cross-party commitment to the UN was symbolized by the participation of leading Republicans in the San Francisco ceremonies.

Fifty-one states gathered to sign the new Charter. All were members of the anti-Axis alliance, though some only recently so. The wartime status of the signatories may have suggested on one level that the UN was to be an alliance of victors, an image that had undermined the moral authority of the League, as we have observed. But the sheer numbers of signatories pointed in another direction – towards a universality of membership that the League never attained. The document to which they put their nations' signatures represented the second attempt in the twentieth century to codify a system of collective security as an alternative to national defence.

The 'Pacific Settlement of Disputes' and 'Action with Respect to Acts of Aggression'

Two sections of the United Nations Charter, Chapters VI and VII, deal with the specifics of international security and set out the role of the organization in guaranteeing it.[4] As we will see, the term peacekeeping does not appear in the United Nations Charter and it is doubtful that such activity was ever contemplated by those drafting its articles in 1944 and 1945. Peacekeeping therefore has no specific identity in international law. This has not deterred scholars and practitioners from attempting to locate it by association with some part of the Charter. In the absence of a clear articulation, peacekeeping has in the past been referred to as a 'Chapter six-and-a-half' activity. This is a legally meaningless term but it nevertheless says something about the nature of peacekeeping. It is, in this view, poised between Chapter VI, which is concerned with the 'Pacific Settlement of Disputes', and Chapter VII, which is the central statement of collective security and deals with 'Action with Respect to Threats to the Peace, Breaches of the Peace, and Acts of Aggression'.

The approach of Chapter VI is essentially 'voluntarist' in that the processes and measures outlined in the Chapter do not involve enforcement by the UN. In this sense it represents an attempt at collective security before the deployment of international military force. The Chapter begins with Article 33 of the Charter, which sets out an extensive menu of procedures to be followed by parties to a dispute, 'the continuance of which is likely to endanger the maintenance of international peace and security'. They are to 'seek a solution by negotiation, enquiry, mediation, conciliation, arbitration, judicial settlement, resort to regional agencies or arrangement, or other peaceful means of their own choice'. Article 34 empowers the Security Council, if it chooses to do so, to determine whether a dispute is likely to pose a threat to peace and security, and Article 36 permits it to 'recommend appropriate procedures or methods of adjustment'. In the event of the parties failing to reach a means of resolving their dispute, Article 37 requires them to refer the matter to the Security Council. At this stage it is open to the Security Council to propose mechanisms of settlement. As this might, implicitly, involve the deployment of peacekeepers there is at least an argument that a legal basis for peacekeeping can be inferred from this part of the Charter.

Alternatively, the Council might view the dispute and the threat it could pose to broader international security as sufficiently serious to be considered under Chapter VII of the Charter. This chapter is in many ways the most significant part of the whole document. It was certainly the most difficult to find agreement on at Dumbarton Oaks. It represented, simply, an attempt to impose on the international system mechanisms of collective security that would succeed where the earlier League experiment had failed. To this end it required far-reaching and burdensome commitments from all Charter signatories. Here once again perhaps we can discern the influence of the legalistic culture of the United States that we touched on when we explored the League Covenant. The lesson to be taken from the failure of the collective security under the League, it seemed, was not that the basic project was flawed, but that its legal structures were insufficiently strong. This second attempt, therefore, would impose clear and unavoidable obligations. The result was a constitution that, potentially, demanded a major qualification of state sovereignty. A measure of the extent of this commitment and the unease it originally generated was Switzerland's decision not to join the United Nations, a position it reversed only in 2002. Despite being widely admired for its good international citizenship (illustrated, for example, by its hosting of the League of Nations headquarters in Geneva), Switzerland viewed the Charter as a treaty commitment that would have compromised its historical neutrality. And, in truth, had the powers given to it under Chapter VII ever been fully exercised by the Security Council, Switzerland's concerns would have been fully justified.

Article 39, with which Chapter VII opens, empowers the Security Council to 'determine the existence of any threat to the peace, breach of the peace, or act of aggression' and to 'decide what measures shall be taken . . . to maintain or restore' peace and security. The range of these measures is presented in Articles 41 and 42. The first of these Articles is concerned with pressures short of military force: economic sanctions, transport and communications blockades and the severance of diplomatic relations. However, Article 42 determined that should 'the Security Council consider that measures provided for in Article 41 would be inadequate or have proved to be inadequate, it may take such action by air, sea, or land forces as may be necessary . . .'. Although the League Covenant did not explicitly rule out military action to enforce collective security, it had little to say on the subject and placed no obligations on members. Now, however, Article 43 of the UN Charter required that all members 'in order to contribute to the maintenance of international peace and security, undertake to make available to the Security Council, on its call . . . armed forces, assistance and facilities . . . necessary for the purpose of maintaining international peace and security'.

These arrangements would effectively have created a UN army that could be raised on need. At an early stage of the planning of the Charter the possibility of an actual standing army was in fact raised. The idea was eventually dropped, but on practical rather than political grounds, which gives a sense of the extent of the ambitions of the wartime planning behind the United Nations. As it was, UN forces would be under the command of a joint staff composed of the military leaders of the permanent members of the Security Council. This was the Military Staff Committee (MSC), which is covered by Article 47. The MSC would be directed by the five chiefs of staff of the permanent members and would be 'responsible under the Security Council for the strategic direction of any armed forces placed at the disposal of the Security Council'.

Article 51, the final part of Chapter VII, appears at first reading to represent an opt-out clause from the far-reaching arrangements that the preceding articles had outlined. The 'inherent right of individual or collective self-defence' was recognized as a legitimate recourse for states under direct assault. In fact, it describes an emergency situation in which a surprise attack may be resisted only 'until the Security Council has taken measures necessary to maintain international peace and security'. In other words, it is not an alternative to Security Council action, merely a preliminary to it. Similarly, the following section of the Charter, Chapter VIII, which deals with 'Regional Arrangements' and which acknowledged the role of local agencies in the maintenance of peace and security, was also only a limited qualification of Security Council control. Article 53 confirmed that the Security Council might utilize regional bodies for enforcement action, but only 'under its authority'. In other words, collective security action might be franchised out, but it could not be undertaken by a competing focus of international authority.

The collective security arrangement of the Charter reflected the concern of its American planners that the history of the League should not be allowed to repeat itself. Urgent decision-making should not be made impossible by unclear and diffuse lines of authority and initiative. The power vested in the permanent members of the Security Council was simply the constitutional embodiment of Roosevelt's idea of a select group of powerful world policemen. It was not an arrangement that was attractive to all of the rank and file membership of the UN, however. At San Francisco some of the more established smaller states opposed this concentration of power, arguing that it was incompatible with the democratic principle of sovereign equality. Australia and New Zealand sought a larger role for the General Assembly in security matters than the Dumbarton Oaks plan had envisaged. A proposal was put by them that the Assembly should approve any enforcement action planned by the Council. But the United States remained adamant that there should be no debilitating seepage of authority. The other permanent members of the Security Council were, of course, happy to agree.

Like the League, the United Nations would be served by a secretariat composed of permanent international civil servants. These would owe their primary loyalty to the organization rather than to their states of origin. At the head of this secretariat, as in the League, there would be a secretary-general. There was, however, a feature of the UN Charter – absent in the League Covenant – that emphasized the UN's determination to make collective security work. The office of secretary-general was to be more than simply an administrative position. The head of the secretariat was to have a personal proactive role in the maintenance of international security. Article 99 of the Charter empowered the secretary-general to 'bring to the attention of the Security Council any matter which in his [*sic*] opinion may threaten the maintenance of international peace and security'. In 1945, before the international system became polarized by the cold war, this was a significant but not a particularly controversial innovation. One potential conflict in the arrangements for the secretary-general was avoided when the United States backed down from its proposal that he or she should be appointed by the General Assembly. Aware of its vulnerability in a forum in which it would be outnumbered by western states, the Soviet Union objected. It was therefore agreed that the responsibility would lie with the Security Council, whose decisions were, of course, subject to veto.

At San Francisco the discussions about who should be appointed as the first secretary-general of the organization underlined the sensitivity of the post. The United States proposed the Canadian foreign minister, Lester Pearson, who was rejected by the Soviet Union as too 'western'. Moscow's own suggestion, the foreign minister of Yugoslavia, was ruled out by the western powers for being too close to the Soviet camp. Eventually it was agreed that Trygve Lie, the foreign minister of Norway, would be a suitable choice. This selection process was a portent of future difficulties. In 1945 Norway was still regarded as largely neutral between east and west; four years later, however, it was a founding member of the North Atlantic Treaty Organisation (NATO) and Lie's position became much more controversial. As the UN divided between opposing camps in the 1950s and 1960s, the neutrality of the secretary-general would become a major area of dispute, particularly in issues relating to the organization's security and peacekeeping functions, as we will see.

Like its predecessor, the new UN was to have a permanent headquarters. San Francisco was a one-off venue (the founding session of the UN there was held in the Opera House). There was no clear agreement or, for that matter, very strong disagreement among the major powers about where the UN should call home. The old League headquarters, the Palais des Nations in Geneva, was not suitable for a number of reasons. For one thing, Switzerland, as we have seen, had opted not to join the United Nations and it would hardly have been appropriate for a non-member to host the general headquarters.[5] But the Geneva building was also inescapably linked with the perceived failure of the earlier institution, and the UN was determined to present itself as a fundamentally new beginning in international cooperation. In addition to the objections to Geneva in particular, there was a wider resistance to the idea of the UN being based in Europe at all. An American location was widely favoured, and not just by the friends and allies of the United States. Many of the smaller member countries felt it would strike a blow against the Eurocentrism that had characterized international relations for centuries past. And, states of the western hemisphere made up a considerable proportion of the UN's initial membership in the years before European decolonization brought an influx of Afro-Asian members. The matter was settled when the American millionaire philanthropist, John D. Rockefeller, bought and presented to the UN a site on New York's East River.

The general consensus over the location of the headquarters building could not, however, disguise the widening rents in the political fabric of the UN. These would have fundamental implications for its role in international security. By definition collective security requires as its starting point a collective will. If it was just about reasonable in 1945 to suppose that this might persist in the post-war system, events soon suggested that it would not. As global bipolarity deepened in the later 1940s and 1950s, it became clear that the hopeful assumptions of the charter-makers at Dumbarton Oaks, and the later optimism of their political masters, were profoundly misplaced. In fairness it must be acknowledged that in the peculiar circumstances of the time – on the path towards final victory in a war of unprecedented scale and ferocity – the commitment of the allies to continued cooperation in the post-war system was to an extent taken for granted. And, of course, in the previous century and a half, major wars had given rise to workable systems of regulation based on cooperation among the victors. We have already discussed the European concert system that followed the French Revolutionary and Napoleonic Wars in 1815. More recently there had been the experience of the League, which had loomed large in the planning of the UN. In both, the wartime allies had maintained reasonably high levels of post-war cooperation. In 1945 the League's major disability appeared to have been the non-participation of the United States, and this was a problem that would not arise in the new institution.

Moreover, the technological basis of the impending cold war was not at all apparent when the Charter was being drafted. In 1945 few if any had an inkling of the profound political impact nuclear weapons would have on international politics and the extent to which their existence would shape the post-war system. The Charter was signed at San Francisco several months before the first use of atomic bombs on Hiroshima and Nagasaki, and the Dumbarton Oaks meeting had taken place more than a year earlier. There had been an awareness that some level of east–west competition was likely after the war, even as the allies were advancing on Germany in 1944 from their respective points of the compass. The general agreement on the importance of having a veto arrangement in the Security Council was an indication of this. But the notion that this competition could create a situation in which two superpowers with unprecedented destructive capacity would confront each other over virtually every conflict anywhere on the globe would have seemed fantastic.

This, however, was what the future held in store. The result was that the Charter's plans for collective security would in effect be irrelevant before they had ever been properly tested. In an elementally divided system all international conflict would inevitably be seen through different, ideologically constructed prisms by each side. Consensus on the rights and wrongs of any crisis would be impossible to achieve. The identity of the aggressor would depend on the political character of any conflict and the broader loyalties of the antagonists. Although the word 'aggression' is used freely in Chapter VII of the Charter, no definition is offered. In reality, though, even if one had been, it is unlikely that it would have made any significant difference. The political judgements of the big powers would not have been subordinated to legal terminology. In the realm of ideology 'aggression' could never be an objective concept. And, of course, without the capacity to agree on the rights and wrongs of an international conflict, the Charter, however legally comprehensive, was an empty vessel as far as collective security was concerned. The veto became not an obstruction to collective security, as some later suggested, but a means of assuring that even a United Nations without enforcement capacities could at least continue to exist.

Collective security tested: the Korean War

The only occasion during the cold war that the UN's collective security powers were invoked – and then rhetorically rather than constitutionally – came in 1950 with the crisis over Korea. By this time the shape of the post-1945 international system was already emerging. During the winter of 1947–48 there was a major east–west confrontation over Berlin, which had been divided into different zones of occupation between the allies at the end of the war. Berlin lay within East Germany, which was now effectively a Soviet satellite, and Russia now sought to complete its control by making the western presence in the city unviable. Land access to Berlin from the west was blocked and the western allies responded with a complex and expensive airlift into their zones. The crisis – in which the UN had only a minimal role – eventually subsided, but the battle lines of the cold war had been clearly marked. Elsewhere, in the parts of eastern Europe from which the German occupiers had been expelled by the Red Army, it was becoming clear that the Soviet presence, asserted through the establishment of local communist regimes, was to be a permanent one.

A parallel situation existed in parts of Asia as well. Korea had been annexed by Japan in 1910 after a troubled history of relations between the two countries stretching far back into history. Although the original act of expansionism little troubled the western powers, during the war against Japan the allies had set the independence of Korea as one of their war aims. However, by the end of the war the situation had become complicated. Like Germany, different halves of Korea had been occupied by the west and the Soviet Union respectively. Moscow had committed forces to the Asian theatre only belatedly in the summer of 1945. This involvement would have been unfeasible while the Red Army was forcing its way westwards towards Germany, but after the Nazi surrender Stalin was able to stake a claim to a place in the Asian settlement by declaring war on an already fatally weakened Japan. At the end of the fighting, therefore, Soviet forces occupied the northern part of the Korean peninsula and American forces the southern part. Korea therefore was divided into two de facto states each ruled by regimes that reflected the ideologies of their occupiers. The delivery of the allies' commitment to creating an independent post-war Korea was not going to be easy in these circumstances.

In the north the Soviets had put in power the local communist leader Kim Il Sung, while in the south the American protégé was Syngman Rhee, who, after elections in 1948, led a pro-western nationalist administration. The new government in the south seemed to see the unification of Korea as best achieved by its absorption of the north. North Korea, for its part, aspired towards the creation of a single communist state as the proper outcome of unification. In both parts of the peninsula local military forces had been built up by the two external patron powers, though Soviet and American troops were withdrawn from Korea in 1948 and 1949 respectively. On the eve of the new decade a fierce war of words developed between two well-armed Koreas confident in their external support, with each insisting on its right to extend its authority over the other.

The overwhelming western majority in the General Assembly meant that the United Nations as an institution favoured the claims of the south and recognized Syngman Rhee's regime as the legitimate representative of 'Korea'. But the Soviet veto in the Security Council prevented the admission of that 'Korea' to the UN. Meanwhile tensions continued to build, and by the beginning of 1950 spasmodic but violent incidents were taking place on the border between north and south. This frontier ran along the 38th parallel of the world map, and this was a geographical term that would become a powerfully evocative political expression in the coming years.

The crisis was considered by the Security Council in unusual circumstances. There was no Soviet delegation present. The USSR was boycotting the Council in 1950 in protest over the continued representation of China at the UN by Chiang Kai-shek's nationalists. The previous year the communists had finally extended their control over all of mainland China and the remnants of the pro-US nationalist regime had escaped to the island of Formosa (later known as Taiwan). Here, too, the large western majority in the General Assembly guaranteed that membership issues would be resolved in favour of the United States' clients and supporters. Although the nationalists had effective control over only a tiny fragment of China's territory and population, it retained the UN seat. Moreover, as China had been considered to be a great power when the Charter was being drawn up, the small group of nationalists on Formosa also occupied a permanent seat on the Security Council with all the associated powers and privileges. Moscow's then ally Mao Zedong now controlled mainland China and its huge population but was denied any recognition whatsoever by the United Nations. The Soviet Union was understandably angered by a situation that seemed to fully justify its early concern over the imbalance of power between east and west in the UN. This situation over the representation of China at the UN persisted until 1971 when a general accommodation was reached between Washington and Beijing, though in the meantime relations between the USSR and Communist China had broken down catastrophically. In 1950, however, the two communist giants were closely allied against the west. The effect of Soviet action in support of Communist China's claims to UN membership, however, was that the Security Council that discussed the Korean crisis was composed entirely of western or pro-western states. And, of course, its decisions were not subject to Soviet veto.

As a result of this, when forces from the north pushed across the 38th parallel in large numbers on 25 June, the Security Council was able to demand their withdrawal back across the border.[6] This was ignored by North Korea, which, it had become clear, was engaged in a wholesale invasion. Still unconstrained by the Soviet veto, the Security Council now called on UN members to assist South Korea against the northern invasion. Significantly, however, this resolution made no reference to Chapter VII of the Charter and was couched in terms of 'recommendation' rather than 'decision'. Even free of the threat of veto, it seemed, the western powers were cautious about attempting to deploy the full battery of the UN's collective security powers.[7] In parallel, the United States had begun to mobilize on its own behalf, moving naval forces into the waters between mainland China and Korea. American forces also conducted sea- and air-launched attacks against northern military formations. Finally, at the end of June, American ground forces from bases in Japan (where there was still a large occupying army) were deployed in support of the South Korean army. America's allies in the region – Britain (which still had considerable imperial interests in Asia), Australia and New Zealand – announced their intention to intervene as well. Meanwhile Washington justified its action in the terms of the UN Charter, invoking Article 51, which, it will be recalled, acknowledged the right to collective self-defence. The Korean War was now under way and attention became increasingly focused on the response of the United Nations.

This response was to be a resolutely pro-western one. Still with a free hand in the Security Council, the western powers now set about creating a Unified Command among the forces fighting against North Korea. This multinational army would be legitimized by the UN and would fight under the UN flag.[8] The Unified Command was put under the control of the commander of American forces in Asia, the hawkish and politically ambitious General Douglas MacArthur. The Unified Command would 'report' to the Security Council rather than be directed by it. The Security Council was not, of course, in a position to provide this direction. Under the terms of Article 47 of the Charter any Security Council command responsibility would have been assigned to the MSC. This was unthinkable, as the chief of staff of the Red Army would have been a key participant.

The arrangement put in place appeared to provide the western coalition (which would grow to involve seventeen states) with United Nations legitimacy as a collective security force.[9] It would not, however, involve risking the politically fatal consequences of attempting to invoke Chapter VII of the Charter. To conform to the procedure established by the Charter the force would, anyway, have to have been formed in the first place with reference to Article 43, which placed military obligations on all UN members. The reality was that the American-led Unified Command was effectively a military alliance engaged in a war against the forces of an opposing alliance. This was a considerable distance from anything foreseen in Chapter VII. As this Chapter represented the beginning and end of the entire collective security system of the United Nations, the western manoeuvre inadvertently pointed up the indelible flaw at the centre of the UN project. Collective security as envisaged by the authors of the UN's constitution was fundamentally unworkable in a bipolar system.

On the ground the western 'UN' forces (two-thirds of which were American) enjoyed considerable success, at least at the beginning. Although the northern forces exploited the shock of their original invasion to push deep into South Korea, in September 1950 a massive western assault from a beachhead at Inchon near the capital, Seoul, stopped the advance. The invaders were now pushed back towards the 38th parallel. But military success for the United States created a major dilemma for the United Nations. With the northern forces once again confined behind their own border, the objective of the UN action had surely been achieved. From an American strategic perspective, however, there was now an opportunity to defeat North Korea and resolve the Korean problem permanently in the interests of the west. Any remaining credibility in the claim that the action was based on multilateral 'collective security' would now disappear and the character of the war as an old-fashioned struggle for domination would be fully revealed.

By this stage the west's free rein over the Security Council had ended. At the beginning of August 1950, faced with what it saw as a western rampage at the UN, the Soviet Union thought better of its pro-Beijing gesture and returned to the Security Council. It did so, moreover, as president of the Council, a position that had passed to it by rota during the summer. Now, with the Soviet veto poised above the table, it was clear that any attempt by the American-led forces in Korea to press their military and political advantage would not be directly supported by the Security Council. The western powers now explored two complementary ways to retain UN legitimacy. First, earlier Security Council resolutions, passed in the absence of the Soviet Union, could be presented as legitimizing continued military action.[10] Second, the west could attempt to move the issue away from the Security Council altogether. In the more favourable forum of the General Assembly there would be no Soviet veto to obstruct western war aims in Korea. There would, instead, be a huge pro-western majority there. Accordingly, in October 1950, the General Assembly was persuaded to adopt a resolution calling on the UN to take control of security 'throughout Korea'. The legal basis of this resolution was questionable. The General Assembly had the right under Articles 10 and 11 of the Charter to discuss issues of international security. It could then make recommendations to the Security Council. But it certainly had no power to authorize military action. For the United States, however, the General Assembly vote was sufficient to sanction the advance of Unified Command forces north of the 38th parallel.

This precipitated a critical change in the nature of the war. As the North Korean forces were being pushed back towards the border, China quickly discerned the risk of a counter-invasion of the north. It duly pronounced this a threat to its own security. But unimpressed by vague threats from a potential enemy that he judged to be exhausted and ill-equipped after decades of revolution, civil war and foreign occupation, MacArthur pressed ahead. In response, Chinese communist 'volunteers' began to cross into North Korea from the Chinese province of Manchuria. The human waves that they now threw against the western forces that had crossed into North Korea reversed the flow of the war once again. The 'UN' forces were now those forced back across a border they had recently crossed in triumph.

Now on the defensive on the battlefield, the United States worked to shore up its position in the UN. It did so by attempting to bring the General Assembly even further into the security arena. America now sought to shift fundamentally the goalposts through which the legitimization of UN military action had to pass. This involved a fundamental departure from Roosevelt's original vision of a UN in which authority for collective security and enforcement were to be concentrated in the hands of the big policemen of the Security Council. In effect, the Charter was now revised to pass power to the General Assembly in the event of Security Council action being stalled by disagreement. In November 1950, at the behest of the American delegation, the General Assembly passed the so-called 'Uniting for Peace' resolution. This permitted the transfer – in certain circumstances – of discussion and decision-making in matters of international security from the Security Council to the General Assembly. The conditions under which this could happen would arise when:

> the Security Council because of lack of unanimity of the permanent members, fails to exercise its primary responsibility for the maintenance of international peace and security in any case where there appears to be a threat to the peace, breach of the peace or act of aggression. [In these circumstances] the General Assembly [would] consider the matter immediately with a view to making appropriate recommendations to Members for collective measures, including . . . the use of armed force where necessary.[11]

The use in the resolution of the exact language of Chapter VII was not accidental; this was no less than an attempt to move collective security power away from the Security Council. The use of the Uniting for Peace procedure did not, as events developed, prove as fatal to the UN's credibility as it might have done. Over the coming years the composition of the Assembly changed radically. New states, many of them former colonies that did not automatically identify with western interests, changed the political landscape in a way that made the procedure much less attractive to those who had designed it. In November 1950, however, it threatened to subvert the entire purpose of the UN as originally conceived.

On the ground in Korea the war continued, with fighting concentrated around the 38th parallel and without any decisive breakthrough by either side. There was a growing concern among the western allies about the nature of the American command. Specifically, General MacArthur's intentions and their implications for the conduct of the war caused considerable suspicion. Increasingly, his gung-ho approach to the conduct of the war grated with both allies and other American military leaders and politicians. His general demeanour was also uncomfortable to many who had a more sober view of how a 'UN commander' should conduct himself. Western leaders in general were becoming more circumspect about the whole undertaking in Korea as the prospect of a quick and triumphant outcome retreated at the beginning of 1951. Finally, in April 1951 after some intemperate remarks that contradicted official American policy, MacArthur was summarily dismissed by President Truman. This proved to be something of a watershed for the western effort in Korea and, belatedly, for the image of the United Nations as an impartial world body. The reunification of Korea under the control of the South, which had been MacArthur's key war aim, was no longer at the top of the public agenda. As a result the war was no longer quite as damaging as it had been to perceptions of the UN's political identity. Long and mistrustful negotiations led in July 1953 to an armistice between the sides in the war that merely reconfirmed the 38th parallel as a de facto international frontier. This was some way short of a peace agreement, and no long-term settlement was ever agreed. In the face of the immensely complex local circumstances where common ground was virtually impossible to locate, this may not have been surprising. But it nevertheless represented a failure for the peacemaking capacity of the United Nations.

The war achieved nothing for the Korean people, North or South. It was a wholly destructive event, unmitigated by any political progress. How did it leave the United Nations? The UN emerged from Korea with an image in the world that fell far short of the hopes of its founders. It had come to look dangerously like a mere western alliance. It may have appeared to its more internationalist-minded supporters that the price of American involvement – supposedly the crucial advance on the League of Nations – had come at a self-defeating price. Not only, it seemed, was the dream of a functional collective security system unrealizable, but the mechanisms that were supposed to realize it were dangerously vulnerable to political exploitation. This was not, it must be said, a widely held perception in western public opinion. The early 1950s was not a notably liberal era. Assumptions about Korea were shaped by the pervasive anti-communism of the time and a considerable degree of racial and cultural prejudice. This meant that western – that is 'UN' – efforts in Korea were not subject to the same critical scrutiny they would be in later conflicts, most obviously that in Vietnam. But beyond the west, among those open to communist propaganda and those nationalists in the European empires who were poised to take control of their new states as decolonization approached, the image of the UN had been badly damaged. Would the United Nations now follow the League into irrelevance and worse, or would it merely formalize itself into the western alliance that many now assumed it to be? Or was there a way forward, an adjustment of role and identity that could give the United Nations a new, genuinely multilateralist role even amid the bipolarity of the cold war? Could the organization find a military purpose that would enable it to lessen cold war conflict rather than contribute to it as had happened in Korea?

4 Peacekeeping resumed

From Palestine and Kashmir to Suez

In Chapter 2, when we discussed the League of Nations' record in peacekeeping, we referred to an exercise undertaken by the UN General Assembly's Palestine Commission in 1948 that laid out the League's experience with multilateral military operations. This, we observed, indicated a continuity in peacekeeping thinking that has often gone unacknowledged. There was certainly an interregnum after the League's loss of relevance and authority and during the early years of the United Nations when its ambitions were focused on its far-reaching plans for enforcement-backed collective security. But with the deep-seated flaws of this new collective security exposed by the Korean crisis, this underlying continuity in the peacekeeping role became more evident. After Korea it gradually came to be accepted that a security role for the UN could be developed, and it could involve the use of military personnel, but it would be a much more modest one than that envisaged by Chapter VII of the Charter.

The bases of this role were, in fact, emerging even before the Korean War. In two parts of what can loosely be described as the post-colonial world – in the Middle East and in South Asia – military units under Security Council control and deployed under the UN flag were already engaged in peacekeeping functions. These operations in Palestine and Kashmir were limited to military observation of ceasefires, but soon different techniques would develop to meet more ambitious Security Council mandates. The relatively modest use of observers in Palestine and Kashmir from the late 1940s was followed in 1956 by the large-scale deployment of a major UN military presence along the Suez Canal. After the Suez involvement, the techniques of peacekeeping were listed and codified in a way that sometimes suggested that the activity was a fundamentally new one rather than what it was: a continuation of an activity with an established history in the international system.

The special attention focused on peacekeeping from the 1950s was perhaps understandable, though, if we consider where we left things at the end of the Korean War. The future of the United Nations as an impartial, multinational actor with a viable security role was in question. Peacekeeping appeared to be a possible answer. Palestine and Kashmir provided some significant indicators about the character of peacekeeping and its feasibility in a bipolar system. Both were in essence crises of decolonization; they were conflicts generated by the adjustment of the sovereign units in the international system by the withdrawal of 'imperial order' in unfavourable environments and circumstances. In Palestine the ending of the British League of Nations mandate was complicated by the establishment of the state of Israel. In Kashmir, Britain's withdrawal from its Indian empire had led not to a single new independent state but partition into new units characterized by contested borders and mutual hostility.

The role that the UN undertook in these conflicts was facilitated by a number of important factors, the presence or absence of which would be central to the success of future peacekeeping projects. First, in both cases there was a peace to keep in that the UN's function was to observe established ceasefires. There was no question of enforcement by the UN against an identified aggressor. Second, and as a consequence of this, the military deployment by the UN was very modest in each case. This meant that contributing states did not feel unduly burdened while the host states did not feel any threat from the intervention. Third, and critically in view of bipolarity, neither Palestine nor Kashmir in the late 1940s was an area of significant east–west competition (though this situation would change). The Security Council therefore had little difficulty in agreeing mandates and supporting the operations once they were under way. In other words, peacekeeping of this sort, in contrast to collective security, was a viable undertaking even in a cold war.

Palestine and the Truce Supervision Organization

Palestine occupied a special position in international politics by virtue of the League of Nation's mandate system, which we discussed briefly in Chapter 2. As it was part of the Ottoman Empire at the beginning of the First World War, responsibility for the territory passed initially to the League after Turkey's defeat. Britain became responsible for Palestine as well as modern-day Jordan and Iraq while France took the mandates for Syria and Lebanon. With the formal dissolution of the League, responsibility for the mandate system passed to the United Nations, which had established a 'Trusteeship Council' for this purpose.[1] Other territories, such as the German colonies in Africa and the Pacific, were effectively absorbed into the empires of the mandated powers. The former Ottoman Middle East, however, where Arab nationalism was already well developed by the 1920s, proved problematic for its new rulers.

Palestine presented particular difficulties. The location of the historical land of Israel, it became the destination for growing numbers of Jewish immigrants from Europe in the inter-war years. This migration, originally orchestrated by the growing Zionist movement as part of a religiously influenced ideology, accelerated dramatically as Nazi power grew in

Europe. Then, after the end of the Second World War, a flood of holocaust survivors began to make their way to the new 'Israel'. As the numbers of these migrants increased there was mounting pressure for the creation of a fully independent Israeli state that would take its place as a sovereign member of the international system. In the meantime, the indigenous Arab population of Palestine feared for its own political future as it saw much of its traditional land being absorbed into the new Jewish entity. It fell to Britain, exhausted and impoverished after the war, to manage this dangerous and increasingly violent situation. British forces were required to turn away 'illegal' migrant ships packed with the desperate survivors of the Nazi concentration camps while suffering terrorist attacks by Zionist extremists already in Palestine. Unwilling to continue with this burden amid the pressures of its own post-war reconstruction, the British government informed the United Nations in April 1947 that it intended to relinquish the mandate the following year.

The UN had difficulty in developing a clear course of action for Palestine after the end of the mandate. A General Assembly committee was established, which recommended the partition of Palestine into two separate political entities. This was, in essence, a recognition of the situation that had developed on the ground. But the committee could not agree on the international status of the new arrangement. The majority favoured two sovereign independent states that would share a single capital, the contested city of Jerusalem, which would remain under international control. A minority on the committee, however, backed a single state with federal components. The two positions reflected the different preferences of Jews and Arabs. The Zionist position strongly backed the majority view that an independent state of Israel should be created. The Palestinian Arabs on the other hand saw their interests as best protected in a federal state with a strong international presence. In September 1947 the General Assembly, meeting in plenary session, opted for the majority proposal.

The positions of America and the Soviet Union were ambiguous. During 1947 the United States appeared to alternate in its view from support of the partition plan to advocacy of long-term direct UN administration, an arrangement that would have been warmly welcomed by the Palestinian Arabs. The Soviet position was even less clear, and it is likely that Moscow simply had no strong view on the issue at this time. Seen from the perspective of the subsequent history of the Middle East, this may appear strange. By the 1960s the superpowers had identified their respective clients in the region and Soviet support for the Arab cause could be taken just as much for granted as American support for Israel. But in the late 1940s the battle lines were not nearly so clear. For one thing, the Israel lobby in Washington was nothing like as powerful as it would later become, and the Truman administration approached the problems of the region in a much more open-minded way than its successors would. Moscow, for its part, was much more sympathetic to Jewish aspirations at this time. Many of the most influential figures among the Jewish migrants to Palestine were east European socialists, and the prospect of a leftist Israel was attractive to the Soviet Union, which was still desperately short of friends in the international system. At all events, by October 1947 both Washington and Moscow appeared to favour a settlement based on a two-state partition. In other words, they had come to support the view of the majority of the General Assembly committee and the one favoured by the Jewish side.

In retrospect, the open-mindedness of the United States and the Soviet Union and their apparent willingness to agree a joint position at this time can be seen as a lost opportunity for the UN. If the organization had approached the Palestine problem in a more creative way, unburdened by considerations of cold war politics, the entire Middle East might have enjoyed a fundamentally different and happier history. But in 1947 there was no means of predicting the central importance that the region and its difficulties would have in international politics in the coming decades. The plain fact was that neither Washington nor Moscow saw the Palestine issue as especially close to their national interests and therefore, quite understandably, they opted for the line of least resistance by accepting the majority position of the General Assembly. Consequently, they supported the adoption of this two-state approach as UN policy in November 1947.[2]

The effect of the adoption of the plan was to increase inter-ethnic violence in Palestine itself at the end of 1947 and the first months of 1948. The issue was now taken up by the Security Council, which – although discussing it at length – seemed incapable of bringing new thinking to the problem. The situation became further confused when the United States announced that it no longer had confidence in the plan adopted in November 1947 and resurrected its plan for the long-term administration of Palestine by the UN. At this point the consensus between Washington and Moscow broke down, with the Soviet Union opposing UN rule, seeing it as an attempt by the west to maintain control in the region. This was, of course, a further illustration of how far the terms of the Middle East conflict would change in the coming years: at this point the United States appeared to back a minority approach strongly favoured by the Palestinians while the Soviet Union wished to defend the creation of a sovereign Israel.

The result of this international uncertainty over the future of the territory was yet a further intensification of violence, which now involved Arab forces from neighbouring countries. The British mandate ended on 14 May 1948 with no clear indication of what was to take its place. Consequently, each side attempted to force the situation in its own interests. Israel immediately declared its statehood and the surrounding Arab states declared war on it. The Security Council was now called upon to deal with an international conflict that in a real sense was of its own making. Its initial efforts were far from successful. Attempts to invoke Chapter VII of the Charter to force an end to the fighting were made by both the United States and the Soviet Union at different points. These were rejected by the antagonists and, therefore, despite the legal possibility of compulsion, were not forced. Eventually, a British resolution was adopted that called for a temporary truce to enable mediation to take place. This mediation effort fell to a Truce Commission, which had been established by the Security Council during the final days of the mandate.[3] A senior Swedish diplomat, Count Folke Bernadotte, was UN mediator at the head of the Truce Commission. With UN secretary-general Trygve Lie he now set about implementing another part of the ceasefire arrangement. The British-sponsored resolution had determined that the mediation efforts should be 'provided with a sufficient number of military observers' to ensure that both sides complied with the truce.[4] In this way the first UN peacekeeping operation came into existence (Map 17). An initial group of sixty-three officer observers was provided by Belgium, France, Sweden and the United States (which was still regarded as neutral in the conflict). These began to arrive in Palestine in June 1948. The operation was called the United Nations Truce Supervision Organization. It quickly became known at UN headquarters and beyond as 'UNTSO', the first of a long line of (not always elegant) acronyms invariably given to the UN's peacekeeping operations.

The deployment of UNTSO helped contain the international dimension to the conflict over Palestine, but fighting continued between forces already in the territory. The UN mediator Folke Bernadotte was to lose his own life amid this pervasive violence; he was assassinated along with a senior French UNTSO official by Jewish extremists in September 1948. Amid the crisis the existence of the state of Israel was consolidated. Neither its Arab neighbours nor the UN could do anything to qualify or delay Israeli statehood. The General Assembly plan that would have seen the progressive and orderly creation of an Israeli state and international control of the city of Jerusalem was abandoned amid the chaos. In May 1949, just a year after declaring its statehood, Israel was admitted to the UN.

The Truce Supervision Organization expanded gradually through the 1950s and 1960s, rising to a maximum deployment of 600. Eventually, UNTSO observers were deployed beyond Palestine itself in five states in the region (Egypt, Israel, Jordan, Lebanon and Syria). The range of contributing powers also expanded dramatically. It has become the longest continuous UN peacekeeping operation and its presence has been critical at key points in the broad Middle East conflict since the late 1940s. The wars of 1956, 1967 and 1973 between Israel and its neighbours all led to an increase in the activities of UNTSO, at least until the peacekeeping forces that were established specifically to deal with the first and last of these crises were in place. In the aftermath of the 1967 war UNTSO represented the only UN military presence in the region. UNTSO has also been used as an emergency 'peacekeeper bank', providing trained and prepared personnel for other undertakings in their urgent initial stages.

The Kashmir crisis and the UN observer group

Within a year the Security Council had established another, in many respects very similar, operation to deal with a crisis over borders and ethnicity elsewhere in the post-colonial world. The British withdrawal from India in 1947 led to the partition of the former empire into approximate ethnic components, the largest being 'Hindu' India and 'Muslim' Pakistan. Geographical borders rarely coincide with ethnic identity, however, and in several places violent conflict ensued between different ethnic communities left to coexist on one side or other of the frontier. The situation in the mountain territory of Jammu and Kashmir (which is normally referred to just as Kashmir) was something of a special case as the conflict here was an international rather than an inter-communal one. Although Kashmir's population was overwhelmingly Muslim, the territory was included in India at the time of partition. This was because local historic conditions were regarded by the British as a key factor in how the border should be drawn. Kashmir was anomalous in this respect as its local ruler was Hindu, and he opted to have his realm included in India rather than Pakistan.

After independence a resentful Pakistan began a series of probing attacks in Kashmir in an attempt to change the territorial settlement and 'straighten' the ethnic frontier. The UN established a Commission for India and Pakistan (UNCIP), which sought to resolve Kashmir's national identity by a process of demilitarization followed by a plebiscite. Political progress, however, was made impossible by continuing violence, and UNCIP's efforts were increasingly devoted to controlling this rather than implementing a long-term settlement. It did eventually manage to negotiate a ceasefire between the sides, however. This was to take effect from midnight on 1 January 1949, though its durability was uncertain in the still febrile atmosphere in Kashmir. The Security Council resolution that originally set out UNCIP's responsibilities had made reference to the deployment of military observers, and this was now used to provide policing for the truce.[5] The United Nations Military Observer Group in India and Pakistan (UNMOGIP) was the result (Map 24). The organization and operational responsibilities of UNMOGIP were based on those of UNTSO in Palestine, though on a smaller scale (its numbers did not go above about 100 military observers and were frequently much lower). Like UNTSO, the operation became a long-term one and the importance of its contribution rose and fell with local conditions. Increasing tension between India and Pakistan in the mid-1960s, the early 1970s and then in 2002 all underlined the importance of a UN presence in the region.

The UN's original plan for the future of the territory to be determined by plebiscite was never implemented, and Kashmir remained a restive part of India, apparently immune to effective peacemaking into the twenty-first century. But, as with UNTSO in Palestine, peacemaking was not the purpose of the mission. UNMOGIP has had a minimalist role, restricted to the observation of opposing forces and the recording and publication of violations by each side. The mere presence of an international military mission has, however, had a restraining effect on the protagonists at key points in their protracted dispute. In this way a relatively modest observation mission is often able to perform a disproportionate peacekeeping function. As in Palestine, the east–west implications of the conflict were not initially very significant – and in contrast to the Middle East, a firm set of opposing client–patron relationships did not develop in south Asia in the coming years. Although Pakistan would come to be seen as a more reliable western ally than India, the cold war did not impinge significantly on the Kashmir issue. The limited contribution of UNMOGIP therefore represented an acceptable political and financial investment for the permanent members of the Security Council. American and Soviet foreign policies were not critically engaged in the conflict but both sides were aware of the danger to their relationship of uncontrolled escalation in Kashmir and, indeed, everywhere else in the system.

Suez and the United Nations Emergency Force

The UN's peacekeeping efforts took a huge leap forward in scale and ambition in 1956 when, for the first time, a substantial force rather than an observer group was deployed. The United Nations Emergency Force (UNEF) was established to act as an interposition force in the Suez Canal area after the short but dangerous three-way war that had been fought there in October and November 1956 (Map 9). So marked was the shift in scale from the Palestine and Kashmir missions that UNEF has at times been considered as the first UN peacekeeping operation. This is misleading, however, as the basic purpose of UNEF, as well as its essential operational characteristics, represented a development on, rather than a departure from, UNTSO and UNMOGIP, though admittedly a large one. The key characteristics of all three operations were neutral reporting, non-involvement in political processes and non-aggressive physical presence. UNEF therefore represented a change in degree rather than in kind.

The Suez crisis came three years into the term of the UN's second secretary-general, Dag Hammarskjöld. Like his predecessor Trygve Lie, Hammarskjöld was a Scandinavian (a Swede) but unlike Lie he was primarily a professional diplomat rather than a politician. His image as a cautious and safe bureaucrat had helped make him acceptable to the Soviet Union at the time of his appointment. Lie had come to be regarded by Moscow, particularly after the Korean crisis, as unacceptably pro-western in his sympathies. Soon, however, Hammarskjöld was exhibiting considerable independence of thought and action, though his fundamental loyalty to the UN as an institution seemed absolute. Faced with the inescapable fact that the collective security ambitions of the organization's founders had been grounded on the rocks of bipolarity, Hammarskjöld sought to elaborate a more realistic but still effective role for the United Nations in the maintenance of peace. He was convinced that the UN could provide a mechanism for what he described as 'preventive diplomacy'. As the term suggests, this involved proactive and pre-emptive intervention in crises – or even just potential crises – before they developed into major conflicts. While preventive diplomacy would not *necessarily* involve the deployment of military personnel, the UN's experience in Palestine and the Middle East, as well as the record of the League before it, suggested that there could certainly be a military dimension to it. In other words, implicit in Hammarskjöld's thinking was a role for UN military forces that could sidestep the basic obstacles facing the application of Chapter VII enforcement. The key was to deploy diplomatic and, where appropriate, limited military efforts before the question of such enforcement even arose.

The first significant opportunity – and test – of this thinking came with another Middle East crisis when the nationalist regime in Egypt took control of the Suez Canal. In so doing, it provoked an imperial reflex reaction from Britain and France and a linked opportunist attack from Israel. Although the war in the region that had been sparked by the end of the Palestine mandate and the declaration of the state of Israel ended with a UN-supervised truce, this was not followed by effective long-term peacemaking. Meanwhile, a rising tide of Arab nationalism in the region, provoked in part by resentment at what was seen as the world's disregard for Arab rights and contempt for the failure of existing weak, often corrupt, regimes in the region to assert these rights, contributed to mounting tensions.

The UN became engaged in attempts to manage the situation at a number of levels. The chief of staff of UNTSO, the Canadian General E. L. M. Burns, met regularly with Egyptian and Israeli commanders along the border in continuing attempts to calm the situation and prevent the escalation of ceasefire violations. Simultaneously, at the political level Hammarskjöld was spending considerable periods in the region engaged in discussion with government leaders attempting actively to implement his model of preventive diplomacy. Had the general backdrop been more stable, he might well have had some success. He had managed to establish a good relationship with his Egyptian interlocutors, though in an early intimation of what would become something of a diplomatic given, Israel showed itself to be suspicious of UN intentions. At all events, the setting was not favourable and the events over Suez in 1956 brought the secretary-general's diplomacy to a halt.

Egypt was regarded by many in the Middle East and North Africa as the natural leader of a new pan-Arabism. In 1954 Colonel Gamal Abdel Nasser had taken power in Cairo after the earlier overthrow of the old pro-British monarchy. Nasser supported the cross-border campaign of *fedayeen* (guerrilla) attacks on Israel while stopping short of launching a full-scale war that he was uncertain of winning. His activism and evident willingness to stand up to 'imperialism', however vaguely defined, enhanced his reputation in the burgeoning 'Afro-Asian' bloc of states and aspirant states emerging from colonial rule in the 1950s. Inside Egypt Nasser was engaged in a massive programme of economic and social modernization. A centrepiece of this policy was the construction of a high dam on the Nile at Aswan. This was intended to drive forward Egypt's economic self-reliance by increasing food production through irrigation schemes, but more important was its potential for the generation of hydroelectricity. The new source of power would give a huge boost to industrial productivity as well as providing electricity to a large part of the population of the Nile delta.

The Aswan Dam was, however, a hugely expensive project that Egypt could not finance without substantial aid from abroad. The undertaking was originally to have been funded by a group of individual state and institutional donors led by the United States and the World Bank. Washington, however, had grown increasingly wary of Nasser's Egypt and its international role. Its strident anti-Israeli rhetoric and support for Palestinian guerrilla activity was part of this; the pro-Israel lobby had grown rapidly in the 1950s and was now a significant factor in Washington politics. But there were wider concerns. Nasser's radical nationalism had taken Egypt closer than was comfortable for the Americans to the Soviet Union. While it was not – yet – a Soviet client state, the Republican administration of President Dwight D. Eisenhower (who had succeeded the Democrat Truman after the 1952 presidential election) decided that a firm signal should be sent to Nasser about the consequences of becoming one. Accordingly, in the summer of 1956 Eisenhower's secretary of state, the resolute cold warrior John Foster Dulles, announced that the United States was withdrawing from the Aswan funding arrangement. This in effect stopped the entire project in its tracks.

Unsurprisingly, Nasser reacted angrily to the threat to the jewel in the crown of Egypt's modernization programme. In July 1956, no doubt with one eye on the impact of his actions in the region and the broader Afro-Asian world, Nasser decided to strike at one of the more visible (and economically significant) symbols of imperialism by nationalizing the Suez Canal. Built by the French in the 1860s and owned by an Anglo-French company, the canal had been a grand imperial project from an age when the nationalist sensitivities of the non-European world were hardly regarded. It was both a statement of European grandeur at the high point of the continent's nineteenth-century power and a very practical economic investment. The Canal, by connecting the Mediterranean with the Red Sea, revolutionized Europe's physical links with its imperial possessions and economic interests in Asia. These had hitherto been reached only by circumnavigation of the African continent. The Canal's significance did not diminish with the decline of the colonial empires or with the development of air transport after the Second World War. Access to oil supplies from the Persian Gulf was now a major preoccupation and the key function of the canal.

Nasser could not have chosen a more sensitive pressure point in his attempt to punish western 'neo-colonialism'. But by the same token he could hardly have picked a more dangerous one. From his perspective the gesture served a number of symbolic and practical purposes. It represented the Egyptian nation's determination to control its own territory by ending a foreign imposition on national sovereignty. The nationalization signalled to the west that economic leverage could work both ways, and it marked Egypt out as a dominant actor in the international relations of the developing post-colonial system. And, of course, by taking control of the canal, Egypt also took control of its revenues, which could, in principle at any rate, be redirected to replace the foreign aid that was to have financed the Aswan project.

For a time, however, it seemed that the gesture might prove to be an empty one. The United States, which in comparison to industrial Europe had only limited national interest in the Canal, seemed unwilling to be provoked. There was little to be gained, in Dulles' view, by squaring up to Nasser. To do so might simply have the effect of validating his claims to leadership in the Middle East and the broader Afro-Asian world. But Britain and France were not so sanguine. The British prime minister, Anthony Eden, was particularly outraged at Egypt's actions. While Nasser presented the nationalization as an anti-colonial statement, Eden, who had been marked by his experience as a minister at the time of the British 'appeasement' of the Nazis in the 1930s, saw the Egyptian president as a new Hitler who had at all costs to be faced down. For a time, however, even the British and French appeared to be pursuing a solution through the United Nations. Hammarskjöld provided his good offices for a series of talks between British, French and Egyptian representatives, and by mid-October it seemed that progress was being made. A Security Council resolution was adopted, laying out agreed principles for a settlement. These included inter alia: free transit through the canal for all states – a reference to Egypt's long-standing refusal to allow Israeli shipping to use the waterway; respect for Egyptian sovereignty; and a proportion of canal dues to be allotted to development projects.[6] But while the British and French appeared to be cooperating with UN attempts to resolve the crisis by negotiation, they were pursuing a secret parallel approach involving military action. In effect, they were conspiring with Israel to deepen the crisis to a point that would 'require' an Anglo-French intervention in the Canal Zone.

On 29 October 1956 Israeli forces crossed the border into Egypt on the pretext of an operation against *fedayeen* bases. An ultimatum was now issued by the British and French governments to both 'sides' to end the fighting and to withdraw from the area of the Canal in the interests of the free movement of shipping. This was to be guaranteed by the intervention of an Anglo-French military expedition. The Israeli assault was therefore just part of a broader conspiracy hatched by Britain and France following the nationalization. The second phase of the plan involved the ultimatum from London and Paris to both parties demanding their withdrawal from the canal and their agreement to its 'protection' by an Anglo-French force. The effect, of course, would have been to reverse the nationalization of the canal, transfer it back to even tighter Anglo-French control and inflict a major humiliation on Nasser. To no one's great surprise Egypt refused to comply, and on 31 October British aircraft bombed the Canal Zone to prepare the way for troop landings, which followed a few days later. In the meantime, Egypt blocked the canal by sinking ships at key points along its course.

The international reaction to the Anglo-French-Israeli conspiracy was immediate and fierce. The Americans, who felt they had been deliberately kept in the dark by their allies, took the lead at the United Nations and convened an urgent Security Council meeting. Here they proposed a resolution calling on Israel to retreat behind the 1948 armistice line separating it from Egypt. Pointedly, it also called on other UN members not to interfere in the situation. This was blocked by Britain and France, along with a subsequent Soviet resolution, in the first ever use by Britain of its Security Council veto.[7] Clearly, the east–west bipolarity that by 1956 afflicted virtually every area of international relations did not appear to apply to the Suez crisis. The western bloc was fundamentally split on transatlantic lines while the United States and the Soviet Union had discovered an area of mutual, if limited, agreement. Ironically, in view of this, at this precise time east–west relations had just touched a new low as Soviet tanks were crushing an anti-communist uprising in Hungary. For Washington, the Anglo-French adventure in Suez had been a reckless diversion from what should have been a propaganda coup for the west. Instead, it appeared to bring the two bloc leaders together in condemnation of an anachronistic piece of imperial petulance.

The irony deepened when the Anglo-French veto of the Security Council resolutions led to the transfer of discussion and decision-making to the General Assembly under the Uniting for Peace procedure (which was now formally invoked by Yugoslavia). In this way the west's adjustment of the UN's rules in 1950, which had originally been designed to outmanoeuvre Soviet obstruction over Korea, was now turned against two key members of the western alliance. An Emergency Session of the General Assembly (its first) now began, which put in train events leading to the deployment of what was by far the UN's most ambitious military venture to date.

As well as from Hammarskjöld, the Canadian foreign minister (and future prime minister) Lester Pearson had a key role in the development of the plans for this United Nations Emergency Force. It will be recalled that in 1945 Pearson had been discussed as a possible founding UN secretary-general. In the intervening period he had been closely involved with the development of the organization in which Canada, along with the

Scandinavian countries and other independent-minded states, had come to play a prominent part. He and the secretary-general now formed something of a diplomatic double act to plan and organize the UN Emergency Force. On 2 November the General Assembly, acting under the Uniting for Peace procedure, adopted a resolution based on the vetoed American draft from the Security Council.[8] This was passed by a large majority, Anglo-French opposition being supported only by Australia, New Zealand and, of course, Israel. Two days later the Assembly passed a Canadian-sponsored resolution drawn up by Pearson that instructed Hammarskjöld to prepare a plan for a military force. By this stage even Britain and France were beginning to see the advantages in wider UN involvement. Their ground forces were now landing in Port Said on the Canal and the whole affair was rapidly turning into a major political crisis, not just internationally but domestically as well. Consequently, they voted with the rest of the General Assembly in favour of the Canadian scheme.

Hammarskjöld's preliminary plan for UNEF was presented to the General Assembly's Emergency Session on 4 November and elaborated two days later.[9] The details embraced a number of key characteristics of UN peacekeeping as it would develop over the coming decades. UNEF personnel would not use force other than in self-defence and would not be a permanent presence. UNEF would have no direct political role in the crisis and would remain only with the consent of Egypt as the 'host state'. The force would not include any significant participation by the big powers. The virtue in these arrangements was that most of the protagonists in the crisis could interpret some aspect of UNEF's deployment as benefiting their own national interests. Crucially, the UNEF plan did not point any fingers at 'culprits'. The UN's involvement made no reference whatsoever to Chapter VII of the Charter and there was therefore no question of an aggressor being identified – had this collective security route been taken, the crisis would merely have deepened. The Security Council, which would have had to retain responsibility, would have remained blocked by British and French vetoes. America's willingness to distance itself from the behaviour of its allies might not have survived if they were to be publicly vilified as aggressor states by the UN and a gleeful Soviet Union. As it was, however, the anxiety of the British and French governments was mounting hourly at this time as the full implications of their adventure became clear. They could now present UN involvement at home as a multilateral 'continuation' of their timely and necessary intervention in a critical situation. But Egypt too saw a number of benefits in agreeing to the force. Its host state power of veto over the undertaking gave it real influence on the character of UNEF. The deployment could be construed by the Cairo regime not as a 'replacement' for the Anglo-French force but as a reproof by the international community to Anglo-French 'aggression'.

The bloc leaders saw the idea of a UN force bringing several benefits. The Soviet Union had strong reservations about the apparent extension of General Assembly authority into the area of military action. This, of course, was in line with Moscow's sense of vulnerability in the veto-free setting of the Assembly. But in this particular case the advantage to the Soviet Union of pushing ahead with UNEF outweighed the broader point of principle. For the United States, the UN intervention was a means of closing over without long-term damage the division that had opened up in the western alliance. It was also a means of containing, if not resolving, a situation that appeared to be on the point of spinning out of control. Only Israel seemed unhappy with the arrangement and declined to offer any real cooperation. The government of prime minister David Ben Gurion refused to permit the deployment of UNEF troops on Israeli soil, and Israeli forces on the ground did not make any great effort to facilitate UNEF's activities. Israeli suspicion of UN involvement in the region, which dated back to the foundation of the state in 1948, if anything deepened with this major military deployment.

Ten offers of contingents from UN members were accepted by Hammarskjöld for the initial deployment. These came from states on three continents that, though not necessarily formal neutrals, nevertheless were widely regarded as independent.[10] Most of them would be approached almost as a matter of routine by secretaries-general seeking future peace-keeping contributors during later phases of the cold war. The advance party of UNEF arrived in the Canal Zone on 15 November 1956 and was put under the command of General Burns, who was transferred temporarily from UNTSO. Within three months UNEF had reached its maximum operational strength of 6,000. In the meantime British and French troops had completed their withdrawal from Egypt in December. Israeli disengagement followed, but only slowly and reluctantly.

The course of UNEF's operations between 1956 and 1967 was marked by general calm in its area of operation. Quite quickly after its initial deployment its numbers were reduced by about a half without any impact on its effectiveness. The continuation of the operation after its initial objective of the withdrawal of foreign forces from Egyptian territory had been achieved was not an explicit part of its original mandate but it made a considerable contribution to the stability of the region. There was an obvious advantage in having a long-term international buffer between Israel and Egypt, invested with the moral force of the United Nations. As a peacekeeping operation with locally defined objectives, however, there was little that UNEF could do about the larger dynamics of the Middle East conflict. Tension between Israel and its neighbours remained high for the rest of the 1950s and in the following decade it increased with the intensification of Arab nationalism. The threat to Israel now came on a number of other fronts as well as the Egyptian one, with hostility growing from Syria in particular. In May 1967 Egypt, exercising its right as host state, requested the withdrawal of UNEF from its territory. Within three weeks a widely expected war – the so-called Six Day War – had begun when Israeli forces pre-empted a planned multi-front attack on its borders led by Egypt and Syria.

Criticism of the then secretary-general, Burma's U Thant, followed for agreeing to the withdrawal of UNEF. How, it was asked, could the UN withdraw its peacekeeping presence from an area when peace was under such obvious threat? Yet for a number of reasons there was no real alternative. Host state consent had been established from the outset as a basic condition for the deployment of the peacekeeping force. Whatever the reasons for its deployment, UNEF represented a foreign presence on sovereign Egyptian territory. There was no possibility in the circumstances of May 1967 that Nasser would have been persuaded to let it remain; Egypt was determined to pursue its own military objectives and the removal of this foreign presence was clearly non-negotiable. For the UN to have disregarded the Egyptian demand would have taken it into new territory wholly alien to the peacekeeping ethos that had developed with UNEF. In practical terms any attempt to pursue this route would have been pointless in any case. Such a move would have had to pass to the Security Council where the Soviet Union would assuredly have used its veto. Moreover, it was highly unlikely that the states contributing contingents to UNEF would have agreed to the use of their troops in such changed conditions. And, anyway, on the ground the small UN force would have easily been pushed aside by the Egyptian army. In fact, UNEF did not complete its withdrawal until 13 June, by which time Israel had occupied Egyptian Sinai, seized the west bank of the River Jordan and had taken the Golan Heights from Syria. In so doing it had sown the seeds of further conflict that would remain unresolved into the following century.

The circumstances of UNEF's withdrawal from Egypt could not overshadow either the real success of the operation or its significance for the future of the use of military forces by the United Nations. The characteristics of the Suez force, in terms of its purpose, composition and operational tactics, came to provide, for better or worse, a basic model for the UN's peacekeeping project as a whole. There was, of course, a hazard in this. Although the undertaking had provided a series of practical lessons and indicated some fundamental rules, the danger was that the particular circumstances of the Suez crisis would not necessarily be repeated in subsequent conflicts. Understandably, however, the success of UNEF was an irresistible signal to UN officials, prominent among them Dag Hammarskjöld himself, who had been searching for an effective post-Korea role for the organization.

Hammarskjöld's Summary Study and the formalization of peacekeeping practice

Two years into the deployment of UNEF Hammarskjöld presented the General Assembly with his Summary Study of peacekeeping practice based on the Suez experience.[11] Much of the study dealt with issues quite specific to that conflict, but its most significant parts were those concerned with aspects of the intervention with potentially broader applications. The United Nations, Hammarskjöld noted, had now 'acquired considerable experience in the establishment, organization and functioning of such an instrument'. A 'study of the operation as a whole', he suggested, 'might afford useful guidance for any future efforts looking forward towards the establishment or use of international United Nations instruments serving the purposes of the kind met by UNEF'. Thus, although aware that the Suez operation had a number of unique features that would not necessarily be present in future emergencies, Hammarskjöld sought to identify for the General Assembly 'certain basic principles and rules which would provide an adaptable framework for later operations which might be found necessary'. These principles can be considered under the general headings of voluntarism, neutrality and non-enforcement.

At the outset of the Summary Study, Hammarskjöld noted that peacekeeping did not involve 'the type of force envisaged under Chapter VII of the Charter'. Without this legal base, the activity had to be an elective one. There were two senses to this. First, there could be no deployment on a state's territory 'without the consent of the Government concerned'. Second, it followed that if Chapter VII was not to be used as the basis of a peacekeeping action then Article 43, with its obligations on member states to 'make available to the Security Council, on its call' whatever military forces were deemed necessary, could not be invoked. They could only be freely offered by contributing states in response to a request from the UN. These principles would 'naturally hold valid for all similar operations in the future'.

As we have seen, peacekeeping in Suez lay outside the scope of Chapter VII in another important respect: it was not concerned with the imposition of an outcome against an act of aggression by an identified wrongdoer. Therefore UN neutrality was an essential starting point for the Suez intervention and for future ones in similar situations. Command and control of peacekeeping forces were to be exercised by the United Nations. The commander of UNEF – and by implication the commanders of future operations – 'would be appointed by and responsible to the United Nations, and . . . his authority would be so defined as to make him fully independent of the policies or control of any one nation'. Furthermore, the force was to be recruited 'from Member States other than the permanent members of the Security Council'. But it was not only the five permanent members of the Security Council who were to be excluded. Contributions would not be accepted 'from any country which for geographical or other reasons might have a special interest in the conflict'. In this regard, the UN 'must give most serious consideration to the views of the host Government' on the national composition of any force, without, however, surrendering its own responsibility in the matter.

The roll-call of the countries originally contributing contingents to UNEF was built around a particular type of state. As we have seen, these countries would later be described as middle powers. They were countries that Lester Pearson would describe as 'big enough to discharge with effect [their] responsibilities [but] not big enough for others to fear' them.[12] In other words, they had the capacity to carry out the mandates given to them by the UN without their military strength being such that it raised suspicions about their own intentions or ambitions in the conflict they had been sent to deal with. As well as being middle-ranking military powers, they were to be, if not formally neutral, then at least perceived as independent in their approach to foreign policy. This was important in relation to the threat of cold war infection, which was present in many local conflicts in the 1950s and 1960s. One of the primary functions of peacekeeping was to act as a firebreak, preventing local conflicts being absorbed into the larger east–west confrontation. This aim would be frustrated if the peacekeepers themselves were closely identified with one or other side in that conflict and their political impartiality therefore questioned.

Taken together, these characteristics of the peacekeeping role were seen by Hammarskjöld as important departures that distinguished peacekeeping on the Suez model from the UN's engagement in Korea. The deployment of 'UN' forces in Korea was, of course, concerned with the enforcement of particular outcomes. The same would be the case with any actions that might at some time in the future be authorized under Chapter VII. In contrast, force was not a primary part of peacekeeping. The use of force in peacekeeping operations must, in Hammarskjöld's view, be restricted to self-defence. He recognized that there was a potential difficulty here 'because of the fact that a wide interpretation of the right of self-defence might well blur the distinction between [peacekeeping] operations . . . and combat operations, which would require a decision under Chapter VII of the Charter'. In an attempt to clarify this problem Hammarskjöld proposed a 'prohibition against any *initiative* [original emphasis] in the use of armed force'. This formulation, if applied, might have closed off the possibility of peacekeepers' actions impacting on the outcome of the conflict they were engaged with. But it was not a practical doctrine on the ground, where pre-emption and 'precautionary force' may be integral components of self-defence. Like much else in the Summary Study, prescriptions for the future conduct of peacekeeping were based on the more or less ideal circumstances of Suez where ambiguities rarely arose and force commanders were only infrequently faced with difficult judgements.

The Summary Study did touch on a central problem for peacekeeping as an institutional undertaking by the UN that had already caused problems for the Suez operation. How was peacekeeping to be paid for? This was another matter bedevilled by the fact that peacekeeping has no clear and explicit identity in the UN Charter. The Soviet Union had expressed reservations about the control of the Suez operation as a non-Chapter VII

Collective security and peacekeeping contrasted

	'Chapter VII' collective security	*The peacekeeping ideal*
Trigger	Act of aggression	Crisis/threat of conflict
Mandate by UN	Enforcement of set outcome	Interposition/observation
Force presence	Imposed	Agreed/host state consent
Contributors	All member states	Middle powers
Legal basis	Charter Chapter VII	Charter Chapter VI/none
Control	Security Council	Security Council/General Assembly
Method	Military force	Moral force/policing

activity when UNEF was first being discussed. At the root of this was Moscow's chronic concern about its relative impotence in the General Assembly in contrast to its permanent member status in the Security Council. Was the Suez force to be treated as a 'normal cost' of the organization and therefore levied routinely on all members via the regular budget? Hammarskjöld, anxious to see peacekeeping adopted as a regular UN activity and absorbed into the institution's fundamental culture, argued that it should be a routine, centrally borne cost. His case was that as peacekeeping was an activity 'based on decisions of the General Assembly or Security Council' it should be paid for 'in accordance with the normal scale of contributions'. In short, peacekeeping should be an obligatory expense for all UN members. For the Soviet Union, however, UNEF as a product of the Uniting for Peace procedure was a General Assembly undertaking not approved by the Security Council. It could not, therefore, be deemed a compulsory expense. At this early stage in the development of peacekeeping some states – mainly Arab ones – proposed another principle in relation to costs. They were of the view that the 'aggressor' should pay. They argued that UNEF and its expenses would not have arisen but for the 'aggression' of Britain, France and Israel, and therefore they should bear the cost of the operation. This was a political statement rather than a viable proposal. It was clear that it would not survive even an initial encounter with the Security Council. But the proposition added a further dimension to what was already threatening to grow into a major issue for the prospects of viable UN peacekeeping in future emergencies. Although not yet a pressing problem at the outset of the Suez operation, it would eventually assume crisis proportions within the United Nations.

In 1958 when he presented the Summary Study to the General Assembly, Hammarskjöld's primary objective was to maintain the positive momentum created by UNEF in order to entrench peacekeeping in the institutional consciousness of the UN. Inevitably, this involved the construction of large propositions on limited premises. In a sense, the UNEF experience was just too ‘easy’ as a starting point. It remains the classic UN peacekeeping operation, not only because it was the first substantial one but because it had few complicated or difficult elements. It emerged from an effective – and extremely unusual – consensus between the leaders of the opposing cold war blocs. It had straightforward, clearly defined and limited objectives. In pursuit of these objectives UNEF was never faced with difficult decisions about the borderline between interposition and enforcement. The force was never physically challenged by the parties to the conflict. Its geographical area of operations was limited and well defined. The main protagonists in the conflict for the most part welcomed the UN intervention, even if for different reasons. Finally, these protagonists were sovereign states. They were full members of the international system with all the constraints on their behaviour that this status imposed. The future would not be so obliging, and Hammarskjöld’s prescriptions would frequently prove impossible to apply.

5 Peacekeeping as immunization

Regional crises in the cold war

The range of peacekeeping activities undertaken by the United Nations in the decade following the start of the Suez operation rarely conformed to the model set out by Dag Hammarskjöld in the 1958 Summary Study. The peacekeeping venture that followed UNEF was also in the Middle East, a successful observation mission in Lebanon, but the next major force deployment was in the former Belgian Congo and began in 1960. This bore virtually no relationship to the Suez operation in its political setting, its objectives or its operational character. Moreover, the institutional context in which the two operations were conceived and then managed in New York could hardly have been more different. The United Nations' next traditional peacekeeping commitment began in Cyprus just as the Congo operation ended. The attitudes of the UN as an institution and of its individual member states towards Cyprus were shaped by the Congo experience. Although the UN had, during the course of the Congo operation, mounted a novel and ambitious operation in West New Guinea that had been wholly successful within the term of its mandate, it was the more negative image of the Congo that raised the apprehensions of potential contributors to the Cyprus force. Where the evident success of the Suez operation tended to encourage unrealistic expectations of what the UN could do for the Congo, the Cyprus commitment was approached with considerable misgivings that by and large proved unjustified, at least as far as the experience of the peacekeepers on the ground was concerned.

The four operations in Suez, Congo, West New Guinea and Cyprus did have something in common with each other – and with the earlier experiences in Palestine and Kashmir. All, at the most fundamental level, were attempts to reduce the pressures put on the international system by the end of empire and the construction of new states that came as a consequence of this. In Egypt the transition to independence had been a protracted and complex one, but the radical nationalism of the Nasser years was just as surely a result of imperial history as the border problems between India and Pakistan in Kashmir. Britain's withdrawal from its mandate in Palestine represented a special type of decolonization, but its consequences were in all meaningful ways a result of the end of empire.

Although the UN's experiences in Congo and Cyprus were in most respects vastly different, there were similarities in that neither solved the underlying causes of each conflict. The withdrawal of peacekeepers from the Congo in 1964 took place at a point of relative calm in the longer cycle of political instability and violence. More than three decades later UN peacekeepers would again be deployed in large numbers in the same country, and would again struggle to make an impact on its endemic problems. In Cyprus the operation first launched in 1964 remains in place more than forty years on, and the inter-communal conflict that brought it into being is unresolved. Both engagements illustrate essential truths about peacekeeping. First, problems of post-colonial adjustment in the international system have frequently been more intractable than imagined when they first emerged. Since the 1960s the cold war has waxed and waned and finally disappeared. Yet a large number of the 'local difficulties', which were seen as minor sideshows to it, continue unresolved. Second, the continuing problems of the Congo and Cyprus underline the crucial difference between peacekeeping and peacemaking. The case of Cyprus in particular shows that peacekeeping can be a technical success in the sense of providing effective interposition between parties in conflict with each other and can dramatically reduce levels of violence. But if the parallel but separate political process of peacemaking is not effectively pursued, the peacekeeping effort will tend to settle into a routine that, in the extreme, can contribute to the perpetuation of the problem it was originally supposed to help resolve.

The UN in the Congo: peacekeeping unravels

Two years after Hammarskjöld presented his Summary Study to the General Assembly he led the United Nations into a peacekeeping effort of unprecedented size and scope. It was a commitment that would see the neat definitions and prescriptions of the 1958 document systematically undermined. The idea of the peacekeeper as a neutral buffer between sovereign states in dispute became meaningless within weeks of the beginning of the Congo operation. So too did the feasibility of the notion that the use of force in UN operations could be restricted to immediate self-defence and, more significantly, that there was a clear border between peacekeeping and enforcement of outcomes. The Congo crisis and the UN's response to it also created a grave crisis for the organization as a whole, and led directly to the death of the secretary-general himself.

The Congo operation (which took the acronym 'ONUC', from the French Opération des Nations Unies au Congo) began in July 1960 and lasted until June 1964 (Map 8). Its scale dwarfed anything the UN had attempted hitherto. At its height the Congo force numbered 20,000 and over its course some twenty-eight UN member countries contributed to it. As the Congo state disintegrated during the second half of 1960, the

UN force was in principle responsible for a country of 2.3 million square kilometres accommodating about 250 separate ethnic groups that were frequently at war among themselves.

The origins of the crisis

The crisis followed the precipitate withdrawal of Belgium, the colonial power, evidently panicked by the first signs of assertive nationalism in the territory. The Belgian state had controlled the Congo since 1898 when an international outcry had led to its removal from the more or less personal possession of King Léopold II. For several years up until this point he had enriched himself from the so-called Congo Free State's rubber and ivory resources through the most brutal use of forced labour. With the disapproving eyes of the world on it, Belgium moved quickly to redress the damage done to national prestige by its monarch and to improve the condition of the Congolese people. This process, though, was one in which the violence and exploitation of the Free State was replaced by what was in some ways an equally repressive paternalism. There was little attempt made to prepare the population for a role in the economic or political life of the territory. The development that did take place was concentrated in the south-eastern province of Katanga and was based on mining. Katanga's resources and their exploitation remained firmly in the hands of European companies, and the area, particularly the provincial capital Elisabethville and the larger mining towns, became subject to extensive white settlement. Katanga was crucial to the Congo's economy as it accounted for some 80 per cent of the territory's trade revenues.

The economic and political complacency of the Belgian government and the European companies involved in the exploitation of the Congo's resources was shaken in 1959 when a series of nationalist demonstrations began in the colonial capital Léopoldville. Belated attempts by the government in Brussels to meet the situation with an accelerated process of education and development failed to still the pressure now building for independence. Unwilling to confront the consequences of resisting this, Belgium agreed a hasty programme for decolonization. The huge territory, despite being wholly unprepared for it, would have its independence at the end of June 1960.

The nationalist movement that had forced the hand of Brussels was dominated by two individuals. The more experienced of these, Joseph Kasavubu, was to become president of the new state. Kasavubu was a Bakongo and therefore represented the largest ethnic group in the Congo, which was concentrated particularly around Léopoldville (eventually renamed Kinshasa after independence) and the south of the country. The other key nationalist leader was Patrice Lumumba who became prime minister of the new state. Lumumba had risen quickly through the nationalist ranks, largely as a result of his skills of oratory. Something of a young man in a hurry, in contrast to the more cautious Kasavubu, Lumumba rapidly adopted a radical political stance that marked him out as a leading personality in the pan-African nationalist movement of the time. There may, though, have been an element of political calculation in this as, unlike Kasavubu, he did not have a large ethnic power base in the Congo and had to build political support by other means.

Meanwhile, in Katanga another personality was about to make a major impact on the Congo's post-independence crisis. This was Moise Tshombe, a local businessman favoured by the European elite in the province. Tshombe became leader of the provincial administration after independence. The extent to which he was truly in charge of events in Katanga was unclear, however, as European interests remained strong and he found himself surrounded by a cohort of white 'advisers'. These three personalities would be central to the multi-layered crisis that the United Nations was called on to engage with in July 1960. But a fourth actor, who would have a much more enduring impact on the Congo's dismal future, would soon emerge on stage. Colonel Joseph Mobutu rose after independence from military obscurity as a non-commissioned officer in the colonial army to become chief of staff of the Congolese armed forces (the Armée Nationale Congolese: ANC).

The declaration of independence in Congo on 30 June precipitated a range of conflicts between different ethnic and regional groups. On 4 July, in the unstable atmosphere created by this, the paramilitary Force Publique, which was in the process of transforming itself into the ANC, the new national army, mutinied over pay and conditions and the continued presence of Belgian officers in its command structure. The mutiny began in Léopoldville but soon spread countrywide, with European civilians among the victims of the generalized violence. Only Katanga – where there was still, effectively, European control of the administration and local paramilitary forces – remained largely untouched through most of the convulsion. When violence eventually threatened there too, the administration invited Belgian troops, still present in the country as part of the independence agreement, to intervene. These along with reinforcements flown into the Congo eventually amounted to a 10,000-strong foreign force that intervened far beyond Katanga. While the situation in Katanga itself was quickly stabilized, the rest of the Congo remained in chaos. Against this background, and with the encouragement of his European advisers, Tshombe decided on 11 July simply to declare Katanga independent of the rest of the country. The secession of Katanga now added another dimension to a crisis already spinning out of control.

The creation of ONUC

In the meantime, Kasavubu and Lumumba had approached the United Nations for help. Initially, this was to be restricted to the training of the

ANC after order had returned, but as the prospect of this became increasingly remote, the Congolese leaders sought a direct UN intervention. At this point the Congo crisis seemed to have at least some factors in common with that of Suez four years previously. Foreign (Belgian) forces had 'invaded' the territory of a sovereign state, ostensibly to restore order but amid accusations of ulterior motives. In Suez these had supposedly involved the protection of the neo-colonial interests of the Canal while in the Congo it was the country's mineral wealth. From the UN's perspective – or more specifically that of Hammarskjöld himself – multilateral intervention would be a means of supporting the structural integrity of the international system through the stress of decolonization. While the main locations of this stress in the 1940s and 1950s had been the Middle East and South Asia, in the 1960s all signs pointed to sub-Saharan Africa. At the beginning of the Congo crisis it appeared that a UN peacekeeping intervention could perform a function very close to that of UNEF. External intervention would, it was hoped, immediately stabilize the situation. It would then offer a face-saving formula to the antagonists. It could be presented by the Léopoldville government as an expulsion of the foreign invasion just as UNEF had been an anti-invasion force in the eyes of the Nasser regime. On the other side, a UN presence could be interpreted by Belgium as a continuation of their – necessary – emergency intervention in just the same way as UNEF had been by Britain and France. But these evident parallels were misleading. In reality the two situations in Suez and Congo were fundamentally different, and ONUC was destined to be an infinitely more challenging project for the UN than its predecessor had been.

In July 1960, however, Hammarskjöld seemed to have few doubts about the rightness of the UN intervention. When the Congolese leaders approached him to seek an intervention 'to protect the national territory of the Congo against the present external aggression which is a threat to international peace', he was quick to respond.[1] For the first time in the UN's history the secretary-general invoked Article 99 of the Charter, which permitted him to take the initiative in presenting matters to the Security Council (see Chapter 3). In the Council, Tunisia, an African non-permanent member, produced a draft resolution calling for a withdrawal of Belgian troops and authorizing the secretary-general to arrange 'such military assistance as may be necessary until . . . the [Congolese] national security forces may be able . . . to fully meet their tasks'.[2] The initiative was backed by both the United States and the Soviet Union. Even at this early stage, however, Moscow was concerned about the extent of the powers being given to the secretary-general in a matter of international security in much the same way as it had questioned General Assembly control of UNEF. The Soviet Union remained, as always, anxious about slippage from the principle of Security Council domination of the security agenda. In another apparent parallel with the Suez affair, the western cold war position of Britain and France seemed to be cross-cut with their older imperialist tendencies. In the Security Council they made a point of expressing their understanding of Belgium's actions. These different positions, mildly enough stated in July 1960, would lie at the heart of a major crisis within the United Nations over the coming months and years.

The Congo's multidimensional crisis

Had the immediate crisis in the Congo been resolved by the arrival of UN troops and an associated Belgian withdrawal, and had the establishment of an effective central government followed, then the parallel with Suez and UNEF would have held. Another 'victory' would have been marked up for the UN's peacekeeping project. But the divergences between the two situations quickly revealed themselves and became ever wider as the UN presence built up. Following the UNEF model and its articulation in the Summary Study, participation by the big powers was restricted to transport and logistics assistance. Hammarskjöld strongly favoured a force made up as far as possible of African contingents. There were only a limited number of independent sub-Saharan states to provide these contingents in 1960. Ethiopia, Ghana, Guinea and Liberia contributed, while the pan-African character of ONUC's composition was bolstered by troop contributions from Morocco and Tunisia from north of the Sahara. Apart from the secretary-general's interest in pursuing what would in later decades be called 'African solutions to African problems', he was also concerned to tie independent Africa into the UN process to reduce the likelihood of their acting on their own in the Congo in a way that could further destabilize the situation. To meet European concerns, two of Europe's traditional neutrals, Ireland and Sweden, were persuaded to contribute as well. Within weeks the force was about 8,500-strong, though even such numbers were hardly adequate given the size of the Congo and the scale of its problems.

The early performance of the force was also affected by the ambiguity of its mandate. The Security Council resolution of 14 July, which had established the operation, had required it both to train local forces and to substitute for them in the interim. Who was to give ONUC its local orders? Maintaining law and order in the chaotic conditions of the Congo would inevitably be a highly political undertaking. Was the UN force to become, in effect, the armed forces of the central government? If so, was there to be a limit to what it would agree to do? For example, how was the UN force to respond to the secession of Katanga – which in the view of the central government was an illegal action? These questions had been inadequately explored in the rush to get UN forces on the ground in the Congo. But in the first weeks of the operation they came to the fore, and began to open a rift between Hammarskjöld and Lumumba. The secretary-general was anxious to avoid UN involvement in the Katanga question. Serious conflict on the ground would have threatened if UN troops had been pitched against Katangese forces. But more significantly for the United Nations and its wider place in the world, Katanga had the potential to throw the organization into conflict and disarray if the breakaway province's foreign friends and enemies lined up against each other.

As if the generalized disorder throughout the state, the continued presence of Belgian forces and the secession of the country's economic power base was not enough for the Congo and the UN to contend with, in September 1960 the central government itself disintegrated. The relationship between Lumumba and Kasavubu had never been a close one, and it deteriorated rapidly in the climate of a hydra-headed crisis in the weeks after independence. It is unclear how far the differences between the two were primarily ideological. In later years Patrice Lumumba would become a posthumous icon of African nationalism and a hero of the international left. To his admirers Lumumba was a victim of neo-colonialist forces that manipulated the Kasavubu faction of the government. In part, though, the conflict was one between two ambitious politicians not comfortable with the constraints imposed by the requirement to share power. But the existence of an ideological schism was quick to be assumed in the atmosphere in the wider world of 1960. Any local conflict risked being viewed through cold war lenses and its protagonists adopted as representatives of one bloc or the other. In the Congo as elsewhere, the local actors at the centre of these perceptions were happy to go along with them for their own purposes. Inevitably then, the self-proclaimed radical Lumumba became a pro-Soviet champion while his enemies were seen as pro-western (either neo-colonialist puppets or tribunes of liberal democracy, depending on the observer). The cold war infection that the UN intervention was in part designed to prevent, quickly entered through the Congo's already gaping wounds.

With the collapse of the Lumumba–Kasavubu government the focus of Congolese politics shifted from the breach between Katanga and the central government to the struggle for control in Léopoldville. The prime minister and the president were each attempting to dismiss the other and take power for himself. The UN's response to the situation, initially at any rate, deepened rather than eased the crisis. The chief representative in Léopoldville was Andrew Cordier, an American. The tactical decisions he now took, relating to access to radio stations and the movement of air traffic, appeared to favour Kasavubu against Lumumba. In truth, Kasavubu's access to a local power base in Léopoldville was the main factor in his relative advantage but Lumumba's foreign supporters were quick to accuse the UN of partiality towards his rival. Cordier's nationality became an issue just as, more broadly, did the almost exclusively western composition of Hammarskjöld's group of advisers on the Congo.

The wrangle exposed a developing truth about peacekeeping as a whole. While not in any way a positive 'anti-Soviet' undertaking, it was one that was dominated by western powers and driven by pluralist western values. In addition to Cordier, virtually all senior UN figures in the Congo at this stage were westerners. ONUC's first commander was a Swede, General Carl von Horn, and his successor an Irishman, General Sean McKeown. The powerful UN head of political operations was another Swede, Sture Linnér. Although Ireland and Sweden were, legally speaking, neutral states, they were still 'western' in their political and economic cultures and systems and in their diplomatic affinities. The initial Soviet support for UN peacekeeping in the Congo was not strong, as we have seen, and it was not likely to be maintained if Moscow came to see the operation as an agent of western interests there. As the view of the force as a means of expelling Belgian forces from the Congo receded, and as the complexity of the situation began to make a mockery of the idea of ONUC as an interpositionary presence in an inter-state conflict, even the qualified acceptance of ONUC by the Soviet Union began to fade. In New York, during the annual General Assembly in the autumn of 1960, Soviet leader Nikita Khrushchev denounced the nature and evident direction of the UN intervention. To the consternation of the secretary-general, this condemnation, carefully couched in the language of anti-imperialist solidarity, attracted some support in the Assembly from the increasingly influential Afro-Asian bloc.

The death of Lumumba and crisis in New York

In mid-September 1960 Lumumba's position was terminally undermined when Mobutu, as army chief of staff, intervened to 'resolve' the crisis. The government, already hardly functioning as such, was suspended. Kasavubu, who obviously saw an advantage in cooperating with what was to all intents and purposes a military coup, publicly supported Mobutu's actions. Lumumba, on the other hand, tried to win elements in the ANC to his support. He failed in this, and his personal position became perilous. In consequence he was forced into the humiliating position of accepting the protection of ONUC, which he considered responsible for his plight in the first place.

These developments brought a further deterioration in the situation at UN headquarters in New York. The Congo had now become a major cold war squabble, with all that meant for the prospects of an effective consensus in the Security Council. Ironically, the Soviet Union now looked to the General Assembly for support. Its original insistence on the primacy of the Security Council and the fail-safe mechanism of the veto derived from its fear of automatic defeat in the western-dominated Assembly. But the process of decolonization was rapidly changing the ideological texture of the General Assembly. Fifty-one states had signed the Charter at San Francisco in 1945, but by 1960 membership had almost doubled to ninety-nine. A large proportion of these newer members were part of the new Afro-Asian grouping. This shift in the balance of power had already been intimated during the

Suez crisis when the Uniting for Peace procedure, originally introduced as an anti-Soviet device, was used with Soviet support against Britain and France. By 1960 the process had moved further. While these new UN members were not necessarily pro-Soviet, they were strongly anti-imperialist and therefore very sensitive to the effect of ONUC's actions in the Congo.

For this reason the Soviet Union was not upset to see the Uniting for Peace mechanism used again after its delegation vetoed a Security Council resolution on the Congo in mid-September 1960.[3] The Emergency Special Session of the General Assembly that resulted became the arena for a major Soviet attack on the secretary-general. Hammarskjöld was accused, in a typically knockabout speech by Soviet leader Nikita Khrushchev, of acting as an agent of imperialism. But the Congo crisis, it soon became clear, was merely the launch pad for the airing of a much wider set of Soviet grievances. Peacekeeping as a general activity, with which – as we have seen – Moscow had never been comfortable, now came under question. If, as appeared in the Congo, peacekeeping operations were 'to be used . . . to suppress liberation movements', Khrushchev warned:

> it will naturally be difficult to reach agreement on their establishment, since there will be no guarantee that they will not be used for reactionary purposes that are alien to the interests of peace. Provision must be made to ensure that no state falls into the predicament in which the Republic of the Congo now finds itself.[4]

But Soviet disaffection went further even than the idea of peacekeeping as a key activity of the UN. The situation had now arrived, Khrushchev argued, 'where the post of Secretary-General, who alone directs the staff and alone interprets and executes the decisions of the Security Council and the sessions of the General Assembly, should be abolished'.[5] The alternative proposed by the Soviet Union was a triumvirate – or 'troika' as it became known. This would reflect the balance of forces in the organization at the time: those of the western alliance, the eastern bloc and the Afro-Asian group.[6] At a stroke Khrushchev had thrown the founding structure of the United Nations into question. The idea of a multinational civil service led by a neutral administrator loyal first and last to the institution had been central to international thinking since the establishment of the League of Nations. The nature of the proposed reform betrayed its origins in that it would have gone a considerable way to changing the balance of power in the organization to the benefit of the Soviet Union. Moscow hoped for a long-term functional alliance with the burgeoning Afro-Asian group built around the common ground of anti-imperialism. Without a 'western' secretary-general, the entire UN agenda could be changed. No longer would the Soviet delegation be forced to use its veto with such frequency (by this point it had cast eighty-eight vetoes and the Americans none) to safeguard its national interests.

The assumption of a natural affinity between the Soviet Union and the Afro-Asian group upon which Khrushchev's plan was predicated proved misplaced, however. This became clear when the support in the General Assembly for the troika scheme was not forthcoming. Soviet standing in the ex-colonial world, it seemed, was not as high as Khrushchev had assumed and the scheme was dropped. Nevertheless, the whole affair sent a serious warning to the secretariat about the vulnerability of peacekeeping to the fall-out from bloc politics. A major advantage of peacekeeping was supposed to be its capacity to work around the constraints of bipolarity in a way that Chapter VII collective security could not. That now seemed to be in doubt.

The Congo crisis continued to contaminate the institutional politics of the UN for the rest of 1960. Despite Mobutu's military intervention in Léopoldville, Lumumba still sought to establish himself internationally as the rightful leader of the Congolese government. In November this battle came to New York when the UN had to determine who should be recognized as the legitimate representative of the Congo for purposes of membership of the organization. The General Assembly eventually came down on the side of the Mobutu-Kasavubu faction, and Lumumba was further marginalized.[7] It was a decision that triggered a sequence of events that would have the gravest consequences for the Congo itself and for the United Nations as an institution. Increasingly desperate about his political situation, Lumumba now took himself out of UN protection in Léopoldville and tried to get to his power base in the town of Stanleyville in the eastern Orientale province. He was quickly captured by Mobutu's ANC and, as an apparently impotent UN looked on, he was transferred to Katanga in January 1961 where he was quickly killed. While Mobutu and Tshombe were directly responsible for his murder, Belgian and American complicity was also suspected. Having just survived the troika crisis, Hammarskjöld was now confronted with an emergency that saw African contingents (those of Egypt, Guinea, Mali and Morocco) withdrawn from ONUC, unprecedented anger among the Afro-Asian delegations in New York and renewed Soviet demands for his replacement.

The Security Council responded to the crisis by arming ONUC with a more robust mandate. Inevitably, this took the UN operation close to – if not across – the dividing line between peacekeeping on the UNEF/Summary Study model on the one side and the sort of enforcement of outcomes associated with Chapter VII action on the other. The new resolution authorized ONUC to 'take all appropriate measures to prevent the occurrence of civil war in the Congo', using force if necessary in the last resort.[8] Although no vetoes were cast, the new instructions to ONUC were not universally supported. France, which was Belgium's closest supporter in the Security Council, objected to its strictures on Brussels, while the Soviet Union dismissed it as inadequate. The United States, however, with the new, more liberal Kennedy administration in the White House, favoured the stronger approach and was supported by Britain.

Katanga and the death of Hammarskjöld

The impact of the new resolution was felt most in Katanga. With Lumumba removed from the scene, Mobutu had no need to sustain a relationship with Tshombe, and the economic spoils of Katanga were a powerful attraction to a Congolese regime that was soon to be notorious for its spectacular levels of corruption. The Léopoldville government, therefore, now began to press for the end of the province's secession. It was supported in this by the General Assembly where the Afro-Asian grouping had not forgotten the background to ONUC's new mandate: Lumumba's abduction and subsequent murder in Elisabethville. The secretary-general and the Security Council were more cautious about raising expectations of dramatic developments. There was nothing explicit in the February resolution about ending the secession of Katanga by force. Such a course of action would rest on a particular interpretation of the term 'prevent the occurrence of civil war in the Congo [using] force, if necessary, in the last resort'. Assuming that Tshombe and his backers could not be persuaded to bend to the UN's will – and this was a fair assumption during 1961 – ONUC would be required to undertake a major military operation against well-armed forces. The Katangese army was misdescribed as a gendarmerie; in fact, far from being a police unit, it was a well-equipped fighting force that relied heavily on European mercenaries. And support for Katangese independence remained strong in some European governments, in particular those of Belgium and France. In short, any UN 'war' on Katanga was likely to be extremely expensive in both military and diplomatic terms.

This was dramatically brought home in September 1961. The previous June Hammarskjöld had appointed the Irish diplomat Conor Cruise O'Brien as his representative in Katanga. O'Brien, offended by the posturing of the Katangese government and its mercenary army, interpreted the February Security Council resolution as justifying the use of force to expel foreign military elements from the province. Accordingly, during August he ordered local ONUC forces to move against the mercenaries. Although he had some initial success, the operation was not properly followed through and ended with a not very convincing undertaking from Tshombe that he would arrange the removal of the mercenaries himself. Personally affronted when Tshombe failed to live up to his promise, and determined that the UN would not be humiliated, O'Brien ordered a second, more muscular, operation. This time ONUC's action appeared to have been more decisive. A considerable number of mercenaries were arrested and others abandoned the province rather than risk falling into UN hands. Tshombe himself fled Katanga, fearing arrest and transfer to Léopoldville in a reverse version of Lumumba's fate the previous January. But some ill-considered remarks by O'Brien to the effect that he had ended the secession of Katanga led to anger in the west and a reprieve for the breakaway regime. Katanga's supporters abroad could not be seen to object to a limited UN operation designed to remove mercenaries under the terms of Security Council resolutions, but the suggestion that the UN had formally ended the secession provided an opportunity to challenge O'Brien's interpretation of the February resolution.

Hammarskjöld now sought to retrieve the situation with some belated 'preventive diplomacy'. A meeting was hastily arranged between him and Tshombe in the latter's refuge in neighbouring Northern Rhodesia (which became present-day Zambia but was then still a white-ruled British territory). At dusk on 17 September 1961 the secretary-general's aircraft crashed on its approach to the Ndola airstrip killing everyone on board. The Congo crisis had claimed its most elevated casualty.

The death of Hammarskjöld brought no immediate change to the situation in the Congo or the UN's peacekeeping role. In the short term, in fact, the battle lines seemed to have been reinforced, with the secession of Katanga if anything further entrenched. But the seeds of a profound change in the UN's approach had been sown. The new secretary-general was U Thant of Burma, a less high-profile personality than Hammarskjöld but a committed international civil servant and a highly competent administrator. More important than this, however, was the fact that he was the organization's first non-European secretary-general. His credibility with the Afro-Asian bloc helped to mediate the UN's difficulties in the Congo to an audience in the emerging Third World that had not always been a sympathetic one. In November 1961, two months after U Thant took office, things moved ahead significantly when ONUC was equipped with yet another mandate by a new Security Council resolution. This was more clearly aimed at ending the secession, and it provoked a British as well as a French abstention. With the United States as a leading supporter of the resolution, however, neither felt able to veto it. The Security Council now condemned unequivocally the secession of Katanga and the presence of foreign mercenaries that sustained it. Secessionist activity was deemed 'contrary to Security Council decisions and [should] cease forthwith'. ONUC, through the secretary-general, was accordingly ordered 'to take vigorous action, including the use of the requisite measure of force' to detain and deport foreign political and military personnel in Katanga.[9] The writing was now on the wall for Tshombe's regime – and for any remaining credibility in the claim that the UN was involved in peacekeeping rather than enforcement in the Congo.

The new mandate was not implemented immediately. During the year following the adoption of the resolution, UN mediators sought to negotiate the end of the secession. But Tshombe appeared either unable or unwilling to grasp the fundamental shift in international attitudes to his regime that followed the death of Hammarskjöld. Foreign governments that had at one time been supportive were now quietly distancing themselves from 'independent' Katanga. With the situation in the rest of the Congo slowly improving, in large part as a result of more effective UN policing, the once potent contrast between a violent and anarchic Congo and a peaceful and orderly Katanga lost some force in the debate. Moreover, the dominance of white elements – financial, political and military – in Katanga had become ever more evident. The actions and attitudes of the white mercenaries who formed the backbone of Katanga's security force became increasingly offensive to public opinion outside Africa. But the Elisabethville regime, perhaps convinced from previous dealings that the UN would not back up its warnings, failed to make any significant move to resolve the crisis.

Completion of the mandate

In the event, military action to end the secession of Katanga began safely within the terms of 'Hammarskjöldian' peacekeeping; it started as a wholly justifiable act of self-defence by the peacekeepers. The increasingly aggressive and disorderly behaviour of the mercenaries in the province culminated in December 1962 with attacks on ONUC installations. For a period of days UN forces failed to respond, and the mercenaries and their political masters evidently assumed that it was business as usual and their actions would, as before, be free of consequences. Their days of acting with impunity were numbered, however. When ONUC finally did react, its self-defence was decidedly robust. Within two days the mainly Indian UN forces had routed the mercenaries with ease, killing, capturing and driving them out of the territory in large numbers. Now bereft of its strong-arm support, the Katanga regime simply disintegrated. The formal announcement of the end of secession was made by Tshombe in mid-January 1963 and a UN-supervised programme to reintegrate the province with the rest of the Congo began immediately.

The end of Katangan secession, along with the return of a degree of stability to the Congo as a whole, created the necessary conditions for the completion of UN operations in the country. The largest, most costly and by far the most politically dangerous peacekeeping venture to date was therefore wound up in June 1964, just short of four years after it began. For better or worse, the impact of UN involvement on the first phase of Congolese statehood was immense. As the blue flag was lowered over UN positions in the Congo in 1964 the country appeared to have benefited from the intervention. It was unified under a central administration, order had seemingly been restored throughout most of its territory and a new regime promising strong government was in power. But the Congo's subsequent history was not a happy one. A year after the end of the UN operation further political instability (in which Moise Tshombe was heavily involved, now at national level) caused Mobutu once again to intervene.

This time he turned himself into the national president, beginning a decades-long, kleptocratic rule. Soon he Africanized both his own name (to 'Mobutu Sése Séko') and that of the country (to 'Zaire'), but the corrupt and dictatorial Mobuto was no paragon of African nationalism. Wisely choosing to act as a reliable agent of the west throughout the cold war, at its end he found himself abandoned by his international friends, and his regime crumbled. The chaotic consequences of this affected the entire central African region – and brought another major United Nations engagement with the country, as we will see.

No equivalent to the post-Suez Summary Study followed the Congo operation. This did not reflect any shortage of lessons for peacekeeping to be learned from the Congo experience. This had systematically exposed the shortcomings of the Suez operation as a template for future peacekeeping undertakings. It highlighted the dangers of engagement in a situation where the idea of a responsive and responsible host state – which had been central to the prescriptions of the 1958 Summary Study – was more or less irrelevant. It also challenged assumptions about peacekeeping as an 'international' activity involving the UN in a straightforward buffer role between sovereign state members of the international system. Finally, the UN's experience in the Congo subverted the notion of a clear division between peacekeeping and enforcement. Nothing would be quite the same again as far as peacekeeping was concerned, a situation well illustrated by the circumstances surrounding the establishment of the next major UN undertaking: that in Cyprus.

Back to basics? The United Nations force in Cyprus

The Cyprus operation is the longest lasting UN peacekeeping force (only the two continuing observer missions established in the late 1940s in Palestine and Kashmir have had a greater duration). When it began in March 1964 few could have expected it still to be in existence more than four decades later. Perhaps more than any other UN involvement, the Cyprus operation illustrates the dangers for the credibility of even very successful peacekeeping in situations where peacemaking fails to advance in parallel.

The elements of the conflict

The island of Cyprus, which lies in the eastern Mediterranean to the south of Turkey and west of Lebanon, has been subject to changing foreign rule throughout history. Its geographical position made it a major strategic prize when the Mediterranean lay at the centre of the western economic and political world. The island was ruled by a succession of dominant regional powers up to the nineteenth century: Greece, Rome, Byzantium,

Genoa and finally Ottoman Turkey. In the second half of the nineteenth century Britain was rapidly emerging as the new imperial hegemon in the region and by an agreement with its then ally Turkey in 1878 it assumed administrative control of the island. After the outbreak of the First World War, which saw the two powers on opposite sides, Britain simply annexed the island. Its peculiar pre-war status under British administration meant that Cyprus was not treated as a League of Nations mandate and it became a British crown colony in 1925. From its days as part of the Hellenic empire Cyprus had been subject to waves of migration from Greece and by the mid-twentieth century the majority of its 600,000 population, about four-fifths, was ethnically Greek. The rest of the population was predominantly Turkish in origin, a product of the years of Ottoman rule. British administration created expectations among the majority population that Cyprus would be transferred to Greek sovereignty as Crete had been in 1913. However, London was reluctant to make any hasty move in the dircction of *enosis* (as union with Greece was called). For one thing, Cyprus remained an important strategic asset, even if the focus of the international system had moved away from the region in the twentieth century. For another, the interests of the Turkish minority, who saw their best option as continued British rule, had to be considered.

Pressure for change intensified after the Second World War as the global movement towards colonial independence gained pace. Britain found itself in a position not wholly different from the one it had laboured under in Palestine. It was responsible for a colonial territory whose future was intensely contested by its ethnically divided population. As Cyprus was a crown colony and not a mandated territory, however, the problem could not simply be laid back at the door of the United Nations as the Palestine issue had. In 1955 Greek Cypriot nationalism took a violent turn, just as Israeli nationalism had in Palestine in the 1940s. The National Organization of Cypriot Struggle – known from its Greek acronym as 'EOKA' – began a campaign of attacks on British forces on the island. While EOKA's methods were not universally supported by Greek Cypriots there was little disagreement with its objective of *enosis*. The most prominent champion of their case was the Cypriot patriarch of the Greek Orthodox church, Archbishop Makarios, who, despite British attempts to silence him through forced exile, emerged as the overall leader of his community. In the meantime the Turkish community was making its anti-*enosis* concerns heard, demanding either the retrocession of the island to Turkey or its partition into two independent micro-states, one Greek and one Turkish.

London was growing increasingly exasperated with what appeared to be a wholly intractable situation, but a breakthrough was provided, unexpectedly, by Greece and Turkey. Despite their intense mutual suspicion over Cyprus and other unresolved historical conflicts, delegations from Athens and Ankara met in Switzerland at the beginning of 1959 and hammered out an agreement between themselves. A meeting was then convened in London at which the British government accepted the Greco-Turkish plan. The settlement proposal involved an agreement that Cyprus would not seek unification with either Greece or Turkey. Nor would it be partitioned. There would be a Greek Cypriot president and a Turkish Cypriot vice president, both of whom would have a veto over decisions affecting security and foreign affairs. The Turkish Cypriots, who made up 20 per cent of the population, were to be guaranteed a proportionately larger role in the civil service and army than their numbers would strictly suggest, and they would have one-third of the seats in parliament reserved to them. Britain was to retain control of two 'sovereign base areas', which would secure its strategic presence in the eastern Mediterranean. Events now moved quickly, with elections in July 1960 leading to independence (and membership of the United Nations) the following month. As expected, Archbishop Makarios became the first president of the new Republic of Cyprus.

Constitutional crisis and inter-communal violence

The speed with which the inter-communal arrangements embedded in the Cypriot constitution had been agreed in 1959 belied their complexity and they soon proved difficult to implement. Moreover, after the initial euphoria of the joint agreement and independence passed, the Greek majority began to question the extent of the concessions that had been made to the Turkish Cypriots. There was a general feeling that the aspiration of *enosis* had been abandoned too easily. On the Turkish Cypriot side there were considerable misgivings about what was seen as the new Greek-dominated state. Consequently, when at the end of 1963 Makarios proposed adjustments to the independence constitution to his Turkish Cypriot deputy and was rebuffed, inter-communal fighting broke out. Both communities suffered in the violence but it was the minority Turkish population that bore the main brunt of it. Although the death toll remained in the low hundreds – not high by the standards of other inter-ethnic conflicts later in the century – there was a broader international dimension that carried a considerable threat for the system as a whole. For a time the sufferings of the Turkish Cypriots threatened to bring a military intervention from Turkey itself. This would in turn have created a significant risk of a response from Greece, perhaps on their common continental border rather than in Cyprus. Significant escalation was a real danger, therefore, and action to contain the violence became urgent.

The initial moves to this end were made by British forces from the sovereign base areas. Britain, in contrast to Belgium in the Congo four years earlier, was fully aware of the political implications of the former imperial power intervening by force in the post-independence politics of an ex-colony, even with the purest of motives. London sought as a matter of urgency, therefore, to internationalize its peacekeeping role. Initially an attempt was made to do this through the agency of NATO rather than the UN. Britain, Greece and Turkey, the three 'guarantor powers' of the Cypriot constitution, were all NATO members. To have dealt with the crisis through the alliance would have avoided the cold war politics in the Security Council that had bedevilled the Congo operation. Cyprus itself was not a member of NATO, however, and the Makarios government was wary about the terms of any intervention being set by an Anglo-Turkish axis hostile to Greek Cypriot interests. The United Nations, with its growing reputation in the 1960s for anti-imperialism, was a much more attractive option to the majority community. The issue therefore passed to the Security Council in February 1964.

For a number of reasons there was limited enthusiasm here for UN involvement. Memories of the Congo were still fresh and there was a concern about what any commitment might hold in store. Just as the Congo operation had been launched on a high tide of post-Suez enthusiasm for peacekeeping, the Cyprus operation was almost grounded on the rocks of post-Congo caution. Beyond this, both the Soviet Union and France had developed, from different premises, national positions that were implicitly hostile to the idea of UN peacekeeping. The Congo loomed large here as well. Moscow was suspicious of the west's apparent control of peacekeeping operations (as suggested by ONUC's evident anti-Lumumbist actions) and France objected to UN 'interference' in national politics (as suggested by ONUC's role in the ending of Katangan secession). Finally, while the Suez and Congo operations, at least at the outset, were designed to deal with conflicts that were clearly international, the Cyprus question was an internal one, albeit with international implications. Was this a legitimate area for the attentions of the United Nations, which, by its own Charter, was forbidden from interfering in internal politics?[10] The internal politics of the Security Council itself, however, eventually guaranteed that action would be taken. Britain was anxious to extricate itself from an uncomfortable unilateral peacekeeping role. The United States was concerned at the impact of the conflict on the cohesion of the NATO alliance, a position shared to a degree by France, which was still at this time a fully participating member of NATO.[11] The Soviet Union for its part was anxious not to set itself against the expressed wish of the Cyprus government for UN involvement. Cyprus was, after all, a potential anti-imperialist ally. And, of course, it was not in the Soviet interest to risk the issue returning to NATO for resolution. This would merely have enhanced the prestige and political reach of the western alliance. But the Security Council commitment that emerged from this tangle of motives boded ill for the management of the operation.

UNFICYP established

Despite these less than optimistic portents, the United Nations Force in Cyprus (UNFICYP) was established by a Security Council resolution in

March 1964.[12] The force was 'to use its best efforts to prevent a recurrence of fighting and . . . to contribute to the maintenance and restoration of law and order and a return to normal conditions'. In fact, the combined effect of British action and the movement of populations during the fighting into consolidated ethnic areas meant that there was little continuing violence for the UN force to deal with (Map 7). But with the experience of the Congo and its high casualties still recent, secretary-general U Thant did not find it easy to construct a force at short notice. British troops remained on the ground but now in blue berets under UN command. This, of course, was contrary to Hammarskjöld's thinking that suggested that permanent members of the Security Council should not be employed directly in peacekeeping, but the specific circumstances of the Cyprus problem dictated otherwise. Beyond the British exception the composition of the force eventually raised by U Thant read like a roll-call of the emerging cohort of newly 'traditional' peacekeepers. Initial contingents were provided by Denmark, Finland, Ireland and Sweden, all emblematic of the middle-power identity. The physical division between the communities, which had been deepened by the violence of the preceding weeks, may have augured ill for a harmonious and integrated future for the Cypriot populations, but it did permit UNFICYP to operate much more in line with classic Hammarskjöldian tactics than had been remotely possible in the Congo. The force was able to interpose itself between the sides (even if they were ethnic communities rather than state armies) and keep an already established peace.

UNFICYP faced few major operational difficulties in the first decade of its deployment. Patient local negotiation improved the atmosphere throughout the island and a de facto inter-communal border was intensively patrolled. In 1967 tensions rose momentarily after incidents in the south-eastern part of the island that Turkey regarded as deliberate provocations by the new right-wing military junta that had just seized power in Greece. Under American pressure, which was easily brought to bear on the largely friendless regime in Athens, the issue was settled by the withdrawal of a contingent of the Greek army that had been stationed on the island. In the meantime UNFICYP had managed to contain the problem on the ground.

UN politics and the peacekeeping finance crisis

The operational success of the Cyprus force disguised grave difficulties surrounding it at the UN institutional level. In addition to post-Congo fears about the physical danger of participation, the resistance that U Thant met from potential contributing states was in part to do with the very uncertain financial basis of the operation. As we have seen, French and Soviet misgivings about UNFICYP derived from broader objections to the whole idea of peacekeeping as an activity not covered explicitly by the Charter. This lack of clear legal standing did not seem to create too many difficulties for UNEF in Suez, but in the Congo it seemed to expose a tendency for UN military interventions to shift in methods and objectives. This, in the Soviet view, undermined the capacity of the permanent members of the Security Council to control issues of international security as the Charter had intended them to do. The key battleground in this conflict centred on the financing arrangements for peacekeeping. In the opinion of Hammarskjöld and later U Thant, peacekeeping should be regarded as a routine expense met from the regular UN budget. For the Soviet Union, however, such an approach was unlawful. Without an identity in the Charter, peacekeeping could not be a 'regular' activity of the organization. Although there had been no objection made to the financing of the smaller observer missions in Palestine and Kashmir from the regular budget, problems arose with Suez, which was not only a much larger and more expensive undertaking but authorized by the General Assembly following its transfer from the Security Council through the Uniting for Peace procedure. Moscow recorded its objections at the outset, but because UNEF did not jar with Soviet interests in any significant way, no major arguments arose. Calm was maintained, too, by the fact that Britain and the United States voluntarily picked up most of the bills for UNEF anyway. But the situation changed with the Congo operation. Although ONUC was established and mandated by the Security Council its performance at many key junctures was denounced by the Soviet Union as pro-western and beyond the rightful limits of the Charter. The Cyprus operation, like that in Suez, did not clash particularly with larger Soviet interests, but now, with the intervening experience of the Congo, Moscow was determined to make its position felt. It had begun to withhold assessed contributions at a relatively early stage in the Congo operation and it now refused outright to pay for UNFICYP. In the meantime, many of the newer, smaller and poorer states that had joined the UN after decolonization in the early 1960s were genuinely hard-pressed to pay the extra peacekeeping assessments. These were growing with the spread of the UN commitment. While each year of UNEF had cost about twenty million dollars, ONUC had cost about 120 million dollars annually.

France shared the general view of the Soviet Union. Its specific objections to the direction of the Congo operation were politically very different from those of the Soviet Union, but like Moscow, Paris had fundamental reservations about peacekeeping as an activity. The government of President Charles de Gaulle took a determinedly realist view of the international system. In this state-centric perspective the whole idea of multilateral military intervention in conflicts was suspect. The UN as an institution should not, in the French view, have 'power' in any meaningful sense. If the big powers wished the UN to enforce an outcome on their behalf, then Chapter VII existed to enable this. But peacekeeping, lacking any clear legal base, potentially undermined this control by sovereign states. The UN therefore had no legal right to require member states to finance it.

In December 1961, as the crisis over the financing of ONUC began to develop, the General Assembly, which was the organ responsible for the assessment of members' payments, laid the issue before the International Court of Justice (ICJ). The result was an 'advisory opinion' by the Court in July 1962 that peacekeeping was indeed a 'regular expense' of the UN that could be levied on members as part of their ordinary assessed contribution.[13] The ICJ, however, had no power to make a binding judgment, and as its opinion conformed with the views of both Hammarskjöld and the United States administration, there was no possibility of Soviet compliance. The acceptance of the opinion by the General Assembly failed to change the Soviet position. Despite the absence of any legal obligation on the Soviet Union to comply with an advisory opinion, Washington sought other means of applying pressure. At the same time it was the United States that saw an opportunity to score some useful points in the contest for Afro-Asian favour in the UN, a contest in which the 'anti-imperialist' Soviet Union had made most of the running. Article 19 of the UN Charter provided a sanction against any member in default of assessed payments in circumstances other than genuine financial hardship: such states could be deprived of their vote in the General Assembly.[14]

The stakes for the United States and the UN were high, however. The Soviet Union made it clear that it would take any move against it under Article 19 as a deliberate provocation that would trigger its withdrawal from the General Assembly. Washington, too, had to be confident that the target audience – the states of the emerging Third World – would see its actions as driven by concern with the well-being of the UN and its peacekeeping responsibilities rather than as a mere propaganda stunt. In the event, Article 19 was invoked, but an elaborate procedural dance was performed to prevent it being fully applied. The opening of the nineteenth session of the General Assembly was delayed from September until December 1964 while a group of UN middle powers sought to find a compromise. Finally, it was agreed that no votes would be called during the session. Although normal discussion and debate took place, no resolutions were presented other than those that could be adopted without a division. In this way the Soviet Union, its allies and France were kept within the Assembly.

The situation was obviously untenable in the long term and at the beginning of the twentieth session, which opened in 1965, it was agreed that Article 19 would not be used in the area of peacekeeping finance. If a threat to the institution had thus been removed, the problem at the root of it remained, however. The states contributing contingents to UNFICYP continued to bear the costs themselves pending a settlement to the financing issue and by the summer of 1964, just months after the start of the operation, peacekeeping funds were in deficit by 112 million dollars. The lack of a sound and dependable basis for paying for peacekeeping had an impact on the conduct of the Cyprus operation into the 1970s, which, had conditions on the ground been more challenging over a sustained period, would have caused major problems for the whole undertaking.

The Turkish invasion

As it was, UNFICYP continued with little incident until 1974 when the Cyprus situation took a dramatic turn. In July of that year Archbishop Makarios was ousted by a coup carried out by Greek Cypriot extremists. The origins of the crisis lay in Greece rather than Cyprus itself. In Athens the military junta, which had seized power in 1967, was under growing domestic and international pressure. In a classic attempt to rally the nation in its support, it raised the long-standing nationalist shibboleth of *enosis*. It was a bad miscalculation. Five days after the coup Turkish forces invaded the island. Initially, the Turkish army seemed to be restricting its activity to the protection of the Turkish Cypriot communities in the north and, by its mere presence, blocking any possibility of the Greeks achieving *enosis*. After a pause of a few weeks, however, the Turkish invasion force continued its advance south into Greek Cypriot areas, provoking a massive movement of refugees. Despite the collapse of the coup (and the rapid fall of the junta in Athens in its wake) Turkey, which itself had a markedly nationalistic government at this time, showed no signs of withdrawing.

The invasion had come so suddenly and after such a rapid course of events that UNFICYP was left unsure of its role. In the event, it provided an invaluable resource in containing the crisis. As the secretary-general (now the Austrian Kurt Waldheim, who had succeeded U Thant in 1972) tried to negotiate a ceasefire between the Turkish army and the Greek Cypriot forces, UNFICYP acted as a classic interpositionary buffer. A Security Council resolution of 15 August demanding that all parties cooperate with UNFICYP confronted Turkey with a dilemma.[15] While there was some sympathy for Ankara's action following the original crypto-fascist coup, it would evaporate very quickly if Security Council resolutions were ignored and UN peacekeepers attacked. The Turkish advance stopped short of occupying the capital Nicosia, and while the presence of UNFICYP positions in the city may have been only a contributory factor in this, it was certainly a significant one. The resulting pause in Turkish operations gave time for diplomatic pressure to be brought to bear on Ankara and for the situation to cool somewhat. In truth, Turkey itself may have welcomed the presence of UNFICYP as an 'excuse' to halt its advance. While Turkey was clearly capable militarily of capturing the entire island, the diplomatic consequence of this would have been grave. The provision of pretexts is an important function of peacekeeping forces, and UNIFICYP performed this role very effectively.

Following the events of 1974 the 'Green Line' dividing the two communities and patrolled by UNFICYP was redrawn and now stretched 180 kilometres across the length of the island. On either side of it a UN buffer zone was created, varying in depth from a few metres in places to several kilometres in others. To the north was a de facto Turkish Cypriot statelet and to the south 'Cyprus' as recognized by the international community. The partition of the island sought by the Turkish Cypriots in the period leading to independence had come about, but its economic and political consequences have been largely negative. The 'Turkish Republic of Northern Cyprus', which was formally declared in 1983, is recognized only by Ankara. The international recognition of the Greek Cypriot state facilitated considerable economic development there after 1974 while there was little change in the northern part of the island.

The failure of peacemaking

The pace of the peacemaking effort in Cyprus has been halting, even stalled at times. Paradoxically, while the end of the cold war opened the way to the resolution of other long-standing conflicts, the intra-alliance character of the Cyprus problem has meant that no fundamental change came with the end of bipolarity. Consequently, there was no new impetus for a fundamental settlement. If anything, the end of the cold war made Cyprus and its problems even less significant to the United States and the western allies than it had been previously. The threat to the unity of NATO became a much less pressing consideration. The situation in Cyprus may, in fact, illustrate an unintended consequence of long-term peacekeeping. If peacemaking is not – or cannot be – pursued in parallel with the presence of peacekeeping forces, the peacekeeping operation itself may mutate into a semi-permanent institution that hampers rather than helps the search for a permanent solution. An entire generation of Cypriots has now grown to middle age in close daily contact with the United Nations. UNFICYP provides the stability and security that this socially dominant age group has grown up with and takes for granted. Moreover, like any permanent garrison, UNFICYP has an important part in the local economy. In this way peacekeeping, despite or even because of its success within the terms that a peacekeeping operation is judged, can become part of the problem rather than part of the solution.

Cold war operations in the Middle East and south Asia

The focus of attention on peacekeeping in the late 1950s and 1960s was understandably dominated by the big forces in Suez, Congo and Cyprus. But as these operations were authorized and deployed, a range of other UN missions was taking place. Although smaller ventures in personnel and cost terms, all of these were of considerable significance to the international politics of the cold war. One operation, in West New Guinea, was an early example of a model of UN intervention that came to be seen as a post-cold war innovation. In the long-term history of peacekeeping, the significance of these relatively small-scale, short-duration operations has tended to be under-appreciated. In fact, they provided a major contribution to the containment of local conflicts within their own regions at particularly delicate junctures in the cold war. They also illustrated some broader truths about the role of peacekeeping in the bipolar international system of the late 1950s and 1960s.

Between 1958 and 1965 three observation missions were established to address regional problems in the Middle East and Asia. Although each of these crises derived from specific local circumstances, all three threatened to import broader problems from the polarized international system of the cold war. The role of UN intervention in these conflicts was to provide immunization against this potential infection. In all three cases the intervention was limited to observation rather than interposition. Two were operational for less than a year and the third for only fourteen months. But together they demonstrated the potential of relatively modest multilateral commitments to bring disproportionately large benefits in the dangerous cross-currents of cold war international relations.

The Lebanon observation group

The Lebanon was placed under French administration by a League of Nations mandate after the defeat of Turkey in the First World War and the dissolution of the Ottoman Empire. Uniquely in the Middle East region, the population of the Lebanon was divided roughly equally between Maronite Christian and Muslim communities. The Christians dominated Lebanese politics under the mandate and received preferential treatment from the French administration. When the country became fully independent in 1946, it did so under a Christian president who shared power with a Sunni Muslim prime minister. In 1956 a new Christian president, Camille Chamoun, came to power at a critical point in Middle East politics. Chamoun put Lebanon at odds with the rest of the Arab states when he refused to support Egypt during the Suez crisis by severing diplomatic relations with France and Britain. In a climate of mounting Arab nationalism, Chamoun's attitude opened the hitherto subterranean divisions in Lebanese society.

Since the end of Ottoman rule many Muslims in the country had been uncomfortable with the religious demography of twentieth-century Lebanon and the political dominance of the Christians. They favoured some kind of unification with neighbouring Syria, a position that became increasingly popular as Lebanese Arabs became alienated from the assertively pro-western Chamoun regime. At the beginning of 1958 Egypt and Syria entered into a much vaunted (though politically insubstantial and short-lived) union as the United Arab Republic (UAR). This was supposed to embody Arab unity through the creation of a new multinational state. The founding of the UAR raised still further tensions within Lebanon and on its eastern borders with Syria. In mid-1958 this febrile atmosphere gave rise to a number of serious incidents of disorder within Lebanon's Muslim communities. Chamoun chose to see this as a Syrian-orchestrated attempt to undermine his government, although there were suspicions in Lebanon that he was talking up the crisis to justify moves to retain power beyond his constitutional term. Whether through genuine concern for the integrity of the Lebanese state or as a piece of political theatre, Chamoun took the matter to the United Nations. There his claims of Syrian (or UAR) infiltration were sympathetically heard by the United States, which, with the Republican Eisenhower administration in power, was pursuing a policy of containment of anti-western regimes wherever they might emerge. The Soviet Union, however, was suspicious of Chamoun and Lebanon's pro-western, anti-Arab nationalist diplomacy. This, along with Moscow's reservations about the whole legal standing of peacekeeping, ensured that the full-scale UN 'force' on the Lebanon–Syrian border that Chamoun originally requested would not materialize. Soviet agreement was achieved for a so-called observer group, however, mainly because the UAR itself welcomed the deployment as a means of proving that the disturbances in Lebanon were home-grown and not imported from the wider Arab world. This was duly authorized on 11 June 1958.[16]

Once again UNTSO performed the role of emergency reserve, providing an advance party of observers that could be transferred from Palestine to Lebanon immediately the Security Council passed the enabling resolution. By the middle of July the United Nations Observation Group in Lebanon (UNOGIL) consisted of a hundred military observers with aerial reconnaissance resources (necessary in the rugged border region) (Map 18). Its initial reports, based on investigations along the border, seemed to support Syrian denials of involvement in the Lebanon crisis. Just at this point, however, the broader regional setting in which UNOGIL was operating changed dramatically when the pro-western Iraqi monarchy was overthrown in a nationalist revolution. Iraq now joined Egypt and Syria in the vanguard of pan-Arab radicalism. This left the western powers with just Lebanon and Jordan as significant allies in the region, and the crisis deepened as Jordan too now complained of UAR infiltration and subversion.

In this new situation Washington was no longer willing to leave the matter to the United Nations. UN peacekeeping in the cold war was frequently about access to what might be described as 'permitted space'. The perimeters of this space depended on the perceptions of east and west about the importance of issues and areas to their own interests in the system at any particular time. Peacekeeping had no role, for example, in the conflicts in Soviet-dominated eastern Europe. At the very time that UN forces were taking up positions in Suez, the Hungarian uprising was being suppressed by Soviet forces with no suggestion of any kind of military role for the UN. Similarly, when peacekeeping forces were deployed along Israel's borders in the early 1970s, the war in Vietnam remained the concern of America and its allies; there would be no UN peacekeeping in south-east Asia until the cold war was over. While Suez and later Sinai and the Golan Heights were regarded as areas where the UN could perform a useful role acceptable to the opposing blocs and were therefore 'permitted' to the UN, eastern Europe and south-east Asia were not. The permitted space, however, could expand and contract from time to time, depending on the specific nature of conflicts within it and the overall state of superpower relations. In July 1958 it suddenly seemed to contract in the Middle East as a result of the Iraq coup. The United States was now determined to become directly involved in a newly significant area of national interest.

The US Sixth Fleet was directed to the eastern Mediterranean and in the second half of July 1958 some 14,000 American troops landed in Lebanon. The UN nevertheless still determined to carry on with its immunizing role in Lebanon, and UNOGIL's numbers were dramatically increased to 600, drawn from twenty contributing states. There was now something of a mannerly stand-off. The American force was garrisoned around the capital, Beirut, rather than deployed to the sensitive border area where the enlarged UN presence was widening its operations. At this point the Americans proposed a return to Chamoun's original plan for a UN 'force' rather than the observer mission, but even with thousands of American troops in the country poised to intervene, the Soviet Union still vetoed the proposal.[17] Over the next weeks the crisis subsided. There was no evidence of significant Syrian interference in either Lebanon or Jordan, and UNOGIL was instrumental in mediating this. It might be argued of course that UNOGIL's presence inhibited any such interference by acting as a de facto interposition force as well as an observer mission. The imprecision of the borderline between these two functions is, in fact, one of the most convincing reasons for describing both types of operations as peacekeeping. But developments in internal Lebanese politics also helped calm the situation after the Americans persuaded Chamoun that he should not seek to extend his presidency. The improvement in the situation provided sufficient cover for the withdrawal of the American force at the end of October 1958. UNOGIL itself was withdrawn from Lebanon by mid-December.

Viewed in retrospect, it may appear that the UN intervention in Lebanon in 1958 was not wholly justified by the conditions on the ground. On the basis of subsequent evidence it would seem that Camille Chamoun's initial complaints against Syria were either mistaken or intentionally manufactured. A major military deployment was not perhaps necessary to establish this. On the other hand, the initial deployment of UNOGIL was not large and its early reports were instrumental in discrediting the claims of the Lebanon government and preventing them from turning into diplomatically dangerous 'facts' by default. Additionally, the presence of UNOGIL and its rapid expansion after the American landings was probably instrumental in keeping US troops away from areas where they might have made disastrous contact with pro-Syrian forces. For these reasons, therefore, and while acknowledging the danger of attempting to construct 'what if' histories, it seems probable that UNOGIL performed a role at a dangerous location on the periphery of the cold war that was out of proportion to the relatively small resources involved.

The observer mission in Yemen

In 1963 the United Nations established a similar military observation mission to address another conflict between a pro-western leadership and radical Arab nationalism. In September 1962 the Yemeni monarchy was overthrown by republican army officers. Here, as in Lebanon four years previously, the local conflict was tied into the larger regional one in the Arab world. This in turn had implications for the balance in the broader system as the old monarchies and the revolutionary nationalists had political and diplomatic affinities with the west and the Soviet bloc respectively.

Yemen lies at the southern point of the Arab peninsula below Saudi Arabia. During the nineteenth century control of the territory was divided between Turkey, which dominated the northern portion adjacent to modern-day Saudi Arabia, and Britain, which controlled the southern part from the port of Aden. British interests were primarily strategic. Aden was on the Arabian coast where the Red Sea flowed into the Indian Ocean and was therefore an important way-station on the imperial trade routes to India and south-east Asia. The value of Aden to the larger British Empire increased enormously after the opening of the Suez Canal in the 1860s. After the First World War, Ottoman Yemen became independent under its local rulers rather than subject to a League of Nations mandate like Turkey's northern Arab territories. The 1962 revolution came about when the ultra-traditional ruling family fell victim to the modernizing pressures from the north, in particularly Nasser's Egypt, whose influence permeated Yemen's educated elite and its foreign-trained officer corps. There was no neat transfer of power to the revolutionaries, however. In Yemen's highly tribalized political culture the forces of conservatism were strong enough to oppose the new regime by force, though not strong enough to prevent them establishing a government. A civil war ensued in which the deposed royalists were supported by neighbouring Saudi Arabia and the new regime was supported by Egypt, which had stationed several thousand troops in Yemen following the revolution.

Both the United States and the UN became involved in the search for a settlement. This eventually bore fruit with an agreement between the two sides in April 1963. The terms of this would consolidate the position of the republican government, but the Kennedy administration now in the White House was more open to establishing workable relationships with the new Arab regimes than its predecessor. The Eisenhower White House tended to regard the emergence of these regimes as a challenge to western interests. Its withdrawal of economic support from Nasser's Aswan plans in 1956 and then its approach to the Lebanon crisis of 1958 were examples of this.

The essence of the Yemen agreement was that the conflict should be localized. This would be brought about by the withdrawal of the Egyptian military presence and the end of Saudi support for the royalist rebels. While the repatriation of the Egyptians could in theory be easily enough verified, the Saudi obligations required a physical presence on the long, remote and inhospitable border. To this end the Security Council created the Yemen Observation Mission (UNYOM) (Map 32). The operation, initially proposed by Jordan in the General Assembly, was established in June 1963 by the Security Council with no real difficulty between the permanent members.[18] Despite the Soviet Union's unhappiness with the management of peacekeeping, which was by now, late in the Congo operation, well established, Moscow raised no strong objection. As with the previous undertakings in Suez and Lebanon, Soviet opposition in principle to peacekeeping was outweighed by diplomatic pragmatism in the particular circumstances. If local friends and clients of the Soviet Union saw it as in their interests to have UN operations established, then Moscow was not going to jeopardize its relationships by opposing them. In the case of UNYOM Soviet reservations were, anyway, lessened by the fact that there was no wrangle over financing. Egypt and Saudi Arabia, the two international actors involved, agreed to cover the costs of the operation between them.

In its fourteen months duration UNYOM drew on military personnel from eleven countries, though its strength never exceeded 200. Given the terrain in which it had to operate, much of its work had to be carried out from the air. In strictly operational terms UNYOM was not a notable success for the UN. At the time of its withdrawal in September 1964 Egyptian forces were still present in the country supporting the republican regime. This was probably an indication that Nasser had miscalculated the impact that the end of direct Saudi support for the royalist fighters would have on the situation. The civil war continued without it. The republican modernizers were not, evidently, as popular in the deeply conservative country as they had claimed and as Nasser had believed. In the meantime Saudi Arabia continued to provide refuge for pro-royalist tribal fighters if not direct military support for them. But in the broad political tapestry of the region and the wider international system UNYOM successfully carried out a classic peacekeeping function. The presence of the United Nations, supported by both superpowers, sent a powerful political signal. It indicated a mutual agreement that the matter would not be drawn into any general bipolar rivalry and that the outcome should be determined within the context of the region. While the situation remained unresolved over the coming years, it did not deteriorate significantly. A general peace agreement was eventually reached through local negotiations in 1970. In the meantime, Britain had withdrawn from Aden and the entire political texture of the Arabian peninsula had changed. In 1963 and 1964, however, Yemen lay within the limited permitted space for cold war peacekeeping in which the superpowers were willing to utilize the UN in their mutual interests. In this the Yemen operation looked ahead to peacekeeping in the period of détente, where the permitted space expanded still further and peacekeeping became virtually a management tool of US–Soviet relations.

India and Pakistan again: the 1965 conflict and the observer mission

The mid-1960s saw UN involvement further east, in an observation mission on the India–Pakistan border following a dramatic intensification of the continuing hostility between them. At the beginning of 1965 a dispute emerged over the Rann of Kutch area at the southern end of the shared frontier. Tensions erupted into violence in August in Kashmir, historically the most incendiary part of the border. As a result, the 1949 ceasefire, which UNMOGIP had been established to monitor, effectively collapsed. Despite a sequence of Security Council resolutions supported by both superpowers and strongly backed by Britain (concerned about the internal Commonwealth nature of the crisis), neither side seemed prepared for compromise. So serious was the situation – and so strong the Security Council consensus – that U Thant proposed the application of Article 40 of Chapter VII of the Charter, which empowered the Council to require parties in conflict to comply with its instruction to cease hostilities.[19] Accordingly, on 20 September the Council 'demanded' that both sides cease hostilities within two days and return to the positions they held before the August fighting (which would have the effect of re-establishing the 1949 ceasefire line).[20] In order to oversee the process in Kashmir UNMOGIP was temporarily enlarged. But the tensions along the rest of the border required the creation of a further military observation mission that could be mandated to operate beyond Kashmir. The United Nations India–Pakistan Observation Mission (UNIPOM) was therefore established (Map 24). Yet again the urgency of the situation meant that UNTSO in the Middle East was used as an emergency source of military observers to permit the mission to get under way as quickly as possible. Hostilities did not cease immediately, however, and the 100 or so military observers provided by twelve states (almost all middle powers) along with the expanded UNMOGIP personnel, operated in difficult and frequently dangerous conditions. Eventually, however, after a further Security Council resolution demanding the cessation of military activity and cooperation with UN personnel, fighting subsided.

It is unclear how far this was an achievement of the Security Council and the UN presence on the ground. It is likely that the two governments involved had begun to comprehend the implications of continued fighting and the consequences of an all-out war. Both the United States and the Soviet Union were applying their own pressures for a ceasefire where they would have most effect – on Pakistan and India respectively. Pressure was being exerted too by Britain and the Commonwealth, which at this time had a greater influence on the international behaviour of its members than it would in the future. But as in Lebanon and Yemen, the UN presence on the ground provided an earnest of the international system's commitment to resolving a conflict that was seen as a threat to peace and security going far beyond the area of fighting. Like the Yemen involvement, too, it was a public signal of the superpowers' mutual acceptance that the crisis was not to be exploited for cold war purposes. Neither India nor Pakistan was to be left under any illusions of bilateral support from their respective cold war patrons. The Soviet Union eventually provided the necessary good offices for a longer-term settlement. In January 1966 it brought both sides together for talks in Tashkent. The agreement worked out here did not settle the problems of the India–Pakistan border; these would flare again dramatically in the future. But it did ease the tension from the particular confrontation of the previous year.

The UN as interim state: West New Guinea

The conflict between the Netherlands and Indonesia over the territory of West New Guinea[21] was another illustration of the stresses put on the international system by the process of European decolonization after 1945. The territory formed the western half of the island of New Guinea, the eastern part in the early 1960s being administered by Australia as the UN Trusteeship of Papua and New Guinea. West Papua had been part of the Dutch East Indies since the early nineteenth century, but when this emerged as the independent state of Indonesia in 1949, the Netherlands excepted West New Guinea from the decolonization agreement and retained control of it. The rationale of the Dutch position was that West New Guinea was ethnically and culturally so different from the rest of the Indonesian archipelago that it could not be considered part of a unified national entity. It proposed therefore to maintain its administrative control until such time as the indigenous population was ready and able to decide its own future. There was some justice in this argument. While Indonesia was, beyond question, a south-east Asian nation, West Papua was part of the South Pacific sub-region of Melanesia. In the early 1960s the limited state of economic and political development in Melanesia was such that decolonization lay some way in the future. Fiji, the first of the Melanesian territories to become independent, did not do so until 1970, and Australia did not transfer power to the new state of Papua New Guinea until five years after that. Indonesia had never accepted the Dutch position, however, and had pressed consistently for the transfer of West New Guinea to its control since its own independence.

The United Nations and the Indonesian campaign for West New Guinea

By 1960 the radical nationalist Indonesian regime of President Sukarno was becoming increasingly vociferous in its claim. Sukarno's campaign was conducted on two fronts. He mounted a global diplomatic offensive that exploited his growing reputation as a leader in the Afro-Asian grouping of states that at this time was beginning to organize itself into a formal 'non-aligned movement'. The campaign also took on a military dimension with Indonesian commandos making incursions against Dutch military installations in West New Guinea. This served to create the – misleading – impression that there was an anti-colonial 'independence war' in progress. Unsurprisingly, the United Nations became a major arena for the diplomatic side of the Indonesian strategy. General Assembly debates on the issue took place regularly from the mid-1950s with Indonesia's position attracting increasing support as the Afro-Asian grouping in the Assembly grew. The issue was never a major preoccupation for the UN, however. West New Guinea was perceived as occupying the exotic periphery of the international system. It generated little urgency as an issue while attention was taken up with what were seen as the more pressing post-colonial problems of the Middle East and Africa. But when U Thant, himself Asian, succeeded Dag Hammarskjöld as secretary-general after the latter's death in Africa, he determined to push for a resolution of the conflict. Accordingly, he persuaded both Indonesia and the Netherlands to agree to UN-brokered negotiations.

Despite a racking up of tensions by the Indonesians in the course of the talks, an agreement was reached in August 1962 that amounted to a concession of defeat on the issue by the Netherlands. The Dutch position had become untenable, largely because of the terms of the cold war at this time. The incipient non-aligned movement within which Indonesia was a key player was increasingly able to flex its diplomatic muscles. It was acquiring considerable leverage against the west, which was concerned at this stage in the cold war not to 'lose points' to the Soviet Union. There was a general fear among western delegations at the United Nations of being seen as 'soft on imperialism', which led to the complexities of special cases such as West New Guinea being disregarded. Nevertheless, the agreement did not amount to an immediate capitulation by Holland, and the plan had some extremely novel features in the role it proposed for the United Nations.[22]

UN 'government': the Temporary Executive Authority

The administration of West New Guinea was to be transferred in the first instance from the Netherlands to the United Nations. Thus, for the first time since the League of Nations Governing Commission for the Saar, an international organization would act as a transitional 'state' (Map 15). The arrangement would pre-date by three decades the Transitional Authority in Cambodia, which has often been presented as the first such venture by the UN (see Chapter 7). This United Nations Temporary Executive Authority (UNTEA) would be headed by an administrator appointed by the secretary-general after consultation with the two states involved. UNTEA would administer West New Guinea from October 1962 until May 1963 at which time the territory would be ceded to Indonesia. In a nod to Dutch concerns over the exercise of self-determination by the population of the territory, a future 'act of free choice' was to take place among the Papuan people to confirm or reject Indonesian sovereignty.

In the meantime, the Temporary Executive Authority would have all the necessary trappings of a state, including an executive wing responsible for security and law and order. This was the United Nations Security Force (UNSF) whose size would be determined by the administrator based on conditions in the territory after the transfer of power to the UN. The Security Force would also have the more traditional peacekeeping role of monitoring the ceasefire between Indonesian and Dutch forces pending the withdrawal of the latter (which was completed by January 1963). This task extended to what amounted virtually to a rescue operation for Indonesian troops who had been dropped by parachute in the jungles and mountains of West Papua. The military observers involved in this part of the UNSF role were drawn from a range of middle powers, but the main body of the Security Force was provided by a single contributor, Pakistan, which provided a contingent of 1,500 soldiers. An Iranian, Djalal Abdoh, was appointed UN administrator with the agreement of both parties. In a delicate piece of diplomatic symmetry, the United Nations flag flew along with that of the Netherlands over the headquarters of UNTEA until 31 December 1962 when the latter was replaced by the Indonesian flag for the duration of UN administration. Ominously for the future political development of the territory, the rapid withdrawal of Dutch officials exposed the scarcity of trained Papuans ready to take their place. There was in consequence a major movement of Indonesian civil servants from Java and other parts of the Indonesian archipelago and these quickly came to dominate the territory's administration in a way alarmingly reminiscent of a colonial government. The withdrawal of UNSF at the end of the period of UN administration in May 1963 was likewise followed immediately by the arrival of the Indonesian military in considerable force.

Operational success, moral ambiguity

The Temporary Executive Authority and its Security Force met fully their mandate of overseeing the smooth transfer of power from the Netherlands to Indonesia and to this extent it was a successful peacekeeping operation. The political morality of the larger process for which the UN was responsible in West New Guinea could be seriously questioned, however. The decades of Indonesian occupation since 1963 have tended to validate the position of the Dutch and others who were sceptical of Indonesia's claim to West New Guinea and its intentions for the territory's future. In 1969 Indonesia undertook the act of free choice agreed under the terms of the 1962 settlement. This took the form of a 'consultation' among Indonesian-controlled 'representative councils'. To no one's surprise these voted unanimously to maintain West New Guinea as part of Indonesia. While there was widespread awareness of the inadequacy of the process, possession is nine points of the law in diplomacy as much as in any other field of endeavour, and there was no appetite in the UN or elsewhere for re-opening the issue. In truth, it is unclear what viable alternative there could have been to continued Indonesian rule. Reversion to UN administration, though legally feasible, would have been politically untenable and immediate independence would have been disastrous for the territory's unprepared population. In subsequent years West New Guinea became a major destination in Indonesia's trans-migration programme, which involved the transfer of populations from the overcrowded islands of Java and Bali and their resettlement in new, less populous parts of the national territory. This led to much of the most productive land being taken from its traditional Papuan owners and given to settlers. Meanwhile, the exploitation of the territory's considerable natural resources by multinational companies licensed by Indonesia brought little benefit to the local populations. Papuan nationalism, which developed some force in the 1970s and 1980s, was ruthlessly suppressed by the authoritarian regime of Sukarno's successor, Suharto.

In some respects it is surprising that the UN's involvement in West New Guinea passed off with virtually no disagreement in the organization. Coming as it did in the middle of the Congo operation it might have been expected that it would have fallen victim to the wider divisions in the UN at the time. The West New Guinea operation was, moreover, initiated by the secretary-general working with the General Assembly and with no formal input from the Security Council. This would seem to be a recipe for Soviet dissent, but some key aspects of the situation prevented this. From the beginning the process was designed to transfer West New Guinea to Indonesia, which at that time was close to the Soviet Union. As in other operations – in Suez, in Yemen, between India and Pakistan – where its friends or potential friends favoured UN involvement, Moscow was happy to put its anti-peacekeeping principles on one side. It was helpful in this respect that there was no difficulty around the question of financing: the UN operation in West New Guinea was paid for jointly by the Netherlands and Indonesia.

As with other successful peacekeeping operations, an important ingredient in the UN involvement with West New Guinea was that all sides derived clear benefits. At the systemic level the west could free itself from thinking too much about the merits and demerits of the solution to a potentially thorny diplomatic problem, leaving its implementation to the UN. For Indonesia the delay in the transfer of power in the territory caused by the temporary UN administration was a price well worth paying for that legitimization. Finally, for the Netherlands, which found it impossible to hold on in West New Guinea in the absence of any diplomatic support, some face could be saved by ceding the territory to the United Nations rather than directly to Indonesia, even if no one was under any illusion that it amounted to the same thing.

At the broadest systemic level, the UN's engagement with West New Guinea kept a potentially difficult issue safely out of the crucible of the confrontation between the western and the eastern blocs. In this regard the UN's function was identical to the one that it had already performed in Lebanon and that it was simultaneously engaged in, with limited success, in the Congo. However important this role might have been for the regulation of the international system, though, the morality of the undertaking as far as the people of West New Guinea were concerned was more questionable. The inescapable truth was that the principle of genuine self-determination for West New Guinea had been sacrificed to the exigencies of international politics. The services required of peacekeeping in the cold war, in other words, were not always compatible with common perceptions of natural justice.

6 Peacekeeping and détente

The Middle East in the 1970s

In the last chapter we discussed the idea that peacekeeping during the cold war took place within a 'permitted area'. This area was political as much as geographical. Its perimeters were fixed by tacit agreement between east and west and excluded issues and regions where core national interests were in play. These were off-limits to multilateral intervention as the superpowers and their allies regarded it as crucial to retain close national control over them. Eastern Europe and Latin America, for example, were spheres of national influence for the Soviet Union and the United States respectively where, whatever crises and conflicts emerged during the cold war, direct UN military intervention was never a serious option. But other areas – in the Middle East, sub-Saharan Africa, south Asia and the Pacific – were open to UN intervention not because they did not involve core interests but because multilateral responses to their conflicts could serve the management of east–west relations by preventing their drift into the larger bipolar contest.

The boundaries of those areas 'available' for UN peacekeeping were, to an extent, elastic. In periods when east–west tension was high, the permitted area contracted, but when the superpowers were able to take a more distanced view of events in the international system, it expanded. The period of détente, which can be dated approximately from the mid-1960s until the later 1970s, was one in which cold war tensions were substantially – if temporarily – reduced. In these years, therefore, superpower attitudes to the usefulness of the UN and the permissible extent of its peacekeeping role were particularly liberal. This situation, and its eventual unravelling, was evident in the changing attitudes of the superpowers to missions already under way, but it was most obviously illustrated by new operations that were established during the period in the Middle East.

The origins and nature of détente

There is no single explanation for the interlude of détente. A number of factors came together to contribute to the lessening of tensions between the superpowers in the 1960s and 1970s. At the most general level, it could be argued that it was the result of a natural ebb and flow in international relations. The cold war had been a characteristic of the international system since the late 1940s while both the United States and the Soviet Union developed their nuclear arsenals and competed for influence throughout the international system. But in the late 1950s and 1960s as the world gradually recovered from the effects of the Second World War, the continued stasis in political relationships was increasingly at odds with the development of a new buoyant global economy and increasingly sophisticated means of communication. In this view, the beginnings of what later became known as globalization dictated adjustments to the stagnant political relationship between east and west.

Whatever the strength of this argument, there were more tangible elements in the equation as well. The increasing sophistication of the nuclear weapons and their means of delivery, which underlay bipolarity (and, in the prevailing view, ensured that the cold war remained just that: cold rather than hot), dictated changes in the political relationship they supposedly served. The Cuban missile crisis of October 1962, which brought the world as close as it had then come to nuclear war, drove home a vital truth. The balance of nuclear capability between the superpowers was such that there could be no question of either winning a war against the other. The age of 'mutually assured destruction' had arrived. Technology meant that the United States and the Soviet Union enjoyed so-called 'second strike capability'. In other words, even an attempt at pre-emptive nuclear attack would be punished by a nuclear counter-attack because missiles deep in underground silos or dispersed across the oceans in submarines would always be able to respond, even if the cities of the homeland had already been destroyed. Any rational understanding of the east–west relationship had to start from an acceptance that it was now based on technically effective mutual deterrence and that it was in everyone's interest to ensure that this was properly managed. An obvious conclusion to be drawn was that the superpowers had to embrace the mutual self-interest implied by this situation and cooperate to avoid – or, where that proved impossible, manage – conflict rather than seek to win in conflict situations. Once this proposition was accepted, the implications for peacekeeping – and its permitted area – became clear. Multilateralism, whether through the United Nations or other agencies, provided a tool by which the superpowers could manage conflict in the system to their own mutual advantage without running the risks associated with direct involvement on the ground.

And, 'cometh the hour, cometh the man'. As these new imperatives began to make themselves felt in the international system, individuals emerged who seemed to understand their dynamics and who were able to manage their application in day-to-day relationships. In Chapter 2 we discussed the ways in which historical phases in the international system can speak over the centuries to later ones. Specifically, we discussed Henry

Kissinger, US national security adviser and then later secretary of state in the Nixon and Ford administrations of the early 1970s. Kissinger, it will be recalled, drew on his academic work on the European concert system after 1815 to formulate a view of international relations that, though still conservative and 'realist', recognized the mutuality of interest of states at the top of the international hierarchy of power. In this view, the different ideologies on which the domestic politics of big powers were founded had little relevance in the international realm. The state of nuclear technology provided a natural impetus towards détente in the historical period in which Kissinger was close to the centre of power; his own intellectual perspective complemented this and he was in a position to provide both a political rationale for superpower cooperation and a policy response that pushed in that direction. For Kissinger, the United Nations could never be more than a collection of states; it could not acquire sovereignty. His vision of the international system was an uncompromisingly state-centric one. But if the UN could not supplant the state, it could certainly be used as an instrument of the state. Specifically, its peacekeeping role could be utilized to manage challenges to the mutual self-interest of the superpowers. In the 1970s these challenges were most threatening in the Middle East.

The Middle East War of 1973

We left the Middle East in 1967 after the forced withdrawal of UNEF when Egypt ended its host state consent (see Chapter 4). The departure of the United Nations coincided, and not by accident, with the Six Day War in June of that year. The war was in large part an attempt by Nasser to save the fading fortunes of pan-Arab nationalism – and in its train a decline in his own prestige was underway since its high point at the time of the Suez crisis. The United Arab Republic, which was established in 1958 and supposedly created a unified state between Egypt and Syria, unravelled in 1961 when Syria withdrew, resentful at Nasser's attempt to dominate the arrangement. Although the Arab nationalist message had prevailed in Iraq with the overthrow of the monarchy in 1958, it made few inroads into Lebanon or Jordan and, as we have seen, it met fierce conservative resistance in Yemen after the revolution there in 1962.

The most certain way of restoring the fortunes of the pan-Arab cause, in Nasser's view, was to strike with other Arab states against the common enemy, Israel. Immediately following the withdrawal of UNEF, Egypt closed the Gulf of Aqaba to Israeli shipping, denying it an outlet to the Red Sea and the Indian Ocean. At this point, early in the evolution of détente, both superpowers sought to restrain their local clients. Israel, however, felt its very existence to be at threat, and launched a dramatic pre-emptive strike. The large Egyptian air force, which would have spear-headed an attack on Israel, was destroyed on the ground before it could be deployed, and Israeli forces swept across Egypt's Sinai Desert destroying enemy tanks and armour across a wide front. From Jordan the Israelis took the west bank of the Jordan river, which included Jerusalem, a prize of huge religious and historical significance. Syria meanwhile lost the Golan Heights on its rugged border area with Israel.

The Israeli victory was total, and there was little interest – or point – in considering a peacekeeping operation in its wake. Israel's fundamental hostility to the UN's peacekeeping endeavours in the region had not been allayed by the secretary-general's acquiescence in the withdrawal of UNEF at Egypt's bidding. The Israeli diplomatic position in the aftermath of its triumph was, anyway, such that it could easily resist pressure to accept a UN presence. The Security Council was closely involved in the aftermath of the war, however. In November 1967 it passed what became one of its best known resolutions since 1945. Resolution 242 called for Israeli withdrawal from the territories occupied during the Six Day War.[1] The fact that the resolution was adopted unanimously, without an abstention let alone a veto, says something about the developing influence of détente on the Security Council's deliberations. Israel, however, refused to comply. To withdraw from the occupied territories would have negated much of the point of the Six Day War from Israel's perspective. A return to the status quo ante would, in the view of the Israeli government, have left the country just as vulnerable to future attempts to 'drive it into the sea' as it had been previously. It now had a buffer of land around its most exposed borders. Despite the obvious complications of controlling about one million Arabs, most of them Palestinians, in the West Bank and the former Egyptian Gaza Strip, Israel judged that this made it more secure. And, beyond geo-strategic calculations, the capture of Jerusalem represented the achievement of a national dream that could not be given up.

The impact of the Six Day War on the Arab states was profound. Far from restoring his reputation, Nasser had seen his standing in the Arab world and beyond decline still further. His popularity in Egypt itself, however, was little affected and he remained in power until his death in 1970 when he was succeeded by Anwar el-Sadat. Sadat was a far less popular figure, and his position as Egyptian president would have to be much more reliant on tangible achievements than Nasser's had been. Consequently, in the face of Israel's refusal to make any significant concessions after its victory in 1967, Sadat began to contemplate yet another war. The Soviet Union had moved swiftly to re-arm Egypt after 1967 and within a short period its air force had been rebuilt and its border defences strengthened with up-to-date missile systems. During the first half of 1973 Sadat and the Syrian president, Hafiz al-Assad, laid plans for a surprise attack similar to the failed one of 1967. Fighting began during a Jewish religious holiday on 6 October 1973 (giving the conflict its familiar name: the Yom Kippur War). The Egyptian assault came through the Sinai desert, scene of some of the most intense fighting in 1967, while the Syrians attacked in the Golan Heights. Exploiting the shock of their strategy, the Arabs made considerable early gains. But once again Israel was able to mobilize quickly and the initiative was soon lost by the Arab side. Israeli forces moved rapidly into Sinai where they encircled the Egyptian Third Army. They were also able to cross to the west bank of the Suez Canal where they neutralized much of Egypt's most sophisticated Soviet-supplied missile defences. Simultaneously, Syrian advances in the Golan Heights were pushed back.

Israel–Egypt: the Second United Nations Emergency Force

Both sides' superpower patrons were caught off-balance by the eruption of the war and appeared to have had no useful advance intelligence about Arab intentions. The initial response in both Washington and Moscow was to rush to the support of their respective clients. Arms supplies were rapidly shipped to both sides, and there was some uncomfortable sabre-rattling between the superpowers themselves. Once the initial confusion and uncertainty passed, however, and the outcome of the war – another Israeli victory – became clear, the influence of détente on superpower calculations began to reveal itself. On 20 October Henry Kissinger, at this time secretary of state in the Nixon administration, travelled to Moscow for talks with his Soviet opposite number, Andrei Gromyko. The purpose of the meeting was to work out the details of a ceasefire and then to agree how it would be imposed. The following day the two superpowers more or less 'informed' their clients that the war was over. The vehicle of this instruction was a short, terse Security Council resolution constructed by the American and Soviet delegations and adopted unanimously. This required a cessation of fighting within twelve hours.[2]

At this point there was a momentary stutter in the process. Israel now had the initiative on the battlefield and was reluctant to lose momentum before it had achieved as much as it could on the ground. Egypt, anxious about the outcome of a continuing Israeli advance and also ready to score a propaganda point or two, immediately accepted the ceasefire demand and called on the Soviet Union and the United States to themselves send a peacekeeping force to impose it. Moscow appeared receptive to this, but Washington would not contemplate such a level of direct involvement. Now the Soviet Union sought to raise the stakes by making reference to its nuclear capability in the region. In response, the United States announced that it would put its own nuclear forces on heightened alert. The apparent reversion to old-fashioned cold war confrontation soon passed, however. It was the result of a diplomatic miscalculation by the Soviet Union that demanded an American response, but the logic of détente soon reasserted itself when Israel complied with Security Council demands and accepted the ceasefire. The next stage was to ensure that the truce was maintained and conditions created for a longer-term settlement of the war. To this end the Security Council, again acting at the behest of the two superpowers, authorized the creation of a second United Nations Emergency Force (UNEF-II) to be interposed between Israel and Egypt.[3]

Secretary-general Kurt Waldheim now had to put together an operation at great speed if it was to take command of a still volatile situation. To do so he requested the immediate transfer of peacekeepers from the force in Cyprus, which at this time, a year before the Turkish invasion, was largely calm. Contingents from Austria, Finland and Sweden were quickly flown into Sinai and were followed a few days later by a company of Irish troops, also from UNFICYP. In a rerun of the arrangements made for the first Emergency Force in 1956, the chief of staff of UNTSO, a Finnish general, was appointed interim force commander. Eventually, thirteen states would contribute personnel to UNEF-II, which Waldheim envisaged would grow quickly to a strength of 7,000 (which it achieved at the beginning of 1974). The force immediately set about delivering humanitarian supplies to the encircled Egyptian army in the Sinai whose plight was becoming desperate. Later, it was able to facilitate the exchange of prisoners of war and take over Israeli positions and checkpoints in Sinai. After the easing of the immediate post-conflict tensions, the UN force faced no significant difficulties from either side during its five-year period of deployment (Map 9).

UNEF-II was the first large-scale operation established since the Cyprus force, which had been set up almost a decade before. In contrast to UNFICYP, of which the then secretary-general U Thant had been the prime mover, the creation of the new Sinai force was to all intents and purposes a joint enterprise by the superpowers. The role of Kurt Waldheim was primarily to support and implement this initiative. Whether this state of affairs was good or bad for the UN and for peacekeeping is a matter for debate. On one side it can be argued that the speed, efficiency and cooperativeness with which UNEF-II was launched illustrated the potential for peacekeeping in an international system relatively free of superpower rivalry. The operational effectiveness of the Congo operation and the financial stability of both it and the Cyprus force had been deeply affected by this rivalry. Now, within one hectic week, a major war had been brought to an end and a peacekeeping operation established. This operation could pursue its mandate confident in the support of the Security Council and the major actors of the international system. Against this, however, is the view that such superpower domination of peacekeeping undermined its claims to offer a genuinely multilateral alternative, however limited in effectiveness, to big-power domination of the international system. In other words, how far could peacekeeping claim to be a truly international activity if it was merely to be another instrument of big power foreign policy? As one writer saw it: '. . . the United Nations in general and the Security Council in particular were pushed further along the road to the point where they became mere elements – however essential – in superpower strategy'.[4]

The advanced level of superpower cooperation over UNEF-II and their mutual commitment to it did bring some historical advances for UN peacekeeping. For the first time a Soviet ally, Poland, provided a contingent for a peacekeeping operation.[5] And, despite the Security Council's explicit exclusion of its own permanent members from participation in UNEF-II, the new attitude towards peacekeeping generated by détente resulted in the Soviet Union itself sending military observers to serve in UNTSO, exactly balancing a longer-standing American contribution. The financing of the new Middle East operation also represented a major advance. Previously, as we have seen, the Soviet Union had been willing fully to support peacekeeping operations where arrangements other than payment from regular funds had been made. The operations in West New Guinea and in Yemen, for example, had been acceptable to Moscow in part because the parties to these disputes had agreed to meet all costs, but the Congo and Cyprus forces had been critically affected by the UN's insistence that they should be regarded as routine costs. The Soviet Union now accepted that UNEF-II could be treated as a 'regular expense' of the organization and its costs could be levied on all members.

The new cooperation on peacekeeping also affected the patron–client relationship in the region. Israel had to put aside its long-standing dislike of UN intervention and fall into line with Washington's larger strategy. It may have been the case, though, that Israel would have been less hostile to UNEF-II than it was to other UN deployments on its borders anyway. The Arab assault of October 1973 had come close to success before the Israeli counter-attack prevailed. Israeli confidence had been shaken and a degree of complacency about its own invincibility that developed after the 1967 war was dispelled. For the first time UN interposition might provide a guarantee to Israel rather than a constraint on its freedom of initiative.

Israel–Syria: the Disengagement Observer Force

Things did not proceed so quickly or so smoothly on the other front of the 1973 war. Syria, like Egypt on the Sinai front, had enjoyed some initial success in the Golan Heights, re-occupying some of the territory taken by Israel in 1967. But here, too, the gain was short-lived and its counter-attack had taken Israeli forces even further into Syrian territory than previously. While international attention was concentrated on the more dramatic circumstances of the Sinai front after the end of the fighting in 1973, the Golan Heights was the scene of frequent clashes and the possibility of the resumption of major fighting there remained high. Serious attention was not given to the Syrian front until the spring of 1974 when Henry Kissinger embarked on a process of so-called shuttle diplomacy between President Assad and the Israeli prime minister, Golda Meir (replaced in the final phase of the process by Yitzhak Rabin).

Both leaders proved resistant to compromise, but Kissinger's persistence, along with background pressure from the Soviet Union, eventually prevailed. A settlement was reached that involved an Israeli withdrawal more or less to its post-1967 positions with a United Nations presence being interposed in most of the territory it evacuated. The exact character of this presence became an issue between the sides, however. Israel, newly anxious about its security, as we have said, wanted a major international presence that would act as a powerful disincentive to any Syrian adventurism on the border. On its side, Syria objected to the idea of a UN 'force', not because of the constraints it would impose on its actions but because it would occupy Syrian rather than Israeli territory (that had been occupied and then evacuated by Israel in the latest fighting). Assad therefore wanted a small observation group to monitor and verify the Israeli disengagement. The outcome was a military and semantic compromise. Instead of the 3,000-strong force favoured by Israel, there would be a UN presence of just over 1,000 troops (Map 17). These would form something called an 'observer force', which would be a hybrid mission somewhere between military observer group and peacekeeping force. The new mission would be supplemented by about 80 observers from the Israel–Syria component of UNTSO who would be responsible for the actual military observation.

Once again, the Security Council fell in line with superpower wishes and the secretary-general was left to work out the details of their implementation. The US-brokered agreement between Israel and Syria was signed on 31 October 1974 and on the same day the Council provided the enabling resolution for the establishment of the United Nations Disengagement Observer Force (UNDOF).[6]

'Détente peacekeeping' had thus taken a further step forward. But, for better or worse, it would not prove to be a long-term phenomenon. By the late 1970s the momentum of détente faltered as the superpower relationship came under strain from powerful pressures in various parts of the system. In the meantime, however, it would retain just enough momentum to ensure the establishment of one further major peacekeeping commitment in the Middle East.

Israel–Lebanon: the 'interim' force

We last focused on Lebanon when we discussed the events of 1958 and the work of the UN observer group set up to determine whether there was significant infiltration from Syria and, if so, to deter it. UNOGIL had been a modest but significant success in the early phase of cold war peacekeeping. Despite this, and developments in the country's domestic politics that helped to calm the situation in the short term, the deep cleavages within Lebanon meant that enduring stability remained elusive. Lebanon enjoyed a level of economic prosperity far beyond anything that its Arab neighbours could aspire to in the 1960s and 1970s, and lifestyles – at least in Lebanon's cities – were the most cosmopolitan in the region. But this apparent sophistication overlay profound and dangerous structural divisions within Lebanese politics and society.

These divisions derived first and foremost from the country's unique and complex ethnic and religious composition that we discussed in the previous chapter, but they were aggravated by the broader Middle East conflict from which there was no escape given Lebanon's borders with Israel in the south and Syria in the east. Following each of the Arab–Israeli wars from 1948, Lebanon had accepted more and more Palestinian refugees. It also took in Palestinians who were expelled from Jordan in 1970 when the government there decided that their activities were a threat to the national interest. As a result, by the end of the 1973 war much of southern Lebanon as well as the capital Beirut (where more than 40 per cent of the country's population lived in the 1970s) accommodated a large, long-term Palestinian diaspora. Now constituting about 20 per cent of the population of the Lebanon, this Palestinian presence had begun to alter the country's already delicate religious and ethnic balance. The demographic change might have been absorbed had the Palestinians been integrated in the political life of the nation. But their loyalty remained to the Palestine Liberation Organization (PLO), the main force confronting Israel over its occupation of Palestinian land. Any gratitude that may have been expected between refugee and host was more than counterbalanced by Palestinian resentment at Lebanon's failure to participate in the 1967 and 1973 wars against Israel. The resentment was mutual, and the Palestinians were seen by the Lebanese elite, Christian and Muslim, as unsophisticated interlopers. In this way the Palestinians and the PLO came to constitute a destabilizing shadow state within an already dangerously unstable country.

In the early 1970s the Palestinians in the south were mounting increasingly frequent and destructive raids across the border into northern Israel. This provoked Israeli reprisals that inevitably became a source of Lebanese nationalist resentment. In the south itself, rightist Christians associated with the Phalangist party began to attack Palestinians. At the national level the Maronite Christians who had dominated Lebanese politics after independence were now a minority – a disgruntled one who sought to restore their position by increasingly violent means. In short, the situation in Lebanon was spiralling downwards towards a civil war that finally erupted in 1975. After a year of extreme violence and destruction, an alliance of Muslim leftists and Palestinians had the upper hand and looked set to inflict total defeat on the Christian-dominated alliance opposing them. At this point Syria, who had been watching the situation with mounting alarm from across the border, intervened. It did so, however, on the side of the beleaguered Christians rather than the Palestinians and

Arab nationalists. At one level this seemed an enormous paradox, as the most radical of the Arab states would have been expected to support the anti-Christian side. But Syria's actions derived from a realist assessment of its own national interest. Outright victory for the Palestinians and leftists, President Assad calculated, would provoke an Israeli invasion to which Syria would be forced to respond. Keeping the Christians in power would at least keep Israel at a distance; and if the Christian government owed its position to Syrian support and knew it, so much the better.

The position was formalized in 1976 when a hastily organized summit of regional states (excluding Israel) approved the formation of a huge Arab League peacekeeping force. This was a prime example of the sort of misuse of the term that we discussed in Chapter 1. In reality, the 'peacekeepers' were almost exclusively Syrian and their methods and objectives could not have been further removed from the prescriptions of Hammarskjöld's Summary Study.

The creation of UNIFIL

Although the Syrian intervention brought some stability to the situation, fighting continued, especially in the south where the PLO confronted both the Israeli army on the border and the Phalangist militias. Ironically, Syrians were reluctant to venture too far or in too much force into the south for fear of provoking an Israeli reaction, but here their caution was counterproductive. The deteriorating situation in the south in fact provoked an Israeli invasion in March 1978. This direct internationalization of the conflict opened the way for UN involvement. As in 1973 and 1974, the main initiative for this came from the United States. In 1978 Washington was orchestrating peace talks between Israel and Egypt that held out the possibility of a historic permanent settlement between the two previously irreconcilable enemies. The rise in temperature throughout the Arab world brought by Israel's invasion of Lebanon was not helpful to this delicate diplomacy, to say the least. The obvious remedy appeared to be a UN peacekeeping operation. Détente was beginning to weaken by this point, however. Cold war sensitivities and tensions of a kind familiar from an earlier era had begun to re-emerge against the backdrop of communist victories in south-east Asia and growing Soviet influence (usually via Cuban involvement) in sub-Saharan Africa. The ready cooperation on the part of Moscow in creating the Middle East peacekeeping operations in 1973 and 1974 was no longer available. The UN operation in Lebanon, therefore, was created just as détente was being eclipsed by the beginnings of what has been described as the 'second cold war'. The UN force's performance in Lebanon over the coming years would be shaped by this circumstance.

Whatever the broader circumstances of its creation, the United Nations Interim Force in Lebanon (UNIFIL) was authorized easily enough by the

Security Council on 19 March 1978, just a few days after the Israeli invasion (Map 18). The Soviet Union did not support its creation though it did not veto it (its representative abstained on the resolution). But there was no prospect, for example, of Warsaw Pact contributions as in the heady days of 1973. According to its mandate UNIFIL was to confirm 'the withdrawal of Israeli forces, [restore] international peace and security and [assist] the Government of Lebanon in ensuring the return of its effective authority in the area . . .'[7] An immediate problem lay in the fact that the central government had not exercised anything like 'effective authority' in the area for a considerable period before the Israeli invasion. Furthermore, to restore peace and security would require the force to confront both Palestinian and Phalangist forces who, with or without an Israeli presence, were intent on destroying each other. Another problem for the UN was that, in the case of UNIFIL, Israel had reverted to its default posture of instinctive hostility to peacekeeping, which it had temporarily suspended in respect of UNEF-II and UNDOF. Washington's sponsoring of the UN force was not well received by its Israeli allies.

The force was composed of contingents from the familiar pool of middle powers, early contributions coming from Canada, Finland, Ireland, the Netherlands, Norway and Sweden. But, unusually, one permanent member, France, also contributed. The French involvement was in some respects analogous to that of Britain in the Cyprus force. It was the former colonial power, having held the League of Nations mandate for Lebanon after the First World War and having had some considerable influence in its politics in the first years of independence. Like Britain in Cyprus as well, however, France carried some inconvenient political baggage into the conflict. Just as Britain was considered closer to the Turkish than the Greek Cypriot community, France had historically favoured the Maronite Christians over Lebanon's Muslims. While these perceptions did not materially compromise Britain's neutral role in UNFICYP, the behaviour and attitudes of the French in UNIFIL raised questions about its impartiality. To some extent, the problem may have been to do with the robustness of French tactics in general rather than the partiality of their application. Unlike most of the other contributors to the force, France had no real tradition or experience of peacekeeping – though it had a long history of colonial pacification and policing. While the Muslims may have perceived the French as pro-Christian, there was equally no affection between the French and the Israeli army. As a result, there was little regret in UNIFIL's area of operations when the French withdrew from the force in the late 1980s.

Within a month of its deployment at the beginning of April 1978 UNIFIL had grown rapidly to a strength of 6,000 (about 50 per cent larger than originally planned). In principle it was responsible for a single large segment of southern Lebanon north from the Israeli border, but in reality its territory was overlaid with a patchwork of rival Palestinian and Christian pockets. The force's prospects of asserting effective control of the area were further damaged by the nature of the Israeli withdrawal. Instead of transferring the frontier areas they had occupied to UNIFIL, the Israeli Defence Force installed its allies, the Christian Phalangist militias, who soon came to constitute a rival focus of power to the UN. The logic of Israel's action was that the Phalangists would provide a more effective (certainly a more ruthless) defence than the long-suspect UN against Palestinian incursions along the border.

From the beginning, therefore, UNIFIL struggled to pursue its mandate. The geographical and political complexity of its area of operations made the idea of interposition meaningless. In the culture of south Lebanon in the late 1970s and 1980s, one in which physical power was paramount, the moral presence of a UN force had little impact. On the contrary, UNIFIL's efforts to follow the principles and procedures of traditional peacekeeping merely exposed what was perceived by the competing factions as its weakness. It is questionable whether UNIFIL as originally constituted in 1978 could have pursued a more effective strategy. Arguably, what was required in southern Lebanon at that time was a large enforcement operation capable of intimidating the local factions into compliance with its instructions and punishing them militarily if they failed to do what was demanded of them. This would not, of course, have been peacekeeping in any meaningful sense and would have required authorization under Chapter VII of the Charter. It might just have achieved two key results, however. It could have stabilized southern Lebanon itself and reduced pressure on the beleaguered government in Beirut. It might also have assured Israel that its security concerns on its northern border were being taken seriously by the UN and that its patronage of the Phalangist militias was not therefore necessary. This approach might just have been an option had the superpower consensus on UN intervention not passed its high point of 1973 and 1974. With détente in decline, however, this was simply not feasible. The Soviet Union would almost certainly have vetoed any resolution attempting to create such an enforcement operation. Instead, Israel, unchallenged by the United States, which itself seemed to have lost confidence in the peacekeeping force it was responsible for creating, had more or less carte blanche to defy the UN, and its Christian allies in southern Lebanon were keenly aware of this.

UNIFIL's difficulties did not come from one side. The Palestinians refused to withdraw from a number of their own positions within the UN's supposed area of command. They also insisted on retaining control of the Mediterranean port city of Tyre. In Israeli eyes this alone proved the weakness of the UN and underlined the necessity of making their own security arrangements in southern Lebanon. UNIFIL therefore did not have freedom of movement within its own notional area of operations – which had been correctly identified as a key requirement of peacekeeping by Dag Hammarskjöld in the Summary Study.

The 1982 Israeli invasion and non-UN peacekeeping

Unable to impose its will on the situation, UNIFIL could do little more than attempt to minimize the damage from the continuing conflict in southern Lebanon. Although the Security Council regularly renewed its six-month mandates, it did not make any of the adjustments to the force that would have enabled it to achieve those mandates. The consequence of this was a further Israeli invasion of Lebanon in July 1982. Responding to a spike in the pattern of cross-border attacks, a 60,000-strong Israeli force now pushed north, brushing UNIFIL units aside as they went. This time their occupation went much further than in 1978 and eventually reached Beirut itself. The basic objective of the Israeli government, now led by the hard-line prime minister Menachem Begin, was to bring a conclusive end to the Palestinian 'problem' in Lebanon. Israel would attempt to impose 'regime change', as it would later be termed, on Lebanon. A new cooperative Lebanese government would expel the Palestinians just as Jordan had done in 1970 and conclude a permanent peace agreement with Israel as Egypt had done four years previously. Although Israel had little difficulty in getting to Beirut, when it arrived, the task of bending the chaotic and complex politics of the Lebanon to its will proved beyond it. After a period of intense fighting in which the principal victims were civilians trapped in the dense streets and alleys of West Beirut, the Israelis did manage to enforce the expulsion of the PLO leadership from the country along with thousands of their supporters. But there was little it could do about the growth of indigenous Muslim radicalism that had been nurtured by the long conflict. This religiously oriented resistance quickly supplanted the more secular Palestinians as Israel's sworn enemies in Lebanon.

As Israel began the forced expulsion of the Palestinians from West Beirut in the second half of 1982 there seemed every possibility that they would find themselves in confrontation with the Syrian army that remained in Lebanon after its intervention to pacify the situation following the outbreak of the civil war in 1975. Although Syria's original involvement had, in effect, been on the side of Israel's allies, the Maronite Christians, its sympathies had shifted over the term of the protracted conflict back to the Palestinians and local Muslim groups. And, of course, Syria's intervention had originally been designed to prevent an Israeli invasion, a motive that could no longer justify restraint. This might have been UNIFIL's moment. A redeployment into Beirut where it could have acted as a meaningful interpositionary presence could have reinvigorated the UN's role in Lebanon. But with détente now a distant memory, Security Council support for this would have been unattainable. The Soviet Union now stood apart from the whole engagement in Lebanon, though its sympathies were with its Syrian friends and the Palestinians. The United States was now closer than ever to Israel and would have resisted any move to which its ally objected – and Israel would assuredly have objected to the imposition of a UN force in Beirut that might have constrained its actions there.

America now embarked on an initiative for the creation of a non-UN peacekeeping operation. This took the form of an exclusively western force, which was deployed in August 1982 and which consisted of 2,000 American, French and Italian troops. This so-called Multinational Force (MNF) did make a contribution by working with both the Israelis and the Syrians to ensure that the removal of about 7,500 Palestinians from West Beirut was achieved without any major fighting. This, however, followed a period of great destruction and loss of life as the Israelis had pounded the area with artillery and air raids rather than risk a direct clash on the ground with the Syrian army. The peace being kept by the MNF was the peace of desolation.

Fatally, this apparent success for the MNF led to an expansion in the American-led western peacekeeping effort. A new force was created (MNF-II) with a strength of about 4,000. The purpose of this operation was to support the weak and demoralized army of the central Lebanese government, which was outgunned by just about every other faction in the country. The western force was also to act as a buffer between the Israeli army and the rapidly expanding home-grown radical Islamic movements that, as we have said, threatened to pose as great a threat to Israel as the PLO had previously. This was a much more difficult, open-ended task than the one just completed by the first MNF. Ironically, it was a mission that UNIFIL might just have managed to perform if given the opportunity and a clear Security Council mandate. But as it was, the obviously western composition of the force meant that it was hopelessly compromised in the eyes of the Muslim groups. Far from being stabilized after the expulsion of the Palestinians, Beirut spiralled down into ever greater levels of violence and chaos during 1983 as the Muslim militias became more and more daring in their attacks against both Christian factions and Israeli forces. The 'peacekeeping' force became engaged increasingly in straightforward street fighting against these Muslim groups as it attempted to impose some sort of peace that it could keep. The final act for MNF-II and the west's attempt at peacekeeping without the UN in Lebanon came in October 1983 when a series of coordinated suicide bomb attacks killed over 300 American and French troops. The operation was rapidly wound up and Beirut left to its own grisly devices.

Lebanon and the end of the cold war

Without an enlarged role in the crisis UNIFIL was consigned to the borderlines of relevance during the Israeli occupation. The idea of the UN force pursuing its original mandate to create the necessary conditions for the resumption of authority by the Lebanese government in southern Lebanon was now absurd. But UNIFIL remained in place, engaged mainly in humanitarian activities while the Israelis and their allies had a free hand in imposing 'security'. In 1985 Israel carried out a partial withdrawal, though it left an extended security zone under its control on the border. By this time, however, the second cold war was beginning to thaw. With President Gorbachev in the Kremlin the bipolar division in the international system had entered its final days. For UNIFIL this meant at least a partial return to superpower consensus in the Security Council. The Soviet Union no longer remained apart from discussion and for the first time began paying its assessed financial contributions to the force. But by this stage it was probably beyond the capacity of even a united Security Council to make any significant impact on Lebanon through UNIFIL or by any other means.

In 2000 a more effective role for the UN opened up when Israel announced its final withdrawal from UNIFIL's area of operations. The UN force would now be responsible for the so-called Blue Line, which had marked the limit of the Israeli presence. For the first time since its deployment UNIFIL could now make a serious attempt to carry out its original mandate to stabilize the area in preparation for the Lebanese state resuming its responsibilities. This had been the tone of secretary-general Kofi Annan's report on the new conditions the Lebanon force confronted, which he presented to the Security Council in May 2000 as Israel withdrew its forces.[8] In 2005 the situation took another important step forward with the withdrawal of Syrian forces. The original mandate was an even more viable objective after this, not just because of the Israeli and Syrian withdrawals as such but because Lebanon – now left to develop its own political future – could install its own, truly independent government. Whatever the role of the United Nations in this new environment, and however effective its contribution, the long history of UNIFIL from 1978 could not have illustrated more sharply an essential truth about the peacekeeping process: it can never be anything but futile without commitment by the local actors and, when necessary, the pressure of their external sponsors.

After détente: the impact on Middle East peacekeeping

Beyond Lebanon, the changing terms of superpower relations after détente had an important impact elsewhere in the Middle East. The Disengagement Observer Force in the Golan Heights proved, like the force in Cyprus, that peacekeeping can be technically successful with the support of the parties to a dispute. But if the relationship between the antagonists does not extend beyond this into an active pursuit of a long-term settlement, then the peacekeeping mission will be in danger of becoming a permanent one. UNDOF continued to provide a 1,000-strong buffer between Israel and Syria into the twenty-first century with no sign that a long-term settlement on the border would lead to its termination in the foreseeable future. Nevertheless, even in the absence of effective peacemaking, UNDOF's function as a force for stabilization in an area of extreme tension should not be underestimated.

A quite different situation emerged between Israel and Egypt, its other main enemy in the 1973 war. UNEF-II, which was interposed between the two sides at the end of October 1973, remained in place until 1979. It was terminated at the insistence of the Soviet Union, which was now deeply hostile to the emerging balance of diplomatic power in the Middle East. With détente now ended, competition for regional support re-emerged as a key part of the bipolar contest and Moscow was resentful at the apparent success of the United States in taking control of the peace process between Israel and Egypt over the previous years. In 1974, when cooperation between the superpowers was still high, Henry Kissinger had undertaken a process of shuttle diplomacy to turn the ceasefire that had been imposed on Israel and Egypt the previous October into a comprehensive disengagement. The Sinai agreement, which was the fruit of this, proved to be the first step towards a long-term political settlement between Israel and Egypt. The territorial agreement involved the reoccupation by Egypt of territory up to the Suez Canal and six miles eastwards into Sinai. East of this there would be a UN buffer zone up to the Israeli positions. A subsequent agreement later in 1974 widened the UN zone and pushed the Israeli line further back to the east.

Although there were day-to-day difficulties between commanders on the ground, at the political level the arrangements proceeded quite smoothly. Persistent external pressure played a large part in this. This came mainly from the Americans, but an awareness of Soviet support behind this was a major factor in the success of the process. As the larger fabric of détente began to unravel, however, it became evident that the key player in brokering the peace was the United States, and Soviet attitudes to the process began to shift. Eventually, in 1978 a full peace treaty was agreed between Egypt and Israel. The formal ceremony involving the Israeli prime minister Menachem Begin and Egyptian president Anwar Sadat took place the following year in March 1979. Appropriately, the venue was in the United States at Camp David, the presidential retreat. The completion of the process that had begun under the Republican administration of Richard Nixon in 1973 took place under the supervision of the Democrat president Jimmy Carter, with America having managed each stage of the protracted process.

During the negotiations leading up to Camp David, it had been assumed that UNEF-II would continue after the agreement was finalized in order to oversee its implementation. But this took for granted continued Security Council support for the force and, as we have seen, by 1979 this was not forthcoming. To the Soviet Union the Camp David agreement had nothing to do with the United Nations, it was in all essentials a piece of American diplomacy. While the co-option of the UN by the United States might have been acceptable during détente, it was so no longer. There was another, more political reason for Soviet resistance to a continued UN role. The peace process between Egypt and Israel had not been well received in the Arab world. For Egypt, which from the 1950s to the 1970s had been the de facto leader of the pan-Arab movement and Israel's most implacable enemy, to make a unilateral peace now was a momentous historical departure in the Middle East. It was not one readily accepted by other Arab states. This posed a dilemma for the Soviet Union. Moscow's earlier support for the consolidation of the ceasefire between Egypt and Israel had been given within the context of the United Nations, even if the running had been made by America. The process had caused no serious difficulties to the historically close Soviet–Arab relationship. Now, however, the peace process had reached a point where Egypt had isolated itself from the larger Arab world, and the Soviet Union was keenly aware of the danger of being associated with this in Arab eyes. The role of UNEF-II in the post-Camp David environment would be fundamentally different from its original one of interposition. The UN, if it remained, would become identified with a western diplomatic process that fulfilled largely western interests. To support this, particularly as a new cold war threatened in the broader system, would have been too much for Moscow. To oppose UN involvement, on the other hand, would consolidate the Soviet Union's position as a friend of the Arab world. UN peacekeeping would not, therefore, be put at the service of American diplomacy and UNEF-II was accordingly terminated in July 1979. Soviet hostility to the Camp David process was both a symptom and a further cause of the decline of détente, which confirmed the onset of the second cold war.

Denied the support of UN peacekeeping, the authors of the Camp David agreement had to look elsewhere for the necessary multilateral support in implementing it. Reluctantly, the Americans set about creating a non-UN force. An agreement between the United States and the two Camp David signatories allowed for the deployment of a 2,500-strong MFO. As the MFO was widely seen as an American alternative to 'proper' UN peacekeeping it proved difficult to bring a sufficient number of experienced peacekeepers on board. This was not due to any concerns over the force's operations or the safety of contingents. The peace that it was to keep (principally by means of military observation) was already solidly established by the time of its deployment. But there was a wariness on the part of the traditional middle-power peacekeepers at involvement in what was widely seen as an American foreign policy initiative. Most participants in the MFO, therefore, have been American allies either in NATO or in other regional treaty organizations. The MFO has evolved into a more or less permanent presence in Sinai, though it has faced no significant operational difficulties as both Israel and Egypt were committed to its success from the outset and neither has shown any interest in it being terminated.

7 New horizons

Peacekeeping and the end of the cold war

In the decade after the creation of the Lebanon operation in 1978 no new UN peacekeeping operations were established. In the following ten years more than twenty new ventures were begun. The reason for this was quite simple: the end of the cold war. UNIFIL in Lebanon began just as détente was beginning to give way to a return to cold war between the superpowers. The second cold war proved to be an even more unfriendly environment for UN peacekeeping than the first. There may have been major conflicts over the political direction of the Congo operation and damaging wrangles over the financing of peacekeeping as a whole in the 1960s and 1970s, but operations were established and in most cases served an important role in maintaining stability on the peripheries of the international system through some very delicate times. In the 1980s, in contrast, such new multilateral peacekeeping as there was took place outside the United Nations when western states constructed forces to help achieve primarily western interests, such as the two Multinational Forces in Beirut and the MFO in Sinai.

The end of the cold war in the late 1980s, when the historic divisions in the Security Council appeared suddenly to have closed, created a wholly new institutional environment from which a reinvigorated peacekeeping could emerge. Within the system as a whole two linked factors determined the new peacekeeping agenda. First, the concept of the permitted area for peacekeeping no longer had much relevance. With superpower rivalry evidently no longer a feature of the international system, all areas – political and geographical – were in principle open to UN peacekeeping. Second, however, there was a corollary to this that greatly increased the demand for peacekeeping. If the superpowers were no longer so interested in safeguarding their cold war spheres of influence, equally they were no longer so committed to managing security within these areas. The removal of superpower influence over their clients had the effect of lifting the lid on some volatile regional mixes. In the 1990s, therefore, not only was there more opportunity for peacekeeping, there was more demand for it as well.

Despite this threat of increased local conflict in the wake of the superpowers' retreat from regions on which they had previously retained a tight grip, the prevailing mood in the United Nations was positive. The decade of the 1990s seemed to promise a new world order in which cooperative multilateralism would have an unprecedented importance in the regulation of the international system.

The new possibilities went beyond the prospect of *more* peacekeeping; they also involved a prospect of *better* peacekeeping. Why should the big powers still be excluded from participating in peacekeeping, for example? If there was no longer a cold war for local conflicts to be pulled into, there was no obvious reason why the one-time cold war rivals should not now become peacekeepers themselves, with all the technical operational advantages that would bring. In the period between the fall of the Berlin Wall in 1989 and the disintegration of the Soviet Union in 1991 both of the old cold war superpowers seemed almost to be in competition once again, this time to outdo each other in their public commitment to the new multilateralism. In the Soviet Union President Gorbachev and his foreign minister Eduard Shevardnadze led a country that had to find a new world role. For a time around 1989 and 1990 it seemed that they might be opting for that of European middle power. At that time the notion was not as strange as it might have appeared later. The Soviet Union had 'lost' the cold war, and there seemed little mileage in clinging to the myth of continuing superpower status. The prospect of national reinvention as a modern north European democracy committed to an activist role at the UN had obvious attractions. At all events, the new Soviet Union now paid off a large part of its debts for peacekeeping (which stood at about 200 million dollars) that had accumulated during the years of Moscow's refusal to accept the organization's right to levy costs. The administration of the elder George Bush in the United States also agreed to pay outstanding dues to the United Nations that had built up in the mid-1980s during the presidency of Bush's predecessor, Ronald Reagan, which had generally been hostile to the UN. Bush, although a Republican like Reagan, seemed ready to embrace the new multilateralism in the general climate of optimism following America's 'victory' in the cold war.

However far short of the grim realities of the 1990s the rhetoric of a new world order might have fallen, the new conditions in the international system did have a profound effect on peacekeeping. In the three years between 1988 and 1991 a series of new, largely observer-based missions were established in regions where a UN presence would have been virtually unthinkable a short time previously. From Afghanistan to the Gulf to Latin America, United Nations operations were created to deal with the debris of conflicts that had hitherto been regarded as core interests of the superpowers and therefore off-limits to multilateral intervention.

The Soviet withdrawal from Afghanistan: the Good Offices Mission

A number of factors underlay the disintegration of détente in the second half of the 1970s, but perhaps the principal event – certainly the point of no-return on the road back to cold war – was the Soviet invasion of Afghanistan at the end of 1979. The east–west rift that opened up over Afghanistan had origins that long pre-dated the cold war and even the Russian Revolution of 1917. In the nineteenth century Afghanistan was the geographical link – and buffer – between the Russian and British empires and became the object of the so-called 'great game' played out between them. The mountainous, inaccessible territory of Afghanistan was home to diverse, fiercely independent tribes and was never effectively occupied by any imperial power. For most of the twentieth century it had been, nominally at any rate, ruled by a monarchy. In 1973, however, the king was deposed in a coup orchestrated by the prime minister, Mohammad Daud Khan, who afterwards presided over a one-party state. The new regime pursued a non-aligned foreign policy, but domestic politics became increasingly factionalized throughout the 1970s and, given Afghanistan's delicate geographical location, the situation attracted increasing concern and attention from the superpowers.

A large but violently factional Communist Party, a reform-minded nationalist army officer corps (who twenty years previously would have been described as Nasserists) and conservative Muslim groups all became engaged in a labyrinthine power struggle. In 1978 a pro-Marxist faction in the military assassinated Daud Khan, opening the way for Communist Party dominance of the government. The murderous internal feuds within the party, however, ensured that this would not be a smooth process. Most of the factional conflict was played out in the capital Kabul and other large cities. But in the meantime, in more remote parts of the country, Muslim opposition to the 'godless communism' of the conspirators turned into a full-scale insurgency. Across the border the Soviet Union grew increasingly worried about the chaos in its neighbour and the impact it might have in its own adjacent Central Asian republics. The Soviet invasion of Afghanistan that began in December 1979, therefore, was not undertaken as an act of brute territorial expansionism. In the dying spirit of détente, which still persisted despite growing stresses, the government of Leonid Brezhnev in Moscow had warned the United States that the crisis in Afghanistan might demand intervention. Moscow's concern was to stabilize the situation while still retaining a friendly regime in power in Kabul. To this end an internal coup was contrived by the Soviet occupying forces and a 'safe' communist leader, Babrak Karmal, imposed.

The response of the American administration of Jimmy Carter was initially one of cautious displeasure rather than outrage. Washington was well aware of the extent of the crisis in Afghanistan (its ambassador in Kabul had been murdered there at the beginning of 1979) and could hardly claim that the Soviet move had come out of the blue. It was even possible to interpret the invasion as a Soviet right under the so-called 'Brezhnev doctrine'. This had developed during détente as a tacit acceptance that the Soviet Union had certain prerogatives within its sphere of influence. In the terms of our discussion of the permitted area of peacekeeping, for example, the Brezhnev doctrine effectively excluded the communist eastern Europe from the range of multilateral intervention. But as Afghanistan had not, until the late 1970s, attracted any particular attention from the superpowers, the general assumption had been that this Soviet sphere of influence applied only to eastern Europe. Recent developments elsewhere on the interface area between the Middle East and South Asia added to the complexities of the Afghan situation. Neighbouring Iran had undergone an Islamist revolution of 1979 that had delivered a major blow to American confidence in the region. American strategists now began to talk of an 'arc of crisis' stretching across the Middle East and Central Asia and enclosing a Pandora's box of threat to American interests.

Even still, had a Pax Sovietica been effectively imposed on Afghanistan and the situation been stabilized, it would probably not have inflicted the damage it did on the superpower relationship and the remnants of détente. But the Karmal regime was incapable of embedding itself in the country. The Islamist insurgency developed into a civil war, which in turn came to be seen abroad as a liberation struggle against the Soviet invader. A change of administration in Washington at the beginning of 1981, which brought the conservative Republican Ronald Reagan to the White House, marked the beginning of a new anti-Soviet approach. In Afghanistan this meant that American weapons and military advisers were showered on the insurgents – or *mujahideen* – who managed to pin down a Soviet force of about 100,000 with a much smaller, demoralized and unreliable Afghan government army in the inhospitable interior of the country. Two decades later the nurturing of Islamic fundamentalism in Afghanistan would return to haunt the United States. The *mujahideen* strength the Americans built up during the anti-Soviet struggle would turn the mountains of Afghanistan into a centre for the indoctrination and training of anti-western terrorists from around the world. But in the 1980s the encouragement of the Islamists' struggle against atheistic communism, and the foreign invader who embodied it internationally, seemed to be an extremely effective strategy on a major front in the second cold war. The Islamists' equal hatred of western materialism and 'crusader imperialism' would find expression in the future.

In the meantime the war brought devastation to large areas of Afghanistan. A huge movement of refugees was created. More than two million Afghanis became externally displaced, many in Iran but the majority in Pakistan, which was also a key base through which western aid for the anti-Soviet struggle was channelled. The remote areas on the Pakistan side of the border also provided bases and training grounds for the *mujahideen*. Relations between the Pakistani government and the pro-Soviet one in Kabul became intensely hostile, adding a further, dangerous international dimension to the civil war.

Afghanistan soon turned into the Soviet Union's 'Vietnam'. The war became intensely unpopular at home as casualties mounted and it became clear that it was inherently unwinnable. When Mikhail Gorbachev came to power in 1985 extrication from Afghanistan became one of his policy priorities. The complexity of the situation meant that this took some time, but in April 1988 the withdrawal of Soviet forces began and was completed at the beginning of the following year. The communist government, which had been held in place by the Soviet presence, was now more or less left to its fate. In the interest of the broader region and the superpowers themselves, however, the international setting in which Afghanistan worked through its internal problems was to be subject to regulation.

The Soviet withdrawal and the wider agreement of which it formed part created the conditions that led to the UN's first peacekeeping involvement in what had been a core area of superpower interest. Hitherto, the UN had played only a very limited role in the conflict. Discussion in the Security Council did not advance, as cold war positions were adopted by the membership virtually as a reflex. In January 1980, when the issue first came before the Council for emergency discussion, deadlock led to the use of the Uniting for Peace procedure and an emergency session of the General Assembly. Although this condemned the Soviet invasion and called for the immediate withdrawal of its forces, Moscow remained unmoved.[1] Some local peacemaking ventures were tried by the UN in 1981 when secretary-general Kurt Waldheim appointed the man who would shortly succeed him, the Peruvian Javier Pérez de Cuéllar, as his special representative in the area, but these came to nothing amid the tangled factionalism of the conflict. But with the 1988 agreement, which of course coincided with a general thawing of east–west relations, a peacekeeping role for the United Nations opened up.

The United Nations Good Offices Mission in Afghanistan and Pakistan (UNGOMAP) was established by the Security Council in May 1988 immediately following the conclusion of the peace accords in Geneva. This was a complex, multidimensional agreement covering relationships between Afghanistan and Pakistan and a commitment by the Soviet Union and the United States to guarantee the peace arrangements. A timetable was also set for Soviet withdrawal, which the United Nations would be responsible for overseeing and verifying. The central role of the two superpowers in the peace process meant that the secretary-general was able to move ahead with the formation of UNGOMAP before the Security Council gave formal approval.[2] A fifty-strong mission of military observers was therefore dispatched to Afghanistan and Pakistan within days of the signing of the agreement in Geneva. As well as the usual peacekeeping middle powers of Austria, Canada, Denmark, Finland and Ireland, UNGOMAP had officers from Poland (which had been the first Warsaw Pact state to participate in peacekeeping, in UNEF-II in Sinai) and from a small but significant newcomer, Fiji, which had already made its peacekeeping debut in Lebanon and which would shortly be making a contribution to peacekeeping out of all proportion to its size.

The mandate of the mission involved three main tasks. UNGOMAP was to monitor the mutual non-interference in each other's affairs of Afghanistan and Pakistan. It was to observe (though not organize) the return of external refugees to Afghanistan. But, most significantly in peacekeeping terms, it was to verify the withdrawal of Soviet forces from Afghanistan (Map 1). As widely expected, UNGOMAP faced no significant obstructions in carrying out its mandate. With both superpowers committed to the peace process there was little likelihood that their respective regional clients, Pakistan and Afghanistan, would create difficulties that could compromise the larger process. The UN's verification of Soviet withdrawal was little more than symbolic. It was unthinkable that the Soviet Union would seek to prevaricate or dissemble on the matter. The main impetus for withdrawal, after all, came from Moscow itself. But the presence of UN military observers had an important symbolic function. It legitimized and made respectable the larger process and acted as a witness to an important shift in the superpower relationship. Providing a certain element of political theatre has always been a significant part of the peacekeeping role, but it was particularly prominent on the stage set up by the end of the war in Afghanistan. The UN presence also acted as a useful distraction from the fact that the war did not in any meaningful sense end for Afghanistan itself. The withdrawal of foreign forces merely left the various factions to fight their internecine battles without the complication of superpower involvement. This was a consequence of superpower involvement in the war that neither was particularly anxious to see advertised. But whatever the subtexts to UNGOMAP's presence in Afghanistan, it carried out its formal mandate with complete success. It was withdrawn in March 1990 just less than two years after its establishment.

After the Iran–Iraq War: the Military Observer Group

While the *mujahideen* battled against Soviet helicopter gun-ships in the mountains of Afghanistan during the 1980s, further west in the so-called arc of crisis a more conventional – and much more destructive – war was taking place between Iran and Iraq. Tensions had grown dramatically between the two neighbours following the Islamist revolution in Iran that deposed the pro-western monarch, the Shah, at the beginning of 1979. The spiritual leader of the Iranian revolution, Ayatollah Ruhollah

Khomeini was in most meaningful respects also the political leader of a Shi'ite Muslim theocracy. Iraq under the Saddam Hussein dictatorship was strongly secular. His regime was, nominally at any rate, the continued embodiment of the Ba'th socialist revolution that overthrew the Iraqi monarchy in the heady period of pan-Arab radicalism in the 1950s. Saddam's Ba'thist Party was dominated not by the majority Shia Muslim sect but the minority Sunni branch of Islam. This arrangement followed a political tradition that stretched back through the days of the British League of Nations mandate to the time of Ottoman rule.

The regime in Baghdad had been taken by surprise by the outcome of the Iranian revolution just as the Shah's western friends had been. Saddam now feared that Shia militancy might spill over into Iraq and threaten his own position, a fear justified in part by Khomeini's personal influence in Iraq, where he had spent many years in exile. In this climate, long-standing disputes over parts of the two countries' joint border escalated into localized fighting. Eventually, in September 1980, Iraq occupied a number of these areas, simultaneously launching a pre-emptive strike against the Iranian air force. Saddam had evidently calculated that the general chaos prevailing in Iran would allow him to seize the disputed areas unchallenged and, more broadly, adjust the balance of power in the region in Iraq's favour. Not for the last time, Saddam's political instincts around foreign adventures were woefully wrong. Iraq's attack had the effect of uniting Iran behind the new regime, which up until then had been far from fully implanted in the country. The region now fell headlong into eight years of particularly horrific war. The common military parallel used to describe the strategy and tactics of this 'first' Gulf War was the western front of the First World War. Opposing trench positions, fought over in 'human wave' attacks often involving the use of poison gas, created monstrous casualty rates.

Western fears of the Iranian regime, with its evident disregard from the day it seized power for the accepted 'rules and regulations' of the international state system, coincided with Soviet fears of the influence of militant Islam in its own southern periphery. As a result, international support was almost wholly behind Iraq (despite the inconvenient fact that it had been the original aggressor). Just weeks after the outbreak of the war the Security Council had sought to arrange a ceasefire and a negotiated settlement.[3] While Iraq had been willing to accept this as a means of consolidating its early gains, Iran rejected it. The Tehran regime saw the resolution as objectively pro-Iraqi and confirmation of western hostility to the Iranian revolution. Most of the rest of the world saw Iran's failure to cooperate with the Security Council as confirmation of the regime's determination to reject established international norms. Throughout the 1980s repeated Security Council attempts to achieve at least a ceasefire failed when Iran refused to cooperate unless Iraq was formally identified as the aggressor. This was an impossible demand as, even if the members of the Security

Council had been willing to consider a resolution denouncing what in many respects was their champion in the region, Iraq would have refused to cooperate anyway.

The breakthrough came in mid-1988. The previous year had seen a significant escalation of the war, with Iranian attacks on international shipping in the Gulf and a consequent build-up of warships from western states. At this point the hopelessness of Iran's diplomatic and military situation seems to have finally percolated through to the leadership around Ayatollah Khomeini. Virtually without a friend in the world, and locked into a static but hugely destructive and costly war, it was clear that for the Iranian revolution to survive, the war would have to be ended. Iran therefore accepted the latest Security Council resolution calling for a ceasefire and substantive peace negotiations to be led by the UN secretary-general, Javier Pérez de Cuéllar.[4] This was followed, at the beginning of August 1988, with a further resolution establishing the Iran–Iraq Military Observer Group (UNIIMOG).[5] Its mandate was to establish ceasefire lines in consultation with the parties and then to monitor observance of them (Map 16). It would also, where possible, take local confidence-building measures to embed the peace pending the conclusion of a permanent political settlement.

The first UN military observers began to arrive in the Gulf the day following the adoption of the enabling resolution. Yet again, the advance party was 'borrowed' from UNTSO on Israel's borders. Over the two and a half years of its operation UNIIMOG grew into one of the largest observation missions the UN had mounted, deploying 400 military personnel at its height. At the time of its withdrawal in February 1991, on the eve of yet another Gulf war, this time between Iraq and the western allies, the two antagonists were hardly reconciled to peaceful coexistence. But UNIIMOG smoothed the way for a cessation of fighting that, while probably inevitable given the depletion of Iran's fighting capacity, might have been much more difficult to sustain in the absence of a substantial UN presence.

Collective security rediscovered? The 1991 war against Iraq and its aftermath

When we explored the re-emergence of peacekeeping after 1945 a key part of our discussion involved the failure of collective security. The large-scale, enforcement-based collective security envisaged by the authors of the UN Charter had proved fundamentally incompatible with bipolarity. Instead, peacekeeping – a voluntarist activity that did not involve identifying aggressors or enforcing outcomes – became the standard mode of military intervention by the UN. With the end of the cold war, the question inevitably arose as to whether the robust system of collective security laid out in Chapter VII of the Charter could now make a delayed appearance in the international system. The question took on a particular urgency early in the immediate post-cold war period. In August 1990, less than a year after the fall of the Berlin wall, Iraq invaded its neighbour Kuwait. The Iraqi justification was that Kuwait's supposed overproduction of oil was driving down world prices to the detriment of other producers. Behind this, however, was a long-standing Iraqi ambition to absorb its small southern neighbour with its huge oil reserves and its extensive coastline on the Persian Gulf. Since the late 1970s the Iraqi regime of Saddam Hussein had been generally favoured by the west as a counter to the power of Iran in the region, and previous misbehaviour had generally been overlooked. Kuwait, a former British protectorate, was itself close to the west, however, and the response of the United States and its allies was unequivocal: Iraq was guilty of a clear 'breach of the peace' and 'act of aggression' within the terms of the UN Charter. The new world order was about to be put to the test.

One view of the UN-legitimized military campaign that was mounted to expel Iraq from Kuwait – Operation Desert Storm, as it was known – saw it as a limited but genuine application of collective security by the United Nations. The Security Council took decisive action under Chapter VII of the Charter with the support of all the permanent members. This led to a majority of those members participating in a military alliance for the purpose of dealing with the aggression of Saddam Hussein's regime and securing the stated United Nations objective of restoring Kuwaiti sovereignty. A more cynical perspective was pitched against this, however. This interpreted Desert Storm as a war of the 'new' west (now expanded to include former rivals in the east) in pursuit of its own collective interests. This coalition of self-interest sought legitimization for its actions by co-opting the name of the United Nations into the process. In other words, the war against Iraq bore a powerful resemblance to that against North Korea four decades previously. While the Soviet Union had been prevented from using its veto by its absence from the Security Council in 1950, in 1990 it was prevented again by its diplomatic feebleness and anxiety to be amenable to the United States in the immediate aftermath of the cold war.

While this sceptical interpretation of the Gulf War strains to draw exact parallels, it was certainly the case that the UN's position in 1990–1 was in some respects similar to the one it had adopted over Korea. Following the invasion of Kuwait in August 1990 the Security Council passed a number of resolutions. These began on 2 August, the day of the initial attack, with a demand for an immediate and unconditional Iraqi withdrawal.[6] This was soon backed with economic sanctions, but Iraq showed no sign of either ending its occupation of Kuwait or entering into meaningful negotiations. At the end of November a key vote – the famous resolution 678 – made clear that force legitimized by the Security Council was likely to be used. Iraq was given 'one final opportunity' to withdraw from Kuwait. But if it failed to take it and fully implement the demands of previous resolutions by 15 January 1991, the Security Council 'authorized' member states 'to use all necessary means' to force it to comply 'and to restore international peace and security in the region'.[7] All of the permanent members voted for resolution 678 with the exception of China, which abstained.

In one view, then, resolution 678 seemed to confirm that collective security was firmly back on the UN's agenda after lying dormant for the decades of the cold war. But on close examination, this was not quite so apparent. For one thing, the Security Council's response to the crisis was driven by the United States. While most of the other members of the Council were willing to acquiesce in this with varying degrees of enthusiasm, it was not, therefore, a wholly collective effort. Moreover, resolution 678 made no reference at all to Chapter VII of the Charter. There was no formal basis in international law for the UN's collective response to the crisis. Member states were merely 'requested' to 'provide appropriate support for the action undertaken' to enforce Security Council resolutions. The use of Article 43 of Chapter VII, however, would have given the Council the power to require this support. In sum, resolution 678 simply backed the efforts of the United States to put together an ad hoc military alliance against Iraq. The similarities with the Unified Command arrangements in Korea were inescapable.

Operation Desert Storm began shortly after the passing of the 15 January deadline laid down in resolution 678. After an initial air assault failed to dislodge the invaders from Kuwait, a full-scale ground attack began in late February and within a few days Iraqi forces had been pushed north back across the border. The major part of the fighting, both in the air and on the ground, was done by the United States and its European NATO allies – another clear echo of the Korean War. The Soviet Union, despite its support for the resolution, increasingly distanced itself from the alliance as war approached. Indeed, during the air campaign before the ground war had begun, bilateral Soviet–Iraqi negotiations led to a peace plan that was rejected by the United States. Throughout the crisis China remained opposed to any military action against Iraq. There were, then, some very large gaps in the Security Council collective.

The Gulf War of 1991 underlined some hard truths about the prospects for collective security. It was not, it seemed, just the existence of the cold war and the resulting bipolar character of the international system that had blocked the development of collective security in the UN system. The difficulties ran deeper, and to some extent the cold war may have been no more than an alibi. When the Charter was drawn up there was a sense that the apparent failures of the League could be 'written out' of international relations simply by creating a more clear, robust and transparent set of legal obligations. But perhaps the failures of the League were rooted deeper in the international system itself, and mere legal formulations were never going to alter the situation in any significant way. In other words, it was in the basic nature of states to define their own national interests and pursue them in their own way. These interests would rarely coincide completely, even among the five permanent members of the Security Council and even without the brute division of the system into two ideological blocs.

The after-effects of this 'second' Gulf War would produce yet another UN military mission. If the Security Council's relationship to Operation Desert Storm and the expulsion of Iraq from Kuwait looked back to its semi-detached pseudo-enforcement role in Korea, it had a more conventional part to play amid the debris of the war. The anti-Iraq coalition ended its operations on 28 February 1991, just a few days after the ground phase had begun. The Iraq–Kuwait border area obviously remained sensitive, however. The Saddam regime had been left in place in Baghdad after the war as the lead allies, the United States and Britain, had decided against pressing their military advantage into Iraq and imposing regime change at that time. They were uncertain of the legal position of such a move and anxious not to jeopardize the high level of international support the war had attracted. Their hope was that the devastating effects of the war on Iraq would bring about a popular uprising against the regime. Their objectives would thus be achieved without the military and political risks of carrying the war to the heart of Iraq. To this end the Shias of southern Iraq and the Kurds in the north were actively encouraged by the allies to rise against Saddam. While the Kurds succeeded in establishing their own de facto state and seceding from Iraq under western protection, the southern uprising faltered and was brutally suppressed by the regime. With Saddam once again unchallenged in Baghdad, the allies were determined that post-war attention should not wander from the border area and that there should be no prospect of Iraq being able to row back against its defeat in Kuwait. From the allies' perspective it was important that the multilateral aspect of the war and its aftermath be emphasized. It would have been possible simply to police the border area as an extension of Operation Desert Storm, but it was politically preferable that the UN be brought into the process. Although the Security Council legitimized the coalition's war and did not take responsibility for it, the UN could be given nominal control of the post-war management of the border.

On 9 April 1991 the Security Council established the Iraq–Kuwait Observation Mission (UNIKOM), which was mandated to monitor the demilitarized zone on the border set up after the Iraqi army had been forced from the area (Map 16). UNIKOM was intended by its presence to deter any violation of the zone by Iraqi forces.[8] The mission grew to an initial strength of 300, which by UN standards was large for an observation mission. Its role was really to act as a human tripwire against Iraqi adventurism. The enabling resolution made direct reference to Chapter VII of the Charter as a signal that the consequences of any attempt to interfere with UNIKOM's work would be serious. On his past record

Saddam Hussein did not appear to be the most rational of decision-makers, and serious provocations on the border could not be ruled out. This concern seemed justified when, at the beginning of 1993, Iraq began to probe the demilitarized zone, ostensibly to recover military equipment left behind during the retreat of 1991. The United States immediately brought the matter to the Security Council and UNIKOM's strength was increased more than tenfold to 3,600. The major part of this was composed of three mechanized infantry battalions, and the enlarged force was empowered to take military action to prevent or punish violations of the demilitarized zone.[9] In one rapid step UNIKOM had passed from observation mission to potential enforcement operation, completely bypassing interpositionary peacekeeping on the way.

Henceforward there were only relatively minor incidents along the demilitarized zone until the next twist in the region's turbulent contemporary history. When, in March 2003, a United States-dominated coalition invaded Iraq with the express intention of deposing Saddam Hussein, the position of UNIKOM became wholly untenable. A significant part of the invasion force was mustered around the demilitarized zone, which effectively ceased to exist with the outbreak of hostilities. UNIKOM remained largely as a paper exercise until October 2003 when it was formally disbanded. For the previous twelve years, however, it had served an important role in imposing stability on the Iraq–Kuwait border. Whether UNIKOM can be regarded as a representative UN peacekeeping operation, though, is questionable. It was deployed originally as a marker of the west's intent to contain the Iraqi regime at a time when the United States and its allies saw it as important that the venture had the respectability of the UN flag wrapped around it. But UNIKOM's authority was not in the end based on moral presence in the Hammarskjöldian peacekeeping tradition. It was clear that transgression of the rules it was sent to monitor would assuredly lead to western military enforcement whether inside or outside of the UN's institutional embrace.

Beyond the Monroe doctrine: peacekeeping in Central America and the Caribbean

We have seen how the political and geographical space open to UN peacekeeping expanded to embrace the Soviet withdrawal from Afghanistan at the end of the cold war. Moscow's claim to pursue its interests unimpeded there and in eastern Europe rested, it will be recalled, on the Brezhnev doctrine that delimited the Soviet Union's spheres of influence around its borders. The United States, too, claimed special rights of intervention over areas on its own periphery, though this 'doctrine' had much the longer historical pedigree. What came to be known as the Monroe doctrine had been formulated by the fifth president of the United States, James Monroe, in 1823. Its original purpose was to warn the European powers against interference in those areas of Latin America and the Caribbean that they did not hold as imperial possessions. Any such interference would impinge on areas of special interest to the United States and would be regarded as hostile activity. By the second half of the twentieth century the focus of the Monroe doctrine had moved from the machinations of the old European imperialists, whose threat had now long passed, to the internal politics of Washington's neighbours and in particular the supposed threat of communist expansion in the region. Throughout the cold war there were repeated American interventions, overt and covert, in states where Washington perceived a political risk. Following Castro's revolution of 1959, Cuba was famously the one that got away in terms of the Monroe doctrine, but many others, from Guatemala in 1954 to Chile in 1973, did not.

From time to time there were real diplomatic tensions between Washington's pursuit of its regional interests and the rights of national self-determination and sovereign independence recognized and guaranteed by the United Nations Charter. In 1965, for example, a coup attempt by leftist officers in the Dominican Republic in the Caribbean brought an intervention by US marines on the pretext of protecting American residents. In reality it was an attempt to impose American control on events and prevent the emergence of a left-wing government. The marines were quickly replaced by – or, more correctly, absorbed in – an Inter-American Peacekeeping Force (IAPF), which was validated by the Organization of American States, but there were few who saw this as anything but American intervention by another name. It was certainly difficult to class it as 'peacekeeping', given that it had been imposed on the Dominican Republic uninvited, and its transparent purpose was to safeguard the interest of the United States. Pressure in the United Nations led to the appointment by U Thant of a Representative for the Dominican Republic who, assisted by a small group of military observers, monitored the actions of the IAPF. It was one of the few cases in the 1960s when UN peacekeeping crossed purposes with United States interests, and the irritation with which Washington reacted to the UN's involvement gave some sense of American sensitivities over its sphere of influence.

Later in the cold war period, in the 1970s and 1980s, a series of challenges to American-favoured regimes in Central America gave rise to so-called 'dirty wars' between American-trained and supported militaries and left-wing guerrilla movements. Any substantial UN involvement in these conflicts was not feasible during the cold war, but with the rapid thaw in superpower relations in the late 1980s and the end of the Soviet Union in 1991, new possibilities emerged. The UN could now play a significant role in stabilizing a sub-system of the international system that had hitherto been both violently unstable and off-limits to meaningful multilateral attention.

The first post-cold war UN undertaking in the region came at the end of 1989 with the establishment of the Observer Group in Central America

(ONUCA – from the Spanish Observadores de las Naciones Unidas en Centroamerica).[10] The operation had a clear inter-state function. Its purpose was to monitor the implementation of an agreement between all four countries of the region – El Salvador, Guatemala, Honduras and Nicaragua – to stop the movement of fighters and supplies across their shared borders and to end the provision of support for foreign revolutionary movements in each other's territory.[11] The principal victim of this external backing for subversion and rebel activity had been Nicaragua (Map 23). The United States-backed 'Contra' movement had beset the leftist government there since soon after it had come to power after the revolution of 1979. This had swept away a long-standing pro-American dictatorship in Nicaragua, and Washington, especially during the years of the Reagan presidency in the 1980s, took this as a challenge to its authority in the region. With the reduction of east–west tensions at the end of the decade, however, and with Nicaragua committed to the democratization of its political system, the Contras no longer had either international purpose or internal legitimacy. America's local allies, therefore, were freed from pressure to provide support for the rebels and were eager to enlist the United Nations in a process aimed at bringing a new stability to the region as a whole.

ONUCA's initial mandate was carried out with more or less total success. Here, as elsewhere, the critical element in this was the commitment of the parties to the process in hand, and there was no question that the states that had signed the initial joint agreement were keen to see it implemented. Having verified the compliance of the parties with their undertakings, ONUCA's mandate was expanded significantly in March 1990 when it took responsibility for the managed (and voluntary) demobilization and disarmament of the Contra forces.[12]

Some months before ONUCA completed its duties in January 1992, a new operation had already begun in the region. In contrast to ONUCA this was primarily an intra-state undertaking. In May 1991 the Security Council established an observer mission in El Salvador.[13] Known as ONUSAL (an acronym of its Spanish title, Observadores de las Naciones Unidas en El Salvador), the operation was mandated to oversee the implementation of a final peace agreement between the pro-American government of El Salvador and the leftist Farabundo Martí National Liberation Front (FMLN) which had been engaged in a ten-year armed struggle against it (Map 10). The UN's task was to supervise a radical reduction in the size of the national armed forces and the reintegration of demobilized soldiers back into society. It was also to assist with the creation of a new police force untainted by the gross human rights abuses of its predecessor. Later, ONUSAL's mandate was expanded to include the observation of elections in 1994. These were held successfully and resulted in the governing party retaining power but with the FMLN, now a political party rather than a guerrilla movement, as the main opposition in parliament. ONUSAL, which was 370-strong and composed of a judicious mixture of Latin American contingents and contributions from long-established middle-power peacekeepers, ended its operations in April 1995 after four years. It did so having successfully completed its mandate, though in an admittedly favourable political climate in which the main parties were committed to the peace process and subject to firm external pressure (in particular from the United States).

Two years later a very similar operation, though one with a much shorter duration, was established for neighbouring Guatemala. The UN Verification Mission in Guatemala (MINUGUA – from the Spanish Misión de las Naciones Unidas en Guatemala) operated for less than three months between March and May 1997 to verify the ceasefire agreement signed between the government and the guerrillas of the Guatemalan National Revolutionary Unity movement (Map 13). The 130 military observers of MINUGUA included officers from both the United States and Russia as well as contributions from Latin America and the usual middle powers. Wholly unremarkable in 1997, the operation, let alone its composition, would have been simply unthinkable ten years previously.

A much more substantial – and problematic – UN intervention in America's backyard came in 1995 with the Mission in Haiti (UNMIH). Throughout the twentieth century Haiti, which shares the Caribbean island of Hispaniola with the Dominican Republic, had endured a history of extreme poverty and shockingly bad government (Map 14). The father and son Duvalier dynasty (François and Jean-Claude, or 'Papa Doc' and 'Baby Doc' as they were known) ruled Haiti through the exploitation of superstition and simple terror from 1957 to 1986. Corruption was endemic and development non-existent. But the Duvaliers had been careful to emphasize their position on the right side of the United States' policy of anti-communist vigilance in the region. As a result they were left largely undisturbed. By the mid-1980s, however, Jean-Claude Duvalier's hold on the country, never as secure as his father's, began to loosen to a point where voluntary exile became the only sure alternative to a violent settling of scores. There followed a period of great instability until in 1990 UN-monitored elections resulted in a popular former priest, Jean-Bertrand Aristide, becoming prime minister. The following year, however, Raoul Cédras, the army commander who had been close to the old Duvalier regime, seized power and drove Aristide into exile. Security Council sanctions along with intense diplomatic pressure led Cédras, whose interest in government beyond its opportunities for plunder had never been evident, to agree to stand down.

UNMIH was first established in 1993 as a primarily civilian mission charged with reforming Haiti's armed forces and police to prevent them interfering in politics in future and with implanting a culture of respect for human rights. It had become clear, however, that Cédras was not prepared to go quietly after all. The position of UNMIH soon became impossible and it was withdrawn. To meet the new situation the Security

Council agreed in July 1994 that a multinational force led by the United States should be formed outside of the framework of the United Nations but with the organization's authority. The force would be empowered to use 'all necessary means' to remove the military from power and facilitate the return of Aristide. This mission in turn was to be replaced by a UN peacekeeping force once the removal of the military had been secured. These somewhat unusual arrangements were designed to meet a number of requirements. First, the non-UN status of the multinational force could more easily be configured for enforcement than a conventional UN peacekeeping operation. By legitimizing the use of 'all necessary means' by the US-led operation rather than giving a similar mandate to a UN force, debates around the application of Chapter VII of the Charter could be avoided. Second, US domination and direction of the multinational force was intended to send a message to the military in Haiti that they would not be dealing with a UN mission rooted in the culture of non-aggressive interposition. In other words, Cédras and his associates would trifle with the new force at their peril.

In the event, the United States, shaken by its then still recent experience in Somalia (see Chapter 10) was markedly unenthusiastic about an armed confrontation with the Cédras regime. The force, about 20,000-strong, was deployed only after negotiations had been undertaken by former US president Jimmy Carter that lubricated the Haiti military's withdrawal from politics with the liberal application of material benefits. In 1995 the US-led force was replaced, as intended, by a UNMIH now entirely reconfigured as a military peacekeeping operation. The force had a strength of more than 6,000 at the outset, drawn from numerous small contingents from the western hemisphere but with a spine of US troops. It was withdrawn the following year after successful elections that confirmed Aristide in power. The peacekeeping force was immediately succeeded for a period by a smaller 'support mission' (United Nations Support Mission in Haiti – UNSMIH), which was concentrated in the capital, Port-au-Prince, where the greatest threat to the stability of the new government was located.

Haiti's problems – social, economic and political – ran deep, and there was to be no easy transition to peace and economic development. The reinstalled government of Bertrand Aristide found itself stumbling from crisis to crisis in the early years of the new century. Widespread social disorder broke out at the end of 2003, which the government struggled to contain. In the meantime, the United States had turned against Aristide, accusing him of creating the instability through his increasingly dictatorial approach to government. In February 2004 he was flown by the United States into exile. The circumstances of his removal from Haiti became the subject of fierce debate. Aristide and his still considerable body of supporters claimed that he had been the victim of what amounted to abduction by the Americans. According to this argument, Washington's real objections to his government derived from its old entrenched fear of left-wing radicalism in the region and its determination to assert the Monroe doctrine even in the post-cold war world. Certainly, elements of the old Duvalieriste armed forces were prominent in the agitation against him, and the true level of continuing support for his policies in Haiti was difficult to judge against the pervasive fear and intimidation of the time. At all events, the crisis of 2004 unfolded without any significant intervention by the United Nations.

Whatever the real circumstances of Aristide's departure, there were clear lessons to be drawn about success and failure in peacekeeping in the region. The evident success of the missions in El Salvador and Guatemala had at their root local conflict dynamics that were absolutely favourable resolution. In both situations the parties immediately involved in the conflicts were committed to the pursuit of a political settlement of what had previously been military struggles. The role of the UN in this was twofold. First, it had a practical contribution to make to the implementation of clearly set-out and agreed programmes. Second, it had what might be described as a ceremonial role in stamping the imprimatur of something called the 'international community' on the completion of these programmes. In Haiti, in contrast, local circumstances were far from favourable to a peaceful outcome at any time during the country's extended crisis. The United Nations, therefore, was required not to move with the grain of a locally generated peace process, as it was in Central America, but to attempt to impose a peace process on parties that could reach no meaningful agreement among themselves. Experience shows that in almost all circumstances this is beyond the possibilities of a peacekeeping intervention.

Constructing the post-cold war state: the Transitional Authority in Cambodia

This was the lesson facing the United Nations in another international sub-system newly opened up to peacekeeping after the end of the cold war. Cambodia, which lies on the western border of Vietnam, had been drawn into the widening conflict in the south-east Asia region in the 1970s. For centuries Cambodia had an important, even hegemonic, role in the larger south-east Asian region. In the nineteenth century, however, it fell victim to European imperial rivalries and was absorbed into the French empire in Indochina. After the Second World War French attempts to reinstate their control after the interlude of Japanese occupation were fiercely resisted in Cambodia as they were by nationalists elsewhere in the region. Cambodia became independent in 1953 and for most of the next two decades it was ruled, either directly or indirectly, by its traditional monarchy in coalition with different political parties.

The worsening situation across the border in Vietnam in the later 1960s inevitably had an impact on Cambodian politics. Prince Norodom Sihanouk, who had attempted, not always consistently or successfully, to steer a neutral path for Cambodia through the region's turbulence, began to lose his once unchallenged popularity in the country and was eventually overthrown in a military coup in 1970. His successor, General Lon Nol, pursued more overtly pro-western, anti-communist policies. His rule, however, was increasingly contested by Sihanouk who, from exile in China, formed a tactical alliance with the Cambodian Communist Party and their Khmer Rouge guerrillas. Civil war ensued, complicated by extensive covert American involvement (of which Henry Kissinger was the moving force). In April 1975 the communists occupied the capital Phnom Penh and the Khmer Rouge began an attempt to construct the most far-reaching social and political revolution. The populations of Phnom Penh and other cities were forced at gunpoint into the countryside to 'remake' themselves and the nation. Years of national insanity now ensued, with the Khmer Rouge leadership under Pol Pot attempting to 'purify' the country through forced labour and eventually mass murder. In the meantime, Cambodia was renamed – with wholly unintended irony – 'Democratic Kampuchea'.

Internationally, the Khmer Rouge regime could call on the support of China, and despite the mounting evidence of the horrors being perpetrated by the state, it maintained its accreditation at the UN. In part, this was dictated by realist calculations about the balance of power in the region. China had always been ambivalent towards the North Vietnamese cause and suspicious of the prominent supporting role of the Soviet Union for it. This concern grew with the unification of Vietnam in 1975, and Beijing saw the Khmer Rouge regime in Cambodia as a counterweight to the influence of its enlarged pro-Soviet neighbour. A trace of this thinking was also detectable in the west, which, while routinely denouncing the atrocities of the Khmer Rouge, still recognized its role as an anti-Soviet pawn in the south-east Asian sub-system. Western sensitivities about renewed Soviet adventurism were high in the second half of the 1970s when détente was beginning to crumble. The Soviet invasion of Afghanistan was still a year away, but difficulties in the superpower relationship had been emerging in Angola and other parts of Africa. And, of course, there was still considerable post-Vietnam war bitterness in the United States following the north's extinction of the American client state of South Vietnam, however predictable this became after its own military withdrawal from the region in 1973.

Tension quickly grew between Vietnam and Kampuchea after 1975. In the afterglow of its national victory Vietnam was keen to stamp its influence on the region. Beyond the dictates of realpolitik, however, it is also fair to say that Vietnam's leadership was genuinely outraged at the situation across its border and was determined to rescue the ideals of communist revolution in Asia from the Khmer Rouge. Finally, in December 1978, Vietnam invaded Kampuchea and had little difficulty in toppling the Khmer Rouge regime. A new Vietnamese-sponsored government was put in place in Phnom Penh. This was far from the end of the crisis, however. China now launched an invasion across its border with northern Vietnam that, although short-lived, brought a new global dimension to the south-east Asian crisis. At the United Nations the new regime in Cambodia (as it was called once again) was denied recognition by an alliance of separate but converging interests shared by the United States, China and the non-communist regional states of the Association of Southeast Asian Nations (ASEAN) who feared Vietnam's growing power. In Cambodia, therefore, while the government of Vietnam's protégé, Hun Sen, remained reasonably secure in power, it was not recognized by the international system as a whole.

Broader developments in this system during the latter part of the 1980s, however, helped to bring movement to the situation in Cambodia. With Gorbachev now in power in Moscow, superpower relations were undergoing rapid improvement. As well as presiding over the transformation of relations with the west, Gorbachev also sought, with some success, to heal the Sino-Soviet split, which had poisoned relations between Moscow and Beijing since the early 1960s. In the region itself Prince Sihanouk had re-emerged as a significant political player. Associated with the Khmer Rouge by virtue of his pragmatic alliance with the communists against Lon Nol in the early 1970s, and subsequently part of an anti-Vietnamese coalition, Sihanouk nevertheless began to explore the possibility of an agreement with the pro-Vietnamese Hun Sen regime. His prestige within Cambodia was still such that his position was taken very seriously in the region and beyond. The possibility of a democratization process that would legitimize a new government of whatever political background was now being actively discussed in the region. Although the permanent members of the Security Council still had their differences on Cambodia, secretary-general Pérez de Cuéllar, with the support of Australia, which at this time was developing a new Asian-focused foreign policy of its own, carved out a key role for the UN in the developing settlement process.

The plan that emerged during 1989 was extremely ambitious. The United Nations would itself provide a transitional government for Cambodia. As well as running the country, this administration would organize and control an electoral process that would give legitimacy to a new Cambodian government. The UN operation would also ensure non-violent relations between the political factions and oversee the withdrawal of Vietnamese forces from the country. Part of this last task involved a process that would become an increasingly common part of peacekeeping mandates in the 1990s, particularly in Africa. This can be conveyed by the abbreviation DDR: demobilization; disarmament; reintegration. In order to stabilize the political process and remove the threat of a reversion to armed conflict it was necessary drastically to reduce the number of fighters available to the various parties. Therefore, the forces of both the Hun Sen government and of the Khmer Rouge were to be subject to reduction through initial concentration in demobilization centres followed by the systematic removal of their weapons. This would be followed by a programme of reintegration of the former fighters back into civilian society. In Cambodia, as elsewhere, this process was to prove an extremely problematic part of the peacekeeping project.

The legal process by which power was to be invested in the UN authority involved the creation of an inactive 'shadow' repository of sovereignty: the Supreme National Council (SNC). Chaired by Prince Sihanouk and composed of representatives of the Hun Sen government and the other Cambodian factions, the SNC would temporarily cede all government power to the UN, though it would retain an advisory role during the period of international control. Once the outline of the plan was agreed by the main parties, UN endorsement, both by the Security Council and separately by the General Assembly, was quickly secured. By this time the long-standing divisions within the Security Council over Cambodia that had opened up during the cold war were rapidly evaporating. The space open to peacekeeping had thus widened yet further. In October 1991 the Agreements on a Comprehensive Political Settlement of the Cambodia Conflict were signed in Paris in a ceremony presided over by secretary-general Pérez de Cuéllar. The agreement referred to the establishment of a UN 'Transitional Authority' and in anticipation of the formal outcome to the Paris talks the Security Council had already approved the creation of an 'Advance Mission in Cambodia' (UNAMIC) to prepare the way for this.[14] The Advance Mission gave way to the United Nations Transitional Authority in Cambodia (UNTAC) in March 1992.[15]

At the time of its deployment UNTAC was the largest, most elaborate and most expensive UN operation ever (Map 4). It was not quite as unique and innovative as some claimed at the time. We have already discussed a predecessor operation that bore many similarities: the Temporary Executive Authority and Security Force (UNTEA/UNSF) in West New Guinea during 1962 and 1963 (see Chapter 5). There, too, the UN had assumed governmental powers during a transition period leading to a change of sovereignty. The Cambodian project was of a fundamentally different scale and involved much higher political risks both for the organization and for the parties to the conflict, however. UNTAC consisted of some 20,000 military and police personnel from forty-six countries at its height in mid-1993. Its administrative functions were carried out by more than 1,000 civilian officials. Although the 1,500-strong Security Force in West New Guinea was large by previous UN standards, it was dwarfed by the commitment in Cambodia. The twenty months of UNTAC cost the United Nations about 1.6 billion US dollars. In West New Guinea the outcome of the UN's involvement was never much in doubt: the territory would be transferred from Dutch to Indonesian control. The UN's function was to ensure that this took place in a secure environment and, in the diplomatic realm, ease the withdrawal of the Netherlands by veiling the reality of Indonesia's victory in the conflict. In Cambodia, not only was the internal security situation much less certain but the potential for major political difficulties during the course of the operation was enormous. Finally, however pressing the West New Guinea issue was to Indonesia and the Netherlands, it was of only scant interest to the rest of the world. Cambodia, in contrast, was a hugely ambitious attempt to manage a major, long-standing and dangerous crisis with clear ramifications for global international relations.

The balance sheet of UNTAC's success and failure has significant entries on both sides. While the external actors – Vietnam, the ASEAN states, China, the United States and Russia – were committed to a successful outcome, the internal parties were less cooperative. The Khmer Rouge in particular created considerable difficulties for UNTAC and continued to pose major problems for Cambodia after the end of the UN operation in September 1993. It became clear soon after its seizure of power in 1975 that the Khmer Rouge was as much a cult as a political movement and its engagement with the rational processes of accommodation, peacemaking and national reconstruction was affected accordingly. In particular, its failure to cooperate with the demobilization and disarmament of its fighters confronted UNTAC with great difficulties. With the Khmer Rouge plainly failing to meet its obligations, the Hun Sen faction was unwilling to disarm unilaterally. The result was frequent clashes between these factions throughout the period of UN control, with violence sporadically directed at UNTAC itself, mostly from the Khmer Rouge.

This violence intensified as the presidential and legislative elections scheduled for May 1993 approached, but the process was deemed by UN monitors to have been free and fair and to have produced a representative result. The new 120-member assembly opted for a political system based on a constitutional monarchy. The monarch (a role now assumed by Norodom Sihanouk) would act as head of state. The government over which he presided was effectively a coalition between Sihanouk's non-communist external opposition grouping and the factions around the former Vietnamese-installed leader, Hun Sen. The intentions of the Khmer Rouge, which remained semi-detached from the process, were unclear.

In the wake of the UN withdrawal in September 1993, Cambodia was far from a stable state and over the coming years was subject to continuing, though largely contained, violence. Yet undeniably the UN administration had facilitated the creation of the basic structures of pluralist democracy in a country whose prospects some little time before the deployment of UNTAC seemed hopeless to many. The country had neither destroyed itself from the inside nor been dismembered from the outside: two feasible possibilities before the Paris agreement and its implementation by the UN. Cambodia was in many ways a test case of the possibilities of post-cold war peacekeeping, but it provided no definitive assessment. It is possible that clearer achievements might have been produced by an operation less constrained by the traditional rules of peacekeeping that

UNTAC was subject to. It may be that much of the violence of late 1992 and 1993 could have been suppressed by a more enforcement-oriented mandate. But paradoxically, perhaps, the unusually high level of UN political authority within the borders of Cambodia in a sense worked against too robust a military approach. The combination of political power and military might would have brought the UN uncomfortably close to a form of multilateral 'imperialism'.

As a litmus test of a 'new' peacekeeping, the Cambodian case illustrated the limitations of UN intervention as much as its possibilities. In doing so, it should have sounded a warning about future undertakings elsewhere in the world. A key assumption about peacekeeping after the cold war was that long-standing conflicts that had involved east–west entanglements would now be relatively easy to resolve. The end of externally contrived mischief and its replacement by cooperation in the search for solutions should have militated towards a new record of peacekeeping successes. In reality, as Cambodia demonstrated and as crises as far apart as Angola and Central Asia would confirm, many supposed 'cold war conflicts' had much stronger endogenous bases than had been realized, and these were not automatically resolvable by an improvement in relations between the big powers, with or without UN involvement. Peacekeeping, as we observed when we contrasted the fortunes of the operations in Central America and in Haiti, can only work when the dynamics of the conflict permit it to. Big-power involvement constitutes one set of these dynamics, local conditions quite another. In Cambodia there was no question that the external powers were behind the peacekeeping effort; the situation locally, however, was not so clear.

Taking stock: *An Agenda for Peace*

As UNTAC began the final, post-election phase of its work in Cambodia in June 1992, the then secretary-general, the former Egyptian foreign minister Boutros Boutros-Ghali, presented his own thoughts on peacekeeping after the cold war to both the Security Council and the General Assembly in a report called *An Agenda for Peace*. In truth, the post-cold war period was well established by this point, and a wide range of new peacekeeping efforts were under way. Most notably, perhaps, a huge commitment had been made in the former Yugoslavia, but a whole set of operations were either ongoing or already completed in Africa. But Boutros-Ghali himself was only recently in office (he had replaced Pérez de Cuéllar at the beginning of 1992), and he was anxious to engage with what he foresaw as an activity certain to occupy much of his efforts. Like Dag Hammarskjöld's Summary Study thirty-four years previously, *An Agenda for Peace* sought to review the possibilities for UN intervention in the international system at a particular historical juncture.

His starting point was the sudden and momentous alteration in the character of the international system brought by the end of the cold war. 'In the course of the past few years,' he noted, 'the immense ideological barrier that for decades gave rise to distrust and hostility – and the terrible tools of destruction that were their inseparable companions – has collapsed.'[16] Hammarskjöld had been writing at a point in the cold war when peacekeeping as a non-enforcement, 'no blame' approach to international crises seemed to offer the UN a limited military role despite the inapplicability of Chapter VII on collective security. Boutros-Ghali, in his turn, was writing against the backdrop of the end of bipolarity and the consequent alteration of the terms on which peacekeeping had been conceptualized by his predecessor in the late 1950s. The origins of *An Agenda for Peace* lay in a special Security Council summit on peacekeeping and peacemaking held the previous January just as Boutros-Ghali took office. The tone of the report was cautious but unmistakably upbeat. This was to be expected amid the flurry of new peacekeeping authorizations and less than a year after Operation Desert Storm from which the UN, despite its essentially marginal role, had emerged with an enhanced reputation for decisiveness in the face of international aggression. *An Agenda for Peace*, therefore, sought to carry forward the new momentum for multilateralism that had recently been generated in the international system.

Boutros-Ghali was cautious about the prospects in the new environment for a revival of full-scale military collective security. The sort of forces envisaged in Chapter VII of the Charter might never 'be sufficiently large or well enough equipped to deal with a threat from a major army equipped with sophisticated weapons'. But this should not mean that the possibilities of Chapter VII should be disregarded. He proposed, for example, that the multinational MSC composed of the military leaders of the permanent members of the Security Council should be revived.[17] And, even short of the strict application of Chapter VII, new means of enforcing the implementation of peace agreements might be considered. One approach could be the creation of 'peace enforcement units'. These would not enforce the decisions of the Security Council per se; that would clearly fall into the ambit of Chapter VII as originally conceived. But a growing difficulty for peacekeeping was the reneging on peace settlements by parties that had already agreed to them. This was a problem currently facing UNTAC in Cambodia, but it would become a prime reason for the 'failure' of peacekeeping operations elsewhere as well, particularly in Africa. In such circumstances military units with heavier armaments than conventional peacekeeping forces and with the backing of the Security Council could force antagonists to meet their commitments by suppressing any attempted return to violence.[18]

Another proposed compromise between increasingly inadequate Hammarskjöldian approaches to peacekeeping and the still unattainable enforcement arrangements of Chapter VII was to be found in the report's discussion of 'regional arrangements'. This, it will be recalled, was the title of Chapter VIII of the United Nations Charter that acknowledged that collective security measures might be initiated not only centrally by the Security Council in New York but by regional organizations operating under its authority (see Chapter 3). This had been no more applicable during the cold war than the centralized version of enforcement-based collective security. The regional agencies that would have been responsible for this collective security during the cold war would have been the military alliances of the opposing blocs. These could not have safely intervened in any area of sensitivity. In fact, they were unsuitable even in 'peacekeeping mode' for dealing with intra-alliance problems let alone ones involving non-alliance members. A NATO peacekeeping intervention in Cyprus in 1964 was rejected, as we saw, and the Warsaw Pact's suppression of the reformist regime in Czechoslovakia in 1968 was hardly 'peacekeeping' in any reasonable sense. Now, though, Boutros-Ghali suggested, 'regional action as a matter of decentralization, delegation and cooperation with United Nations efforts could not only lighten the burden of the (Security) Council but also contribute to a deeper sense of participation, consensus and democratization in international affairs'.[19] Although not made explicit in *An Agenda for Peace*, the regionalization of peacekeeping would also offer a way out of the growing resource problem caused by the recent expansion in peacekeeping.

The secretary-general nurtured no illusions about these resource issues. The new pressures for the creation of peacekeeping operations had deepened the financial difficulties that had always surrounded the activity. Although the permanent members of the Security Council were now, at least in their pronouncements, committed to paying their dues, the problem of unpaid assessments went much deeper into the broader membership of the UN. Operational commitments for the current year of 1992 (including the extremely expensive Cambodia operation) were calculated at three billion dollars. In Boutros-Ghali's words, 'a chasm [had] developed between the tasks entrusted to [the UN] and the financial means provided to it'.[20] To bridge this chasm he proposed the creation of a 'reserve fund' for peacekeeping operations that would enable them to be established without the requirement to wrest prior financial commitments from UN members. Underpinning this, he suggested, should be a 'peace endowment fund' of one billion dollars.[21] The accrued interest on this investment would be disbursed to meet the costs on ongoing operations. The problem of personnel resources, Boutros-Ghali suggested, should be met by member states making prior commitments to participate in peacekeeping. If members entered agreements indicating 'the kind and number of skilled personnel they will be prepared to offer the United Nations as the needs of new operations' arose, the constant hand-to-mouth pressure on peacekeeping planners in the UN secretariat would be lessened.[22]

While *An Agenda for Peace* attracted considerable attention from peacekeeping practitioners and analysts (by whom it was generally well received), it seemed to have little tangible impact on the thinking of those best able to implement its recommendations – the permanent members of the Security Council. Although the relevance of much in the report would become more and more evident over the coming years, no concrete steps were taken in the Security Council to implement its proposals. At the beginning of 1995, on the occasion of the fiftieth anniversary of the United Nations, Boutros-Ghali produced a *Supplement to An Agenda for Peace* as a personal position paper. The tone was considerably less optimistic than in the original report. The post-cold war world now, in Boutros-Ghali's view, was less one of opportunity for peacekeeping than one of grave challenge. The 'different world that emerged when the cold war ceased [was] still a world not fully understood'.[23] *An Agenda for Peace* had been issued at a time of hope. It came immediately after a sequence of positive developments, including the apparent success of Operation Desert Storm and the unprecedented deployment in Cambodia. But the future was not to justify this optimism, however reasonable it seemed in mid-1992. The wide alliance built around the war against Iraq proved ephemeral, and the reformism of the last days of the Soviet Union had given way to a new, often resentful, post-Soviet Russian nationalism. This did not amount to another cold war, of course, but it put an end to the notion of the Soviet Union reinventing itself as a new progressive European middle power as seemed possible during the Gorbachev period. The humiliation of the UN in Bosnia lay just ahead, as did the abject failures of the operations in Angola and Somalia and the UN's inability to prevent genocide in Rwanda. These were complex situations, and it was perhaps beyond the capacity of any external intervention to significantly improve them. And there were peacekeeping successes ahead as well, notably in Mozambique. But by 1995 the public perception of peacekeeping was one of inadequacy at best and general failure at worst. The two and a half years between the original *Agenda for Peace* and its sadder, wiser *Supplement* saw the evaporation of much of the euphoria about the end of the cold war and the prospects for a new multilateralism.

East Timor: portmanteau peacekeeping

Viewed in hindsight, 1995 represented something of a nadir for post-cold war peacekeeping rather than a marker of deepening failure. The balance of the following years was positive overall. In a number of new undertakings the UN, partly as a result of some of the bitter experiences of the mid-1990s, redeemed the peacekeeping project in general. New partnerships between the UN and other agencies were experimented with and new configurations of military and civil action were introduced. One of the most notable successes for this second phase of post-cold war peacekeeping took place between 1999 and 2005 in East Timor. The UN's commitment there embraced virtually the range of peacekeeping and ancillary activities undertaken by the organization hitherto. It provides a prime example of the 'multifunctional peacekeeping' that has been seen as typical of post-cold war multilateralism.

From Portuguese colonialism to Indonesian annexation

As in Cambodia, the UN's earlier venture into multi-role peacekeeping in south-east Asia in the 1990s, the crisis in East Timor grew directly out of the changed conditions in the international system after the end of bipolarity. East Timor, which lies within the Indonesian archipelago, had been a Portuguese colony, one of the few remnants of that country's once extensive Asia empire. Until the Second World War East Timor occupied one half of an island in the vast archipelago of the Netherlands East Indies. In 1949 this was transformed into the new state of Indonesia (with the exception of West New Guinea whose own experience of UN peacekeeping we have already discussed). East Timor, however, remained under Portuguese control and – despite some nationalist pressure and the ease with which it could have been done – Indonesia resisted the temptation to seize the small imperial remnant in the midst of its national territory.

The situation changed dramatically in 1974, however, when a military coup in Lisbon set off a chain of events that led to the final dissolution of the Portuguese empire. The attention of Portugal and the wider world in this process was focused on the much larger and economically and diplomatically more important African territories, particularly Angola and Mozambique. East Timor was, if not ignored, then certainly left in a state of limbo while these larger problems were dealt with. In this situation the anti-colonial movement in East Timor found a voice (which in truth had not been much heard before the Lisbon coup). Throughout Portuguese Africa at this time Marxism was the dominant ideology among the successful liberation movements and their example was followed by the main East Timorese movement: the Revolutionary Front for an Independent East Timor (Frente Revolucionária de Timor-Leste Independente – Fretilin). The Indonesian government now saw both a threat and an opportunity. The fiercely anti-communist regime of President Suharto had come to power after the bloody overthrow of the supposedly pro-communist nationalist Sukarno in 1966. The prospect of a Marxist-oriented micro-state in the middle of the national archipelago, therefore, was particularly offensive to the government in Jakarta. The idea of a new, weak and potentially pro-Soviet entity in the region was not relished by Indonesia's powerful western friends either. The possibility therefore arose of Indonesia now being 'permitted' to extinguish the threat through forced annexation. Accordingly, at the end of 1975, immediately following what may or may not have been a significant visit from American secretary of state Henry Kissinger, Indonesian forces invaded and occupied East Timor.

For the next quarter of a century East Timor suffered multiple horrors under Indonesian rule. Taking to the territory's rugged mountain spine, Fretilin conducted a long, punishing guerrilla war against the occupiers. In response, Indonesian reprisals cost the lives of thousands, and conflict-related famine cost many thousands more. In all, about a quarter of the population of just over a million died during the occupation. Although the United Nations adhered to the legal fiction that East Timor remained a Portuguese territory, Indonesia had free reign to impose its will by force without any significant challenge by the western powers. With the end of the cold war, however, the situation began to change in East Timor as in so many other hitherto 'sensitive' parts of the bipolar system. In Asia, as in Africa and Latin America, continued support for the dictatorial regimes that had served western geo-strategic interests in the age of bipolarity were no longer necessary and had become politically costly. In 1998 President Suharto, now bereft of external support, resigned in the face of a reform movement weary of his regime's political repression and pervasive corruption.

The following year, now faced with meaningful international pressure, his successors agreed to an externally supervised referendum in East Timor that would determine whether its people wished to remain part of Indonesia (though with a degree of local autonomy) or become an independent state. To no one's surprise the overwhelming majority – more than three-quarters of those who voted in the September 1999 poll – chose the second option. As the scale of the vote for independence became clear, local pro-Indonesian 'militias' with the support of the Indonesian military in the territory launched a campaign of terror and destruction that left about 1,000 people dead and resulted in a quarter of the population fleeing the territory. The Indonesian government was either unwilling or unable to restore order. The UN civilian Mission in East Timor (UNAMET), which had been created in June 1999 and which was responsible for organizing the vote and overseeing the implementation of its outcome, became a particular target of the militias and was forced to evacuate most of its staff.

Ending the violence: the 'coalition of the willing'

The first of a series of differently configured peacekeeping interventions now began. The International Force in East Timor (INTERFET) was not a UN force as such but a so-called 'coalition of the willing' (Map 15). The lead power in INTERFET was Australia, Indonesia's neighbour across the Timor Sea and an increasingly active regional player in the 1990s. In addition to its Australian core INTERFET included contributions from a number of key Asian states, including Indonesia's ASEAN partners, Malaysia, the Philippines, Singapore and Thailand. This structure was politically well geared to the situation. While there would have been little confidence in East Timor or abroad in a force led by one of Indonesia's regional friends, their participation eased Jakarta's reluctance to agree to an international force on what many in the country persisted in seeing as 'Indonesian' territory. That the venture was, in legal terms, not a United Nations operation (it was merely 'agreed to' by the Security Council) also helped secure Indonesian acquiescence because nationalist feeling against the UN still ran high after the outcome of the UNAMET-organized referendum. Although granted the authority to use 'all necessary measures' to restore peace and security in the territory and guarantee the safety of UNAMET staff, INTERFET met no resistance when it was deployed in late September. While prepared to spread a reign of terror over the civilian population, the militias and the remaining Indonesian military in the territory showed no enthusiasm for confronting more than 8,000 well-equipped international troops.[24] But a major task of reconstruction faced the United Nations as the orgy of violence in the first half of September had left much of the capital, Dili, and other centres in ruins.

In February 2000 the second phase of peacekeeping in East Timor began when INTERFET was replaced by a new, formally UN operation. INTERFET had created the necessary diplomatic buffer between East Timor as a de facto part of Indonesia and East Timor as a nascent independent state. Indonesia was now more distanced from the issue and therefore less sensitive to the form and composition of the international presence in the territory. At the end of September 1999 the Indonesian and Portuguese governments had agreed to the formal transfer of East Timor to the United Nations, and it became wholly appropriate that the UN itself should provide the necessary peacekeeping and security forces. Accordingly, at the end of October 1999 the Security Council voted to establish the new mission, the Transitional Administration in East Timor (UNTAET).[25] This would consist of a military element of 9,000 troops as well as more than 1,600 civilian police to fill the vacuum left by the Indonesian withdrawal. A large part of the INTERFET force remained, now under UN command and alongside new contingents from Europe, Africa and Latin America.

Towards statehood: the UN administration

Beyond its peacekeeping and security functions, UNTAET would be the temporary 'state' in East Timor, providing all political, economic, social and judicial services. In the description of the UN Department of Peacekeeping Operations, UNTAET was to be 'an integrated, multidimensional peacekeeping operation fully responsible for the administration of East Timor during its transition to independence'.[26] The task facing UNTAET was daunting. With no history of local administration before the Indonesian occupation that could be 'restored', the new state had to be built from scratch. These difficulties were aggravated by the social and material damage inflicted during the years of Indonesian annexation and then in the violent convulsion of September 1999. The return and reintegration of refugees became a major part of UNTAET's work. This was complicated by a security situation that, although generally manageable, caused continuing difficulties for the international administration and the peacekeeping force. The border with the Indonesian western part of the island remained dangerous as occasional incursions were made by the remnants of the militias that had fled the territory with the arrival of INTERFET.

Specific local conditions made the job achievable, however. The relatively small population and the fact that they were overwhelmingly supportive of the state-building efforts of UNTAET were major factors. Another was the unusual competence and authority of the local leadership of mainly Fretilin veterans poised to take over the new state. In August 2001 the (now former Marxist) party took fifty-five of the seats in the new eighty-eight-member legislature, and the following April the Fretilin leader Xanana Gusmão, who had spent most of the previous ten years in an Indonesian jail, was elected to the presidency with nearly 83 per cent of the vote. On its independence on 20 May 2002 East Timor became the first new addition to the international state system of the twenty-first century.

On the same day UNTAET ceased to exist, having fulfilled its mandate of bringing East Timor to statehood. This marked not the end of the UN's role in the territory but the beginning of a new phase of engagement. UNTAET was immediately replaced by a smaller successor operation, the Mission of Support in East Timor (UNMISET), which had already been approved by the Security Council.[27] This latest version of peacekeeping in East Timor represented a more familiar type of UN deployment than UNTAET, which had been to all intents and purposes the armed forces of a UN state. UNMISET, in contrast, was a peacekeeping and support mission deployed within an independent host state and operating under a formal status of forces agreement. UNMISET, like its predecessor, had to confront continuing security problems on the frontier with West Timor, but in April 2005, under pressure from the United Nations, Indonesia signed a permanent border agreement with East Timor during a highly symbolic official visit by the Indonesian president to Dili. The following month UNMISET was wound up, having been judged by the Security Council to have completed its mission.

In the three years between 1999 and 2002 East Timor had been the subject of a sequence of distinct and varied multinational interventions designed to manage its transition from annexed territory to full member of the international state system. The case of East Timor, therefore, would seem to provide a powerful justification for the view that the post-cold war period saw the emergence of a distinctly 'new' peacekeeping. The innovation supposedly lay in the multifunctional character of such operations. Military, policing, humanitarian and political roles were, it was argued, combined in this form of intervention in a way that they were not in peacekeeping during the cold war years. Yet examination of the separate components of the international engagement with East Timor does not fully support the assertion that it was in any essential way different from what had gone before. The referendum organization and supervision undertaken by UNAMET in 1999 would have been recognizable in the League of Nations seventy years earlier. This was succeeded, after the territory's descent into violence, by INTERFET, a 'coalition of the willing'. This type of operation also had its precedents in the history of multilateral intervention. In the 1990s an American-led operation in Somalia and French ones in Rwanda and the CAR had been 'approved' by the Security Council as alternatives to 'UN' peacekeeping operations. But the phenomenon had already put in an appearance during the cold war – in the form of the American 'Unified Command' in Korea in the early 1950s. The Temporary Executive Authority that succeeded the INTERFET coalition followed the precedent not just of UNTAC in Cambodia but that of West New Guinea, another contested 'Indonesian' territory in the early 1960s where the UN had also provided a transitional government. Finally, the Mission of Support that was the final component of the multinational involvement in East Timor was a largely 'traditional' peacekeeping support mission to a country with inadequate national resources to meet security threats on its borders. The Observer Group in Lebanon had performed a similar function as long ago as 1958.

It is therefore difficult to sustain the argument that the end of the cold war inaugurated a distinctly new phase in the *operational* role of peacekeeping. Unquestionably there was an increase in the frequency of peacekeeping interventions, but this has been a matter of quantity rather than quality. There was, though, a clear difference at the *political* heart of peacekeeping after the cold war. Peacekeeping as a means of inoculating local crises from the dangers of big-power involvement and embroilment in a broader global contest was now irrelevant. So was the notion of areas being off-limits to peacekeeping. The disappearance of core spheres of superpower interest and therefore influence – areas that had to be guarded against multilateral interventions – meant that no part of the system was any longer beyond the legitimate reach of peacekeeping. It is in this sense that the end of the cold war created a 'new peacekeeping'. But the novelty lay in number rather than kind. Nowhere, perhaps, was this widened field of peacekeeping activity more evident than at the geo-political centre of the old bipolar balance, Europe and the former Soviet Union, to which we turn next.

8 The break-up of Yugoslavia and the Soviet Union

Peacekeeping and the end of the multinational state

In the last chapter we made frequent reference to the idea of peacekeeping taking place within a permitted area designated according to big-power perceptions of their own core interests and we explored the impact of the end of the cold war, which widened this area to embrace areas such as Latin America and south-east Asia. But nowhere, perhaps, has the expansion of post-cold war peacekeeping into areas hitherto off-limits been more evident than in Europe and on its eastern borders. Peacekeeping here had previously been confined to the special case of Cyprus; now the possibilities were more or less unlimited.

Although the peacekeeping activities undertaken in Europe and the former Soviet Union in the 1990s were not concerned with the consequences of conventional decolonization as they had been in the Middle East, Asia and Africa in the 1950s and 1960s, there were underlying similarities. Just as the end of the colonial empires and the consequent emergence of new states created stresses in the post-Second World War international system, so the break-up of what can be described as 'multinational states' into more numerous, supposedly 'mono-national states' generated similar strains in the post-cold war system. The greatest humanitarian, political and diplomatic difficulties were caused by the disintegration of Yugoslavia where the emergence of almost all the successor states led to conflict and violence. In contrast, in Czechoslovakia, for example, the dismantling of the state may not have been completely trouble-free, but it took place without serious conflict and therefore without recourse to any peacekeeping intervention. The end of the Soviet Union lay between these two poles. While the process of transition itself was remarkably smooth given the potential for serious conflict, in the immediate post-Soviet period difficulties emerged between a number of the successor states that in turn brought external intervention. These peacekeeping operations were intended to manage difficult inter-ethnic relationships that were often aggravated by the re-emergence of historical claims and counterclaims. Many of these operations involved complex inter-agency arrangements between different external organizations. On occasion these joint ventures in peacekeeping brought their own problems which undermined the success of the interventions. In this respect the performance of the UN in the former Yugoslavia in particular produced one of peacekeeping's least glorious chapters. But there, as in other undertakings from Lebanon in the 1970s to Rwanda in the 1990s, the culpability of 'the UN' cannot be easily disentangled from the policy decisions of the big powers that determined its mandates and provided its resources.

The end of Yugoslavia

Yugoslavia was a product of the First World War. After the defeat of Austria-Hungary and Turkey the allied powers were faced with the problem of what to do with their imperial possessions in Europe. Elsewhere in the world the mandate system seemed to provide a practical and ethical answer. But in Europe, where the major battles of the war had been fought and where the rhetoric of self-determination was loudest, the allies were impelled towards the immediate creation of new states. These states, however, had to be viable as potential members of the international system. This ruled out the simple creation of a series of new micro-states from the various post-imperial territories of the south Slav region. The Balkans had long been a focus of instability in the system – most recently it had played a major part in the crisis leading to the outbreak of war in 1914 – and the allies saw it as essential to create effective state structures there. To this end, Serbia, which had fought on the allied side during the war, was made the centrepiece of a new state composed of former territories of the defeated empires, from Slovenia on the borders of Italy in the north to Macedonia deep in the southern Balkans.

The new state of Yugoslavia embraced a range of cultures and religions: Catholic in the north and west, Orthodox in the east and Muslim in the centre and south. In its first decades, circumstances allowed Yugoslavia to evade some of the difficult issues raised by its wide multi-ethnic composition. Nation-building was helped initially by the post-imperial enthusiasm of its component parts, which encouraged cooperation among the various territories. Then, during the Second World War, invasion and resistance helped pull the country together. The key personality in Yugoslavia's partisan war against the German occupation was the Communist leader Josip Broz, known universally as Tito. After the war the Communist hold on power was such that there was no question of the country returning to the constitutional monarchy imposed on it at its creation. Tito accordingly became president of the Federal People's Republic of Yugoslavia, which was composed of semi-autonomous 'republics' based on the historical ethnicities of the region. Communist though he was, the powerful and independent-minded Tito would not meekly deliver Yugoslavia into a satellite relationship with the Soviet Union of the type being established across eastern Europe in the post-war period. Yugoslavia remained independent of any close relationship with either of the cold war blocs and pursued a formal policy of non-alignment, finding most of its friends outside Europe.

Tito's death in 1980, however, raised questions about the continued viability of a united Yugoslavia. The passing from the scene of the powerful, unifying national father figure precipitated a new micro-nationalism within a number of the federal units that would have been unthinkable while he remained in power. These pressures fermented through the 1980s and then merged with the broader wave of nationalist fervour released with the fall of the Berlin Wall and the sudden contraction of Soviet power in eastern Europe. Many Slovenians, Croatians and Bosnians had now come to see Yugoslavia less as a successful multinational state than as an exercise in Serbian imperialism. It was a view that the Serbian leader, Slobodan Milosevic, did little to dispel from his power base in Belgrade (which, tellingly, was historically the capital of both Yugoslavia and Serbia).

Croatia: peacekeeping marginalized

In June 1991 both Slovenia and Croatia declared themselves independent of Yugoslavia. In the case of Slovenia, which was overwhelmingly mono-ethnic and which was seen beyond its borders as a 'west European' entity rather than Balkan one, the break was quickly consolidated after a short sharp conflict between the Yugoslav army and local forces. Croatia was different, however. It was much more typical of Yugoslavia as a whole in that its population was a mixed one with considerable minorities from the country's other ethnicities. Perhaps fatally for the prospects of a peaceful secession by Croatia, its largest and most powerful minority was Serbian. The Serbian community in Croatia – which comprised about 12 per cent of the population – was violently opposed to separation from Serb-dominated Yugoslavia and in Slobodan Milosevic they had a reliable and powerful ally. The Serb-dominated Yugoslavian National Army (JNA) was now ordered to prevent Croatia's secession from the federation, and a full-scale war ensued.

The diplomatic climate in Europe in 1991 was relatively positive and self-confident. The dramatic changes of the previous two years had been successfully absorbed by the continent's states and institutions. There was considerable optimism that the future would bring a historically unprecedented level of regional cooperation underpinned by pan-European democracy. The onset of the crisis in Yugoslavia, therefore, was seen to some extent as an opportunity as well as a threat. It would be a test of the new security architecture of Europe, a chance for the post-cold war region to prove its cooperative capacity. The initial intervention in Croatia, therefore, was made not by the United Nations but by the European Community (as it was then called), which deployed observers in the first phase of the fighting. Peacemaking efforts were also undertaken by the Organization for Security and Cooperation in Europe (OSCE), a pan-continental institution that grew out of the cold war-era Conference on Security and Cooperation in Europe (CSCE). These proved wholly ineffective, however, and were largely ignored by the warring factions.

The European effort was also compromised by differences in the Community over the merits of the Croatian case. Germany was strongly sympathetic to Croatian aspirations for independence while France was more understanding of the Serbian position. Britain, whose foreign policy at this time was determined on a particularly narrow view of national interest, was anxious to avoid too close an involvement in what threatened to mutate into a major international crisis. The nature of the conflict progressively worsened, with the first exercises of what would become known throughout the former Yugoslavia as 'ethnic cleansing' – the consolidation of ethnic domination of whole areas by the expulsion and worse of minority populations – being undertaken by both Croats and Serbs in their respective parts of Croatia.

The United Nations first became involved at the end of September 1991 when the Security Council imposed an arms embargo on the parties to the Croatian conflict. This was followed by a joint UN and European effort to broker an agreement. A series of meetings in Geneva in November between Croat and Serb representatives seemed to hold out a promise of this. But in a pattern that was to repeat itself throughout long years of war in the former Yugoslavia, apparent agreement was quickly lost as positions changed and prior undertakings were broken. In February 1992 Boutros-Ghali, who had just succeeded Javier Pérez de Cuéllar as secretary-general, persuaded the Security Council that a peacekeeping operation would be necessary to drive the settlement process forward. It was a risky proposition as both the Croats and the Serbs had shown themselves to be unenthusiastic about the idea. The Council accepted Boutros-Ghali's arguments, though with considerable misgivings, and the UN Protection Force (UNPROFOR) was established.[1] The main purpose of UNPROFOR, which would grow to a strength of 14,000 over the following year, was to establish and secure United Nations Protected Areas (UNPAs) in Croatia where large numbers of ethnic Serbs were concentrated (Map 6). By this means it was hoped that the JNA and Serb irregular forces could be persuaded to withdraw. This in turn would facilitate the negotiation of a political settlement.[2] In addition, UNPROFOR would monitor so-called Pink Zones where there were significant concentrations of Serb communities outside the Protected Areas.

A fragile truce was maintained throughout 1992 that would almost certainly not have persisted without the UN presence. In the febrile climate, however, tensions did not subside, even if a slide back to general war was held in check by the peacekeepers. At the beginning of 1993 the situation erupted into widespread violence once again when Croat forces launched attacks on Serbs in the Pink Zones. Serb irregulars responded by seizing weapons they had surrendered to UNPROFOR the previous year, and the UN force was pushed to the margins of the conflict. The problem in Croatia was that after the establishment of UNPROFOR the peacemaking process that its presence was designed to facilitate did not advance. Instead, it faced increasing obstruction from both sides.

At the root of this obstruction was the fact that the apparent cause of the conflict – the fate of the Croatian Serb population – was in a sense merely a red herring. The real issue was the independence of Croatia. Although this had been accepted, if warily, by some in western Europe and beyond as a fait accompli, in Milosevic's Serbia the situation provoked deep nationalist resentment. Unpalatable though the proposition might be, the conflict was simply not amenable to resolution by peacekeeping. The UN's presence in 1992 had restrained the parties and no doubt saved lives, but its larger effect had merely been to delay a reversion to war. The fundamental conflict could only be resolved between parties with directly opposed positions that offered little space for accommodation. At the end of 1993 the military situation in Croatia was such that, taken along with the pressures on Serbia elsewhere in the former Yugoslavia, Belgrade was left with no option but to accept Croatia's independence.

Fighting between the ethnic factions inside Croatia continued for another two years, though in this later phase the conflict had no significant international dimension. UN peacekeepers remained on the ground nevertheless. Subsequent UN missions grew out of UNPROFOR and went on to make an important contribution to post-conflict adjustment in Serb-populated areas of Croatia. Their confidence-building role was particularly important in the former Serb-populated UN Protected Areas, which were taken over, after negotiation, by the Croatian government. The Confidence Restoration Operation (UNCRO) was put in place during 1995 at the end of the armed conflict for this purpose. Later, the Transitional Authority in Eastern Slavonia, Baranja and Western Sirmium (UNTAES) oversaw the extension of Croat government authority to these ethnic Serb areas between 1996 and 1998. The final UN presence was the Mission of Observers in Prevlaka (UNMOP), which operated in the Prevlaka Peninsula from 1996 to 2002. This area, which included the historic city of Dubrovnik, was on the border between Croatia and Montenegro (which, with Serbia, formed the rump of Yugoslavia after the break-up of 1991–2). But the fundamental issue of Croatian independence from Yugoslavia and Serbia's opposition to it was resolved on the battlefield and in spite of rather than because of the peacekeeping effort. With neither a peace to keep nor negotiating space between the opposing positions of the antagonists on which one could be built, UNPROFOR could never be more than marginal to the conflict in Croatia.

Bosnia: peacekeeping shamed

In the spring of 1992, while the fragile temporary truce was maintained under UNPROFOR supervision in Croatia, another war of secession had broken out in the geographic centre of the disintegrating Yugoslav state. Fighting in Bosnia-Herzegovina (normally referred to simply as Bosnia) had been anticipated with dread in Europe after the war in Croatia began.

The ethnic make-up of Bosnia was particularly complicated and the unexpected ferocity of the violence in Croatia, where the ethnic balance was relatively simpler, was a very bad omen. The fears of the other European states were to be proved all too justified as Bosnia descended into the most destructive and savage conflict in the continent since the Second World War.

In Croatia the ethnic dimension to the crisis had been essentially a two-way affair between native Croats and local Serbs. In Bosnia the picture was considerably more complicated. The Bosnian majority – some 43 per cent of the population – was Muslim, an inheritance from the years of Ottoman rule of the area. Religion did not feature prominently in what had traditionally been a tolerant and open society, though, at least in the larger towns. There was in addition, however, a very large ethnic Serb minority (about 31 per cent of the population). The Serbs, to a greater degree than their counterparts in Croatia, nursed something of a sense of superiority in relation to the Muslim majority. The ethnic complexity was further deepened by the presence of a significant Croat population, which made up around 17 per cent of Bosnia's population. Bosnia therefore had an especially tangled political and cultural geometry that threatened to make any conflict that broke out there especially destructive and difficult to manage.

By the end of 1991 such a conflict seemed increasingly inevitable. Under 'normal' circumstances the Bosnian leadership might have been willing to remain within a federal Yugoslavia as long as it continued to be genuinely multinational. However, the secession of Slovenia and Croatia raised the prospect of Bosnia being transformed into a component of the 'greater Serbia' that increasingly formed part of the populist rhetoric of Milosevic and other Serbian nationalists in Belgrade. Therefore, in April 1992, just less than a year after the declarations of independence by Slovenia and Croatia, Bosnia announced its departure from Yugoslavia. Fighting erupted almost immediately, with Bosnian Serb forces targeting the capital and seat of the new 'national' government, Sarajevo.

UNPROFOR deployed

The UN's initial, highly optimistic plan was that once UNPROFOR had successfully completed its mission in Croatia a group of about 100 military observers would be transferred from it to various flashpoints in Bosnia to act as a preventative international presence (Map 3). But the situation in Bosnia rapidly moved beyond the point where the mere moral force of UN personnel could have any impact. Those military observers who were deployed early in the conflict, for example to the historic city of Mostar which was divided between Bosnian Muslims and Croats, had to be hurriedly withdrawn. Throughout the summer of 1992 Boutros-Ghali worked to find a diplomatic solution to the crisis, and sanctions were imposed on Yugoslavia in response to its deployment of the JNA in Bosnia. But the warring factions were beyond such pressure and, reluctantly, the Security

Council agreed to a major expansion of the UNPROFOR presence in Bosnia as a primarily humanitarian intervention.[3]

The main objective of UNPROFOR at this time was restricted to the delivery of supplies to isolated and besieged populations in the remoter parts of Bosnia. Large tracts of the mountainous country had been cut off by the fighting and the Bosnian Serbs especially were blocking aid supplies to Muslim areas as a deliberate tactic. There was mounting concern about this situation as the severe Bosnian winter began to set in, raising real fears of a major humanitarian disaster. In this respect the role of UNPROFOR was very similar to that of the first UN operation in Somalia that had been established in the same year. Both were primarily humanitarian interventions rather than either traditional interpositionary peacekeeping or peace enforcement operations. Neither the African nor the European venture was destined to succeed, however. With the benefit of hindsight it is, of course, easy to point to the critical failures in the UN's approach to intervention at this early stage. In August 1992, a month before the decision to expand UNPROFOR's humanitarian role in Bosnia, the Security Council had invoked enforcement powers. A resolution was passed calling on UN members to take individually 'or through regional agencies or arrangements . . . all measures necessary' to guarantee aid deliveries in Bosnia.[4] The UN did not impose this responsibility on itself, but the reference to 'regional agencies' was a hint to NATO, which under the 'Regional Arrangements' of Chapter VIII of the Charter would have been empowered to intervene in force. No such intervention took place, however. As a result, the will of the international system was tested and found weak by the Serbs who acted increasingly without fear of consequences.

This was evident when a Security Council-declared 'No-Fly Zone' (NFZ), which was intended to prevent the Serbian air force from attacking Bosnian Muslim targets, was systematically ignored by Belgrade.[5] Although not evident at the time, this was the provocation that set in train events that would lead to the defeat of the Serbs and, in the longer term, the end of the Milosovic regime in Belgrade. The road to this final outcome was to prove an immensely dark and destructive one. On its route there would be humiliation and disgrace for the UN and a catalogue of tense and bad-tempered inter-agency squabbles around the intervention. The final act would in fact take place beyond Bosnia itself, with a last outburst of Serbian nationalist aggression in Kosovo. But the unleashing of overwhelming international force against the Serbian regime there could be traced clearly and directly back down that troubled road to Bosnia.

The arrival of NATO: the inter-agency relationship

In March 1993, at the end of a bitter winter of Serb attacks against the Bosnian Muslims that displayed a mounting contempt for the UN, a further Security Council resolution called for the NFZ to be enforced by 'regional arrangements'. This time NATO heeded the call.[6] Britain, France, the United States and Turkey announced that they would immediately make aircraft available to patrol the NFZ. In this way NATO became directly tied in to the intervention in Bosnia, where its role would shift and change over the coming two years to a point where, effectively pushing the UN aside, it would enforce a peace on the country.

While the secretary-general was obviously grateful and relieved that NATO air power was now deployed in support of UNPROFOR, at the outset of the arrangement no clear definition of the relationship between the two institutions was laid down. This was now an inter-agency intervention without either being entirely clear about the limits and extent of the power of the other. Given the precedence of the United Nations Charter in international law, the UN would have been the lead organization. But the situation was complicated by the fact that NATO, though a 'regional agency' in political and geographical reality, was arguably not one in the legal sense covered by Chapter VIII of the UN Charter. Neither Yugoslavia nor any of the successor states to it was a member of the alliance. NATO was, in other words, acting 'out of area' in Bosnia. The relationship with the UN, therefore, could not be satisfactorily defined under Chapter VIII, which covers the use of regional agencies in matters of international security under Security Council authority. And there was a further complication. Although three of the Security Council's permanent members were also in NATO, two emphatically were not. China, which had played no direct part in the ending of the cold war and remained suspicious of the intentions of the western alliance, stood on the margins of the Security Council's engagement with the former Yugoslavia. Russia, through both geography and history, was more closely involved. Moscow had two reasons to be wary about the NATO role in the former Yugoslavia. First, there was a long-standing sympathy in Russia for the Serbs who were fellow Orthodox Christian Slavs. The targets of NATO in Bosnia, whatever diplomatic euphemisms might be employed, were Serbia and the Bosnian Serbs. Second, post-Soviet Russia had by 1993 moved on from the new world order enthusiasms of the Gorbachev years and was hostile to NATO's expanding influence in eastern Europe, particularly among the former Soviet allies of the Warsaw Pact. With this ambiguity and suspicion surrounding its presence there, NATO in Bosnia could only provide 'a framework within which a group of states happened to be joined', rather than a formal partner of the Security Council.[7]

There were difficulties on the other side of the NATO–UN relationship as well. The monopoly of military power lay with NATO. It is unlikely that NATO would have accepted the subordinate position in the relationship assigned to regional agencies by Chapter VIII even if it had been a legal possibility. In October 1994 the NATO secretary-general, Willy Claes, dismissed quite unambiguously any idea that NATO was an adjunct to the

UN in Bosnia; the organization was not, he stated, 'a sub-contractor of the United Nations'.[8] It would be wrong, however, to allow later developments, when NATO seized the lead role in Bosnia, to create an impression of a resolute and determined military alliance tied uncomfortably to a weak and indecisive UN peacekeeping operation. NATO members, for a variety of reasons of national policy, were as reluctant as the Security Council to commit to enforcement action from the outset. The United States, though willing to criticize the performance of UNPROFOR, repeatedly declined to contribute troops to it. There were also intra-alliance differences among the European members of NATO rooted in the historical sympathies and attitudes we touched on earlier. Germany and France as well as Greece and Turkey had different views on the merits of each side's case in Bosnia. Additionally, a number of European members of NATO were also providing contingents for UNPROFOR and would have been especially vulnerable to attack if NATO had become perceived as an anti-Serb combatant. For most of the course of the Bosnian war, therefore, NATO's stance was no more aggressive than that of the UN.

The one area where there was some friction between NATO and the United Nations was in their differences of attitude and approach to air strikes against Serb ground forces breaching UN resolutions. Here the gap between the peacekeeping and the war-fighting mindset of the respective organizations was apparent. The secretary-general's representative in Bosnia was the Japanese diplomat, Yasushi Akashi. His delegated powers were considerable and put him in effective command of UN operations. As such, he was responsible for decisions about when and if NATO support should be called upon. Throughout his time in Bosnia, Akashi showed marked reluctance to use the NATO air power at his disposal. While his caution was no doubt motivated by genuine diplomatic and humanitarian motives, the result was to confirm the Serbian impression of a weak and indecisive multinational intervention. During 1994 and the first half of 1995 UNPROFOR, although it had by this time reached a formidable strength of more than 34,000, was increasingly subject to Serb aggression. This grew in step with the failure of the UN to use the NATO air power available to it either in direct tactical support of its forces or in punitive strikes against Serb assets. Sarajevo was the target of daily artillery and sniper attacks by the Bosnian Serbs that went largely unpunished, despite the presence of NATO warplanes in the skies above the city. In the meantime, fighting was intensifying in the central part of the country between Muslims and Bosnian Croats who were supported by units of the Croatian army.

The apparently endless and multidimensional conflict in Bosnia reached a bloody climax in July 1995. The Bosnian Serb army, now utterly contemptuous of UNPROFOR and untroubled by NATO's extremely limited use of air power, marched into the UN safe area of Srebrenica.

This was one of a small number of centres that had been designated to give safe haven to Muslim victims of Serb ethnic cleansing in eastern Bosnia. These areas had previously served a useful purpose when the determination of the UN to safeguard them had been made clear to the Serbs. The previous March, for example, a strong and credible threat of NATO strikes in defence of UN military observers on the ground had ended Serb attacks on the safe area of Gorazde. Now, however, the Serbs – under the direct command of their military leader, Ratko Mladic – met no resistance from the Dutch UNPROFOR contingent charged with the protection of the Srebrenica safe area. In front of the eyes of the humiliated UN troops virtually the entire male population of the town was herded on to trucks and driven to massacre sites in the surrounding hills. The death toll, though never fully established, was in the region of 8,000.

Srebrenica represented the greatest operational failure of peacekeeping in the UN's history. While the Rwandan genocide in 1994 had resulted in perhaps a hundred times the number of deaths at Srebrenica, the UN's culpability on the ground in that situation was much less. The UN force in Rwanda had neither the military capacity nor the mandate to control events. The blame for this lay in New York and the capitals of the permanent members of the Security Council and not with the peacekeeping operation on the ground. In Bosnia, in contrast, UNPROFOR was directly mandated to protect the safe areas. NATO aircraft patrolled the horizon, capable of inflicting massive damage on the Serb forces in the Srebrenica area and elsewhere in Bosnia. There could, moreover, be no illusions on the part of the Dutch and others about the fate of the Muslims under their protection after three bloody years of Serb atrocities in Bosnia. The events of July 1995 were, in short, a low point for the entire peacekeeping project and arguably the most disgraceful chapter in the history of the United Nations to date.

From peacekeeping to enforcement

Srebrenica marked the end of 'peacekeeping' in Bosnia. In its aftermath the enforcement option, which had always been available, was finally embraced. Now, partly as a result of a shift in the attitude of the American administration, partly because European public opinion finally began to stir after Srebrenica and in the face of the unrelenting Serb attacks of Sarajevo, NATO was finally ordered into action. The peacekeeping culture of the United Nations, which had dominated the intervention in Bosnia and which had been personified by Yasushi Akashi, was now supplanted with an uncompromising 'war-winning' approach. Although NATO's resort to decisive force had been constrained by intra-alliance politics and the risk aversion of many of its members, the organization remained first and foremost a military alliance. Once the diplomatic ground was cleared within the membership, NATO had no real difficulties in acting as a combat force. Throughout August and September 1995 NATO aircraft subjected the Serbs to intense and sustained attack, quickly exposing the limitations of the Bosnian Serb army when confronted by the modern technology of war that the alliance unleashed. The legal basis for the NATO campaign – aptly titled 'Operation Deliberate Force' – was unclear, but this concerned few outside Serbia and the Serbian areas of Bosnia. There was certainly no longer any reference to the 'dual key' held by both the UN and NATO that was supposed to determine the use of air power in Bosnia.

Within weeks Bosnian Serb military assets had been so reduced that there was no alternative to negotiation. In November 1995 Serbia, Croatia and Bosnia were, in effect, directed to participate in American-brokered negotiations in Dayton, Ohio. The agreement, eventually signed in Paris, involved the creation of two Bosnian 'statelets': a Muslim–Croat entity and a Serb one. The arrangement would be guaranteed by a NATO 'implementation force' (IFOR). The Bosnian war was therefore ended despite, rather than by, the efforts of its participants. This outcome appears to contradict a basic rule that we have asserted repeatedly in our exploration of the possibilities and limitations of peacekeeping up to now: that peace cannot be imposed if the necessary local preconditions do not exist. In the Bosnian case, however, it was not 'peacekeepers' who imposed the peace but a powerful regional military alliance whose members had made it clear that the continued conflict was not acceptable to their own national interests. In these circumstances, however unhappy and resentful the parties may have been at the terms of the settlement, they had no option but to accept it – along with the foreign administrators and military force put in place to implement it.

The United Nations was involved in the legitimization of these arrangements. A Security Council resolution following the Dayton agreement transferred all authority from UNPROFOR to IFOR, which would continue to be under NATO command.[9] A small police operation, the Mission in Bosnia and Herzegovina (UNMIBH) remained under UN control but its functions were restricted to support and training of local police forces. In all meaningful respects the UN had been sidelined by NATO. Over the previous year there had been a fundamental reversal in the balance of authority between the external actors involved in Bosnia, one which represented the ascendancy of enforcement over peacekeeping. The irony in this was that, having enforced peace, IFOR had created conditions in Bosnia that permitted it to operate on a day-to-day basis according to standard peacekeeping rules that would have been quite familiar to Dag Hammarskjöld. In Bosnia, however, these peacekeeping rules had currency only because of an initial demonstration of overwhelming force.

Macedonia and Kosovo: peacekeeping in the aftermath of international enforcement

South of Bosnia in the territory of the former Yugoslavia lay the ancient nation of Macedonia, or at least the portion of it that had been incorporated into the Yugoslav state after the First World War. The historic territory of Macedonia had been divided between Greece, Bulgaria and Serbia at the outbreak of the First World War. In the post-war settlement the part controlled by Serbia became a component of the new Yugoslavia. When Yugoslavia began to disintegrate, Macedonia constituted its southernmost republic and, like Slovenia at the other geographical extreme of the country, it did not host any significant Serb diaspora. Its declaration of independence in September 1991, therefore, provoked none of the violence that erupted in Croatia and Bosnia. Nevertheless, Macedonia remained close to the epicentre of the violence that descended on the Balkans in the early 1990s. Understandably, there was considerable nervousness in the new state that it could fall victim to a spillover of violence from its neighbours' crises. As well as having a border with Serbia and its troubled 'autonomous area' of Kosovo, Macedonia also had a frontier with Albania, another former communist state in upheaval in the 1990s.[10]

This was not the most promising regional environment for the new, under-resourced state to have to establish itself in (Map 20). In November 1992 the government of the 'Former Yugoslav Republic of Macedonia' (FYROM), as the country was formally known, approached Boutros-Ghali with a request for the deployment of military observers to its borders to monitor their security.[11] The secretary-general in fact went further, recommending a battalion-strength deployment of more than 700 troops and observers that would be provided by an expanded UNPROFOR.[12] The Macedonian Command of UNPROFOR was unique in being the one component of the UN peacekeeping effort in the former Yugoslavia that had an American contingent. There was some scepticism about Washington's motives in offering its 300-strong contribution to UNPROFOR in Macedonia. There were suspicions that its primary purpose was to deflect criticism of America's refusal to provide troops for UNPROFOR in the more dangerous conditions of Bosnia where they could have added immeasurably to the force's credibility.

In March 1995 the Macedonia operation was detached from UNPROFOR (coincidentally on the eve of the draw-down of the Protection Force that followed the Dayton agreement on Bosnia at the end of the year). The new mission was the Preventive Deployment Force (UNPREDEP), which by the end of the year had established a line of observation posts along the border with Yugoslavia between which mobile patrols were carried out. At this point Macedonia's borders were among the most 'observed' in the world. Almost, it appeared, in compensation for continuing failure in Bosnia, the whole architecture of European security seemed to be brought to bear on Macedonia in a vast preventive effort. As well as UNPREDEP there was an observer mission from the OSCE, an institution whose early involvement in the Yugoslav crisis carried the high expectations of those who hailed a new post-cold war European security and which signally failed to live up to them. There was also a European Commission monitoring mission in FYROM.

Whether all this attention was actually necessary in the mid-1990s is open to question. Ironically, however, just at the point in the crisis of the former Yugoslavia at which a major UN presence would have been fully justified in Macedonia, UNPREDEP was withdrawn when China vetoed the renewal of its mandate. The security situation across the border in the Serbian territory of Kosovo had deteriorated markedly during the conflicts in the other parts of the former Yugoslavia. Kosovo was not a 'republic' of the Yugoslav Federation in the same way as Slovenia, Croatia and Bosnia had been. Its status was the lesser one of 'autonomous area', over which Serbia exercised control. The indigenous population of Kosovo were ethnically Muslim Albanian (known as 'Kosovars'), but there was a considerable Serb population, and the area's history gave it an almost mythic place in the narrative of Serbian nationhood. Throughout much of the lifespan of Yugoslavia, Kosovo had been a restless political entity and was therefore more than vulnerable to the ripple of violence that spread from other parts of the old Yugoslav state in the 1990s. At this time, too, heightened Serbian nationalism made itself felt in the discriminatory administration and policing of Kosovo and contributed to growing Kosovar resentment.

In 1996 a long campaign of largely non-violent agitation for greater autonomy was met with increased Serbian repression. In consequence, Kosovar nationalism took a military turn with the birth of the Kosovo Liberation Army (KLA). Within two years the territory was close to outright war, with the KLA fighting pitched battles against the JNA and local police and paramilitary forces. Atrocities against the civilian population, an inseparable part of the conflicts elsewhere in the former Yugoslavia, became common. Apparently now inured to the condemnation of the international community, the Milosevic regime failed to respond to external criticism of its policies, and intensified its offensives against the KLA and its supporters in early 1999. This hard-line nationalist response seemed to make political sense for the regime in Belgrade, which was still licking its wounds after the disastrous wars in Croatia and Bosnia. If Milosevic assumed that the diplomatic manoeuvrings and evasions that had worked for him through the early 1990s still constituted a viable policy, however, he had badly miscalculated. Srebrenica and its impact on the conscience of the west had completely changed the rules of the game. Britain and the United States now took a lead in getting a NATO commitment to decisive action. After the failure of negotiations hastily convened in France, a bombing campaign was launched against Belgrade and other targets in Serbia and in Kosovo itself. During the ensuing war Serb forces attempted to ethnically cleanse Kosovo of its Albanian population, a futile undertaking that merely stiffened NATO's resolve to impose its own peace on the territory. Thousands of Kosovars flooded across the border into Macedonia with lesser movements into Albania and the Yugoslav republic of Montenegro.

It was indicative of how far the narrative of conflict in the former Yugoslavia had moved on since the mid-1990s that no serious consideration was given to a UN military intervention in Kosovo. The 'peacekeeping phase' that had been so unsuccessful in Bosnia was simply removed from the Kosovo crisis where first recourse was to NATO enforcement (Map 26). Tellingly, too, this enforcement was undertaken unilaterally by the alliance with no reference to the regional collective security arrangements of Chapters VII and VIII of the United Nations Charter. In the case of the former Yugoslavia at least, the end of the cold war had not cleared the way for the application of the remedies planned in 1945. Chinese and probably Russian vetoes would almost certainly have blocked Article 43 action against Serbia. By acting as a military alliance NATO simply presented a strategic fait accompli that the other major powers, however resentful, had little option but to accept. The UN role began only after the imposition of a NATO peace in June 1999, which a ruined Serbia had no option but to accept. The UN involvement took the form of the Interim Administration Mission in Kosovo (UNMIK), which was to work with both the European Union and the OSCE to provide basic services in the territory. Military security remained firmly in the hands of NATO.

In contrast to the other post-conflict areas of the old Yugoslavia, Kosovo occupies a constitutional limbo in the international system. The other component parts that broke away went on to build new nation states (however haltingly in the case of Bosnia). Kosovo, however, cannot be considered either as a feasible candidate for independent statehood or, realistically, as still a part of Serbia. The problems for the fabric of the international state system caused by the end of Yugoslavia therefore remain to be fully resolved. The convulsions of the 1990s brought the full gamut of international intervention, but none of this – from peacekeeping to uncompromising enforcement – proved right for all of the complexities involved in the break-up of such a socially and ethnically diverse multinational state.

Aftermath to the Soviet Union

The parallel situation further east, in the vast territory once occupied by the Soviet Union, brought somewhat different problems for the international system. At root, though, the fundamental question was the same as that posed in the former Yugoslavia: how the system was to absorb with minimum upheaval a series of successor states emerging from an imperfect process of disaggregation. While in Yugoslavia the primary cause of conflict lay in the refusal of the existing state's dominant entity – Serbia – to accept the actual process, in the former Soviet Union the dominant entity – Russia – seemed to come to terms with the change to its former position. The difficulties emerged here in the next phase of adjustment: the establishment of effective relations among the newly created states themselves. This was not a general problem throughout the former Soviet Union. When the violence generated by the secession of only four states from Serbian-dominated Yugoslavia is considered, then the relatively peaceful creation of fourteen new independent entities (excluding Russia itself) from the republics of the USSR is in many respects remarkable. Indeed, eleven of these new states immediately joined with Russia to form a new regional organization, the Commonwealth of Independent States (CIS).[13]

Admittedly, in some regions of the former Soviet Union the adjustment has led to conflicts that have not been subject to peacekeeping. A cease-fire in the long-running separatist conflict in the Trans-Dniester region between Moldova and Ukraine has been enforced by Russian troops, though the OSCE has had a monitoring role there. The same body in its earlier incarnation as the CSCE had much grander plans for a peace-keeping role in one part of the former USSR. In 1992 a major conflict broke out between the Transcaucasus states of Armenia and Azerbaijan. At issue was the position of the predominantly ethnic Armenian enclave of Nagorno-Karabakh in Azerbaijan. The United Nations declined to intervene there, deciding instead that it would provide an opportunity for Europe's new post-cold war regional security arrangements to prove themselves. Accordingly, in 1994 the OSCE proposed to create its own large-scale multinational force to secure peace in the area. The operation was to be subject to Security Council approval under the 'regional arrangements' of Chapter VIII of the Charter, but otherwise it was to be a wholly OSCE undertaking. Continuing fighting in Nagorno-Karabakh led to the OSCE quietly suspending its plans, however, and restricting its intervention to the provision of good offices. Elsewhere in the former Soviet Union, 'foreign' intervention was ruled out for constitutional reasons. The war in Chechnya, where separatists sought to establish a new independent state after the dissolution of the Soviet Union, has been one of the most destructive and deadly of all the conflicts in the region. But the long-drawn-out crisis in Chechnya has been a 'domestic' rather than an international one as the territory at issue lies within the internationally recognized borders of Russia.

In two parts of the CIS, Georgia and Tajikistan, post-Soviet conflicts with cross-border implications have led to United Nations involvement. In both cases, however, Russia and the CIS have had a prominent role in the peacemaking and peacekeeping processes. This has meant that the UN missions in the countries have pursued a new type of mandate.

They have been 'secondary peacekeepers' with responsibility for monitoring or liaising with the activities of the local agency, which in both Georgia and Tajikistan was a CIS peacekeeping force. The approach was not unique to the former Soviet Union. As we will see, while these operations were under way, the UN was involved in similar arrangements in west Africa (see Chapter 10). These inter-agency relationships were more successful in the Soviet successor states where the UN's main partner was, after all, one of the permanent members of the Security Council.

Georgia-Abkhazia: instability, secession and regional intervention

The Republic of Georgia lies at the eastern end of the Black Sea between Russia in the north and Turkey in the south. This location made Georgia the object of a centuries-long struggle for dominance by two great empires, Russian and Ottoman. Russian control was more or less established in the second half of the nineteenth century but was contested by a vigorous Georgian nationalism right up to the Bolshevik revolution of 1917. In the ensuing disorder throughout the former Russian empire, Georgia declared itself independent and was recognized as such by the First World War allied powers. But in 1922 the territory was re-annexed to Russia when, on the order of Stalin who was himself a Georgian, the Red Army marched into the capital Tbilisi. For the next seven decades Georgia, along with Armenia and Azerbaijan, formed the three Transcaucasus republics of the Soviet Union.

With the Gorbachev reforms of the late 1980s, nationalist politics began to flourish once again in Georgia, and the territory declared itself independent of the USSR in April 1991. Georgia had long been famous – or notorious – for the depth and extent of its patrimonial political culture and the often violent intrigue that surrounded it. These features were evident in the new, authoritarian regime of Zviad Gamsakhurdia, which took power after the break from the Soviet Union and which soon found itself under extreme pressure. At the beginning of 1992 Gamsakhurdia was deposed and replaced by a State Council, the most prominent figure on which was the former Soviet foreign minister and Gorbachev ally Eduard Shevardnadze. The highly factionalized political culture of Georgia, however, meant that the old regime was not likely to go quietly, and Gamsakhurdia supporters posed a continuing challenge to the new government. Simultaneously, violent secessionist pressures provoked by the centralizing tendencies of the post-Soviet regime grew in the northern areas of Abkhazia and South Ossetia on Georgia's border with Russia. Mounting tensions led, in the summer of 1992, to an attempt by the local leadership in Abkhazia to sever the territory completely from Georgia. The ensuing fighting between the secessionist forces in Abkhazia and the

Georgian army led to the death of about 200 people and an outflow of refugees across the border into southern Russia.

Attempts by Moscow to negotiate a settlement between the Abkhazians and Georgians met with little success initially, but in the summer of 1993 a fragile ceasefire came into force. This was to be followed by the progressive demilitarization of the Abkhazia flashpoints and the reintegration of the territory with Georgia. At this point the United Nations was approached to provide military observers. In August 1993 the Security Council obliged by creating the Observer Mission in Georgia (UNOMIG).[14] Before the agreed body of military observers had been deployed, however, the never fully effective ceasefire broke down and the UN involvement was all but suspended (Map 12).

The crisis had nevertheless been internationalized by the prospect of a UN observer mission and in May 1994 a new agreement (developed not by Russia alone but by mediators from the UN and from the OSCE) was signed by the parties in Moscow. While largely similar to that of the previous year's arrangement in its political terms, the prospects for the implementation of the new agreement were to be bolstered by the presence of a Russian-led CIS peacekeeping force. UNOMIG would now have a revised and expanded mandate. Its 136 military observers would, in addition to patrolling the demilitarized area in Abkhazia, monitor the operations of the CIS force.[15] While there was no general return to fighting in the following years during UNOMIG's deployment, the situation in Abkhazia and the elaboration of its long-term relationship with Georgia advanced very little. The year 2001 in particular saw great tension, and a situation arose in which UNOMIG personnel were abducted by Abkhazian forces, something that the unarmed military observers could do nothing to prevent, reliant as they were on the CIS force for their security. The Russian-led peacekeepers performed adequately in immensely difficult political and operational circumstances. Neither the Abkhazian nor the Georgian leaderships seemed either able or willing to control their own forces. As a result, ceasefire violations were common and the progress towards a sustainable political settlement perpetually frustrated.[16]

Continued instability in Georgia itself did nothing to create the basic political conditions that would make a settlement involving reintegration attractive to the Abkhazia separatists. In November 2003, after eleven years in which little had been done to tackle the country's widespread poverty, crime and corruption, the government of Eduard Shevardnadze was overthrown. The role – or more correctly the identity – of the CIS force itself became an issue in the crisis, with Georgia's centuries-old nationalist suspicions of Moscow's intentions stirred up once again. Shevardnaze's past in the upper levels of the old Soviet leadership raised questions about Russia's neutrality in the political campaign to oust his regime. Consequently, the presence of a large Russian military force in Georgia, peacekeeping role or not, caused great suspicion in a political culture in which suspicion had long occupied a central place. In Georgia, as elsewhere, peacekeeping carried out by a dominant regional power is fraught with difficulties that the UN as a global body is usually free of. In Abkhazia, while the UN was able to perform its 'secondary' role quite successfully within its limited terms, the CIS force had to learn a lesson long-familiar to their United Nations counterparts: that without the basis of sustainable peace in the political relationships at the centre of a conflict, it is virtually impossible to impose one, regardless of the strength or commitment of the external forces involved.

Tajikistan: civil war and dangerous borders

The Central Asian Republic of Tajikistan became independent of the USSR in September 1991. Its government, though, remained markedly pro-Russian, largely because the leadership of the old Communist Party retained a strong grip on the country's political system even after independence. This apparently smooth transition from Soviet Republic to independent state, however, belied complex and combustible political realities. For many years before the end of the USSR Tajikistan had seen repeated anti-communist, pro-Islamist agitation. In the 1980s this had been a cause of considerable concern to Moscow because of Tajikistan's long southern border with Afghanistan where Soviet troops were struggling against the Islamist resistance of the various *mujahideen* groups. In 1992, after the independence of Tajikistan, a series of anti-government, mainly Islamist demonstrations in the capital Dushanbe set the fuse for a destructive civil war. In the coming years some 50,000 people were killed and about 12 per cent of the country's population were turned into refugees, with some 60,000 crossing the border into Afghanistan.

Here, as in Georgia, Russia led attempts to find a settlement. To this end it assembled a meeting between Tajikistan and its former Soviet Central Asian neighbours, Kazakhstan, Kyrgyzstan and Uzbekistan, in Moscow in September 1993. Here it was decided that a CIS force should be established for Tajikistan. The Collective Peacekeeping Forces in Tajikistan, as the venture was called, had the task of stabilizing the situation in the country in order to smooth the way to peacemaking between the sides. Specifically, it was to provide security for the distribution of humanitarian aid to the thousands of internally displaced civilians and create conditions that would allow them and those who had fled out of the country to return to their homes. The CIS force had some success in its mandated tasks, though in truth the convulsion of violence over the previous year had left the government and its enemies with little energy or resources left to continue the struggle. This did not mean, though, that a long-term peace agreement was easily arrived at; the political positions of the sides were barely reconcilable. Eventually, however, talks held in Russia and in Iran led to an outline agreement in September 1994, part of which involved a supervisory role for the United Nations. On the urging of secretary-general Boutros-Ghali, the Security Council agreed to the creation of a small 'Mission of Observers in Tajikistan' (UNMOT) in November 1994. The mandate of the mission was to verify the maintenance of the ceasefire, to maintain contact with the parties to the conflict and provide good offices when required (Map 30). UNMOT was also to liaise with the CIS peacekeeping operation but not, as in the case of Georgia, to monitor its activities in any supervisory sense. It was to maintain similar contacts with an OSCE political mission that was also engaged in the peacemaking effort.

For some time after the 1994 agreement the situation seemed to be improving, but in July 1995 there was a major incursion of opposition forces across the border from Afghanistan (at this time a virtually stateless territory fought over by different warlord and Islamist factions) and the civil war resumed. When another agreement was reached in 1997, again under Russian and Iranian pressure, the role of UNMOT was expanded to include involvement in an agreed programme of demobilization, disarmament and reintegration of fighters.[17] Although the following years were punctuated by further outbreaks of fighting, political momentum was achieved and elections in 2000 opened the prospect of a sustainable settlement. The poll followed shortly after the withdrawal of UNMOT in May 2000 when the Security Council judged it to have successfully completed its mandate. Russian forces remained in the still troubled region, however.

Peacekeeping in Europe and among the successor states of the Soviet Union after the cold war proved both more necessary and more complex than those hailing a new world order in the late 1980s and early 1990s had expected. Certainly it was to be predicted that in principle Europe would be part of the radically widened area open for multilateral peacekeeping once the bipolar spheres of interest ceased to exist. But it was not anticipated that peacekeeping would be necessary in fact. The popular European view in 1990 was that peacekeeping would remain – and expand – as an essentially Third World activity. The necessary, and for the most part desirable, adjustments to the European sub-system were expected to take place in a fundamentally 'civilized' environment, through the mechanisms of newly installed – or restored – democratic systems. As we have observed, in many places this was the reality. Germany was unified and Czechoslovakia 'un-unified' through democratic if not always amicable processes. But few predicted the dark chaos that would descend on the centre of Europe with the break-up of Yugoslavia or the extent of the external intervention that would be required to restore order to that part of the system.

The political complexity of the peacekeeping response in Europe and the former Soviet Union added to the problem of its unexpectedness. The end of the cold war saw Europe's own institutions enter a phase of considerable optimism and self-assurance. The European Community (as it was then called) had been steadily enlarging since the early 1970s and now looked forward to a dramatic growth in both its numbers and its political authority. In particular, the discourse of a common foreign and security policy for the Community was forging ahead. The CSCE in Europe was transforming itself into a permanent 'organization' – the OSCE – which was intended to have a major role in the security affairs of the states of the two cold war blocs whose relations had been transformed. NATO, the former western alliance, was engaged on a major exercise in institutional self-preservation as it sought to invent a new role for itself relevant to a transformed system in which its original purpose had suddenly become irrelevant. If peacekeeping should become necessary in Europe, therefore, Europe itself would surely be equipped to provide it.

It did not work out this way, however. At the outset of the Yugoslavian crisis, European Community and CSCE/OSCE involvement proved largely ineffectual, and the involvement of NATO, arguably 'out of area', proved disproportionate and possibly counterproductive. The much vaunted new European security architecture was therefore either inadequate or inappropriate to the peacekeeping requirements of Croatia and Bosnia. The United Nations, as the only institution with the necessary experience and 'culture' of peacekeeping, was therefore called upon to undertake an enormous intervention. That this intervention failed to 'solve' the problems of the former Yugoslavia was due to the fact that these particular problems were simply insoluble through the sort of interpositionary peacekeeping that UNPROFOR was configured to carry out. This would not necessarily be the case elsewhere in Europe or the former Soviet Union. When, after the massacres at Srebrenica, this truth became impossible to evade, the necessary enforcement action was undertaken by the institution best equipped to undertake it: the regional military alliance. While this was, perhaps, the only route forward in the particular circumstances of the former Yugoslavia, it was not 'peacekeeping'.

In the former Soviet Union, however, NATO was clearly not an option for any intervention role, whether an enforcement one or otherwise. Here too the other components of the post-cold war security architecture proved of limited use. The CSCE/OSCE performed a number of important mediatory functions in various successor states, but it did not have the capacity to mount significant peacekeeping operations, a truth that became evident after its aborted plans for peacekeeping in the Nagorno-Karabakh conflict between Armenia and Azerbaijan. The obvious regional body to assume the role of peacekeeper (and if necessary 'enforcer') among the former Soviet republics was the CIS. But there were difficulties for the CIS deriving from the dominance of Russia in the organization. Here too, then, the United Nations had a key role to perform, though one adapted to the realities of the new post-Soviet regional sub-system. The UN, by mounting relatively modest operations in Georgia and Tajikistan, could give the necessary degree of international legitimacy and respectability to Russian and CIS efforts.

The story of peacekeeping in Africa, to which we turn next, bears a number of similarities to the experience in post-cold war Europe and the former Soviet Union. In Africa, too, a local institutional architecture existed, at both the continental and the regional level. But there as well questions around both the adequacy and appropriateness of local peacekeeping efforts led inescapably to extensive United Nations involvement.

9 Africa I

Decolonization and contested legitimacy

The extremes of success and failure in peacekeeping have nowhere been as sharply illustrated as in sub-Saharan Africa. We have already had a sense of how wide the spectrum of performance and outcomes can be in a single operation: that in the Congo between 1960 and 1964, which we explored in Chapter 5. The subsequent record, from the late 1980s onwards, has embraced great successes (for example in Namibia and Mozambique) and some of the worst peacekeeping disasters (as in Somalia and Rwanda). This contrasting record has been due to the particular character of most of the conflicts to which peacekeeping has responded in Africa. The classic Hammarskjöldian model has been a rarity in the continent. The inapplicability of the inter-state buffer form of peacekeeping to African realities was evident from the outset of African peacekeeping in the Congo. There, post-Suez confidence in the potential of peacekeeping for the management of crises on the political perimeter of the cold war system was tested to breaking point as, one by one, the tenets of the original model were found wanting.

Peacekeeping and the African State

'Traditional' inter-state peacekeeping *has* taken place in Africa, most recently between Ethiopia and Eritrea after their war in 1998. There have also been military observer missions on the familiar pattern of the Middle East and south Asia, the clearest example being that between Chad and Libya in 1994. These 'straightforward' interventions in conflicts between sovereign states, however, remain untypical of peacekeeping in Africa where external intervention has been primarily an 'intra-state' activity. Although African conflicts have generally had an international *dimension* (UN interventions would, after all, be 'illegal' otherwise), their primary sources have been internal. Frequently, they have been 'international' in the sense that in many parts of Africa there has historically been a discontinuity between ethnic and political borders. The Great Lakes region, which encompasses a constellation of some of Africa's most unstable states, is just the most striking example of this. Elsewhere, though, antagonists have deliberately 'internationalized' internal conflicts because they have seen a tactical benefit in doing so. This has been a feature of a number of conflicts in the west African region. In other parts internal crises have become international because they have reached a point at which the state has simply ceased to exist as a unit of the larger system, thus threatening the integrity of the whole. This happens when a 'failed state' passes to the next stage of entropy and becomes a 'collapsed state'.

The state and its apparently endemic weakness has indeed lain at the root of virtually all peacekeeping interventions in post-colonial Africa. This gives rise to an obvious question: is peacekeeping in Africa a 'unique' activity, distinct from that in, say, the Middle East or Asia? Or have UN interventions in Africa simply been more frequent and more dramatic than elsewhere. Put another way, is there anything inherent to UN interventions in, for example, Mozambique, Angola and Somalia that distinguishes them from others in, say, Cyprus or Lebanon or Cambodia? It is in fact difficult to locate anything wholly unique in the nature of Africa's conflicts. Underlying conditions similar to those in any African crisis have prevailed elsewhere throughout the history of peacekeeping. Africa's 'specialness', if it exists, lies in the frequency of conflict and its intensity rather than its intrinsic character. We can identify three phenomena, none unique to Africa but particularly toxic in their effects there, that have contributed to its disproportionate claim on the global peacekeeping effort since the 1990s. First, there is the effect of the withdrawal of externally imposed order. Second, there is the exceptionally high level of African 'dependency' in terms of the global economy, which has stifled economic development and contributed to domestic unrest and conflict. Third, there is the stress in a number of African polities between the idea of the sovereign territorial state and underlying political cultures that are rooted in older forms of social relations.

We have already spoken of the end of the cold war as having a double-sided effect on the development of peacekeeping. Yes, the end of bipolar sensitivities widened the political and geographical areas open to peacekeeping but, at the same time, the loosening of the grip of the superpowers on their spheres of political influence created new conditions for conflict among the ex-client states. In Africa this was a dual-layered phenomenon. First, decolonization in the 1960s and 1970s removed the order imposed by the imperial powers. The new post-independence frontiers, which were based entirely on colonial borders, in many places exposed a mismatch between ethnic and national loyalties and generated tensions between the recently formed territorial states. Second, Africa underwent the process of superpower 'withdrawal' that we have just described. In the north-east of Africa in particular this was a major contributing factor in the spread of factional violence within states and tensions between states.

Throughout Africa these tensions were exacerbated by a general failure of economic development. While other parts of the post-colonial world, most notably in Asia, overcame 'underdevelopment' to a point where they became major actors in the global economy, in Africa this did not happen. Whether African underdevelopment was the result of the deliberate manipulation of the 'world system' by the dominant states of the north, as dependency theorists argued, or whether it was due to factors internal to African states themselves has been hotly debated since the 1970s. Those who see Africa's problems as externally generated point to underdevelopment not as an unfortunate condition to be overcome but as an intentional 'policy' imposed on the global system by the states of the north in order to safeguard their own relative advantage. African development, in this view, would threaten the economic dominance of the north and therefore had to be suppressed. The result has been poverty-fuelled conflict that has frequently been the object of peacekeeping interventions.

One does not have to dismiss entirely the position of the dependency theorists in this debate to acknowledge that their opponents have offered some interesting alternative arguments that point to local 'cultural' reasons for underdevelopment. It is possible to portray 'statehood' in Africa as an ultimate act of colonialism. The modern state, the basis of the Westphalian system, is a western construct that emerged organically from western political culture. Indigenous African culture before the irruption of the European imperialists was usually 'patrimonial'. That is to say, it was based on duties and obligations between rulers ('patrons') and the ruled (their 'clients'). The geographically delimited state, even where it might have existed, rarely played any part in this. When they ended their imperial adventure in Africa, however, the European states sought to 'impose' the forms of the territorial state on their former colonies because they could conceive of no alternative arrangement. This was what the inflexible structure of a state-based international system demanded. Tensions between post-colonial 'statism' and the re-emergence of patrimonial forms of relationship from a still robust pre-colonial political culture contributed both to conflict and to the state's inability to deal with it.

Together these interconnected factors – economic dependency and friction between underlying political culture and imposed forms of governance – produced a propensity for conflict throughout post-colonial Africa. By 2005 this had brought into being twenty UN peacekeeping operations in or between seventeen different African states. It is possible to classify these undertakings in different ways. There is, for example, some regional logic to the peacekeeping experience in Africa, with common factors linking conflicts in southern Africa and distinguishing them from those in, say, west Africa. A straightforward chronological approach to exploring African peacekeeping is also possible, though not perhaps very revealing of underlying linkages. For our own exploration, however, we will focus on function, and examine the peacekeeping record in Africa on the basis of what particular operations set out to achieve.

First, we will look at those 'conventional' inter-state operations that have taken place in trans-Saharan Africa and the Horn of Africa. Next, we will consider the role of peacekeeping in managing problems surrounding decolonization and the transfer of power to post-colonial regimes. The Congo in the early 1960s, which we have already examined in the context of the cold war, would be an obvious example of this peacekeeping role, but there were others that involved the United Nations in the 1990s, most notably Namibia and the Western Sahara. Then we will explore post-colonial crises of state legitimacy that have emerged as the state comes under challenge either from groups excluded from power within it or from the outside by other states or their clients. The list here is a lengthy one and includes Angola, Mozambique, Rwanda, Burundi, the CAR and Côte d'Ivoire. Then, in the next chapter, we will examine the peacekeeping response to the ultimate challenge Africa has posed to the international system: the disintegration of the territorial state as a viable unit. The problems of the 'collapsed state' go beyond difficulties around decolonization or even post-colonial legitimacy. They involve the effective disappearance of the state as a national and international actor and its replacement by rudimentary forms of political organization often involving so-called 'warlordism'. These are not, of course, watertight categories sealed off from each other. Many African conflicts could be said to lie between these sub-divisions. But some framework of classification, however imperfect, is necessary if we are to make sense of the enormous complexity of African conflicts and the peacekeeping response to them.

'Conventional' peacekeeping in Africa

In some respects the rarity of inter-state peacekeeping in Africa is surprising. While the predominance of intra-state operations is not unexpected in the political and social setting of Africa, it might be thought that there would also be a frequent need for interposition forces on state borders. After all, these borders were, famously, arbitrary colonial constructs, supposedly designed for the convenience of imperial exploitation rather than as rational 'national' divisions. Yet only two interventions out of the many peacekeeping ventures in Africa have been concerned with border disputes between sovereign states. On examination, however, this is not perhaps quite so surprising. For one thing, the notion that the colonial frontiers that formed the basis of the borders between the independent states of Africa were drawn haphazardly with rulers on maps is misleading. For the most part imperial cartographers established borders along obvious geographical barriers, whether rivers, mountain ranges or lake shores. This did not prevent the division of ethnic groups by colonial frontiers but, logically, it reduced it. Second, whatever the imperfections of the territorial division of Africa imposed by the imperialists, it was accepted in its entirety by post-independence governments. The prospect of re-arranging the continent was simply too daunting for states and organizations already facing major political and economic challenges. Serious border disputes leading to military conflict are not common in Africa, despite the sheer number of national frontiers concentrated in its land-mass. The type of state-to-state international wars that were familiar in twentieth-century Europe, Asia and Latin America have been rare in Africa. Before the 1990s there were really only two such conflicts, both during the 1970s: those between Ethiopia and Somalia and between Tanzania and Uganda. Consequently, there have been only two peacekeeping operations designed to manage conflicts between African states. One of these, between Chad and Libya, was a classic (though very modest) military observation mission.

In May 1994 a small group of officers from the United Nations operation then under way in Western Sahara was seconded to the UN Aouzou Strip Observer Group (UNASOG) on the disputed Sahara border between Chad and Libya.[1] The operation followed a long period of political instability in Chad during the 1970s and 1980s in which Libya, under unpredictable President Muammar Gaddafi, had been deeply involved in its support of favoured factions. In the late 1980s the pro-western, anti-Libyan faction leader Hissène Habré managed to drive Libyan troops who had entered Chad from the north back towards the common border region of the Aouzou Strip.

This development highlighted the absence of any agreed delimitation of the desert frontier. The colonial powers in Chad and Libya – France and Italy respectively – had never reached a definitive agreement, largely because of the Strip's remoteness and lack of economic or strategic interest. Chad and Libya now submitted the issue to the ICJ for arbitration, both confident of a finding in their favour. In the event the ICJ determined that the Strip belonged to Chad, and it became necessary to effect the withdrawal of Libyan forces and installations from the area. The uncharacteristic cooperativeness with which Libya had submitted the issue to the ICJ did not survive the finding against it. But, however reluctantly, it chose not to reject the outcome and agreed that its withdrawal could be monitored by the UN (Map 5). The observer group was extremely small, never exceeding fifteen in number, and it encountered no difficulties from either party. UNASOG was a small-scale and in some respects insignificant peacekeeping operation. But against a contemporary background of an apparent collective failure of African peacekeeping (in Somalia, in Rwanda, in Angola) it provided a limited, but significant, morale boost for those who insisted in the face of the apparent evidence that the UN could make a significant contribution to the resolution of Africa's conflicts.

Between Ethiopia and Eritrea: interposition in the Horn of Africa

In April 1993 the new state of Eritrea came into being in the Horn of Africa. Eritrea had been an Italian colony taken over by the allies during the Second World War and in 1952 it had formed a federation with independent Ethiopia. The fears of Eritrean politicians that this would be a prelude to annexation by the larger state were realized ten years later when it was reduced to the status of a province of Ethiopia. The separatist campaign began soon after and intensified in the 1970s and 1980s. Immediately after Eritrean independence in 1993 relations with Ethiopia were remarkably cordial considering the nature of the two countries' past relationship. For a time both states were held up as exemplars of the predicted 'African renaissance' of the 1990s. The personal relationship between their two leaders, Meles Zenawi of Ethiopia and Isaias Afwerki of Eritrea, was cooperative and amicable, and the two countries remained closely integrated economically. These positive outward signs, however, disguised underlying tensions. Joint currency and financial arrangements maintained between Eritrea and Ethiopia were delicate and difficult to manage. And in the mid-1990s Eritrea was acquiring the reputation of difficult neighbour, following diplomatic spats with both Sudan and Yemen. There was, therefore, less surprise in the region than outside it when a border war broke out between Eritrea and Ethiopia at the beginning of May 1998.

The immediate cause of the war was a dispute over a not very significant 400-square-kilometre patch of land in northern Ethiopia around the town of Badme. Although each side blamed the other for initiating the fighting, it is probable that the situation was engineered by Eritrea, regardless of who fired the first shot. The front rapidly expanded and intense fighting, resulting in high military and civilian casualties, continued for the next two months. By July 1998 military conflict had subsided, but there was every indication that the war was far from over. Eritrean forces now occupied Badme and appeared to have achieved their territorial objectives. But Ethiopia remained capable of inflicting considerable punishment on its smaller neighbour. The straightforward nature of the conflict – an 'old-fashioned' war between two countries over disputed territory – and the previously 'good character' of the antagonists meant that there was no shortage of potential mediators ready to become involved. Italy, the United States and the Organization of African Unity (OAU), as well as the UN secretary-general Kofi Annan, all offered their good offices.[2] But the various settlement plans proposed were based on an initial return to the territorial status quo ante, which was unacceptable to Eritrea as it would have involved it surrendering its gains. In February 1999, however, Ethiopia launched a bloody counter-attack which drove the Eritreans out of Badme. After this they became much more receptive to the idea of an externally brokered peace.

United Nations, African and American negotiators worked throughout 1999 to find an acceptable formula. In the meantime, the costs of the war – human, economic, political and diplomatic – were beginning to press on both sides. Agreement was finally reached at talks in Algiers in mid-2000. A 'Temporary Security Zone' (TSZ) was to be established between the two opposing armies and this buffer would be patrolled by a UN force. This was intended to create the conditions for the negotiation of a permanent territorial settlement between the two states. Accordingly, the Security Council approved the formation of the UN Mission in Ethiopia and Eritrea (UNMEE) in September 2000.[3] The initial force, composed of contingents from Canada, India, Kenya and the Netherlands, quickly rose to a strength of 5,600 and was immediately deployed in the TSZ.

In the following years the UN presence provided a very effective line of separation between the sides and, despite regular peaks in tensions, there was no return to war on the border (Map 11). However, rather like the UN force in Cyprus, UNMEE threatened to become a successful peacekeeping operation trapped in position by an inadequate peacemaking process. Although an international border commission reported on the territorial dispute at the centre of the conflict (largely in favour of Eritrea) there was no decisive move towards a permanent settlement. The continuing UN presence allowed both sides to maintain their positions – both political and military – at minimum cost. The political price of movement appeared to be too high for states that, although well established and stable by sub-Saharan African standards, were still vulnerable to popular pressures against compromise.

Managing decolonization

The Congo operation of the early 1960s was, as we saw, a United Nations response to the consequences of a deeply flawed decolonization. Steering the international system through the often heavy weather of the end of empire was, for secretary-general Dag Hammarskjöld, a major task for the UN in general and its peacekeeping role in particular. The geographical focus of this would change as patterns of decolonization altered. The late 1940s and 1950s had seen difficult transfers of power in the Middle East and South Asia. By the 1960s attention had turned to Africa where the decolonization process promised to be even more complex and certainly more extensive.

In the early 1960s, therefore, there was a reasonable expectation that the Congo operation might be the first of many in Africa. In the event, however, peacekeeping did not become a feature of the major epoch of African decolonization. With few exceptions Belgium's other African territories, along with the much larger British and French empires south of the Sahara, passed to independence with little conflict. Difficulties would follow in many of these territories, as we will see, but the actual transfers of power took place remarkably smoothly. By the end of the 1960s there was little left to decolonize. The only European empires still to be dismantled were those of Portugal and Spain, though there were special difficulties around the existence of white minority regimes in South Africa and Rhodesia. The apparently orderly end of empire in Africa in the 1960s was no doubt a relief to those who had predicted the process would demand a major peacekeeping effort. The general optimism amid which the operation in the Congo was launched had evaporated when the danger and complexity of the situation there became plain. After that experience it is doubtful whether the United Nations would have been capable of responding to any significant demand for more peacekeeping to ease African independence. The resource cost of the Congo and the likely reluctance of contributors to supply forces for similar missions would have been major obstacles. Moreover, the damage inflicted on the UN itself by the Congo affair as it was pulled into politics of the cold war would have given pause for thought to even the most enthusiastic partisans of peacekeeping in New York.

If the nature of African decolonization in the 1960s relieved the UN of a potentially burdensome responsibility, by the late 1970s and 1980s, when problems were beginning to accumulate in Africa, peacekeeping in general had fallen dormant as détente gave way to a newly intensified period of bipolarity. Conflict in Africa in fact had played a part in this process. Perceived communist adventurism in the former Portuguese territories, particularly Angola, and growing competition for strategic advantage in the Horn of Africa had damaged détente some time before the Soviet invasion of Afghanistan at the end of 1979. With the beginning of the end of the cold war in the late 1980s, however, in Africa, as elsewhere, multilateral approaches to conflict became possible. The stored-up 'backlog' of such difficulties in Africa was enormous. It was in Africa, in fact, that the long period in which no new UN peacekeeping had been initiated came to an end in 1989. Among the earliest post-cold war operations were two which dealt with unusual but pressing problems of delayed decolonization in south-west and north-west Africa respectively.

'Transition assistance' in Namibia

'South West Africa', as modern-day Namibia was known, had been a German colony until the end of the First World War when it passed under a League of Nations mandate to South Africa. In 1946 the mandate was superseded by a Trusteeship arrangement under the new United Nations. South Africa, a regional state itself sharing a border with the mandated territory, was obviously in a different position from the other Trusteeship powers in Africa that had in all practical terms grafted the territories in trust to their own empires and prepared them for decolonization accordingly.[4] The South African government in Pretoria was attracted by the idea of simply annexing the territory instead. South West Africa, though physically large, was mostly desert and had a population of barely more than one and a half million. It had a long Atlantic coastline, however, which was important both strategically and economically to South Africa. Its fertile coastal strip had also been subject to white South African settlement during the period of the mandate. In the interior, South African companies began to exploit the territory's rich mineral resources, including precious metals and diamonds.

During the 1960s pressure mounted on South Africa, both from the UN and in the territory itself. The rapid expansion of the Afro-Asian presence in the UN in the 1960s had increased demands on the Security Council to take a harder line on Pretoria's evasion of its responsibility to bring South West Africa – by then increasingly known by its 'African' name, 'Namibia' – to independence. At the same time the South West African People's Organization (SWAPO), under the leadership of Sam Nujoma, had begun a guerrilla war of liberation. In 1970 the Security Council formally terminated the South African Trusteeship, making its continued occupation of the territory unlawful.[5] This position was confirmed by the ICJ the following year in a judgment that also required all states to refrain from any action that could sustain South Africa's presence in the territory.[6] The situation changed radically in 1975, however, with the independence of Angola under a pro-Soviet Marxist regime. The effect of this was probably to delay Namibia's decolonization until after the end of the cold war. Namibia now took on a new strategic importance for South Africa as a buffer with a hostile state that before had been a 'friendly' Portuguese colony. South Africa was now able to present its occupation of Namibia not as an attempt to extend the frontiers of apartheid in Africa but as an act of solidarity with the west. Although this was publicly dismissed as an unacceptable argument in the west, it undoubtedly had an effect – one that deepened as détente gave way to cold war once again. In the meantime the security situation in the territory and its impact on the larger region worsened dramatically. SWAPO now had a safe rear base in southern Angola from which to mount attacks on South African forces in Namibia. In response, South Africa launched incursions across the border into Angola. The presence of some 50,000 Cuban troops in Angola with whom the South Africans often clashed gave the situation a potentially serious cold war dimension. The South African occupation of Namibia and the Cuban presence in Angola therefore became linked in east–west diplomacy. In 1975 a self-appointed Contact Group composed of the five western members of the Security Council at that time (Canada and West Germany, which were non-permanent members, along with Britain, France and the United States) had begun a protracted diplomacy along with secretary-general Kurt Waldheim in search of a generally acceptable settlement. This led in 1978 to the adoption of a resolution that laid out the framework for an agreement based on free elections in the territory and a transfer of power overseen by a UN Transition Assistance Group (UNTAG).[7]

The plan immediately went into suspended animation. South Africa knew that free elections would mean the end of its rule in the territory. But more significantly, the return of the cold war and the Reagan administrations in Washington in the 1980s (and the Thatcher one in London) had changed the broader international setting of the Namibian problem. There was little enthusiasm in the west for the straightforward transfer of power to a Namibian regime friendly to pro-Soviet Angola. By this time Washington's approach to apartheid South Africa was based on a policy of so-called 'constructive engagement'. For all its manifest faults, the argument ran, the government in Pretoria was indisputably anti-communist. Washington would not, therefore, press Pretoria into a settlement that it did not consider to be in the west's broader interests.

In the later 1980s the global picture began to change, and this had implications for southern Africa as well as every other region whose politics had been shaped by cold war rivalries. South Africa's self-proclaimed role as bulwark against international communism was a rapidly devaluing currency as the Soviet 'threat' dissolved. At the same time, Moscow's support for the Marxist government in Angola and its Cuban ally became more conditional. In parallel with this changed international climate, the warring parties on the ground were becoming painfully aware that there was going to be no easy or obvious victory. Bloody stalemate prevailed in southern Angola and northern Namibia with little prospect of a military breakthrough on either side. The losses of the South African Defence Forces (SADF) raised comparisons with Vietnam among the white middle classes whose sons were liable to be conscripted and sent off to the battle zone. On the other side, Angola had known no peace or stability since its independence, and Cuba was increasingly hard pressed to sustain the human and economic demands of its presence in the country. An agreement was therefore reached at the end of 1988 that was based substantially on the 1978 Security Council resolution but with a plan for the withdrawal of Cuban forces from Angola grafted on to it. The scheme was endorsed by the Security Council in January 1989 and this finally brought UNTAG into material existence. The UN was committed to the deployment of a force of 4,650 troops and military observers by April 1989.[8]

The UNTAG that was eventually assembled in Namibia was a significantly smaller force than that foreseen at the time of the original 1978 resolution that had been based on a 7,500-strong presence (Map 22). UN commanders on the ground were unhappy with this as the force's mandate was multifaceted and potentially extremely demanding. Its responsibilities included the monitoring of a far from widely comprehended ceasefire arrangement across a vast terrain. It had in addition to oversee the demobilization of SWAPO fighters and the garrisoning of the South African troops. Then, with the stand-down of the SADF, the UN force would become responsible for law and order throughout the country. And, eventually, UNTAG would have to oversee a potentially violent election campaign and ensure the safety and integrity of the poll itself. The stretched resources of the operation were almost to cause its failure even before it had properly started. Just as the permanent ceasefire was about to take effect, a large force of SWAPO guerrillas moved across the Angolan border into northern Namibia in apparent defiance of the peace agreement. The South African government now demanded that the situation be dealt with. The secretary-general's representative in the country, Martti Ahtisaari (a Finnish diplomat who would later become his country's prime minister) had few options. The UN force had yet to be fully deployed and would probably have been inadequate in the crisis even if it had been. Eventually, Ahtisaari gave in to South African pressure and agreed that the SADF could engage the infiltrators. The result was a full-scale battle that left some 300 SWAPO fighters dead. The incident enraged African opinion and shook supporters of the peace process worldwide. The peacekeeping operation had been seriously compromised before it had even started to deal with its formal mandate. The UN had, it appeared, acted hand in glove with the forces of apartheid in Namibia whose presence had long ago been declared illegal by that same UN.

The process was put back on track only with great difficulty, but there was no comparable crisis during the rest of the UN presence in the territory. There was much tension to be managed, particularly as the scale of its likely defeat in the elections became clear to the South African government. While it had accepted that Namibia would become an independent state at the end of the process, Pretoria had hoped to retain its influence through the local pro-South African party, the Democratic Turnhalle Alliance (DTA). From early in the campaign, however, it became clear that SWAPO would have a convincing victory. A spoiling campaign of South African 'dirty tricks' began but had little effect on the march of events. When the elections were held in November 1989, just seven months after UNTAG's arrival, SWAPO's victory was all but absolute.[9] As predicted, UNTAG's resources were stretched during the process, but they proved sufficient in the end. In March 1990, less than a year after the arrival of the first UN troops, Namibia became independent under the presidency of Sam Nujoma. The appearance on South Africa's now sharply contracted border of a regime ruled by its former guerrilla enemies might have been expected to lead to long years of low-level conflict. But the larger tide of African history would soon change the situation utterly. Simultaneously with Namibia's independence, South Africa began on the road to majority rule. Within a very short time the whole diplomatic character of southern Africa had been transformed, with Namibia and the new South Africa becoming close regional allies.

The Angolan dimension to the linked diplomacy around Namibia's independence, which involved the withdrawal of Cuban forces, proved a text-book exercise in successful military observation by the UN. As the final agreement on Namibia was signed, Angola and Cuba approached secretary-general Pérez de Cuéllar with a request for an observation mission to oversee the withdrawal process. On 20 December 1988 the Security Council approved the formation of the Angola Verification Mission (UNAVEM).[10] The operation was a small one with about seventy observers in the field through most of the process. Its mandate was to verify the withdrawal of all Cuban military personnel from Angola through agreed air and sea ports. This it fulfilled several weeks ahead of the agreed date of June 1991 (Map 2).

Angola's future was not, as we will see, as fortunate as that of Namibia in the aftermath of this UN intervention, but as far as the secretary-general and the Security Council were concerned, the linked process had been a victory for peacekeeping. Twin solutions to grave long-standing problems in southern Africa – Namibian independence and Cuban withdrawal from Angola – had been agreed through successful UN peacemaking and implemented through effective UN military involvement. The UN's first venture back into the peacekeeping role after a decade of politically enforced inactivity had been successful and provided a good omen for the organization's role elsewhere in the post-cold war world. This optimism was not to be generally justified, as far as Africa was concerned at least. The success of the Namibia–Angola venture lay principally in the circumstances surrounding the peace process. Put at its simplest, each key actor was behind the settlement and committed to see it succeed. South Africa sought extrication from an increasingly unsustainable war. SWAPO discerned more or less total victory in its fight for independence. Angola wanted peace on its borders and the opportunity to focus on its internal problems. Cuba sought relief from an expensive and apparently limitless commitment to Angola. Behind these frontline actors the big non-regional players in the Security Council urged their respective clients on, making clear the lack of alternative to the settlement. Peacekeeping in these circumstances, as we have argued, is rarely an unsuccessful activity. But they were not circumstances that pertained in many other parts of Africa either at that time or in the future.

Western Sahara: the elusive pursuit of a referendum

A clear illustration of this was provided by another crisis of decolonization at the other geographical end of the continent. The large desert territory of Western Sahara sits on Africa's Atlantic coast, bordered in the south and east by Mauritania and in the north by Morocco, with a small frontier in the north-east with Algeria. From the late nineteenth century the territory was held by Spain, though effective imperial occupation did not go far beyond the coastal strip and was contested by the nomadic clans of the interior. In the twentieth century the territory acquired some importance as a source of phosphates, which gave Spain some return from what had been a largely uneconomic imperial conceit. The territory was little affected by the main wave of anti-imperialist nationalism that passed through the continent in the 1950s and 1960s, but in 1973 an anti-Spanish guerrilla campaign was launched by the Polisario movement that gave a unified political direction to the resentments of the desert clans.[11] The start of this anti-colonial struggle attracted the attention of the territory's neighbours. Morocco had a long-standing historical claim to Western Sahara pre-dating Spanish colonialism, while Mauritania was anxious not to be cut out of any eventual settlement that could bring it some desperately needed economic benefit. Algeria, at this time a leading Third World radical, supported the Polisario's struggle for independence and allowed it to establish rear bases across the border in the Algerian Sahara.

In 1975 Spain came to an agreement with Morocco and Mauritania by which 'independence' in February 1976 would be followed by the partition of the territory between its two neighbours, with the northern two-thirds passing to Morocco and the southern third to Mauritania. The transfer of power brought an intensification of the Polisario's efforts as it confronted a massive build-up of Moroccan and Mauritanian forces in the territory. On the political front the nationalists formed a government in exile, declaring the 'Saharan Arab Democratic Republic' (SADR) in Tindouf in the Algerian Sahara. The struggle went well for the Polisario for the first few years after the Spanish departure, culminating in 1979 with the withdrawal of Mauritania, leaving Morocco to lay claim to the entire territory. Morocco had in the meantime become more adept at the type of warfare it was forced to conduct in Western Sahara. The Moroccan strategy involved the improved use of air power and the construction of a sand wall – or 'berm' – around the greater part of the territory to counter Polisario raids from across the Algerian border. The struggle soon settled into stalemate.

The Western Sahara issue had proved a thorny one for the OAU, which, as the leading regional organization, had quickly been drawn into the diplomatic conflict. While Morocco was a powerful and influential member of the OAU, there were other African states in the late 1970s and 1980s that were strongly sympathetic to the Polisario. Aside from Algeria, the 'Afro-Marxist' states of Portuguese-speaking Africa backed the Polisario's struggle, and many other sub-Saharan states resented what they saw as the 'imperialism' of Morocco, which they did not fully acknowledge as a truly 'African' state. The OAU therefore sought to pass responsibility to the United Nations. Protracted 'proximity talks' were undertaken by secretary-general Pérez de Cuéllar who negotiated with the Moroccan government and Polisario separately (Morocco arguing that direct talks would imply recognition of the SADR). The result was an agreement that a referendum would be held in the territory to determine its future status. This would be organized and supervised by the United Nations, which would deploy a peacekeeping force in support of the process.

The plan was formally accepted by Morocco and the Polisario in August 1988, though the UN operation was not put in place by the Security Council until April 1991 when the Mission for the Referendum in Western Sahara (MINURSO, from the French Mission des Nations Unies pour l'Organisation d'un Référendum au Sahara Occidental) was authorized.[12] The peacekeeping part of the operation was relatively modest in size, never exceeding 300 personnel (Map 31). The operation had, after all, been established to oversee the implementation of an agreed settlement plan, and there was no expectation that its authority would be seriously challenged. The process begun in 1991, however, was to be one of the most tortuous and frustrating that the UN had ever engaged in. The original date planned for the referendum, January 1992, soon proved hopelessly optimistic. It was one thing for the parties to agree to a referendum in principle, but implementation was another thing. The main matter of contention was the extent of the electorate. Who would be entitled to vote? How could a largely nomadic population that traditionally did not fully acknowledge desert borders be identified as 'Western Saharan' and registered accordingly? What was the status of the large population of Moroccan migrants who had been moved into the territory since Spain's withdrawal? These and other questions soon formed a new battleground between Morocco and the Polisario, with the UN – which was responsible for arriving at acceptable answers – caught in the middle.

Early planning assumptions based on the recent experience in Namibia, ostensibly a very similar undertaking, were soon proved to be misplaced. The fundamental problem was that Morocco (which supposedly paralleled the 'South African' role in Western Sahara) was not resigned to seeing the territory become an independent state under the Polisario (the 'SWAPO' of the territory). Morocco intended to hold on to Western Sahara and there was no 'linkage' (like the Cuban withdrawal from Angola) that could persuade it otherwise. Moreover, western pressure on Morocco was not applied with the same force as it had been on South Africa. There was much less of a diplomatic price to be paid by western states for their sympathy towards Morocco than there was in the South African case. In short, the dynamics of the conflict were simply not configured to settlement in the way that they had been in Namibia. The UN operation consequently became bogged down in endless prevarication from Morocco with secretary-general Kofi Annan reporting in 2004, twelve years after the original schedule for completion of the referendum, that an end to the affair now 'appeared more distant today' than ever before.[13] As in Cyprus, peacekeeping in Western Sahara had been largely successful as 'peacekeeping'. There had been very little overt violence during the period of its deployment. MINURSO's observation and interpositionary functions along the Algerian border had no doubt deterred confrontations between

Moroccan and Polisario forces. But without effective peacemaking there was no real way forward. And without the acceptance of meaningful compromise by the parties – of the type evident over Namibia – such a peace would remain elusive.

Dealing with contested legitimacy

Beyond conflicts that can be directly traced to contested or imperfect decolonization, Africa has been victim to another class of crisis that, though having origins in the imperial experience, is not so immediately rooted in the transfer of power. In many parts of Africa independence settlements have given rise to 'deferred' problems around the legitimacy of the states formed in the wake of imperial withdrawal. These have often had at their root clashes between the 'in-group' of patron and clients that 'inherited' the state from the departing colonial power and other ethnically, regionally or, more rarely, ideologically defined 'out-groups' resentful at their exclusion from power and the resources of the state. When peace agreements have been reached by the parties to these conflicts, often under pressure from external actors, the United Nations has frequently been enlisted to oversee their implementation. The feasibility of these agreements has varied widely, and the UN has, therefore, often found itself attempting to maintain a rapidly crumbling peace to which the parties have been insufficiently committed at the outset. The civil wars in Angola and Mozambique, both former Portuguese territories that found themselves suddenly independent in 1975, were two examples of UN involvement in such situations that provide examples of sharply different outcomes. Long-simmering ethnic divisions in the former Belgian territories of Rwanda and Burundi also brought UN involvement – which in the first case became inextricably linked with the genocide of 1994. The former French areas of Africa, often seen by outsiders as unusually stable regions in sub-Saharan Africa, have also had their share of problems that in the cases of the Central Africa Republic and Côte d'Ivoire the UN was enlisted to help deal with.

Repeated failure: Angola

We left Angola in the upbeat atmosphere generated by the success of the independence process in neighbouring Namibia and the smooth and efficient withdrawal of Cuban forces from Angolan territory. At this early stage in the post-cold war period general optimism about the prospects for a more peaceful and stable international system went hand in hand with a tendency to overstate the importance of superpower rivalry in regional problems. This manifested itself over Angola in an assumption that the civil war that had afflicted the country since before independence in 1975 could be simply resolved now that the superpowers no longer had an interest in backing 'their' different sides. The Soviet Union's support for the governing Popular Movement for the Liberation of Angola (MPLA – Movimento Popular de Libertação de Angola) had been countered by American backing for the rebel National Union for the Total Independence of Angola movement (UNITA – União Nacional para a Independência Total de Angola), with South Africa and Cuba acting as conduits between the respective patrons and clients. These two secondary actors had been removed from the stage by the Namibia settlement, and the big powers now undertook to 'sort' the underlying conflict in Angola in the expectation that the elements of a permanent settlement would easily fall into place.

This, though, grossly underestimated the depth of the local roots to the Angolan civil war. Ethnic and regional divisions separated the sides more fundamentally than any imported global ideologies, and the long destructive civil war had deepened the visceral hostility between them. Angola, moreover, was immensely rich in natural resources and control of the state held material benefits fiercely defended by the MPLA elite and equally fiercely coveted by the UNITA leadership under the unpredictable but charismatic Jonas Savimbi. Evidently undeterred by these local realities, however, the United States and the Soviet Union along with Portugal, the former colonial power, secured a 'settlement' at a meeting between the sides held near Lisbon in May 1991, just as the last Cubans were leaving Angola under UN verification. These 'Acordos de Paz' (peace accords) set a timetable for legislative and presidential elections to establish a post-civil war administration. In the presidential contest Savimbi would run against the incumbent, the MPLA's José Eduardo dos Santos. The other main component of the agreement was the creation of a new national army drawn from both sides.[14] A United Nations peacekeeping force was to oversee the process. The participation of the United States and the Soviet Union in the arrangement guaranteed that the Security Council would support the plan, and the second UN Verification Mission in Angola (UNAVEM-II) was accordingly established at the end of May 1991.[15] This co-option of the UN by the superpowers was reminiscent of the 'détente peacekeeping' in the Middle East after the 1973 war. In Africa, however, it would not have the same success.

UNAVEM-II was required to implement a deeply flawed settlement in the negotiation and formulation of which the UN had played no part. Mistaken assumptions about the ease with which the peace process would take place because of the withdrawal of external support for the war led to a catastrophically under-resourced operation that even at its peak was less than 500-strong (Map 2). This small force had to oversee and police elections while at the same time planning and implementing a demobilization, disarmament and reintegration programme for former combatants that it had no capacity to enforce. In these circumstances, in fact, UNAVEM-II performed quite creditably. A ceasefire was maintained, and successful elections took place in September 1992, just fifteen months after the mission's deployment. These were judged by external monitors to be free and fair, and for a time it looked as though the process might just succeed. The parties were, after all, publicly committed to it, having been put under pressure by their respective foreign backers. But the terms of the electoral contest were dangerously unsuited to the conditions of Angola at this time. The time frame between agreement and elections was inadequate in the context of a civil war that had been going on for seventeen years. The polls were based on a 'winner-takes-all' outcome in which either the MPLA or UNITA would have control of the country; there was nothing for the loser. In these circumstances support for the process was easily given when the prospect of victory seemed high; when things began to look less certain, however, support was equally easily withdrawn. This is precisely what happened when Savimbi saw defeat looming during the election. UNITA abandoned the process citing, quite disingenuously, electoral malpractice, and returned to war.[16] The small UNAVEM presence was now confronted with combined rival forces of about 150,000, and it could do nothing to keep the peace.

The next attempt to end the conflict began a year after the resumption of the war when the representative of secretary-general Boutros-Ghali, the Malian diplomat Alioune Blondin Beye, arranged talks between the MPLA and UNITA in the Zambian capital Lusaka. UNITA's grudging agreement to participate in this process was partly due to the Security Council's threat to impose sanctions against it.[17] At Lusaka Savimbi seemed to accept the validity of the 1992 election result, and the talks turned to the nature of post-settlement government. To tie him into the process Savimbi was offered a post in the new administration, an advance on the 1991 agreement that had denied the loser any position at all. After this apparent initial cooperation, however, Savimbi reverted to character, returning to his headquarters in the Angolan interior and evading all attempts to enlist him in the post-Lusaka process. Nevertheless, with so much already invested in the arrangement, the Security Council established another peacekeeping force to help drive the process forward. The third Verification Mission (UNAVEM-III) was authorized in February 1995.[18] Learning from the mistakes that had trammelled its predecessor, the new operation was to be a much more formidable one, with 7,000 infantry troops as well as 250 military observers and 360 civilian police. There now followed a period of years of obfuscation and temporization by Savimbi, who continued to refuse to engage in any substantial way with the process. Although the ceasefire between UNITA and MPLA government forces held reasonably well and a new 'unity and reconciliation government' was formed (which included some UNITA dissidents who broke with Savimbi), the country remained as far from a permanent durable peace settlement as ever. The demobilization and disarmament process advanced only haltingly amid suspicions that UNITA was doing the absolute minimum to keep the process alive and nothing that would materially advance it.

In mid-1997, in an apparent attempt to create momentum, the Security Council agreed to replace UNAVEM-III with a new, much reduced operation that would be responsible for the 'conclusion' of the process. Balking at a fourth UNAVEM, the Security Council called the new operation the Observer Mission in Angola (MONUA – from the Portuguese Missão de Observação das Nações Unidas em Angola).[19] But the conditions for successful peacekeeping were simply not present. By 1999 Angola had slipped back into war. The next three years saw UNITA weakened on the battlefield and enfeebled by the application of UN 'smart sanctions' targeted on its leadership. Peacekeeping on the ground had in the meantime been acknowledged by the UN secretariat and the Security Council as largely pointless amid the intractable dynamics of the Angolan conflict. The entire tragedy was a testament to the capacity of one powerful and charismatic figure to defy not just local pressures for conflict resolution but the entire peacekeeping resources of the United Nations. Quite simply, there seemed to be no way forward as long as Jonas Savimbi remained in the equation. Stalin's famous dictum was brought inescapably to mind: 'no man, no problem; death solves everything'. And so it transpired. In February 2002 Savimbi was located by government forces in a remote part of eastern Angola and killed. Within days the war was virtually at an end and a peace settlement agreed, the terms of which were largely dictated by the government.

Angola was obviously not the finest hour of UN peacekeeping. Yet the successive operations there were not wholly useless. Ceasefires were maintained for at least part of the period in which UN forces were present and an immeasurable contribution was made to humanitarian support. It is difficult to see what other course the UN could have taken. Once involved at the behest of the United States and the Soviet Union in 1991 it could not abandon its peacekeeping effort, however paltry its results. The UN and Angola became, in a sense, shackled to each other until time and circumstances made disengagement possible. Once again, the lesson was plain: without a genuine commitment to peace on the part of the antagonists, peacekeeping could be no more than a costly, meaningless exercise. It may be possible to allow a situation to evolve in the hope that the necessary commitment might emerge, but in Angola the likelihood that it would not should have been clear to the United Nations long before its withdrawal, let alone Savimbi's necessary death.

Success at first attempt: Mozambique

The UN had a strikingly different experience in the other former Portuguese colony in southern Africa, Mozambique. The conflict in Mozambique had a number of similarities to that in Angola. In both states Marxist liberation movements that had been engaged in guerrilla wars against the imperial presence had formed the post-independence regimes following the collapse of Portugal's authoritarian government in April 1974. In contrast to the MPLA in Angola, which had come to power amid a civil war that had been well under way before the Portuguese abandoned the country, Frelimo (Front for the Liberation of Mozambique – Frente para a Libertação de Moçambique) in Mozambique had received the transfer of power from Portugal in 1975 against only weak political opposition. This, however, disguised considerable difficulties, both internal and external, that in the years following independence would come together to pull the country down into a hideously destructive civil war.

Frelimo's attempts to impose a revolution based on the centralization of political and economic power clashed with traditional sources of authority and modes of economic production. The state was insensitive to local cultural concerns that were routinely dismissed as backward and 'obscurantist'. There was also a regionalist dimension to post-independence politics in Mozambique in that the political leadership of Frelimo was seen as predominantly 'southern' and its military cadres disproportionately 'northern', leading to a certain sense of exclusion among the population of the centre of the country. All of this may have been manageable given the time and the opportunity for the revolution to prove itself. However, Mozambique came to independence in a period of great regional tension. On its central western borders the illegal white regime of Rhodesia, which had declared unilateral independence from Britain in 1965, was confronted by a growing nationalist insurgency. With the end of the Portuguese presence in Mozambique and its replacement by a radical African government, a completely new front opened up in the Rhodesian war as the insurgents could now use Mozambique as a base. By the late 1970s internal discontent in Mozambique was being manipulated by the Rhodesian intelligence services, and different Mozambican dissident groups and individuals were brought together by them to form Renamo (Mozambican National Resistance Movement – Resistência Nacional Moçambicana).

In the late 1970s Renamo was a considerable but largely localized problem for the Mozambican government, one restricted to the centre of the country adjacent to the Rhodesian frontier. The settlement of 1980, which brought the end of white rule and Rhodesia's transition to independent Zimbabwe, would, Frelimo hoped, bring an end to the matter. By this stage, however, white South Africa was just beginning its long-drawn-out terminal crisis. Although the South African government seemed less concerned about the Frelimo regime in Mozambique than it was about the MPLA in Angola, by the early 1980s it was becoming anxious about its 'encirclement' by hostile states. It therefore took over sponsorship of Renamo from Rhodesia with the result that the insurgency in Mozambique became a civil war fought on a wide front through much of central and southern Mozambique. Neither the government nor the rebels seemed capable of forcing any decisive turn in the war. This was a situation that suited South Africa, as the long destructive conflict reduced Mozambique's capacity to support the African National Congress (ANC) campaign against white rule. A supposed peace agreement between South Africa and Mozambique in 1984, the Nkomati accord, which was based on undertakings to end the two countries' support for Renamo and the ANC respectively, failed to produce significant results when the South Africans reneged on their obligations. As a result, the war in Mozambique dragged on with horrific consequences throughout the 1980s.

By 1990 both the internal and the regional setting had changed significantly. Frelimo began to move away from the rigidities of economic centralization and the one-party state, though the apparently endless war, along with a series of climatic disasters, had reduced the Mozambican state virtually to an empty shell. Additionally, the Soviet Union, with Mikhail Gorbachev now in office, was no longer the reliable ally it once had been. In South Africa, too, things were changing rapidly. At the beginning of 1990 Nelson Mandela was released from prison and it was clear that the days of white minority rule – which underlay Renamo's external support – were numbered. Both sides, then, had every reason to seek an exit from the war. The first negotiations were facilitated by an Italian missionary agency active in the country and then, following encouraging initial movement, responsibility was taken over by the Italian government. Negotiations continued over more than a year until October 1992 when an outline agreement was reached between Frelimo and Renamo.

Up to this point the United Nations had played no prominent role, but there was a general assumption, given its involvement elsewhere in Africa by this time, that it would be engaged in the implementation process. The two sides were divided about the extent of this role. Frelimo regarded United Nations involvement and the deployment of foreign peacekeepers as an implicit qualification of its own sovereignty. Renamo, in contrast, saw a UN presence as an acknowledgement of its standing as a major actor on equivalent terms to Frelimo. Ultimately, though, the extent of the UN role – which was considerable – was dictated by the immediate requirements of the peace process rather than the political preferences of the parties.

The UN Operation in Mozambique (ONUMOZ – from the Portuguese name Operação das Nações Unidas em Moçambique) was established by the Security Council in December 1992, though the principle that the UN was to have a central role had been accepted by the Council immediately after the signing of the 'General Peace Agreement' (GPA) between Frelimo and Renamo the previous October 1992.[20] The UN had multiple tasks in the peace process. It was to chair the Supervision and Control Commission that was to oversee the entire implementation of the GPA (Map 21). ONUMOZ was also to organize and monitor presidential and legislative elections in which the key contestants would be Frelimo and Renamo (which rapidly transformed itself into a political party). The government's presidential candidate would be the incumbent, Joaquim Chissano, who would face the Renamo leader, Afonso Dhlakama. Most onerously, perhaps, the UN was to be responsible for the demobilization, disarming and dispersal to their home areas of government and Renamo soldiers. To enable it to fulfil this mandate the force was to be a large one with about 7,000 personnel.

The road to the elections that were held at the end of October 1994 was far from smooth. Both sides put obstacles in the way of the process, particularly in relation to the demobilization of fighters. Constant external pressure was applied by, among others, Nelson Mandela in neighbouring South Africa who, during the course of the UN operation in Mozambique, had emerged as sub-Saharan Africa's leading statesman. Even at the ultimate hour, the entire peace process was put in jeopardy when Dhlakama threatened to 'do a Savimbi' and pull out of a contest that he now looked set to lose. A mixture of pressure and bribery kept him onside, however, and he reluctantly accepted his and Renamo's defeat in the presidential and legislative elections respectively. It was far from an electoral rout, anyway, and Renamo now provided a strong parliamentary opposition.[21] ONUMOZ left Mozambique in December 1994, just weeks after the confirmation of the election results. As well as ensuring free and fair elections the outcome of which was, however grudgingly, accepted by all parties, ONUMOZ successfully completed the complex and delicate demobilization process. Mozambique now settled down to a sustained period of political stability that allowed a quite remarkable process of reconstruction to take place. Within a few years of the country being written off by many as beyond any kind of redemption, it had become something of a model for successful development in sub-Saharan Africa.

Contrasting outcomes: comparing peacekeeping in Angola and Mozambique

The conflicts in Angola and Mozambique were in many respects very similar. Both states came into being under Afro-Marxist regimes – the MPLA in Angola and Frelimo in Mozambique – following long liberation wars that ended with the sudden collapse of the Portuguese imperial state. Both were pro-Soviet states at a time when détente was giving way once again to cold war. The civil wars in each were fought between the government and internal opposition groups – UNITA and Renamo – that were sustained by extensive external support. The peace processes in each were very similar in substance. They were based on ceasefires followed by elections for a new, pluralist form of government accompanied by a demobilization and disarmament process designed to remove the risk of a reversion to violence. Why then was the outcome of United Nations intervention so different in each? There were four crucial differences between Angola and Mozambique that fundamentally affected the dynamics of the conflict in each country and therefore determined the outcome of the UN's peacekeeping projects.

First, while Renamo had local support, particularly in the central regions of Mozambique, its position was fundamentally different from that of UNITA in Angola. UNITA had a long history of rivalry with the MPLA in the anti-colonial struggle stretching back to the 1960s. Renamo, in contrast, had been a creation of the white Rhodesian regime that had then been adopted by the South African security apparatus. It was therefore less rooted than UNITA and much more vulnerable to changes in the international setting of the conflict (such as the end of the apartheid state in South Africa). Second, Renamo never acquired the military capacity of UNITA. By the 1990s UNITA had become a conventional army capable of fighting set-piece battles. Renamo, in contrast, remained a dispersed guerrilla movement. It was, therefore, probably incapable of returning to the war (as UNITA had been after the electoral defeat of 1992) despite Dhlakama's posturing during the peace process. Third, while we can identify a 'Savimbi factor' in Angola we cannot talk of a 'Dhlakama factor' in Mozambique. Renamo simply did not have the same charismatic leadership as UNITA – nor its ruthless central control. Renamo fighters were much more anxious than UNITA ones to be demobilized and to return home. This was clear on the eve of the 1994 elections when Dhlakama threatened a boycott, a threat that was relatively easily averted by the UN. The difference between Savimbi and Dhlakama – and the differences between UNITA and Renamo – made the zero-sum, winner-takes-all result foreseen by both peace processes in the early 1990s feasible in Mozambique but fatally flawed for Angola. Finally, Mozambique was, in a strange way, blessed by having few of Angola's riches. With no oil or diamonds to be won by the antagonists there was less economic impetus to the war there.

By the early 1990s there was little sustaining the war in Mozambique while that in Angola was still impelled by multiple drivers. In retrospect it should perhaps have been evident to those experienced in the peacekeeping process and aware of its history that the dynamics of the Angolan conflict in the early 1990s put it beyond the capacity of external intervention to resolve. In Mozambique, in contrast, the conflict had unwound to such a degree that, if the UN was not exactly pushing on an open door, it did not take much of a shove from the outside to break the lock.

Rwanda: peacekeeping amid genocide

The horrors of Rwanda in 1994, widely regarded as a culpable failure of peacekeeping, underline the points we have just made in comparing the situations of Angola and Mozambique. In Rwanda, too, the parties in a civil war had arrived at an agreement that the UN was called on to help implement. Here, as in Angola but in contrast to Mozambique, the commitment of the parties to seeing the agreement through fell far short of what was necessary to permit successful peacekeeping. The consequences in Rwanda were more concentrated than those in Angola where the death toll was much higher but spread across many years. But the underlying obstacles to conflict resolution faced by the peacekeepers in both countries were very similar.

The origins of genocide: history and ethnicity

Rwanda sits at the geographical centre of Africa, and its ethnic and political difficulties radiated outwards through the continent. Its conflict was a major contributory factor in the wider crisis of the region in the 1990s and the 2000s. The primary ethnic and political divide in Rwanda was between the majority Hutu and the minority Tutsi peoples. Although the Tutsi composed only about 10 per cent of the national population, their power and influence had been disproportionate both before and during the colonial period. A Tutsi monarchy had ruled Rwanda for centuries before the arrival of the Germans in the nineteenth century. Following a common practice, the colonial state maintained the existing structures of power, though under its own control. The Tutsi therefore continued to constitute the administrative and economic elite in the colony. When Germany was divested of its colonies after the First World War, Belgium, to whom the League of Nations mandated the territory (largely because of its border with the Congo), saw no reason to alter this situation. At independence in 1962, however, the imperial writ ended, demographic logic asserted itself, and the Hutu now took power. Inevitably, the reversal of power relations created great tension. In 1963 these erupted into violence, resulting in many Tutsi crossing into neighbouring Uganda where they formed the Rwandan Patriotic Front (RPF). Over the coming years this developed into a formidable political and military opposition to the Hutu regime.

A spasmodic cross-border guerrilla war continued through the 1970s and 1980s, its tempo rising and falling with inter-ethnic tensions in Rwanda. By the early 1990s the RPF posed a serious threat to the regime, which had become increasingly reliant on foreign support (particularly from France) for its survival. This critical stage in the conflict coincided with the post-cold war, post-apartheid rhetoric of 'African renaissance', and external pressure mounted on both sides to reach a settlement. Initially, the prospects for agreement seemed reasonable. The Hutu did not form a single, anti-Tutsi bloc; there was a considerable liberal, forward-looking group of Hutus that sought accommodation and were prepared to cooperate with the RPF. But there was also a powerful hard-line faction that resisted any settlement with the ethnic 'enemy' from the outset. Despite this, the view of the Hutu president of Rwanda, Juvénil Habyarimana, and his counterpart, the RPF leader Paul Kagame, who had reached a peace agreement in Arusha in neighbouring Tanzania in August 1993, was that the settlement process could succeed with sufficient external involvement.

UN engagement and the response to the killings

The United Nations had already contributed to the peace process through the provision of a small military observer mission on the Uganda–Rwanda border (Observer Mission Uganda–Rwanda – UNOMUR) to confirm that no RPF infiltration was taking place in the truce during the negotiations. Now the two sides sought a much larger peacekeeping operation that would, in effect, have policed the implementation of the agreement (Map 25). By this stage in the rapid expansion of post-cold war peacekeeping, however, this was not feasible. Boutros-Ghali proposed a much more modest monitoring operation that left responsibility for 'peace enforcement' with the parties themselves. The Security Council authorized the creation of the Assistance Mission for Rwanda (UNAMIR) in October 1993.[22] This was commanded by a Canadian brigadier-general, Romeo Dallaire, who was transferred from the observer mission on the border, and included a significant contingent from Belgium, the former colonial power.

The fragility of the peace process was evident from the outset. There was little trust between the sides even at the higher levels that had been directly involved in the negotiations. More ominously, it was clear that a considerable section of the Hutu political class remained unreconciled to the power-sharing arrangements that the agreement envisaged. The demobilization and disarmament process that was central to the settlement soon stalled and Hutu extremist voices became louder and more influential. General Dallaire's communications with New York turned increasingly anxious in the first months of 1994 as the prospect of a violent convulsion loomed. The explosion came on 6 April when a plane carrying President Habyarimana and his Burundian counterpart was shot down as it approached Kigali, the Rwandan capital. This was almost certainly the work of Hutu extremists who, with this one blow, removed the architect of the 'sell-out' to the Tutsi enemy and created the conditions for the systematic extinction of the entire Tutsi population, ending by genocide the need for any peace process.

Among the first victims were moderate Hutus who had participated in the Arusha settlement. These included the acting prime minister, Agathe Uwilingiyimana, whose supposed protectors, a detachment of Belgian UN troops, were abducted and later killed by Hutu soldiers. Whether planned or not, this proved to be effective in setting nerves on edge in New York, and contributed to the Security Council's failure to act quickly and decisively to attempt to end the killings. In his subsequent, self-exculpating memoir of his time in office, Boutros Boutros-Ghali recounts his desperate attempts to engage the permanent members of the Council with the crisis.[23] There was no enthusiasm for a greater level of commitment, however. There were a number of reasons for this, and given the retrospective denunciations visited on the 'failure of the UN' it is important to be aware of them.

The early UN casualties raised serious questions about the availability of contributors to an expanded UN force. As it gradually became clear that the genocide was planned and orchestrated, an act of 'policy' rather than a chaotic outburst of violence, the extent of the risk facing any force that attempted to end it also became evident. There was among some advocates of action at the time a mildly (and unconsciously) 'imperialist' mindset that assumed that a robust intervention by even a relatively modest force of well-equipped, trained and disciplined outsiders would immediately overawe the *genocidaires* and end the killings. This was never a possibility. Not only was the killing a determined and 'rational' process (in the sense of having a thought-out objective), it was taking place throughout the country in hill villages and lakeside towns as well as in Kigali. A truly massive intervention would have been required to end it by force.

But it was probably events beyond Rwanda that were primarily responsible for the refusal of the members of the Security Council to accept a major role in ending the genocide. By the middle of 1994 the post-cold war peacekeeping commitment – in Africa and elsewhere – was on the point of becoming unsustainable. Huge, expensive and hazardous undertakings were in progress in the former Yugoslavia and in Cambodia. In the meantime large-scale operations continued in the Middle East. In Africa itself the UN was committed to major peacekeeping ventures in Western Sahara, Angola and Mozambique, as we have seen. But in particular, an expanded commitment to Rwanda was made virtually impossible in the wake of the failure of intervention in Somalia. The United States especially – whose support for any such scheme was more or less essential – was rethinking the whole idea of participation in peacekeeping in the aftermath of its experience there (see Chapter 10). The 'UN' as an institution made mistakes in Rwanda, especially in the period before the genocide began when it failed to respond effectively to intelligence reports about the preparations for the coming orgy of killing. But the UN's failure to expand its commitment after the genocide began was to be explained in terms of national foreign policies rather than institutional failure.

The aftermath to genocide

The attempt at genocide ended not as a result of external intervention but with the victory of the RPF in the civil war that had resumed after the killing began. In the meantime 'peacekeeping' of a peculiar sort had been offered late in the day by France, whose intervention in Rwanda (Operation Turquoise) was accepted by the Security Council in its anxiety to distract attention from its own inactivity. The French intervention created a so-called 'humanitarian protection zone' in the south-west of Rwanda. The RPF was convinced that the object of the mission was not to save Tutsis from the *genocidaires* but to protect those *genocidaires* – France's old Hutu allies – from impending punishment as Hutu power collapsed around them. In any case, as a peacekeeping project Operation Turquoise was largely pointless. The victory of the RPF was complete by the middle of July 1994. In the previous months some 800,000 people had been massacred, and the reputation of UN peacekeeping, rightly or wrongly, had been profoundly damaged.

UNAMIR remained in Rwanda until March 1996. Now known as UNAMIR-II, its role changed after the genocide to one of humanitarian assistance. It performed this role with some success as the country began to grapple with the massive social and economic consequences of the events of mid-1994. Its performance in this later period, creditable though it may have been, was inevitably overshadowed by its perceived failure during the killing time. In the longer term, the lack of will on the part of the members of the Security Council to grasp the nettle of decisive intervention underlined the continued relevance, even after the cold war, of the immunizing purpose of peacekeeping. Having been left to spiral out of control, Rwanda's crisis began to infect the larger central African region and helped precipitate a transnational crisis that, over a longer period, cost many more lives than the genocide of 1994.

Getting it right? Burundi

The major impact of this spillover from Rwanda was, as we will see, in the Congo where UN peacekeepers first operated in Africa. However, another of Rwanda's neighbours, Burundi, was also affected, and more than a decade after the Rwandan genocide a UN force was deployed there to help implement another peace treaty (coincidentally also signed in Arusha in Tanzania) between Hutu and Tutsi factions. Like Rwanda, Burundi had been a German colony that passed under League mandate to Belgium after the First World War. The two territories were administered together by Brussels but became separate states at independence in 1963. Although the ethnic balance between Hutu and Tutsi and their respective historical roles were largely the same in each territory, the post-independence state in Burundi retained a more complex distribution of power between the two ethnicities. Despite this, however, Burundi had its own blood-smeared history of inter-group violence, and descended into civil war in the 1980s. Hutu refugees from Burundi in fact contributed to the tensions in Rwanda and bolstered the power of the hard-liners who would eventually be responsible for the genocide.

In the aftermath of the Rwanda crisis the UN was, unsurprisingly, reluctant to become too directly involved in Burundi. At the same time, Africa itself was anxious to experiment with 'African solutions to African problems' and Burundi became something of a testing ground for local peacemaking and peacekeeping by the OAU (which evolved into the 'African Union' in 2002). This intervention by the African Mission in Burundi (AMIB) was designed to implement the Arusha agreement of August 2000, which, like its predecessor for Rwanda, was built around a demobilization, disarmament and reintegration programme for fighters and the establishment of a power-sharing administration. Regional intervention met with mixed success, however, amid suspicions of the intentions of powerful local participants such as South Africa. In 2004, therefore, as sporadic violence continued, the Security Council approved the creation of the UN Operation in Burundi (Opération des Nations Unies au Burundi – ONUB) which would absorb the AMIB forces into the UN command.[24]

The initial phase of ONUB appeared to be relatively successful. It was inconceivable ten years after the Rwandan genocide that the UN would be complicit in any repeat of that level of violence. This was probably well understood by the parties to the conflict in Burundi and was, perhaps, one positive aspect of the spectre of Rwanda on the UN's peacekeeping efforts in Africa. The fundamental problem for peacekeeping was the same in Burundi as in Rwanda and in Angola before that: could the operation be viable when the social and political dynamics of the conflict were simply not 'aligned' towards peace? Considerable doubt remained after the arrival of ONUB about the degree of commitment to the Arusha agreement among the Burundi factions. While violence on the scale of Rwanda in 1994 might be improbable, a long-term peace in Burundi was not to be easily achieved. Whether this situation, in Burundi or elsewhere in Africa, could be altered by the existence of the 'peace enforcement units' proposed by Boutros-Ghali in *An Agenda for Peace* for precisely these circumstances is questionable. The experience of peacekeeping in Africa in the 1990s seems to suggest that enduring peace can only grow organically, so to speak, from its local roots. It can be fertilized but not implanted by external peacekeepers.

The limitations of *Francophonie*: the Central African Republic and Côte d'Ivoire

The Burundi situation, in which the UN took over regional peacekeeping efforts already in place, was not unique in African peacekeeping. Successive French governments of both right and left have prided themselves on France's 'special relationship' with its former sub-Saharan colonies and other French-speaking African countries that constitute the semi-formal *Francophonie* ('French language') grouping. This relationship has frequently involved direct military intervention by France, often in support of regimes that have proved friendly to Paris whose legitimacy has been challenged by opposition groups. The peculiar role of France in Rwanda, both before and after the genocide, can be seen in the context of its relationship with the Francophone Hutu regime against the Tutsi rebels who had acquired an Anglophone identity by virtue of their exile in Uganda. French interventions, whether graced with the name peacekeeping or not, have not always been successful. The accusation of neo-colonialism will always lie in wait for former colonial powers intent on maintaining their influence, and the United Nations has on occasion provided a useful exit route for France from its post-imperial African ventures.

Lying on the northern border of the Congo, the territory that eventually became the CAR was incorporated into French Equatorial Africa in 1910 and became independent fifty years later. Its post-independence history was a colourful one, though the tones were mainly dark. In 1966 its post-colonial government was overthrown by the army chief, Jean Bédel Bokassa, who plunged the country into almost fourteen years of outrageous misrule (including its conversion into the 'Central African Empire' with himself as Emperor). For most of his period in power France appeared to regard him as an acceptable ally, but in 1979 when his behaviour began to exceed all bounds, French troops intervened. Although the pretext for the intervention was the protection of the expatriate community, the reality was that the French had come to facilitate Bokassa's overthrow, which duly took place. A period of instability followed, with civilian and military regimes alternating in the capital, Bangui. In 1993, however, the CAR followed the general trend of the time in Africa towards multi-party elections. These led to the presidency of Ange-Félix Patassé, a former Bokassa ally who had reinvented himself as a democratic politician. In the CAR as elsewhere, however, the mere fact of open elections (often the result of external pressure) did not lead automatically to stable and effective government. An underlying culture of patrimonialism persisted.

The legitimacy of Patassé's regime came under frequent challenge. The army in particular was restive over its pay and conditions. These discontents were shared by the large public service generally, as the yawning gap between the rhetoric of modern governance and the reality of political clientelism became obvious. There was also a significant regionalist dimension to instability in the CAR, as the beneficiaries of the regime's patrimony came predominantly from the president's own northern region while the army was traditionally recruited in the south. When a military mutiny in 1996 threatened to precipitate a civil war, France and the CAR's Francophone neighbours negotiated the 'Bangui Accords', which provided a settlement framework. There was an obvious difficulty over implementation of the agreement, however, as the army, which would normally have been expected to police the process, was itself a party to the conflict. To meet this, France undertook to organize and lead an Inter-African Mission for the Supervision of the Bangui Accords (Mission Interafricaine de Surveillance des Accords de Bangui – MISAB) composed of both French troops and contingents from other Francophone states in the region. This was subsequently legitimized by the Security Council at the request of the African participants in the venture who were anxious that with continuing tensions threatening to spill over into violence their role should be internationally accepted.[25]

By the end of 1997 the burdens of the task were telling on France and it began to prepare an exit strategy. This would involve the withdrawal of French transport and logistical support, which was essential for the functioning of MISAB. The whole peacekeeping operation would be jeopardized if an effective alternative could not be found. This 'plan B' was to be the UN, which both France and Patassé wished to involve for different reasons. For France the UN would provide cover for its withdrawal, and for Patassé direct Security Council involvement in an operation that would secure him in power was obviously very attractive. The project was an unusual one in that the existing African contributors to MISAB agreed to continue under UN command. Thus reassured about the organization of the force, the Security Council voted in March 1998 to create the United Nations Mission in the Central African Republic (MINURCA, from the French name Mission des Nations Unies en République Centrafricaine). The gap left by the withdrawal of French specialists was filled by elements from Canada, Egypt and Portugal.[26]

The transition from MISAB to MINURCA took place smoothly, though the underlying political and economic problems that required the peacekeeping presence were not easily resolved. Neither the UN nor the Francophone African contributors were prepared to see the operation become a permanent fixture in the crisis, however, and the force was withdrawn in February 2000. It left behind a situation that was hardly closer to a final settlement than it had been when the original MISAB had first been deployed. In June 2001 Patassé narrowly survived a military coup – this time by calling on the help of Libyan troops, whose 'peacekeeping' skills were somewhat less refined than those of the UN. Once again, the futility of peacekeeping in a local environment in which the conditions for a viable peace simply did not exist was driven home. For France, however, the UN operation was wholly successful, representing as it did the transfer of responsibility for an expensive and diplomatically hazardous post-colonial project from Paris to New York.

A similar sequence of events led up to the UN peacekeeping operation in Côte d'Ivoire (the Ivory Coast) where the organization also took over from French and regional attempts at conflict resolution. From the time of its decolonization in 1960, Côte d'Ivoire was one of France's closest allies in west Africa. For thirty-three years after independence the country was ruled by the pro-western Francophile president Félix Houphouet-Boigny, and it enjoyed a level of political stability and economic prosperity unusual in the region. As a result, it became a magnet for economic migrants and political refugees from neighbouring countries. The death of Houphouet-Boigny while still in office in 1993 ushered in a period of violent instability, however. During his long, highly personal, rule he had done little to groom a replacement. The result was a protracted power struggle between prospective successors. Eventually, a hotly contested presidential election in

2000 saw Laurent Gbagbo, a veteran opposition figure active throughout Houphouet-Boigny's long reign, installed as head of state.

Never secure in power, Gbagbo soon abandoned his original left-wing, trade unionist credentials and adopted the rhetoric of Ivorian nationalism. This contributed to new disorder, with violence now aimed at the large migrant population. But the manoeuvre failed in its aim of closing national ranks around the president. Instead Gbagbo's attempts to claim a national power base actually tended to highlight his lack of one. Perceptions of his 'southern' identity and loyalty now added to long-standing resentment in the predominantly Muslim north, which had historically felt excluded from national power and its associated patrimony.

In September 2002 an army faction rebelled in the capital Abidjan and in northern centres, pushing the country towards an ethnic and regionally based civil war. While the rising in the capital was easily put down by troops loyal to Gbagbo, the rebels managed to establish themselves in the north, effectively splitting the country in two. The crisis quickly brought outside mediation attempts. Both France and the leading regional organization, the ECOWAS, became involved. While each of these was willing to provide good offices, there was considerable reluctance about committing troops to a peacekeeping venture. An ECOWAS plan for a force of 2,000 quickly ran into the sand when member states found excuses not to participate. While France deployed troops ostensibly to protect the large French expatriate community, any more activist role would have been opposed by Gbagbo's supporters, whose angry nationalism had been deliberately pumped up by the president. A peace plan brokered by France in May 2003, which would have brought rebel elements into the government, was initially accepted by the president, but he then distanced himself from it as the extent of his supporters' anger against it began to manifest itself. In the meantime anti-French and anti-migrant anger grew, further destabilizing the country.

A reluctant Security Council eventually committed the UN to a peacekeeping operation in February 2004. The Council's reservations were practical ones in that there was patently no peace to keep and therefore little prospect of operational success. But there was also an element of high politics involved that had nothing to do with the situation in Côte d'Ivoire itself. The Bush administration in Washington, it was reported, had resisted early French proposals for UN involvement in reprisal for the failure of the government of Jacques Chirac to support the invasion of Iraq in 2003.[27] By the beginning of 2004, however, it was clear that no actor other than the UN would be able or willing to engage with the crisis. The resulting moral pressure on the organization became irresistible. The United Nations Operation in Côte d'Ivoire (UNOCI) had the relatively large authorized strength of 6,240, drawn initially from ten member states, six of them African. It was mandated to observe and monitor the ceasefire associated with the dormant settlement agreement of May 2003 and to liaise with government and rebel forces as well as French army contingents in the country and in this way to establish stability.[28]

There was, in reality, no immediate likelihood of the peacekeeping operation achieving these objectives. There was no ceasefire to monitor, the truce having crumbled along with the political prospects of the 2003 agreement. Government, rebel and French forces were mutually hostile to each other and could provide no basis for national confidence-building. UNOCI's role was restricted to the – not negligible – responsibility for patrolling along with the French a buffer zone between the positions of the government forces in the south and the rebels in the north. But in Côte d'Ivoire as in the CAR, the real purpose of the UN presence was to fill a necessary space left by the failure of other agencies to settle the fundamental problem. In this way the 'international community' remained engaged in an obviously dangerous conflict, although the arrival of a 'peace' to keep had to await a fundamental shift in local attitudes and conditions.

In all the conflicts we have looked at in the last section of this chapter, from Angola to Côte d'Ivoire, the intervention of peacekeepers was designed to sustain and preserve the fabric of states whose regimes were subject to intense pressure. In none of them, however, had the situation slipped to a point where the fundamental *existence* of the state as a political and territorial unit in the international system was under question. In other words, these operations were concerned with 'failing' states rather than 'collapsed' states. This second category, of which several examples were evident in Africa from the 1990s, is the subject of the next chapter.

10 Africa II

Peacekeeping in stateless terrain

In a number of African territories peacekeepers have been deployed in conditions that were different from those examined in the previous chapter. In parts of the continent internal conflict – with and without external interference – reached a point where the state to all intents and purposes ceased to exist. Here it was not just a question of a challenge being mounted to the state with a consequent impact on its effectiveness; the underlying weakness of the state meant that the challenge brought about its collapse. The role of the peacekeeper, therefore, has been to fill a violent – literally 'anarchic' – vacuum rather than to facilitate peacemaking between the state and its opponents. The line dividing these two peacekeeping roles is not a firm one. By the end of the 1980s, for example, the Frelimo state in Mozambique was so beleaguered by the challenge from Renamo and its foreign backers that it barely performed the minimum functions required of statehood. Similarly, the control of the MPLA regime in Angola during the war against UNITA did not extend over the state's territory in its entirety. But in neither case did the state 'collapse'; in both countries the primary role of peacekeeping was to oversee settlements designed to draw things back from such a disaster. In contrast, in Somalia, in Liberia and in neighbouring Sierra Leone, as well as in the Congo where the UN had its first experience of peacekeeping in Africa, the disintegration of the state had gone much further.

In the early 1990s the Canadian political scientist Robert Jackson introduced the concept of the 'quasi-state'.[1] This was an entity whose 'stateness', defined by behaviour and capability, was questionable, but whose claim to be a state was tacitly accepted in the international system for pragmatic reasons. The governments of these territories, so far as they had governments, may have been useful allies in the cold war, for example. But the more substantial reason for the external acceptance of what may often be the fiction of statehood is that, in a system based on territorial units called states, to question or reject the statehood of these units would open a can of political worms best kept firmly shut. At a certain point in a number of African territories in the 1990s, however, this mutually convenient illusion became unsustainable. 'Failing' states became 'collapsed' states and it was necessary for the international system to fill the vacant space. Frequently this was driven by genuine humanitarian concern amid the appalling consequences of state collapse, but intervention was also determined by the necessity to maintain the basic fabric of the state-based system.

If peacekeeping in such circumstances was merely a matter of supplanting the collapsed state with externally supplied administrative and security services, then the role, though burdensome and expensive, would be relatively straightforward. By the early 1990s, as we have seen, the UN already had experience of this sort of activity from West New Guinea and Cambodia. But the realities of state disintegration in Africa have usually been more complex and dangerous. It has invariably been accompanied by violent factionalism as different groups have fought over the debris. The term 'warlordism' was often used in a loose way to describe this. Local leaders, usually associated with particular regional or ethnic interests, would confront each other either in competition for the economic spoils of the territory or simply to prevent the restriction of their own local power by others. In 1998 a firmer definition was given to the term, at least in relation to its manifestation in west Africa, by the American writer William Reno. 'Warlordism', he suggested, describes a situation in which 'rulers' have no particular interest in the control of the state as such. They are not primarily concerned with achieving comprehensive political command of a 'country', but only in securing local power to enable them to exploit available economic resources.[2] The reconstruction of a viable state would, in fact, challenge their interests, as it would curtail their power. Peacekeepers, as the agents of an international system set on just such a rebuilding of 'conventional' politics and accountable government, are seen as a major threat by warlords and their supporters. Peacekeeping in these conditions, therefore, is not about building on a clean, clear space left by the collapsed state; it tends to be a journey amid the very unstable and dangerous rubble.

Somalia: peacekeeping defeated

The situation faced by the United Nations in Somalia in 1992 could be traced directly to the end of the cold war in Africa. Independent Somalia had come into being in 1960, coincidentally on the same day as the Congo. It was a product of an agreement between Britain and Italy to combine their two 'Somaliland' colonies into a single independent state. The colonial history of the two territories had been far from calm and peaceful. Both British Somaliland in the north and the larger Italian territory in the south had seen frequent local uprisings by the patchwork of different clans that had always coexisted uneasily in the region. Early apprehensions about the future of the new state, however, appeared to have been misplaced. For the first nine years of its existence Somalia was largely stable and peaceful, and came to be seen as something of a model for successful African statehood.

In 1969, however, things took a more violent turn following a military coup led by General Muhammad Said Barre. Following the coup Said Barre promptly installed himself as head of state and, co-opting the fashionable rhetoric of the time, proclaimed Somalia a revolutionary socialist state. There was little evidence that the regime was truly committed to the radical transformation of Somalia's deeply conservative Muslim society, however, and Said Barre's ideological posturing was seen by the outside world as merely opportunistic. Revolutionary solidarity certainly did not extend to relations with neighbouring Marxist Ethiopia, whose weakness Said Barre sought to exploit in 1977 when he attempted to take the Ogaden region from it. This resulted in one of the very few conventional interstate wars in the history of post-colonial Africa. It was one that Somalia lost disastrously when Ethiopia enlisted the support of its Soviet and Cuban friends. Said Barre confirmed his reputation for opportunism when he responded to the ensuing political crisis by switching cold war allegiance. Henceforward Somalia would be a western ally. The United States viewed the Somali regime with some suspicion, not to say distaste. But the end of the 1970s was a critical point in superpower relations with the rapid unravelling of détente. The Horn of Africa, with its Indian Ocean coastline and its proximity to the Arabian Peninsula, was assuming an ever increasing strategic significance at this time. The result was that Somalia was admitted, if not exactly welcomed, into the society of western client states in sub-Saharan Africa.

Lacking wholehearted external backing and fatally weakened in the eyes of clan rivals by the debacle in the Ogaden, the regime of Said Barre was challenged by factional opposition throughout the 1980s. When the end of the cold war removed even the conditional support of the west (now no longer concerned with a Soviet 'threat' in the region), the regime's fate was sealed and Said Barre was deposed in January 1991. In the highly factionalized politics of Somalia there was little prospect of a stable succession. The pragmatic anti-Said Barre alliance of clan-based rebel groups disintegrated as soon as its immediate objective had been achieved. As one writer put it, now 'bad government was replaced by no government'.[3] The militarily dominant faction that now fought for control of Mogadishu, the Somali capital, was Mohamed Farah Aideed's Somali National Alliance (SNA), but Aideed was not capable of imposing his control on either the capital or the country as a whole. The result was a brutal civil conflict that soon produced a humanitarian disaster in a country that even at the best of times enjoyed very limited food security. Attempts by aid agencies to relieve the worst of the suffering were made virtually impossible not just by the fighting but by the chilling tactics of the competing factions, which utilized hunger and the control of food as a weapon. Throughout 1991 all of the apparently unstoppable horrors of Somalia were beamed into western homes and the 'CNN effect' began to make itself felt with mounting pressure on national politicians to 'do something'.[4]

The first UN operation in Somalia

The problem, of course, was what this 'something' should be and who should 'do' it. The UN secretariat and then the Security Council itself became involved in the crisis at an early stage and attempted to reach a settlement through mediation, but when this proved impossible, the peacekeeping option became unavoidable. The practical difficulties involved in this were immense, however. In previous UN operations, most obviously in the Congo, there had been obvious problems about the nature of the host state, even about the extent to which there *was* one. But there had always been a sufficiently 'state-like' entity with which to negotiate the practicalities of deployment, at least in the initial stages. In Somalia there was none. Where, therefore, did this leave the central peacekeeping requirement of 'host state consent'? What would be the legal status of any peacekeeping operation in Somalia in the absence of a status of forces agreement with the national government? By the northern summer of 1992 these questions were no closer to being answered than they had been at the outset, but pressure on the permanent members of the Security Council from their own electorates for intervention had become well nigh irresistible. By his own account, secretary-general Boutros Boutros-Ghali was also urging the members of the Council on, contrasting 'their indifference to the horrors of the Horn of Africa with their preoccupation with the "rich man's war" in the former Yugoslavia'.[5] It was therefore agreed that a substantial UN Operation in Somalia (UNOSOM) would be deployed at four centres in the country with a mandate to ensure the distribution of humanitarian aid.[6] In the meantime the difficult legal and practical questions around an intervention in a war-torn stateless territory were put on one side

From the beginning UNOSOM was beset by operational difficulties (Map 28). Aware of the new threat to their approach of using hunger and control of the food supply as a tactic, the factions obstructed UN operations at every opportunity. Initially it proved impossible to deploy units to the four designated strategic centres and the UN force was concentrated in Mogadishu. There, its units were subject to more or less constant harassment by the various 'militias' – often merely gangs of heavily armed, drugged-up teenagers – who ruled the streets. The Security Council was now in a dilemma. Its response to the various pressures to act in Somalia had been to establish UNOSOM. But this had evidently failed, and now not only was public pressure maintained but the options available to meet it were diminished. Withdrawal was unthinkable, but would an escalation in the level of enforcement be militarily wise or, given the fickleness of media-driven public opinion, politically acceptable? A release from this bind came from an unexpected source. The United States, which had been among the most cautious of the permanent members of the Security Council at the outset of the commitment, now offered to supply an American military force that would itself, with UN blessing, provide the necessary enforcement of the humanitarian writ.

There has been much conjecture about the motives behind the American offer. The most cynical interpretation was that the Bush administration in its last weeks had deliberately concocted a poisoned chalice to pass on to the new president, Bill Clinton, who was about to take office at the beginning of 1993. There was certainly a high level of dislike between the two men and their entourages, which was unusual in presidential politics. But other explanations are more likely. The American offer came in the still warm afterglow of Operation Desert Storm in the Gulf in which a UN-legitimized, American-led coalition had successfully ended the Iraqi occupation of Kuwait. The rhetoric of a 'new world order' (a term first deployed by President Bush himself) still had some resonance. And, coming as it did in the dying days of his presidency, the Somali crisis offered George Bush an opportunity to mark his place in history as a global humanitarian. Finally, of course, America more than most countries was subject to the continuing 'CNN effect', which after the evident failure of UNOSOM's initial efforts was stronger than ever. Whatever the motives – political or psychological – for its creation, the so-called Unified Task Force (UNITAF) was, quite simply, an offer the Security Council could not refuse.

The Unified Task Force

At the beginning of December 1992, secure in the American promise to take over the operation in Somalia, the Security Council passed an unusually frank resolution. UNOSOM had been 'an inadequate response to the tragedy in Somalia'. Enforcement action under Chapter VII of the Charter was now the only way forward and 'all necessary means' were permitted to UNITAF.[7] The intention was that the American force would simply overawe the factions in Somalia, which were now treating the UN force with contempt, and deliver a sharp lesson about respect for international opinion. UNOSOM would remain in existence during UNITAF's deployment and then resume its full functions in the transformed conditions in place when the American force withdrew.

This, at any rate, was the plan. The reality proved to be rather different. 'Operation Restore Hope', as the Americans called it, began on 9 December 1992 when the initial detachments of what would eventually be a 37,000-strong force arrived in Mogadishu. The event was carefully stage-managed. The first troops came ashore, D-Day-fashion, from landing craft on (wholly peaceful) beaches around the capital with the main audience provided by the international press. The event had its purposes, however. The show of martial force was designed to send a message to the militias that the international presence in Somalia was now of a different order from the 'weak' UN operation. But it was also an attempt by the Americans to determine rather than to follow the 'CNN effect' by assuring the home audience that what they had demanded had been delivered.

To some extent this was the reality. The American force did secure aid routes throughout the country much more successfully than UNOSOM. It did so without any significant confrontation with the militias who had indeed, it seemed, been 'overawed' by the display of American force. But this apparent success belied a more fundamental failure. There was a significant bureaucratic 'back-story' to the development of the UNITAF plan in Washington before it was presented to the Security Council. The impetus for intervention had come from the White House and the State Department. The military leadership in the Pentagon had been much less enthusiastic. General Colin Powell, then chairman of the US joint chiefs of staff (later secretary of state in the first administration of President George W. Bush), imposed important conditions. UNITAF's role should be restricted to the distribution of humanitarian aid in designated areas only. It should also have as short a duration as possible and should pass responsibility back to UNOSOM at the first feasible opportunity. One of the reasons for the apparent ease with which UNITAF's operations were completed was, therefore, that they were considerably restricted in scope. Most crucially, UNITAF did not undertake what many regarded as a key task of any effective intervention: the disarming and dispersal of the militias. The initial impact of the Americans' arrival, therefore, faded during the period of UNITAF, and the situation inherited by what would become UNOSOM-II was far from the stabilized and secure one foreseen in the original plan.

UNOSOM-II and the collapse of the mission

The UNITAF 'interlude' lasted for six months, with UNOSOM-II taking over responsibility for peacekeeping functions at the beginning of May 1993. The Americans retained a dominant position in the country, however. Some 4,000 US troops were incorporated into UNOSOM and operated alongside contingents from thirty other UN member states. In addition, several thousand American troops remained independent of UNOSOM as the 'United States Joint Task Force in Somalia'. Lines of command and the distribution of responsibility were now dangerously tangled. Although UNOSOM was placed under the nominal command of a Turkish general, he had an American deputy. More significantly, the key role of secretary-general's representative in the country was performed by a retired American admiral, Jonathon Howe. In a situation that demanded the clearest and most streamlined peacekeeping arrangements, the reality was divided responsibilities and parallel command structures.

Amid this, Mohamed Aideed, with some justification, began to denounce the favourable treatment that the intervention forces seemed to be extending to his rivals. As the strongest warlord in military terms, Aideed had become, almost inevitably, the 'enemy' in the eyes of American forces not schooled in the tenets of interpositionary peacekeeping. Fatally, the American position was so dominant in Somalia that the norms of the peacekeeping culture were not transferred to them as they customarily had been to new national participants throughout the peacekeeping experience. Clearly, American involvement with earlier 'UN' operations did little to change the underlying mindset of its forces. In Korea the Unified Command had an enemy; in the Gulf Operation Desert Storm had an enemy. Now, the Americans had assigned that role to Aideed, and the other components of the international intervention in Somalia were drawn into the arrangement. In the first week of June 1993, a month after the transfer of authority to UNOSOM-II from UNITAF, members of the large Pakistani contingent in the UN force were attacked by Aideed's militia in different parts of Mogadishu. In all, about thirty UN soldiers were killed. The ensuing crisis crystallized the dangers of the confused command and control of the multilateral force. On 6 June, the day following the fighting, the Security Council, on the initiative of the Americans, passed a resolution calling for 'all necessary measures' to be used to bring the perpetrators of the attacks to 'trial and punishment'.[8] UNOSOM-II and American forces now launched a series of attacks on Aideed's SNA. Admiral Howe demanded that Aideed himself surrender to the UN, and the UNOSOM-II force commander was ordered to pursue him if he failed to do so.

However understandable American anger at the ruthless and cynical Aideed, their policy of demonization proved disastrously counterproductive. The series of attacks mounted on Aideed's south Mogadishu strongholds inevitably inflicted 'collateral damage', as the military euphemism has it, and thousands of Somalis who might, with more sensitive handling, have remained supportive of the UN's efforts were alienated from the international force. Aideed, ever alert to the political possibilities of crisis, now presented himself not as a faction leader but as a Somali nationalist persecuted by the world's last superpower intent on nefarious neo-colonialist ends. The CNN effect that the American forces had sought to manage in their own interests had now turned against them, and political enthusiasm in Washington for the Somalia venture was fading rapidly in the summer and autumn of 1993. Apparently locked into a set pattern of behaviour by the logic of its original position, however, American – and therefore UN – forces on the ground continued to target Aideed and his SNA.

This culminated in what for the United States became the defining moment of the Somali conflict. Its media-captured images would horrify the home audience and a few years later a fictionalized version would become a hugely successful Hollywood film. On 3 October 1993 two American Blackhawk helicopters were downed by militia fire while attacking targets in south Mogadishu. Tellingly, the operation had been planned and ordered by the United States special forces command in Florida and launched without consultation with either UNOSOM-II or even Admiral Howe who were simply informed of it as it got under way. American special forces units who were despatched to rescue the crews of the helicopters themselves became trapped in the hostile side streets and alleys of south Mogadishu. It now fell to (mainly Malaysian) UNOSOM-II forces to extricate the Americans, which, at the cost of considerable casualties, they did. Countless Somalis were killed in the fighting but it was the eighteen American fatalities that proved significant for the future of peacekeeping in Somalia and, in the longer term, the future of the country itself. A few days after the fighting President Clinton announced that all US troops would be withdrawn from Somalia by the following March. Other contributors to UNOSOM-II felt that in the circumstances that now prevailed and in the absence of American firepower they would have to follow suit.

Consequences and lessons

The next months saw the steady contraction of the multinational effort in Somalia. Aideed the 'enemy', if that he was, had effectively defeated the will and the might of the international community. All attempts to capture him were abandoned as the Americans and the UN planned their departure from a country that was in no better a state than it had been when they arrived. Somalia now became emblematic of the 'failure' of peacekeeping. What had gone wrong? Perhaps the fundamental problem lay in the hybrid nature of the intervention. It began with UNOSOM as an attempt to apply traditional peacekeeping methods to a novel situation. Rather than interpose themselves between two obvious antagonists, the peacekeepers were to use their moral presence (and not their weapons) to ensure the distribution of aid. What had not been fully considered, however, was that the control of aid was itself a weapon in the ongoing conflict and that the UN's attempt to control it was therefore not a 'neutral' action. International public outrage at this brought a transformation in the nature of the operation and in the actors controlling it. With UNITAF it ceased being a 'UN peacekeeping operation' and became an American enforcement one. But UNITAF was constrained by bureaucratic politics in Washington and did not in the event 'enforce' effectively enough. Specifically, it failed to disarm the militias. When the baton passed back nominally to the UN in the form of UNOSOM-II the intervention had plunged into a hopeless identity crisis. What was its objective? What means were to be used to achieve them? Who was in control of their pursuit? These crucial questions were never properly explored, let alone resolved.

The consequences of the failure of the Somali intervention were considerable. Somalia itself continued to defy the 'rules' of the international system by remaining a stateless territory on an apparently permanent basis. Following the humiliation of the multilateral effort in the early 1990s there was little enthusiasm for further intervention, though after the terrorist attacks on America in September 2001 a new concern developed in the west about the dangers inherent in 'stateless' territories, particularly in the Muslim world. There were consequences that went beyond Somalia, too. As we observed in the previous chapter, the Somalia experience contributed to the reluctance of the Security Council to take any decisive steps to end the genocide in Rwanda in 1994. In May of that year, seven months after the American losses in Mogadishu and when the killing in Rwanda was at its height, America's policy towards peacekeeping was sharply qualified. The Clinton administration produced 'Presidential Decision Directive no. 25' ('PDD25'). Entitled 'Policy of Reforming Multilateral Peace Operations', this placed limits on future support for peacekeeping, restricting it to situations involving direct American interests.[9] The Somalian experience, therefore, helped curtail American enthusiasm for participation in peacekeeping and also fed an underlying resentment of the UN and its activities always evident in some sectors of American politics and society.

Beyond the impact on its domestic politics and subsequent approach to multilateralism, America's involvement in Somalia pointed up an important truth about post-cold war peacekeeping. The original Hammarskjöldian model excluded big-power involvement because of the risk of the importation of cold war tensions into conflicts that peacekeeping was designed to exclude them from. The assumption that the end of the bipolar divide would have removed the bar to superpower involvement came under question with the Somalia intervention. In Somalia at least two big-power attributes displayed by the United States proved counterproductive to the intervention. First, regardless of the existence or otherwise of bipolar divisions, big powers will always be vulnerable to the accusation of 'neo-colonialism', and this will remain a potent weapon in the armoury of any local actor who wishes to play the nationalist card. Second, big powers do not easily acquire the operational assumptions of the peacekeeper. While the notion of a 'peacekeeping culture' can be overstated, certain strategic and tactical approaches to intervention are more easily acquired by middle and small powers than by those whose military traditions and political expectations are grounded in identifying enemies and seeking their defeat. Yet ultimately these factors, while significant, were probably not the critical elements in the failure of multilateral intervention in Somalia. In truth, the potential for nation-building in a situation in which the necessary local structures were so weak and conflict so intractable may simply have been beyond the capacity of any intervention to resolve.

Liberia: experimenting with inter-agency peacekeeping

In September 1993, six months after its inglorious withdrawal from Somalia, the UN became involved in a quite different but equally intractable crisis on the other side of the continent in Liberia. Here, too, the 'state' as commonly understood had ceased to function. The UN's initial involvement was a politically complicated though militarily limited one that lasted for almost exactly four years until 1997. The UN withdrew at this point from a situation that was far from stable. Then, in 2003, it entered into a much more substantial commitment that, while stabilizing the situation, encountered great obstacles in helping to establish a permanent peace.

The background: Liberia's historical 'particularism'

The history of Liberia, which forms the background to its contemporary difficulties, is unique and complex. The Liberian 'nation' was the product of a nineteenth-century American movement to resettle freed slaves in their west African 'homeland'. The first ex-slaves (whose origins in reality may have lain anywhere in west or central Africa) arrived in the area in 1821 and 'Liberia' was proclaimed an independent state in 1847. Its peculiar status meant that it remained off-limits to the European imperialists scrambling over the rest of the continent in the second half of the nineteenth century, but in a very real sense an act of colonization was taking place in Liberia. The new arrivals formed an elite that controlled all aspects of Liberian politics and the economy from Monrovia, the capital they constructed and named for the fifth president of the United States, James Monroe (whose 'doctrine' we discussed in Chapter 7). These incomers populated the coastal area. The 'native' Liberians of the interior had the status of second-class citizens if and when they came into contact with the structures of the state, and were largely left to their own devices when they did not. The economic basis of the country for most of the twentieth century lay in rubber production in which native Liberian labour was brutally exploited by the Americo-Liberian elite. As might be expected, considerable resentment grew among the original population as it was brought into contact with the state.

The long period of generally inefficient and corrupt Americo-Liberian rule ended in 1980 with a coup that brought Samuel Doe to power as Liberia's first 'indigenous' president. His capricious and violent regime, however, did not bring improvement to the lives of the Liberian people, whether on the coast or in the interior. Vital American aid was suspended as the economy was grossly mismanaged and plundered of what it did produce in the interests of Doe's own Krahn tribe. Consequently, when in 1989 a group of rebels led by the Americo-Liberian Charles Taylor, once a Doe supporter, crossed over the border from Côte d'Ivoire, it met with some early success. The incursion marked the beginning of a protracted conflict that would claim perhaps 300,000 lives – more than 10 per cent of the population – over the next fourteen years.

The ECOMOG intervention

Although Liberia's neighbours in west Africa were divided in their sympathies – with the Francophone states generally supporting Taylor's rebellion and the Anglophone ones opposing it – determined attempts were made to find a settlement. The situation was complicated by a generalized outbreak of factional opportunism as the Doe regime began to crumble. Taylor was not the only would-be warlord with designs on the country's resources. In August 1990, faced with the apparent impossibility of finding an effective negotiated settlement, the Economic Community of West African States despatched a Military Observation Group (ECOMOG) to Liberia (Map 19). In reality, this was far from an 'observation' mission. ECOMOG was a formidable force of several thousand troops who were drawn mostly from the Anglophone countries of the region and most prominently from Nigeria, the regional hegemon. Through the largely unrestrained use of force ECOMOG managed to take control of the capital and the surrounding area by the end of 1990, but by this time the Liberian state had effectively ceased to exist. Doe had been murdered after being captured by one of the rebel factions and chaos reigned beyond the enclave around Monrovia held by ECOMOG. Taylor, now in control of by far the most powerful faction, correctly identified ECOMOG as his most formidable opponent.

Taylor's political strategy now was to portray the war as a nationalist struggle against a foreign enemy, in much the same way as Mohamed Aideed did in Somalia. In a country with only the most limited sense of national identity, however, this availed him little. His military challenge to ECOMOG was defeated in 1992, and he was forced to pay lip service to a 'settlement' negotiated between the factions in Cotonou, the capital of Benin, which would give him an opportunity to pursue power through an electoral process. The situation remained volatile, however, and the longer the fighting continued the more the role of ECOMOG came under critical scrutiny. There were two aspects to the growing reservations about ECOMOG's role in Liberia. The first was political and diplomatic. The dominance of Nigeria raised questions about the neutrality of the force. Nigeria and the other Anglophone states, after all, were known to be hostile towards Taylor. Second, the behaviour of the ECOMOG force on the ground caused concern abroad. Not only was the designation of 'observation group' wholly misplaced, its conduct was hardly that of a peacekeeping force either. Not only did its use of force tend to be recklessly indiscriminate, its soldiers were notorious for their general misbehaviour.[10]

The inter-agency experiment

To address these problems of 'regional peacekeeping' two adjustments to ECOMOG's position were proposed. First, other non-ECOWAS African contingents – from Tanzania and Uganda – joined the force under the auspices of the OAU. The second initiative was to bring the United Nations into a kind of 'sleeping partnership' in the operation. The United Nations Observer Mission in Liberia (UNOMIL) was therefore created to 'monitor, verify and report on' the activities of ECOMOG in implementing the Cotonou agreement. The operation was approved by the Security Council in September 1993 with an authorized maximum strength of 300 military observers.[11]

On one view this was an intriguing new departure for UN peacekeeping. It could be seen as an early attempt to implement one of the suggestions just recently presented by Boutros-Ghali in *An Agenda for Peace* in which he proposed, it will be recalled, the increased 'regionalization' of peacekeeping under the overall supervision of the Security Council. There were, however, too many loose ends left in the arrangement for this to work effectively. UNOMIL was not the interlocking, mutually supportive combined effort originally conceived by its planners. The reality was the existence of two separate multinational military interventions in Liberia that viewed each other with mutual suspicion and failed to mesh into the intended integrated whole. There was from the beginning considerable inter-agency tension. On one side ECOMOG resented the implicit 'policing' of its efforts by UNOMIL, which the west African commanders regarded as out of touch with the harsh realities of operational conditions in Liberia. On the other, UNOMIL, which only for a short time approached its maximum strength, was reliant for its security and freedom of movement on the ECOMOG force that it was supposed to be supervising. These practical and political difficulties within an insufficiently defined relationship gradually saw UNOMIL's activities confined to Monrovia, leaving ECOMOG a free hand outside the capital and making the UN operation's mandate to supervise activities in the border zones unachievable.

The elections that were central to the Cotonou agreement and that were supposed to have taken place in 1994 were repeatedly delayed as fighting between the factions and between the factions and ECOMOG continued. Among all this UNOMIL was little more than a passive observer. Presidential elections took place finally in 1997 and resulted, to the dismay of the ECOMOG force, in the victory of Charles Taylor. Liberia now had a warlord head of state, legitimized by an electoral process that emerged from a protracted and costly inter-agency peacekeeping effort. To the surprise of few, Taylor's presidency was not a success. Despite continued ECOWAS and UN involvement in the post-conflict peacebuilding process, nothing was done to bring about any reconciliation of the former warring factions. The regime was responsible for the wholesale abuse of human rights. It failed to tackle the essential reform of the country's security apparatus – which remained in the hands of Taylor's former rebel movement. As a result, by mid-2003 Liberia was in the midst of a civil war of a savagery unmatched even by the conflict of the mid-1990s. Taylor, now largely friendless in the region as a result of his interference in the politics of most of his neighbours, faced an onslaught on the capital by a coalition of former enemy factions fighting under the substantially misleading name of Liberians United for Reconciliation and Democracy. After a long period of violent stand-off Taylor was persuaded – with guarantees of legal immunity – to leave Liberia for exile in Nigeria. This left the country once again without a functioning state, though the loss was not widely felt in the wake of Taylor's chaotic misrule.

The UN assumes the lead role: the mission in Liberia

Following discussions with regional governments secretary-general Kofi Annan brought a plan to the Security Council in September 2003 for the creation of a large-scale, multi-functional peacekeeping operation, the UN Mission in Liberia (UNMIL). This 15,000-strong force was to be responsible for supporting a new transitional coalition government by acting in effect as its security force. It would also implement the now customary demobilization, disarmament and reintegration process for former fighters. UNMIL would liaise with the principal regional agencies – ECOWAS and the AU – to ensure that the transnational dimensions of peacemaking in Liberia – a growing preoccupation among neighbouring states – were given proper prominence.[12]

The adoption of Annan's resolution by the Security Council was eased by the fact that the secretary-general had persuaded the United States to bear the main part of the operation's considerable cost.[13] The White House of George W. Bush was not by predisposition a supporter of multilateralism through the UN. But the place and time of the operations were significant. The United States, as we have seen, has a special historical relationship with Liberia, fundamentally different from that with the rest of sub-Saharan Africa. Washington had been stung by criticisms of its apparent reluctance to become involved earlier in the crisis of 2003, when US marines were stationed off-shore but failed to intervene when the violence was at its most intense. By funding the UN operation Washington could redress the damage its earlier reluctance had done to its standing in Africa. More broadly, by the late summer of 2003 Washington was seeking to repair its general relationship with the United Nations, which had been severely damaged by the invasion of Iraq the previous spring. With the apparent initial success of the American-led war now questioned by a growing insurgency in Iraq, the United States sought to internationalize the crisis, and cooperation on Liberia offered at least one element in a rapprochement with the UN.

Security of the funding base for the peacekeeping operations aside, however, there was to be no easy escape from Liberia's vast, acute and deeply embedded difficulties. There, as elsewhere, the UN operation ran the risk of becoming 'institutionalized' and mutating into an integral component of the crisis itself. There was no easy answer to this dilemma. In Liberia the task of building a cohesive nation with an effective state enclosing its political and economic life was inevitably going to be a complex and long-term one. The lesson from 1997 for the UN was that premature withdrawal from the process, rather like the inadequate administration of antibiotics, could only create greater problems that demanded more far-reaching intervention in the future.

Sierra Leone: reviving the state

A similar pattern of international involvement can be seen in Liberia's neighbour to the north-west, Sierra Leone. The responsibility for peacekeeping here, as in Liberia, was initially undertaken by the regional forces of ECOWAS with the UN in a 'supervisory' role. Here, too, an inadequate and poorly managed initial intervention led eventually to the requirement for a much more substantial one with clearer lines of responsibility and command. In Sierra Leone the fundamental crisis of the state was not created by the disintegration of central authority as it was in Liberia, however, but in the hopeless fragility of central authority in the face of the warlord challenge.

As in Liberia, the history of Sierra Leone was shaped by the slave trade. The territory was used as a landing place for slaves rescued at sea during the British navy's anti-slaving patrols in the nineteenth century. Unlike Liberia's unique political experience, Sierra Leone had a more typical history in the context of west Africa as a British possession and came to independent statehood in 1961during the main wave of African decolonization. Relatively rich in resources and with a higher level of educational provision and attainment than many of its neighbours, Sierra Leone enjoyed enviable stability in the first three decades of independence. This political calm, however, overlay a gradual process of economic decline which fed disaffection in particular regions and among certain groups. As in Liberia, there was a social cleavage between the more developed coastal areas and the interior. Inland, economic opportunities for even well-educated young people were very limited. The slow build-up of resentment and tension came to a head in the early 1990s, fed actively by Charles Taylor's deeds across the border in Liberia. Taylor's Liberian insurgency acted initially as a destabilizing force in border areas as the Sierra Leone Army (SLA) was deployed to repel incursions across the poorly demarcated frontier. The disruption and dislocation caused by the sudden appearance of a not always well-disciplined military meant that the Liberian rebels came to be seen as a model among disenchanted youth on the Sierra Leone side of the border. This gave added momentum to the emergence of a home-grown insurgent movement, the Revolutionary United Front (RUF), led by a former soldier, Foday Sankoh.

Although the RUF was far from a well-organized or effective fighting force, it managed, through a combination of its own ruthless brutality and the inadequacy of the SLA to establish itself in significant parts of the interior. Its rebellion meanwhile had an impact on national politics, leading to the steady militarization of government through a series of army coups. For Charles Taylor, the Sierra Leone insurgency brought an accretion of economic and military benefits, and he was not slow to exploit it in pursuit of them. The chaos in Sierra Leone's border areas gave him access to the region's rich diamond deposits. In addition, by feeding the crisis in Sierra Leone, Taylor saw an opportunity of reducing the pressure he was under from the Nigerian-dominated ECOMOG forces in Liberia. And indeed, during 1993 a large component of the west African force in Liberia was transferred to Sierra Leone to support anti-RUF operations there (Map 27). Soon ECOMOG had more or less supplanted the ineffective SLA as Sierra Leone's main security force.

In one key respect the operational situation in Sierra Leone was much worse for the ECOMOG force than it was in Liberia. By the mid-1990s the RUF constituted a single challenge to ECOMOG and what was left of the Sierra Leone state. In Liberia, in contrast, much rebel effort was expended on inter-factional fighting, which reduced the overall military challenge to ECOMOG. By the first months of 1995 the 2,000-strong ECOMOG force was engaged in a desperate defence of the capital, Freetown, against an apparently unstoppable RUF advance. Only the engagement by the government of a South African based 'private security company' (or mercenary venture, in less euphemistic terms), Executive Outcomes (EO), turned this particular tide. Together, ECOMOG and EO forces were able to push the RUF back into the interior and, eventually, to force Foday Sankoh to the negotiating table. This led to a series of elections in 1996, which produced a new, democratically legitimized Sierra Leone government under the presidency of a former UN official, Ahmad Tejan Kabbah. The peace did not hold, however. Kabbah proved a less than inspiring leader and presided over a period of political drift during which the RUF was able – after the withdrawal of EO – to rearm and regroup. In May 1997 another military coup saw Kabbah flee the country and the installation of an army major, Johnny Paul Koroma, as president. The incompetent and unpredictable Koroma, aware of the extent of the rebel challenge and clearly daunted by it, now declared himself sympathetic to the RUF, turning the factions of the SLA under his control (the army had been divided over his coup) against the ECOMOG force, which still, by default, backed the former, now absent, government.

UN involvement in Sierra Leone up to this point had been restricted to offers of good offices and minor mediatory roles. Already heavily committed to a range of peacekeeping operations in Africa, and aware of the huge complexities of the conflict, the Security Council made a virtue of encouraging 'African solutions to African problems' and was happy to leave the main peacekeeping and peacemaking efforts in Sierra Leone to ECOWAS. By the middle of 1998, however, pressure was growing for a more active UN role. During the previous year ECOMOG, once again supported by bought-in mercenary support (now from EO's British sister company, Sandline) and with local tribal help, had regained the initiative and expelled Koroma from Freetown. In the meantime, Foday Sankoh had been arrested during a visit to Nigeria and was now detained there, leaving the RUF without a figurehead. In these altered conditions Kabbah felt it safe to return to Freetown. His position was still extremely weak, though. On the initiative of Kofi Annan, himself a west African, the Security Council agreed to take much the same route as it had in Liberia – its very limited success there notwithstanding – and create a 'supervisory' operation to monitor ECOMOG 'peacekeeping'. In July 1998, therefore, the Observer Mission in Sierra Leone (UNOMSIL) was formed to oversee 'the role of ECOMOG in the provision of security' and its 'respect for international humanitarian law'.[14]

If UNOMSIL was designed to consolidate the position of the Kabbah regime through the presence of UN observers, it proved disastrously inadequate. Although Koroma's forces had been dispersed by pro-government offensives in the previous year, a rump of former SLA soldiers had been able to join with the RUF in the interior where the rebel movement was little affected by the absence of Sankoh, whose leadership had for some time been more nominal than real. Far from diminishing, therefore, rebel activity intensified in the second part of 1998 and into the next year. An attack on Freetown in January 1999 was only repelled by pro-Kabbah forces with great difficulty. The UNOMSIL presence had in the meantime been reduced to single figures as its mandate became impossible to fulfil in the prevailing conditions of total war.

Implementing a settlement: the UN mission in Sierra Leone

The crisis of January 1999 brought it home to the UN and other international actors in Sierra Leone that there was little future in the current arrangements. Kabbah had been saved only at the eleventh hour, and even then it was predominantly foreign forces (ECOMOG and Sandline) that had done the job. In the future he might not be so lucky, and a successful state could not be built on the permanent presence of external forces anyway. However distasteful it might be – and given the foul record of RUF brutality it was inevitably extremely distasteful – a peace settlement would have to be reached that would bring the rebels into some sort of power-sharing arrangement. Accordingly, under pressure from the

UN and leading members of the Security Council, Kabbah agreed to a deal arranged in Lomé in Togo in July 1999 by President Clinton's personal envoy, Jesse Jackson.

By the terms of the agreement the RUF would be brought into a new national government and in return would agree to demobilize and disarm its fighters. This approach represented a potentially dangerous reversal of the sequence of peace implementation elsewhere in Africa in that the rebels would receive their political reward before meeting their part of the bargain. Given the extreme unpredictability of the RUF and the large question marks over the nature of its leadership, this was hazardous indeed. To meet the problem, the UN followed a similar route in Sierra Leone to that in Liberia a few years later. The largely ineffectual monitoring operation established to oversee the peacekeeping efforts of other agencies was supplanted by a large UN force with wide-ranging responsibilities. The United Nations Mission in Sierra Leone (UNAMSIL) was created by the Security Council in October 1999. With an authorized strength of 6,000 it was to cooperate with the Kabbah government and the former rebels in implementing the Lomé agreement.[15] The ECOMOG force would remain in the meantime, largely to reassure Kabbah's supporters of their own security.

The tasks facing the UN operation were Herculean. The Lomé agreement had been the product of external pressure rather than any impetus towards peace among the antagonists. Nowhere before in Africa – from Angola to Western Sahara to Rwanda – had such a situation had a satisfactory outcome. In Sierra Leone, moreover, the rebels were notoriously unpredictable and unreliable interlocutors. The country was awash with weapons held in the hands of some 45,000 fighters whose willingness to give them up and return to uncertain futures in their home areas was very far from certain. The composition of the United Nations force was also questionable. Neither the United States nor Britain, who had been the principal advocates of the Lomé agreement, were willing to participate, and the force was made up in the majority by African and Asian states with limited collective experience of peacekeeping work. Soon a pattern of obstruction and evasion familiar in other failed settlement agreements was emerging, with the RUF finding excuses not to demobilize and for excluding UN troops from its areas of control.

Against this threatening background, the ECOMOG force, which remained crucial to the limited peace that prevailed, prepared to withdraw. Its principal contributor, Nigeria, had borne virtually all the costs of the operation and the pressure was beginning to tell in the domestic economy. The pull-out began at the end of 1999 and continued over the following months. The effect was soon felt. Although Annan successfully lobbied the Security Council for a doubling of UNAMSIL's strength and an expansion of its mandate, the removal of battle-hardened ECOMOG troops familiar with local conditions led to a rapid deterioration in the security situation. RUF fighters, far from presenting themselves for demobilization and disarming as required by the Lomé agreement, now began to probe the resolution of UNAMSIL units in a way that they would not have contemplated with the ECOMOG force. The rebels found that the UN forces had little appetite for fighting. Provocations grew into major confrontations and mass abductions of usually unresisting UNAMSIL troops by RUF groups. It soon became clear that the RUF could, and almost certainly would, launch another assault on the capital, now undefended by either ECOMOG or mercenary forces, and simply abandon the Lomé process, which in any event it had hardly engaged with.

The situation, which was potentially the greatest crisis for peacekeeping in Africa since the Rwanda genocide six years previously, was retrieved not by UN forces who appeared paralysed by the RUF's aggression but by a semi-clandestine British intervention. Taking a leaf from a book more commonly associated with the French in Africa, marine commandos and paratroops were inserted into the Freetown area, ostensibly to secure the evacuation of British nationals from the country. It soon became clear, however, that their orders went much further, and it emerged that British special forces had been deployed in other key areas of the country. Once again, foreign forces had been required to save a Sierra Leone 'government', which, it seemed, was incapable of demonstrating even the most basic requirements of statehood. The small but decisive unilateral intervention by Britain also raised some hard questions about UN peacekeeping in Africa at the beginning of the new century. Had nothing been learned from the failures of earlier peace processes that the UN had been supposed to implement? And, at the operational level, why had UNAMSIL, a large force with a far-reaching mandate, been so supine in the face of challenges from ill-organized and untrained gangs of rebels? Even in the strict minimalist terms of peacekeeping set out in the Hammarskjöld era, the right of self-defence was fully acknowledged. Was the apparent impossibility of this operation so demoralizing to its participants that even basic military instincts were dulled?

These were important points, but in the changed and improved circumstances that now prevailed in the country they were not pressed. During the crisis Foday Sankoh, who had inexplicably turned up in Freetown, was arrested after narrowly escaping being lynched by a crowd who had identified him in the street. With Sankoh in jail, with RUF activities considerably curtailed by British operations and with a reinvigorated UN force (which was expanded to a strength of 16,000 in 2001), the rebels were forced to accept the deployment of UNAMSIL throughout the country. Charles Taylor's baleful influence on the situation was also removed as his energies were increasingly focused on preserving his own 'government' in Monrovia rather than encouraging mischief across the border. It was now possible to construct a new peace plan to replace the Lomé agreement, which had disintegrated amid the fighting of 2000. This was signed with a minimum of negotiation in the Nigerian capital Abuja in November 2000. The new arrangement gave a much more limited role to the RUF than Lomé had. The rebels, in their reduced circumstances, had little option but to accept. After some initial temporizing, the demobilization, disarmament and reintegration process got under way with little further obstruction.

The journey back to some sort of normality for Sierra Leone would be a long and hard one. The country was more or less wrecked economically and had suffered traumatic social dislocation. The role of UNAMSIL in the process of reconstruction was important and effective; its role in preparing the conditions for this reconstruction – in other words, its performance as a peacekeeping force in time of crisis – was neither.

Back to the source: the Democratic Republic of Congo

We end our exploration of peacekeeping in Africa where we began it: in the Congo. Our earlier examination of the Congo finished with the country in the grip of the Mobutu dictatorship, which established itself after the end of the UN operations in 1964. Mobutu exercised absolute power in the Congo (which was renamed Zaire in 1971), presiding over a regime that became emblematic of the continent's post-independence malaise. Autocratic, brutal and corrupt to the ultimate degree, Mobutu remained secure in power throughout the cold war as a reliable friend of the west. His control of the massive territory, after all, denied it to less ideologically attractive alternatives, and Congo/Zaire's economic and geographic importance enabled him to project western interests far beyond his borders. Even after the end of the cold war, when he was more embarrassment than use to his western friends, he had so reduced and intimidated the internal opposition that he was able to remain in power for several more years. In 1997, however, he was finally deposed.

Regional crisis and the end of the Mobutu regime

The circumstances of Mobutu's fall were significant, both in relation to broader regional conflicts that we have examined and for the future troubles that would afflict the country and to which the UN would be required to respond. Following the victory of the Tutsi-dominated RPF in Rwanda, thousands of Hutu refugees fled across the border into eastern Zaire, either in fear of reprisals or to evade justice for their role in the genocide. This great population movement created considerable instability in Zaire, disturbing its own ethnic relations. The situation was further complicated by the RPF's justified fear that the Hutu refugee camps in Zaire had become bases for Hutu incursions back into Rwanda. Consequently, Rwanda gave its support to the leader of a long-standing but largely dormant anti-Mobutu rebel movement in eastern Zaire, Laurent Desiré Kabila. Energized with the support of the Rwandan army, Kabila's insurgency was able to topple an ailing and now friendless Mobutu in May 1997. His end, therefore, could be traced directly to the events in Rwanda in 1994.

Mobutu's successor had come to power almost entirely on the basis of external backing, however. Kabila's regime was not grounded in widespread national support, and his record as an opposition figure had not been a distinguished one. To the surprise of few who knew him, Kabila showed little interest in or capacity for mobilizing the nation in the enormous task of social and economic reconstruction after the decades of misrule by Mobutu. A change of name from Zaire to the DRC seemed about the limit of Kabila's interest in reform. Beyond this he gave every appearance of merely replacing Mobutu at the head of his own corrupt, patrimonial regime. When his foreign backers turned against him, therefore, as they did little more than a year after he came to power, Kabila's regime was thrown into crisis. His mistake had been to attempt to free himself and his armed forces from what was effectively Rwandan control. This was unacceptable to the RPF government in Kigali, and the Rwanda army in the DRC now moved against him. Soon the crisis had triggered a generalized war between a patchwork of ethnically based factions in the DRC that quickly acquired a wider central and southern African dimension. The involvement of both Rwandan and Ugandan forces on the anti-Kabila side was balanced by that of Angola, Namibia and Zimbabwe, who intervened to prop up Kabila. Other African states became less directly involved, principally through supplying arms to one or other of the sides. The reason the conflict proved so contagious lay partly in the location of the DRC at the heart of a complex of troubled ethnic and political relationships in the Great Lakes region of Africa. Beyond this, however, lay the Congo's enormous natural wealth, which acted as a magnet to the political and military elites of many African states intent on self-enrichment in the vast, effectively stateless territory. The result was what the American secretary of state, Madeleine Albright, described in the United Nations as 'Africa's first world war'.[16]

Initially there was no enthusiasm in New York for a major UN intervention in the crisis. The tangled complexity of the conflict, both in its internal aspects and its broader international ones, was such that it was not clear what effective mandate a United Nations force could be given. Peacekeeping in Africa was, anyway, still a sensitive subject for the Security Council in these last years of the century when Somalia and Rwanda were still recent memories, with Angola serving as a continuing witness to the limits of intervention, and with bloody confusion reigning in Liberia and Sierra Leone. The United Nations had, it seemed, finally taken on board the simple and inescapable truth that a peacekeeping intervention, however much conditions on the ground appeared to demand it, was unlikely to succeed unless the foundations of a durable settlement were already in place locally. There could be no peacekeeping without a clear indication that the parties to the conflict in the DRC, both domestic and international, were serious about finding an accommodation.

The Lusaka agreement and the creation of the UN mission

A pointer in this direction was provided in July 1999 following a series of meetings between most of the significant actors in the Congo held in the Zambian capital, Lusaka. This was based on the familiar template of demobilization and disarmament of fighters followed by externally supervised elections for a new national government. An interim peace agreement on these lines was signed, which included an invitation to the United Nations to provide a large peacekeeping force to oversee its implementation. The operation would involve 'peace enforcement units' of the sort envisaged by Boutros-Ghali in *An Agenda for Peace*, which in principle would permit decisive action against parties evading their commitments. Anxious to maintain the momentum towards a settlement, secretary-general Kofi Annan responded quickly and positively to the Lusaka plan. He did not understate the difficulties of the proposed UN role when urging the Security Council to agree to intervene. The commitment 'would be large and expensive [requiring] the deployment of several thousands of international troops and civilian personnel. It [would] face tremendous difficulties and will be beset with risks'.[17] Thus cautioned, the Security Council agreed to the establishment of the United Nations Organization Mission to the Congo, which would be known by the acronym MONUC from its French title Mission de l'Organisation des Nations Unies en République Démocratique du Congo.[18]

Displaying due prudence, the secretary-general did not immediately authorize a major despatch of peacekeepers. He insisted that the deployment of MONUC must be in careful phases, with objectives achieved at the end of each before the next would begin. Initially the operation was restricted to the despatch of liaison officers who were to be attached to the various Congolese factions and neighbouring states involved in the conflict. Annan's wariness proved justified. The ceasefire on which implementation of the Lusaka agreement was predicated did not endure. By the beginning of 2000 fighting had resumed in various parts of the Congo. Then in May a further, wholly unpredicted dimension was added to the conflict when the anti-Kabila alliance between Rwanda and Uganda broke down and the two foreign armies began to fight each other in eastern Congo. The prospects for success of any UN 'peace enforcement units' that might have been deployed in this situation could only be guessed at, but it is unlikely they would have been good. As it was, by the middle of 2000 MONUC consisted only of about 200 military observers (Map 8). Even this relatively small deployment became a pawn in the bewildering political game under way in the DRC. In a development reminiscent of the UN's earlier involvement in the Congo in the 1960s, Kabila's government, which barely controlled even the capital by this stage, orchestrated 'popular' demonstrations against the UN for its supposed ineffectualness. His real concern was that a concomitant of any effective peace would most probably be his own removal from power. In these deeply unpromising conditions the secretary-general held off from any further deployment of MONUC.

The situation changed radically in January 2001 when the now isolated and increasingly irrelevant Kabila was murdered, apparently by his own bodyguards. He was immediately succeeded, in true patrimonial style, by his son Joseph. There was now a flutter of optimism as the new president appeared to be a more reasonable interlocutor for both political opponents and peacemakers than his father. For Annan, the altered disposition in Kinshasa justified taking a major step forward in the UN intervention. There was still no question of fielding the large 'peace-guaranteeing' force originally envisaged after the Lusaka agreement, but he proposed that the military observation element of the operation should be increased to a strength of 550. Additionally, a security force of 2,300 would be sent, which would not have an enforcement function but would be responsible primarily for the safety of UN installations and the protection of its humanitarian activities.[19]

The UN presence was held at this level and committed to this relatively modest mandate for most of the next two years, during which little progress was made towards the implementation of the Lusaka agreement. In fact, in some respects the situation deteriorated as the apparently permanent warfare in parts of the country led to new would-be warlords emerging to exploit the chaos for their own, usually material, ends. In one important respect the situation did improve during 2002, however. A large part of the foreign intervention ended when Rwanda, Uganda and Angola withdrew their forces from the country. Although foreign influence, especially Rwandan, continued to be exercised through local factions, for the UN the situation became politically more manageable. Consequently, in December 2002 Annan persuaded the Security Council to dramatically increase the size of MONUC to 8,700 with a new, more direct mandate to sustain the fragile and far from perfect peace in eastern Congo, which had emerged between the local factions after the withdrawal of the foreign armies.[20] The following two years saw further expansion to 10,800 in July 2003 and then to 15,650 in October 2004 and finally to a ceiling of 16,700 in mid-2005.[21]

During the later phase of this expansion MONUC became involved in sporadic but often intense fighting with warlord factions in eastern Congo. This did not have the same political impact on MONUC's role as the fighting that its 1960s predecessor had engaged in. But this was not, perhaps, such a positive advance. It spoke more of the UN's absorption into the routine round of low-level conflict into which the Congo war had settled. The role of the UN in the DRC in the 2000s appeared, for better or worse, to be that of an only occasionally engaged spectator. In contrast, ONUC had been a key political player in the Congo of the 1960s, and its actions and inaction had a major impact on the conflict. The possibility that the DRC's problems were resolvable through the implementation of a formally structured peace agreement seemed to become more rather than less remote as its snarled and twisted local conflicts ground on. Peace, when it comes, may well be the result of total internal exhaustion rather than positive external intervention. It may be at that point that the role of the UN will become most significant.

The involvement of the United Nations in Somalia, Liberia, Sierra Leone and the DRC took peacekeeping an immeasurable distance from the prescriptions of the 1950s. Against the experience of intervention in the brutal and ever-shifting anarchy of those parts of Africa in the 1990s and 2000s, the idea of peacekeeping as formalized interposition between opposing states appears to belong to a distant historical era. In the conflicts we have explored in this chapter the UN and other peacekeeping agencies have operated in a stateless environment, forced to deal with unpredictable interlocutors whose objectives were frequently opaque. The peacekeepers have been forced constantly to consider the interests and intentions of actors in the broader international region in which they were operating. In such circumstances, the fundamental question of whether peacekeeping is actually 'worth it' must occasional force itself into the consciousness of even the most committed multilateralist. The urgings of neo-conservative writers such as Edward Luttwak that we should 'give war a chance' to resolve such conflicts rather than engage in dangerous, expensive and ultimately futile peacekeeping efforts can at times seem compelling.[22] But against this must be set the positive arguments for intervention, however marginal its effect may be on such deep and intractable conflicts. Peacekeeping may not have 'solved' the problems of Somalia, Liberia, Sierra Leone or the DRC, but it is difficult to argue convincingly that it has aggravated them. Between these two points there is a space in which lives have been saved, aid distributed and peacemaking opportunities facilitated. And, even putting all that aside, the peacekeeping presence in conditions that otherwise might seem utterly irremediable has served to allay the sense of total isolation and abandonment on the part of people who would otherwise be wholly bereft of any psychological or material support.

11 Peacekeeping and the international system in the twenty-first century

Looking back to look forward

One of the themes of this book has been the continuity of purpose that has characterized peacekeeping from the early twentieth century to the early twenty-first century. In pursuing this, we have challenged the idea that the underlying function of peacekeeping has undergone any significant *qualitative* change since the end of the cold war. Nevertheless, it is the case that there has been a significant *quantitative* transformation in the occurrence of peacekeeping since the late 1980s. More peacekeeping operations took place in more parts of the international system in the 1990s than in any preceding decade. This raises questions for the future. A very few years into the post-cold war era there were already clear signs that peacekeeping demand threatened to outstrip supply in the sense that available resources – institutional, human and financial – were becoming unequal to the range of crises on which they had to be expended. New approaches were proposed, for example by Boutros-Ghali's *An Agenda for Peace*, and some were tried, in west Africa and in Europe, with mixed results. The twenty-first century, therefore, began with peacekeeping in something of a crisis, though a slow-burning one that remained manageable in the short-term.

The predicament for peacekeeping is primarily about who is going to undertake it at the point, if it arrives, where the United Nations can no longer sustain the continuing high level of demand. Although we inhabit what might reasonably be described as a 'post-post-cold war' world, there is little sign of a lessening in this demand. A number of pertinent questions therefore arise. What types of relationship are likely to develop between the UN and the various 'partner' peacekeeping agencies that have appeared in parts of the international system, particularly since the early 1990s? Are there alternative institutions capable of actually supplanting the UN as independent peacekeepers without any such partnership? For want of a reliable crystal ball we cannot provide definitive answers to these questions. But by identifying certain signs and trends and relating them to the narrative of peacekeeping in the twentieth century, we can at least clarify the issues and suggest likely scenarios for the new millennium. We can also examine the response of the United Nations itself to the new challenges of peacekeeping and how the organization sees its own role developing in the new century.

A widening pool of providers?

The prospects for a widening institutional participation in peacekeeping beyond the United Nations itself was a frequent point of debate in the 1990s as the demand for multilateral intervention surged at the end of the cold war. There was, of course, no inherent reason why peacekeeping had to be the primary task of the UN itself. As we have seen, its predecessor, the League of Nations, was just one provider of multinational military forces in the inter-war years. At that time ad hoc arrangements between politically appropriate force contributors was the most common means of policing the various territorial plebiscites undertaken in Europe after the First World War. Later, during the cold war, prevailing political considerations meant that the UN was not always considered the most suitable provider, either by the organization itself or by the parties on the ground, and forces were constructed from other international coalitions. This was the case, for example, in Lebanon and on the Egyptian–Israeli border in the 1980s.

Most of the post-cold war experimentation with new forms of provision did, however, involve the United Nations in some role or other, either as a partner in a multi-agency operation or as a legitimizing body. There were a number of reasons for this persistence of United Nations primacy. The presence of the UN in most peacekeeping arrangements, however much it may have remained in the background, was in part due to the organization's claim to supreme legal authority in matters of world peace and security. In 1945 the Charter had been intentionally designed to set the United Nations above all other institutional actors and to equip it with the necessary powers of compulsion to permit it to maintain this position. These were laid out in Chapter VII of the Charter. Although the possibility of a security role for regional organizations was acknowledged, this would, according to Chapter VIII, be performed only at the behest and under the control of the Security Council. The far-reaching enforcement powers of the Charter did not survive polarization of the international system that followed on the heels of the new organization. But assumptions about the continuing monopoly of multilateral military action by the UN persisted, and were given impetus by the development of peacekeeping in the 1950s and 1960s. This perception of the UN's role gained renewed force in the 'new world order' rhetoric that emerged from the rubble of the Berlin Wall in the late 1980s and early 1990s. Both the 'victorious' west and the 'defeated' east found common ground in their support for a reinvigorated United Nations. UN legitimization of the war against Iraq at the beginning of 1991 was one obvious confirmation of this.

As the 1990s progressed, however, the central role of the UN in matters of international security became increasingly qualified. There were three main elements to this, which were to some extent interlinked. The first was simply a question of resources. Faced with the new demands of the post-cold war system, the organization was barely able to continue to mount peacekeeping operations on the same basis as it had in the 1950s, 1960s and 1970s. Second, as UN peacekeeping 'failures' began to mount in the mid-1990s – in Bosnia, in Somalia, in Rwanda – the possibility that more effective peacekeeping might be provided by other agencies with different interests and attributes inevitably came to be discussed. Third, the idea gained ground that regional self-sufficiency in security matters was a virtue in itself and ought to be encouraged. Peacekeeping by a single, western-dominated global organization could, from some viewpoints, come uncomfortably close to a form of neo-imperialism.

The challenge to the idea of United Nations primacy presented by these developments did not (in practical terms it could not) completely and immediately supplant the UN's peacekeeping role. What emerged instead were a series of new arrangements in which the United Nations entered into various relationships with other international actors in the provision of peacekeeping. The UN's partner in Liberia and in Sierra Leone was ECOWAS (and its military force, ECOMOG). In Bosnia the UN's opposite number was NATO, and in the former Soviet Union the CIS. These were not trouble-free arrangements, as we have seen. There were obvious problems touching on both the political motivation and the operational competence of these partners. Regional powers have regional interests that may clash with the Hammarskjöldian condition of political neutrality in peacekeeping. This is the other side to arguments about local knowledge and cultural affinity that are sometimes presented in support of peacekeeping by regional institutions and neighbouring states. Additionally, small, poorly trained and inadequately equipped armies do not make the best peacekeepers, whether in neighbouring countries or anywhere else. There were also difficulties in the inter-agency relationship itself. In both west Africa and Bosnia the UN's long-developed peacekeeping culture was frequently not compatible with the perspectives of its partner organizations, which were more attuned to war-fighting and enforcement.

A second, different inter-agency approach was rather more effective in achieving peacekeeping ends in the 1990s. This involved not a UN partnership on the ground but UN legitimization of 'coalitions of the willing', groups of contributors, or even single states, who sought to accomplish mandates approved by the Security Council. The record here is not one of unalloyed success either. The French-dominated Operation Turquoise in Rwanda in 1994, for example, had both questionable objectives and limited impact. But the Australian-led force in East Timor (INTERFET) in 1999 and early 2000 was wholly successful in ending violence and creating the conditions for effective peace-building. The American Unified

Task Force in Somalia in 1993 lies somewhere between these two in terms of success. It eased the humanitarian plight of many thousands but it failed to tackle the conditions underlying the country's descent into anarchy.

Both these forms of 'partnership peacekeeping' are likely to continue in the new century, and as experience accumulates, they will almost certainly become more effective. The difficulties surrounding peacekeeping undertaken wholly by non-UN agencies are deep seated, however. In Africa, in particular, political and operational obstacles to 'African solutions to African problems' will not be easily or quickly overcome. In 2002 the creation of the AU, which was designed as a more effective replacement for the OAU, raised expectations of a new beginning for African conflict management. Unlike more local African regional organizations such as ECOWAS, the AU could, it was hoped, intervene in African conflicts while remaining free of accusations of political interest or bias. But resource issues remained a problem for most AU states capable of contributing to its peacekeeping role.

The AU's most significant contribution in the first years of the new century was in the Darfur region of western Sudan. In 2003 a rebellion broke out here among the black African population against the central government in Khartoum, which was accused of favouring Sudan's northern 'Arab' people. In the first two years of fighting between the rebels on one side and the Sudanese army and Arab ('Janjaweed') militias on the other nearly 200,000 people died. Another two million fled as refugees across the desert border into neighbouring Chad. In response to the crisis the AU established an African Mission in Sudan (AMIS) and deployed a peacekeeping operation, the Darfur Integrated Taskforce (DITF), which was supposed to protect the civilian population and supervise local ceasefires.[1] The military task in the vast desert region was daunting, however, and the demands on the resources of the contributing African states were immense (Map 29). As a consequence, deployment was very slow and the 3,000-strong force was fundamentally inadequate to the mandate set for it. Planned increases in the size of the force have foundered as national resources have proved inadequate to meet the need. The result has been the gradual, reluctant engagement of the UN in a conflict it had sought to leave in the hands of the local agency. While the Security Council had supported the efforts of the AU in Darfur, it resisted any more direct involvement in Sudan. Eventfully, however, in mid-2005 a UN Mission in Sudan (UNMIS) was created and some 1,400 troops deployed to the country as a whole (Darfur was only one component of a much larger and older conflict between its African and Arab peoples). It was questionable whether the limited UN response would add significantly to the AU's efforts. The plan adopted by the secretariat provided for an operation involving 10,000 troops and police, but it was unlikely that the UN would easily recruit sufficient contributors and resources to reach this.[2]

The Darfur crisis and the response to it may illustrate the very real danger in a certain approach to peacekeeping partnership in the global south. A well-intentioned initial response by the local agency may prove unable to make a significant impact on the situation. In the meantime the United Nations, which is fundamentally reluctant to become closely involved, resists the logic of this situation and remains at a distance. Then, when circumstances reach a point where action becomes unavoidable, the UN response is inadequate to meet the needs of the ever growing crisis.

What of conflicts elsewhere in the system in which better resourced non-UN agencies may become involved? At the beginning of the twenty-first century the north does seem to have the appropriate institutions to perform the functions of multinational intervention without material support from the UN. NATO proved its military capacity in the former Yugoslavia and emerged from the complex of crises there with some credit. As we saw, however, this 'capacity' lay in the realm of enforcement rather than peacekeeping in the interpositionary sense. Another large NATO multinational force was deployed in Afghanistan after the American-led war to remove the Taliban regime at the end of 2001. The International Security Assistance Force (ISAF) there had reached a strength of 8,500 by 2005 and was characterized by NATO itself as a 'peacekeeping' operation (Map 1). Its activities were also legitimized by the UN Security Council. But just as NATO's operations in the former Yugoslavia were concerned with enforcement, ISAF could be seen from a certain perspective as part of the machinery of the west's post-war 'occupation' of Afghanistan rather than 'peacekeeping'. There is also a question to be resolved around NATO's 'proper' area of operations. Yugoslavia was not itself a NATO member, though it was, arguably, located in NATO's area of strategic interest. Afghanistan is not, and NATO's 'out of area' operation there tends to enhance the impression of ISAF as part of the post-war pacification of the country. This is not to say that NATO could not emerge as an effective peacekeeping agency on more traditional patterns. There are signs that it could. For one thing, among its members are some of the most venerable of the UN's middle-power peacekeepers, such as Canada, the Netherlands and Norway. Other members such as Britain, France, Germany and Portugal have also had extensive recent peacekeeping experience. But even taking account of this, NATO's transition from military alliance to multinational peacekeeping agency is as yet some way from complete.

Another potential alternative peacekeeping provider, one much discussed in the first years of the new century, is the European Rapid Reaction Force (ERRF). Agreement to establish the ERRF was reached by the European Union in 1999. It was to be based on earmarked contributions from member countries, which would make up a force of 60,000. This was not to be an 'EU army', but in principle the force could be assembled rapidly from its national components when required. Its primary function was to be a peacekeeping one, and early proposals suggested that it could make a significant contribution in Africa. As in the case of NATO, the ERRF would be able to call on the experience and expertise of long-standing UN force contributors such as Austria, Ireland and Sweden. The ERRF project failed to advance significantly in its first years, however. Part of the problem was that its real purpose was political rather than military. It was not called into being primarily to meet a particular operational need. The Force was supposed to symbolize the ever-advancing process of European integration as the Union widened its membership and deepened its supranational authority in the post-cold war world. As the advance of the broader European project faltered in the new century, especially after the divisions opened up in 2003 over the Iraq war, so the ERRF failed to develop into a viable peacekeeping agent. In the longer term, though, the European Union might offer a real alternative to the United Nations as a peacekeeping provider. But its prospects will be conditioned by the balance that the EU achieves between its institutional authority and the individual national interests of its member states. The EU, much more than the UN or even NATO, remains a work in progress in this regard. In the first years of the twenty-first century the balance perhaps did not lie sufficiently on the side of the institution for a basis for successful peacekeeping to be in place. In this situation the ERRF's performance – most especially perhaps in Africa where European national post-colonial interests can still frequently collide – could be fatally compromised.

However the twenty-first century ends for peacekeeping, its early years suggest that the United Nations will continue to occupy a central position in its provision for some time. Various types of partnership will continue to develop, whether in the form of joint deployments, legitimization of other agencies' operations or the encouragement of 'coalitions of the willing'. Political factors, resource limitations or both would, however, seem to ensure that it will take some time for other actors to establish themselves as autonomous, alternative providers of peacekeeping.

Images of peacekeeping in the twenty-first century: the Brahimi Report

The United Nations cannot be accused of institutional complacency in the face of these and other uncertainties facing peacekeeping in the new century. Within the organization the shortcomings of aspects of peacekeeping in the 1990s, and the extent to which these contributed to major failures, has been widely acknowledged. Institutional failure is, as we have repeatedly emphasized, only one part of a story that is determined to a great extent by the national policies of the big powers. The capacity of the United Nations itself to shape the politics of its dominant members is very limited. Within the range of reform and revision available to it, however, the UN has been far from inactive. At the beginning of the book we made reference to the Brahimi Report, which was presented to the United Nations in 2000.[3] This was the fruit of a 'high level panel' investigation set in motion by secretary-general Kofi Annan. Chaired by UN under-secretary-general and former Algerian foreign minister Lakhdar Brahimi, the panel of ten senior diplomats and military officers was set the task of producing a 'comprehensive review of the whole question of peacekeeping operations in all their aspects'.

In contrast to Boutros-Ghali's *An Agenda for Peace* eight years previously, which was concerned with broad principles for post-cold war peacekeeping, the Brahimi report dealt in precise and often technical detail with the UN's efforts at the end of the 1990s, and made very specific recommendations to improve them. A number of key points in the report, however, touched on long-unresolved dilemmas for the broader politics of peacekeeping. These have resonated across the decades since the 'ideal' conditions of the first Suez deployment in 1956 failed to replicate themselves for later operations. How can peacekeeping operate in environments where there is no stable peace to keep? What is the proper relationship between 'preventive diplomacy' and peacekeeping? How is the necessary consent of parties to be managed? What is the proper extent of the use of force in peacekeeping? What are the rights and responsibilities of contributing states? How should peacekeeping mandates be formulated? Finally, what are the prospects for the 'regionalized' peacekeeping of the type we have just discussed?

Reviewing the post-cold war experience of peacekeeping, Brahimi observed that peacekeepers have been concerned with conditions 'where conflict has not resulted in victory for any side . . . operations thus do not deploy into post-conflict situations so much as they deploy to create such situations'.[4] This was undoubtedly the case in the majority of UN commitments in the 1990s and in several before then. Differing responses to such circumstances by peacekeepers and their political overlords in the Security Council contributed to the disastrous outcomes for operations from Somalia to Bosnia to Rwanda. There was no clear doctrine setting out the relationship between the different components – military and political – of peace missions. The report proposed a much closer integration of peacekeeping as an operational activity and the political process of peace-building (or peacemaking).

As we have seen, the mismatch between the military and political processes is not a uniquely post-cold war phenomenon. Cyprus provides one of the starkest examples of successful peacekeeping and unsuccessful peacemaking. But the relative stability that Cyprus enjoyed (at least after 1974), even in the absence of a long-term settlement of its problems, was untypical of the much more volatile and violent conditions in other later theatres of peacekeeping. The intensity of peacekeeping activity in the post-cold war period therefore exacerbated the basic problem. But in a sense there should never have become a problem. Peacekeeping developed in the 1950s as a component part of what Dag Hammarskjöld characterized as 'preventive diplomacy'. The deployment of international military forces in this sense was part – and not necessarily an essential one – of a larger international process. Like much else to do with peacekeeping, this model did not bear the test of time. Soon, peacekeeping became a first line of international crisis management rather than a phase in a larger diplomatic strategy. The Brahimi report urged what in effect would be a partial return to the original approach (though it did so without acknowledging the historical precedent). The language in 2000 was not that of 'preventive diplomacy' but of 'conflict prevention'. It amounted to much the same thing, however. 'Prevention', the report stated, 'is clearly far more preferable for those who would otherwise suffer the consequences of war, and is less costly for the international community than military action, emergency humanitarian relief or reconstruction after a war has run its course'.[5] This overall strategy of prevention, Brahimi argued, must be based on the integration of the efforts of the UN with those of other international actors. Specifically, the UN itself should engage in 'the more frequent use of fact-finding missions to areas of tension. . .'.[6] The recommendation was an important one, but it was not novel. It was a reaffirmation of the value of older approaches and practices that, if properly implemented, could help revive the peacekeeping project as articulated half a century earlier.

One of the central requirements of peacekeeping operations laid down in that earlier time, which has survived perhaps better than others, is that of 'host state consent' – or in the context of intra-state peacekeeping, consent by the parties. According to this principle, operations cannot be mounted without at least the acquiescence of the state on whose territory it will operate or that of the factions in a civil conflict. Once again, Suez provided an unsatisfactory original template for this. In the next large operation after UNEF, in the Congo, the consent of the host state was freely given; that state then promptly imploded leaving the UN holding the ring. Elsewhere, as in the former Yugoslavia and Angola, for example, consent although initially forthcoming became at best grudging as UN operations did not produce the preferred outcomes of the host state. At the extreme, as we have seen in some African operations, forces have deployed in circumstances where a meaningful host state simply did not exist. The Brahimi report did not propose any fundamental departure from the principle of consent, but it did qualify its absolute importance. 'Consent', the report noted, 'may be manipulated in many ways by the local parties.'[7] But, once deployed, peacekeepers have irreducible responsibilities, which they should discharge regardless. While initial consent of the parties involved in a conflict must remain a condition for deployment, attempts to place conditions on it or to restrict the freedom of initiative of the UN force must be resisted.

Here the crucial issue of the use of force arises. If the parties are to attempt to obstruct the peacekeepers for whatever reason, how is the UN to respond? In one of the more controversial (and important) parts of the report, the panel urged a new 'robustness'. Forces must be equipped and authorized to defend themselves and those under their protection. UN forces should not 'cede the initiative to their attackers'. In this regard the report makes an extremely important distinction between 'impartiality' and 'neutrality' in peacekeeping. Impartiality must:

> mean adherence to the principles of the Charter and to the objectives of a mandate . . . Such impartiality is not the same as neutrality or equal treatment of all parties in all cases for all time, which can amount to a policy of appeasement. In some cases, local parties consist not of moral equals but of obvious aggressors and victims, and peacekeepers may not only be operationally justified in using force but morally compelled to do so.[8]

This was a passage haunted by the ghosts of Rwanda and Srebrenica. Its adoption as a principle of peacekeeping in the twenty-first century, however, will be conditional on its acceptance by two crucial constituencies: the permanent members of the Security Council who determine mandates and the member states who are required to carry them out. Faced with a repeat of the circumstances in Rwanda in 1994, would the big powers take a different course of action in the future? The optimistic answer would be that another 'Rwanda' is unlikely to follow in the wake of another 'Somalia', and therefore the context would be different; the 'right' decisions would not be subverted by the still open wounds of the recent past. And, of course, shame and guilt will always have a part in shaping future behaviour. But on the pessimistic side lies the inescapable fact that big powers have their own perceptions of their own interests, which will shift from time to time and from place to place but which will always shape their judgements about international responsibilities.

The role of the contributing states in determining new approaches to the use of force comes at the next stage. Even with a mandate permitting 'all necessary means', will these means be used if they threaten the safety of UN soldiers on the ground? Perceptions of national interest are obviously involved here, too. Brahimi's answer to this perhaps lacked necessary 'realism' (in both the routine and theoretical senses of the word). When seeking troops for peacekeeping the secretary-general:

> must be able to make the case that troops contributors and indeed all member States have a stake in the management and resolution of the conflict, if only as part of the larger enterprise of establishing peace that the United Nations represents.[9]

This emphasis on the interconnectedness of national interests is obviously admirable as an approach to international responsibilities, but it would not have been easy to convince Dutch public opinion that it was in the interests of the Netherlands for its soldiers to have been killed fighting off Bosnian Serbs in defence of Bosnian Muslims at Srebrenica. It was far from clear that UN member states, whether as permanent members of the Security Council or as force contributors, were any more inclined to see UN troops involved in 'robust' peacekeeping at the beginning of the twenty-first century than they had been in the middle of the twentieth.

Central to the degree of force that peacekeepers will be required to use, of course, is the specific job that they have been deployed to undertake. The question of force mandates has from the outset been at the heart of the peacekeeping experience and is the greatest single determinant of a mission's success or failure. The earliest UN operations in Palestine and Kashmir were set the quite straightforward task of monitoring ceasefires. Although the UN's first major force, established for Suez in 1956, had wider, interpositionary functions, these were clearly defined and, in the particular diplomatic setting of the operation, easily performed. It was in the Congo in the early 1960s that the question of the peacekeeping mandate first arose as a political and operational 'problem' – and it did so in dramatic form. The uncertain and shifting responsibilities of the peacekeepers in the Congo derived from a sequence of changing Security Council mandates. These moved from the original one of interposition between Congolese and Belgian forces at the beginning to the enforced ending of Katangan secession at the endgame. On the way confusion and resentment was created among force contributors and, more damagingly, among the permanent members of the Security Council. Later, the UN force in Lebanon, which had been established in the twilight of détente, was soon forced to operate in the environment of the second cold war and was consistently denied a mandate that would have given it a significant role in the unfolding crisis in the 1980s. In 1994 the Rwanda genocide was carried out against the background of the Security Council's refusal to change the mandate (and enhance the resources) of the UN force already deployed in the country in a way that would have permitted it to intervene. Earlier, in Angola in 1991, another class of mandate problem had arisen when the second verification mission was charged with implementing a deeply flawed peace plan that the UN itself had played no part in arranging. These were operations in which the mandate question had particularly grave consequences, but it has been an issue for many more UN undertakings both before and after the end of the cold war.

Brahimi's proposal to meet the type of problem that had arisen in Angola was that the United Nations should demand and verify that 'certain minimum standards' were present in peace agreements if it was to participate in their implementation. To this end UN 'adviser-observers' should be present during the negotiations that produce such peace plans.[10] Where the United Nations itself is responsible for the mandate, the report proposed a number of ways in which the prospects of successful execution could be improved. The UN secretariat should not 'self-censor' when planning operations by proposing 'what it presumes to be acceptable to the [Security] Council politically'. UN members 'must not be led to believe they are doing something useful for countries in trouble when . . . they are most likely agreeing to a waste of human resources, time and money'.[11] Force contributors should have an input into the formulation – and alteration – of mandates as well as the secretariat and Security Council, in order to reduce the risk of initial misperceptions leading to damaging consequences on the ground. Finally, the report warned implicitly of the dangers of over-compensation after Rwanda through the imposition of a blanket mandate on UN forces requiring them to protect all civilians in all circumstances. This was not a practical possibility and the 'potentially large mismatch between desired objective and resources available to meet it raises the prospect of continuing disappointment . . .'.[12] It is probably the case, though, that Brahimi was preaching to the already converted in the matter of mandates. The lesson may have taken some time to learn after the Congo operation in the early 1960s, but the problems generated by mandates that were either ambiguous or simply unachievable were too obvious to ignore after the mid-1990s.

Despite the many experiments in multi-agency peacekeeping in the 1990s, which we have discussed in some detail, the panel dealt in a surprisingly cursory manner with the question of non-UN peacekeeping. In contrast to Boutros-Ghali in *An Agenda for Peace* in 1992, Brahimi saw little potential for peacekeeping by regional organizations in the near future. While acknowledging the value of inter-agency cooperation in the areas of conflict preventions and post-conflict peace-building, the report was doubtful about extending this to peacekeeping as such. The panel did not engage with the manifest political obstacles to regional peacekeeping; its concerns were practical ones. Caution was appropriate 'because military resources and capability are unevenly distributed around the world, and troops in the most crisis-prone areas are often less prepared for the demands of modern peacekeeping than is the case elsewhere'.[13] Instead, the capacity of all states to contribute to United Nations operations can be enhanced by the provision of training and equipment. The peacekeeping project, the report seemed to suggest, should remain a primarily systemic rather than a sub-systemic one, though participation in it should be facilitated and encouraged in all parts of the system.

It is unlikely that this could be the last word on the issue. At the beginning of the twenty-first century there are strong forces at the centre pushing peacekeeping out for regional attention. Simultaneously, there are peripheral forces tending to pull peacekeeping provision away from direct UN responsibility. The spiralling costs of peacekeeping and the increasing difficulty in enlisting sufficient contributing states makes the regionalization of peacekeeping no less attractive to the UN in the mid-2000s than it was in the mid-1990s. There is little sign that these practical imperatives are likely to disappear. Meanwhile, provision of peacekeeping has become in a sense a rite of passage for regional organizations, a mark of their effectiveness and legitimacy. This organizational mindset was evident among the security institutions of post-cold war Europe in the early 1990s and soon became prevalent among African and other regional bodies, as we have seen. It is a reasonably safe prediction that the global–regional balance will be one of the most important facets of the politics of peacekeeping in the years to come.

The Brahimi panel was commissioned to look forward. Its task was to propose ways and means of sustaining the peacekeeping efforts of the United Nations in the new century after the problems and pressures it had been subjected to in the last decade of the old one. But a reading of the report has the effect of underlining the long narrative of peacekeeping, one which, although given a new tone by the end of the cold war, begins many decades earlier. The key political problems faced by peacekeeping in the new century were posed in particularly acute form in the 1990s, but they first arose long previously. Peacekeeping where there is no peace was an issue in the 1990s, certainly, and caused difficulties for the UN from Bosnia to Somalia; but it was as much of a problem in the Congo three decades earlier. Similarly, the necessity of properly integrating the peacekeeping function with the larger conflict resolution process was as evident in Cyprus in the 1960s and 1970s as it was in Africa in the 1990s. And so it goes on, in relation to the consent of parties, the degree of force permissible in peacekeeping and the critical importance of properly formulated mandates. It was principally the peculiar intensity of peacekeeping demand and supply in the 1990s rather than the emergence of a distinctly 'new' peacekeeping that required the hard thinking that has taken place over the past decade or so.

Just as the problems facing the provision of peacekeeping speak as much of continuity as they do of recent change, so the essential political purposes of peacekeeping also remain largely the same after the cold war as before it. Clearly, the configuration of the international system at any particular time will have an impact on the immediate aims of peacekeeping. The fundamental alteration of the political and territorial disposition of Europe after the First World War required international forces to serve particular purposes. The rapid growth of states in the international system that came with decolonization after 1945 demanded a particular type of peacekeeping. The cold war meant that peacekeeping had an especially important 'immunizing' role. The interlude of détente in the system meant that in the 1970s peacekeeping became to an extent an instrument of superpower cooperation. The huge changes in international relations brought by the end of bipolarity presented peacekeeping with new immediate purposes, such as the dismantling and re-ordering of state frontiers and the management of conflicts previously controlled by the superpowers in their own spheres of influence. The destruction that threatened a number of African states at a particular economic and political conjuncture in the post-independence period imposed yet another requirement on international peacekeeping. But through all of these different phases and conditions there runs a thread. Whatever the precise terms of any crisis that called for a peacekeeping response, and whatever the specific aims of that response, the underlying purpose has always been the same. It has been to stabilize an international system that, more than four centuries after the Treaty of Westphalia, still has as its basic unit the sovereign, territorial state. Despite the current pressures on this long-standing structure of international relations, and it is undeniable that the disparate processes of globalization are imposing real pressures, the fundamental purpose of peacekeeping remains unchanged in the first decade of the twenty-first century.

Maps

Source of maps: US Central Intelligence Agency

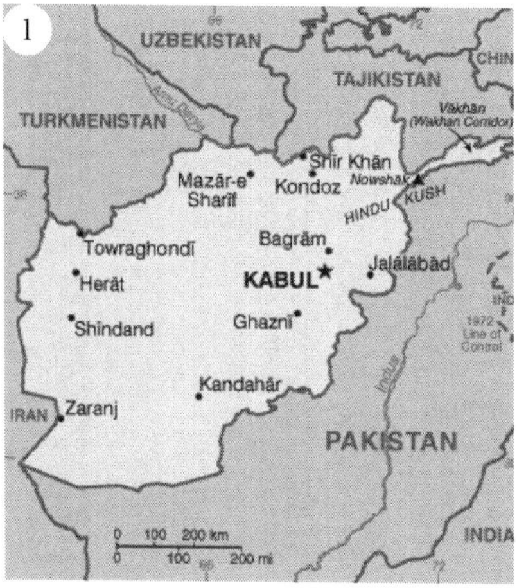
1
UZBEKISTAN
TAJIKISTAN
TURKMENISTAN
Vākhān (Wakhan Corridor)
Mazār-e Sharīf
Kondoz
Shīr Khān
Nowshak
HINDU KUSH
Towraghondī
Bagrām
KABUL
Jalālābād
Herāt
Shīndand
Ghaznī
Kandahār
IRAN
Zaranj
PAKISTAN
INDIA
Indus
1972 Line of Control
0 100 200 km
0 100 200 mi

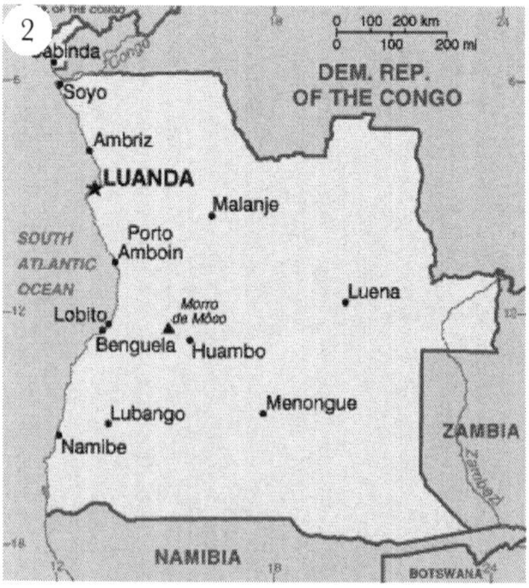
2
0 100 200 km
0 100 200 mi
DEM. REP. OF THE CONGO
Congo
Cabinda
Soyo
Ambriz
LUANDA
Malanje
SOUTH ATLANTIC OCEAN
Porto Amboin
Luena
Lobito
Morro de Môco
Benguela
Huambo
Lubango
Menongue
Namibe
ZAMBIA
Zambezi
NAMIBIA
BOTSWANA

3
40 km
20 40 mi
CROATIA
Sava
Danube
Prijedor
Bosanski Brod
Bihać
Republika Srpska
Brčko
Banja Luka
SER. AND MONT.
Tuzla
Zenica
CROATIA
SARAJEVO
Republika Srpska
Federation of Bosnia and Herzegovina
Goražde
Mostar
Maglić
SERBIA AND MONTENEGRO
Adriatic Sea
CROATIA
ALB.

4
THAILAND
LAOS
Sisŏphŏn
Siemréab
Stœ̆ng Trêng
Bătdâmbâng
Tonle Sap
Mekong
Pŏuthĭsăt
Kâmpóng Chhnăng
Krâchéh
Phnum Aôral
Kâmpóng Cham
Krŏng Kaôh Kŏng
PHNOM PENH
VIETNAM
Kâmpóng Saôm
Kâmpôt
Gulf of Thailand
0 50 100 km
0 50 100 mi
South China Sea

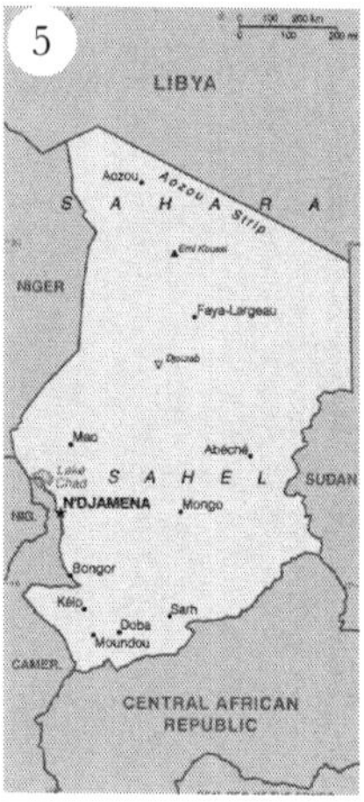
5
LIBYA
Aozou Strip
S A H A R A
NIGER
Faya-Largeau
Abéché
S A H E L
SUDAN
N'DJAMENA
Mongo
Bongor
Sarh
Doba
Moundou
CENTRAL AFRICAN REPUBLIC

6
AUSTRIA
HUNGARY
SLOVENIA
Danube
ZAGREB
SER. AND MONT.
Sisak
Osijek
Rijeka
Vukovar
Omišalj
Pula
BOSNIA AND HERZEGOVINA
Zadar
Dinara
Šibenik
Split
Adriatic Sea
Dugi Rat
Ploče
SER. AND MONT.
Dubrovnik
ITALY
0 30 60 km
0 30 60 mi

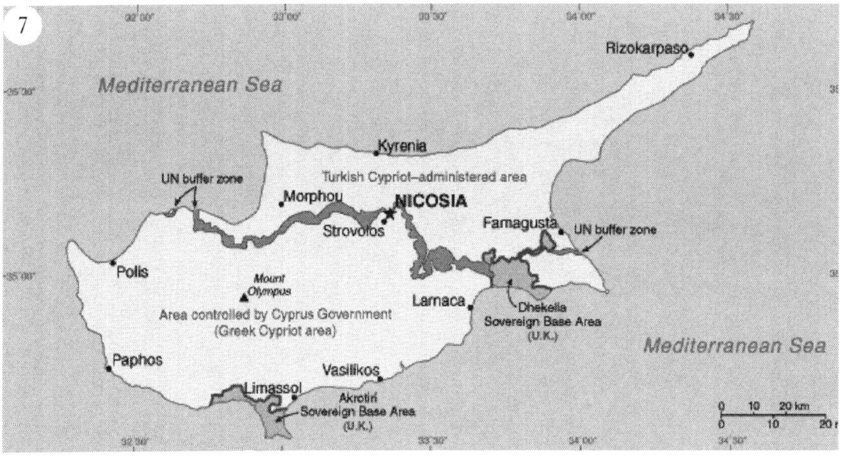
7
Mediterranean Sea
Rizokarpaso
Kyrenia
UN buffer zone
Turkish Cypriot–administered area
Morphou
NICOSIA
Strovolos
Famagusta
UN buffer zone
Polis
Mount Olympus
Larnaca
Dhekelia Sovereign Base Area (U.K.)
Area controlled by Cyprus Government (Greek Cypriot area)
Mediterranean Sea
Paphos
Vasilikos
Limassol
Akrotiri Sovereign Base Area (U.K.)
0 10 20 km
0 10 20

8
C.A.R.
SUDAN
CAMER.
Gbadolite
Congo
Bumba
REP. OF THE CONGO
Kisangani
Pic Marguerite
UG.
Equator
Mbandaka
GABON
Goma
RW.
Bukavu
Kindu
BURU.
ANG.
KINSHASA
Ilebo
Matadi
Kikwit
Kananga
Mbuji-Mayi
TANZ.
Boma
Banana
Tshikapa
Kalemie
Lake Tanganyika
ANGOLA
Kolwezi
Likasi
Lubumbashi
0 200 400 km
0 200 400 mi
ZAMBIA

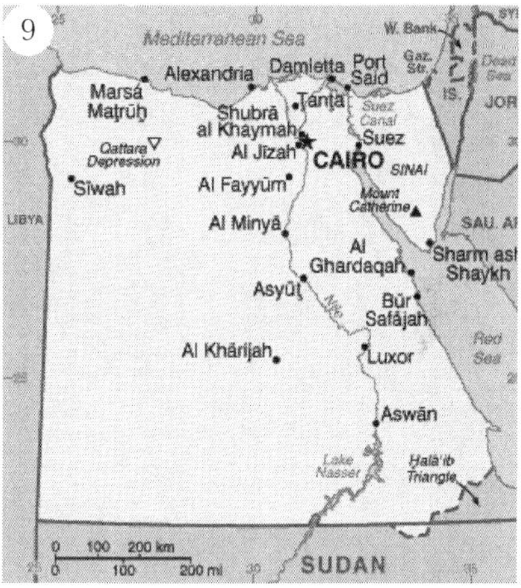
9
Mediterranean Sea
W. Bank
Gaz. Str.
Dead Sea
IS.
JOR.
Alexandria
Damietta
Port Said
Marsá Maţrūḩ
Ţanţā
Suez Canal
Shubrā al Khaymah
Suez
Qattara Depression
Al Jīzah
CAIRO
SINAI
Sīwah
Al Fayyūm
Mount Catherine
LIBYA
Al Minyā
SAU. AR.
Al Ghardaqah
Sharm ash Shaykh
Asyūţ
Nile
Būr Safājah
Red Sea
Al Khārijah
Luxor
Aswān
Lake Nasser
Ḩalā'ib Triangle
0 100 200 km
0 100 200 mi
SUDAN

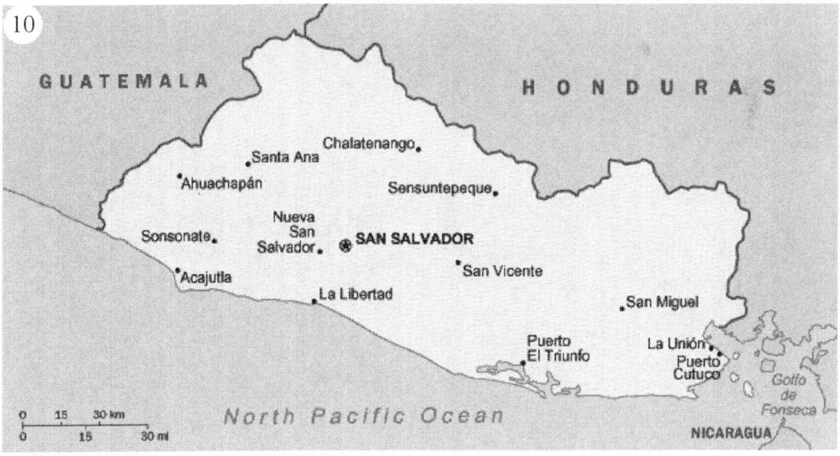
10
GUATEMALA
HONDURAS
Chalatenango
Santa Ana
Ahuachapán
Sensuntepeque
Nueva San Salvador
SAN SALVADOR
Sonsonate
San Vicente
Acajutla
La Libertad
San Miguel
Puerto El Triunfo
La Unión
Puerto Cutuco
Golfo de Fonseca
0 15 30 km
0 15 30 mi
North Pacific Ocean
NICARAGUA

11

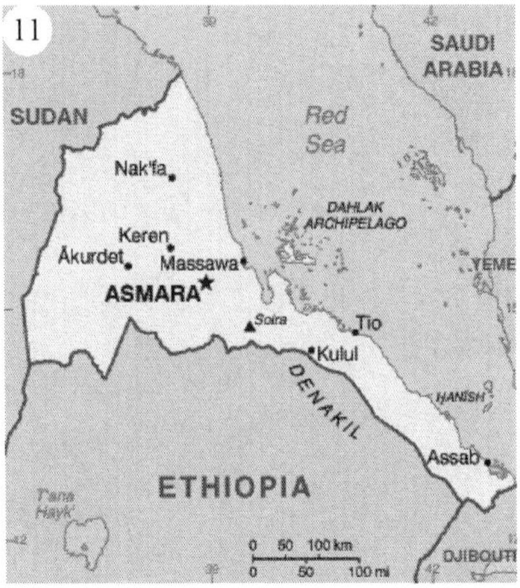
SAUDI ARABIA
SUDAN
Red Sea
Nak'fa
DAHLAK ARCHIPELAGO
Keren
Åkurdet
Massawa
ASMARA
Soira
Tio
Kulul
DENAKIL
HANISH
Assab
ETHIOPIA
T'ana Hayk'
0 50 100 km
0 50 100 mi
DJIBOUTI

12

0 20 40 km
0 20 40 mi
ABKHAZIA
GREATER CAUCASUS MOUNTAINS
RUSSIA
Mt'a Shkhara
Sokhumi
Zugdidi
SOUTH OSSETIA
KOLKHET'IS DABLOBI
K'ut'aisi
Black Sea
P'ot'i
Sup'sa
Ts'khinvali
Pankisi Gorge
Mtkvari
Gori
LESSER CAUCASUS MTS.
TBILISI
Bat'umi
AJARIA
Akhalts'ikhe
Rust'avi
Akhalk'alak'i
TURKEY
ARMENIA
AZERBAIJAN

13

MEXICO
Flores
BELIZE
0 50 100 km
0 50 100 mi
Bahía de Amatique
Lago de Izabal
Puerto Barrios
Cobán
Huehuetenango
Quetzaltenango
Zacapa
Mazatenango
GUATEMALA
HONDURAS
Champerico
Puerto San José
Puerto Quetzal
North Pacific Ocean
EL SALVADOR

14

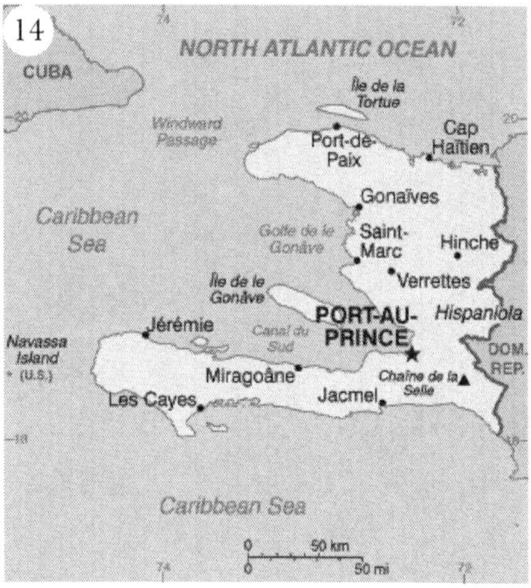
NORTH ATLANTIC OCEAN
CUBA
Île de la Tortue
Windward Passage
Port-de-Paix
Cap Haïtien
Gonaïves
Caribbean Sea
Golfe de la Gonâve
Saint-Marc
Hinche
Verrettes
Île de la Gonâve
Jérémie
PORT-AU-PRINCE
Hispaniola
Canal du Sud
Navassa Island (U.S.)
Miragoâne
Chaîne de la Selle
DOM. REP.
Les Cayes
Jacmel
Caribbean Sea
0 50 km
0 50 mi

15
VIETNAM
THAILAND
Gulf of Thailand
PHILIPPINES
Philippine Sea
South China Sea
NORTH PACIFIC OCEAN
BRUNEI
MALAYSIA
MALAYSIA
Pulau Ligitan
Pulau Sipadan
Celebes Sea
Medan
SINGAPORE
Borneo
Pekanbaru
Equator
Kalimantan
Sumatra
Sulawesi (Celebes)
Biak
Palembang
IRIAN JAYA
Puncak Jaya
Ambon
Java Sea
Makassar
JAKARTA
Semarang
Madura
Cirebon
Java
Surabaya
Banda Sea
INDIAN OCEAN
Cilacap
Denpasar
Kupang
EAST TIMOR
Arafura Sea
Timor Sea
0 200 400 km
0 200 400 mi
AUSTRALI

16
TURKEY
unnamed peak
Arbil
Mosul
As Sulaymaniyah
SYRIA
Kirkuk
IRAN
Buhayrat ath Tharthar
Samarra
BAGHDAD
Ar Ramadi
Ar Rutbah
Buhayrat ar Razazah
Tigris
Karbala
Al Kut
An Najaf
Euphrates
An Nasiriyah
Al Basrah
Umm Qasr
SAUDI ARABIA
KUWAIT
Persian Gulf
0 50 100 km
0 50 100 mi

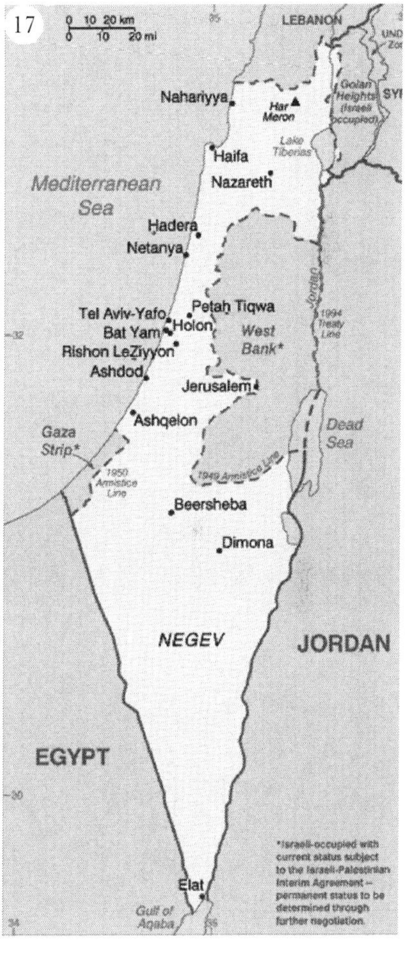
17
0 10 20 km
0 10 20 mi
LEBANON
Nahariyya
Har Meron
Golan Heights (Israeli occupied)
SYRIA
Lake Tiberias
Haifa
Nazareth
Mediterranean Sea
Hadera
Netanya
Jordan
Petah Tiqwa
Tel Aviv-Yafo
Holon
West Bank*
Bat Yam
1994 Treaty Line
Rishon LeZiyyon
Ashdod
Jerusalem
Ashqelon
Dead Sea
Gaza Strip*
1950 Armistice Line
1949 Armistice Line
Beersheba
Dimona
NEGEV
JORDAN
EGYPT
*Israeli-occupied with current status subject to the Israeli-Palestinian Interim Agreement – permanent status to be determined through further negotiation.
Elat
Gulf of Aqaba

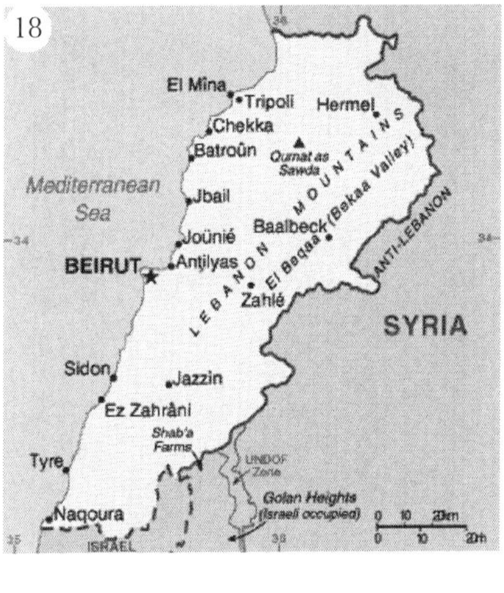
18
El Mina
Tripoli
Hermel
Chekka
Batroûn
Qurnat as Sawda
LEBANON MOUNTAINS
Mediterranean Sea
Jbail
Baalbeck
El Beqaa (Bekaa Valley)
ANTI-LEBANON
Joûnié
BEIRUT
Antilyas
Zahlé
SYRIA
Sidon
Jazzin
Ez Zahrâni
Shab'a Farms
Tyre
UNDOF Zone
Golan Heights (Israeli occupied)
Naqoura
ISRAEL
0 10 20km
0 10 20mi

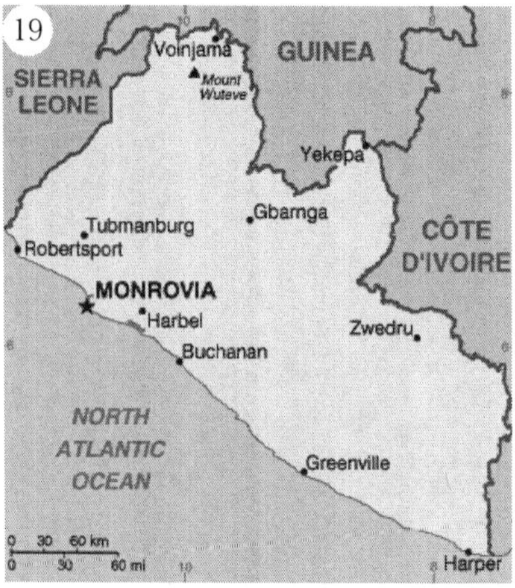
19
GUINEA
SIERRA LEONE
Voinjama
Mount Wuteve
Yekepa
Gbarnga
Tubmanburg
Robertsport
CÔTE D'IVOIRE
MONROVIA
Harbel
Buchanan
Zwedru
NORTH ATLANTIC OCEAN
Greenville
Harper
0 30 60 km
0 30 60 mi

20
20 40 km
20 40 mi
SERBIA AND MONTENEGRO
Kumanovo
BULGARIA
Tetovo
SKOPJE
Golem Korab
Gostivar
Veles
Štip
Vardar
Kičevo
Strumica
Prilep
Lake Dojran
Lake Ohrid
Lake Prespa
Bitola
ALBANIA
GREECE
Aegean Sea

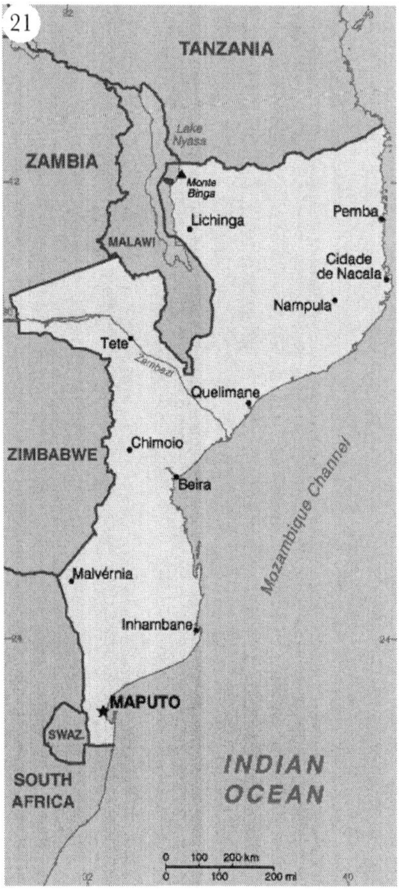
21
TANZANIA
Lake Nyasa
ZAMBIA
Monte Binga
Lichinga
Pemba
MALAWI
Cidade de Nacala
Nampula
Tete
Zambezi
Quelimane
Chimoio
ZIMBABWE
Beira
Mozambique Channel
Malvérnia
Inhambane
MAPUTO
SWAZ.
SOUTH AFRICA
INDIAN OCEAN
0 100 200 km
0 100 200 mi

22
ANGOLA
ZAMBIA
Katima Mulilo
Ondangwa
Rundu
Namib
Grootfontein
Swakopmund
Gobabis
Walvis Bay
WINDHOEK
BOTSWANA
Kalahari Desert
Desert
South Atlantic Ocean
Rehoboth
Lüderitz
Keetmanshoop
Karasburg
SOUTH AFRICA
0 100 200 km
0 100 200 mi

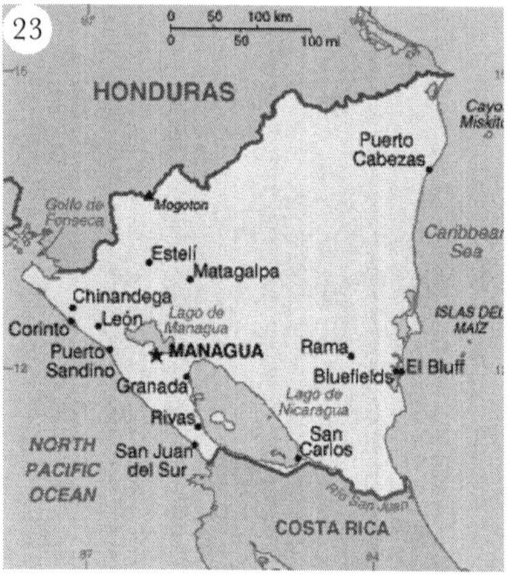
23
0 50 100 km
0 50 100 mi
HONDURAS
Cayo Miskito
Puerto Cabezas
Golfo de Fonseca
Mogoton
Caribbean Sea
Estelí
Matagalpa
Chinandega
ISLAS DEL MAIZ
Corinto
León
Lago de Managua
Puerto Sandino
MANAGUA
Rama
El Bluff
Bluefields
Granada
Lago de Nicaragua
Rivas
San Carlos
NORTH PACIFIC OCEAN
San Juan del Sur
Río San Juan
COSTA RICA

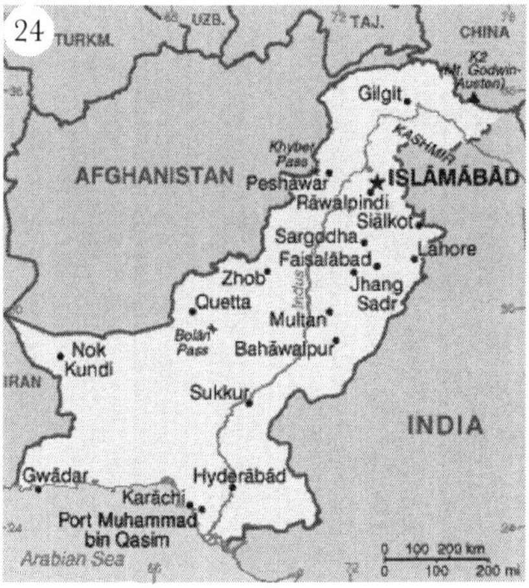

24

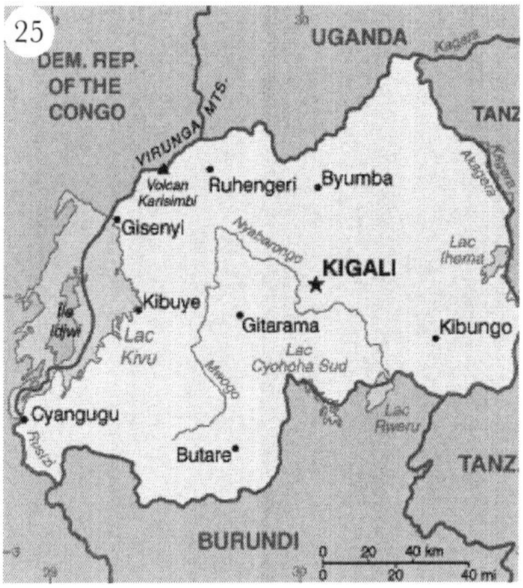

25

26

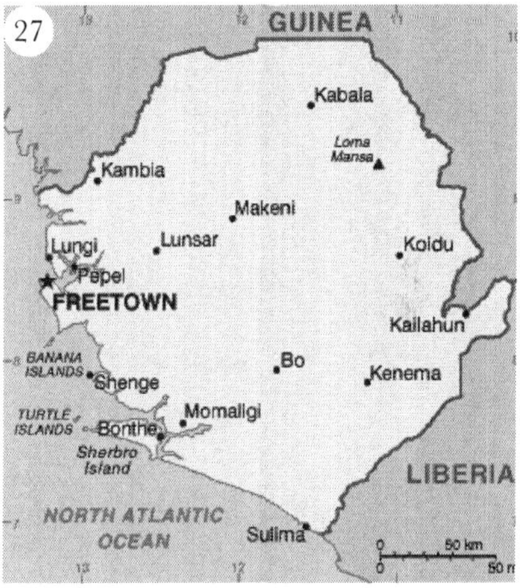

27

28

29

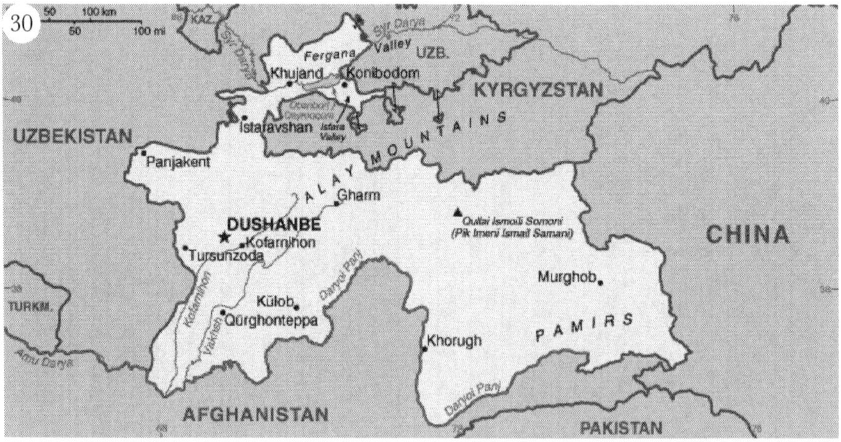
30
50 100 km
50 100 mi
KAZ.
Fergana Valley
UZB.
Khujand
Konibodom
KYRGYZSTAN
Istaravshan
UZBEKISTAN
Panjakent
ALAY MOUNTAINS
Gharm
DUSHANBE
Kofarnihon
Tursunzoda
Qullai Ismoili Somoni
(Pik Imeni Ismail Samani)
CHINA
Murghob
TURKM.
Kūlob
Qūrghonteppa
Khorugh
PAMIRS
Amu Darya
Daryoi Panj
AFGHANISTAN
PAKISTAN

31
Canary Islands
(SPAIN)
MOROCCO
Laayoune
(El Aaiún)
Semara
Cabo Bojador
Bu Craa
ALGERIA
North Atlantic Ocean
Guelta Zemmur
Ad Dakhla
MAURITANIA
Bir Gandús
0 100 200 km
0 100 200 mi

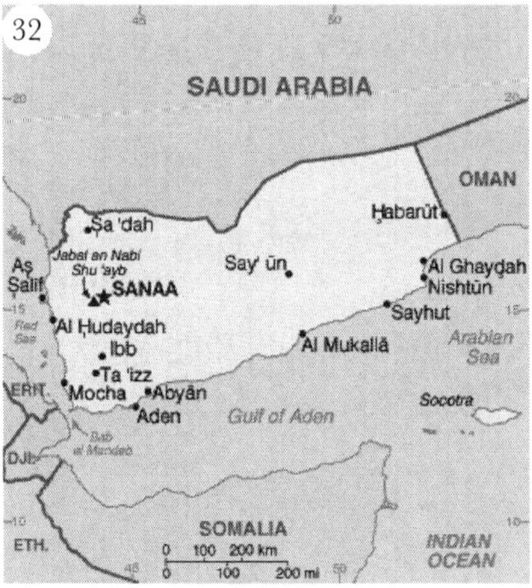
32
SAUDI ARABIA
OMAN
Ḩabarūt
Şa 'dah
Jabal an Nabī Shu 'ayb
Aş Şalīf
SANAA
Say' ūn
Al Ghayḑah
Nishtūn
Sayhut
Al Ḩudaydah
Ibb
Al Mukallā
Arabian Sea
Ta 'izz
Mocha
Abyān
Aden
Gulf of Aden
Socotra
ERIT.
DJI.
SOMALIA
ETH.
0 100 200 km
0 100 200 mi
INDIAN OCEAN

Notes

1 The dimensions of international peacekeeping

1 Alan James, *The Politics of Peacekeeping* (London: Chatto & Windus, 1969), p. 9.
2 'Report of the Panel on United Nations Peace Operations' issued as United Nations Documents A/55/305 (General Assembly); S/2000/809 (Security Council), 21 August 2000, paragraph 12.
3 Among the more prominent cold war era American works on peacekeepers were: A. M. Cox, *Prospects for Peacekeeping* (Washington DC: Brookings Institute, 1967); Larry Fabian, *Soldiers without Enemies* (Washington DC: Brookings Institute, 1973); D. W. Wainhouse *et al.*, *International Peacekeeping at the Crossroads* (Baltimore MD: Johns Hopkins University Press, 1973). It is interesting that the leading British writer on peacekeeping of this time, Alan James, is much more alert to its pre-1939 manifestations. See Alan James, *The Politics of Peacekeeping* (already cited in note 1) and *Peacekeeping in International Politics* (London: Macmillan, 1990).

2 Peacekeeping before the UN

1 Kissinger's fascination with the European concert system and its contemporary relevance went back to his doctoral thesis which was later published as *A World Restored: Metternich, Castlereagh and the Problems of Peace 1812–22* (Boston MA: Houghton Mifflin, 1957).
2 Bourgeois outlined his basic theories in his 1896 book, *Solidarité*. He lived to see his vision realized in the League of Nations of which he remained an enthusiastic partisan until his death in 1925.
3 The Fourteen Points in their entirety can be found at www.yale.edu/lawweb/avalon/wilson14.htm.
4 The Covenant of the League of Nations can be found at fletcher.tufts.edu/multi/www/league-covenant.html.
5 The mandate system was covered by article 22 of the Covenant. Turkey's possessions in the Middle East were mandated to Britain and France. Germany's African empire was mandated to Britain, France and South Africa, and the administration of its Pacific territories passed to Australia, New Zealand and Japan. The United Nations, which inherited responsibility for the system, redefined mandated territories as 'trusteeships'.
6 General Assembly document A/AC.21/W.18, 22 January 1948.
7 Treaty of Versailles, article 109. The text of the Versailles treaty can be found at www.yale.edu/lawweb/avalon/imt/menu.htm.
8 The Klagenfurt plebiscite was covered by article 49 of the Treaty of St Germain. The terms of the treaty can be found at www.austlii.edu.au/au/other/dfat/treaties/1920/3.html.

9 F. P. Walters, *A History of the League of Nations* (Oxford: Oxford University Press, 1960), p. 146.
10 Treaty of Versailles article 49. Found at www.yale.edu/lawweb/avalon/imt/menu.htm. The fifteen-year period of international administration began in 1920 when the treaty came into force.
11 Walters, *History of the League of Nations*, p. 586.
12 Ibid., p. 592.

3 Collective security revived

1 The full text of the Atlantic Charter can be found at www.yale.edu/lawweb/avalon/wwii/atlantic.htm.
2 Quoted in Amos Yoder, *The Evolution of the United Nations System* (3rd edition, London: Taylor & Francis, 1993), p. 26.
3 Roosevelt in particular was unhappy at what he saw as an assault on the basic principle of the General Assembly, at one point threatening to press for representation for the (then) forty-eight individual states of the United States if the Soviets persisted in their demands for seats for each of their republics.
4 The United Nations Charter can be found at http://www.un.org/aboutun/charter/.
5 The Palais des Nations in Geneva did, however, house the UN's European office and continued as the headquarters of a number of the specialized agencies associated with the organization.
6 Security Council resolution S/RES/82 (1950), 25 June 1950.
7 Security Council resolution S/RES/83 (1950), 27 June 1950. The resolution 'recommended' that 'Members of the United Nations furnish such assistance to the Republic of Korea as may be necessary to repel the armed attack and to restore international peace and security'.
8 Security Council Resolution S/RES/85 (1950), 31 July 1950.
9 Combat units were contributed by: Australia, Canada, Belgium, Colombia, Ethiopia, France, Greece, Luxembourg, the Netherlands, New Zealand, the Philippines, Thailand, Turkey, South Africa, Britain and the United States. Denmark, Italy, Norway and Sweden supplied medical units.
10 Interestingly, this was the essence of the strategy adopted by the United States and its allies nearly half a century later to justify the invasion of Iraq in 2003 when it became clear that the Security Council would not pass a new resolution explicitly permitting military action.
11 General Assembly Resolution GA/RES/377A, 3 November 1950.

4 Peacekeeping resumed

1 The Trusteeship arrangements that supplanted the League's mandate system was embodied in Chapter XII (Articles 75–85) of the Charter.
2 General Assembly Resolution G/RES/181 (II), 29 November 1947. Britain abstained on this vote.
3 Security Council resolution S/RES/48, 23 April 1948.
4 Security Council resolution S/RES/50, 29 May 1948.
5 See Security Council Resolution S/RES/47 (1948), 21 April 1948.
6 Security Council Resolution S/RES/118 (1956), 13 October 1956.
7 Security Council Documents S/3710, 30 October 1956 and S/3713/Rev.1, 30 October 1973.
8 General Assembly Resolution G/RES/997 (ES-I), 2 November 1956.
9 Report to the General Assembly by the secretary-general. A/3289, 4 November 1956 and A/3302, 6 November 1956.

10 The contributors of initial contingents were Brazil, Canada, Colombia, Denmark, Finland, India, Indonesia, Norway, Sweden and Yugoslavia.
11 General Assembly Document A/3943, 9 October 1958.
12 Quoted in Larry Fabian, *Soldiers without Enemies* (Washington DC: Brookings Institute, 1973), p. 94.

5 Peacekeeping as immunization

1 Request from the Government of Congo, Security Council Document S/4382, 12 July 1960.
2 Security Council Resolution S/RES/143 (1960), 14 July 1960.
3 Security Council Document S/4523, 17 September 1960.
4 General Assembly Document A/PV.869, 23 September 1960.
5 Ibid.
6 Ibid.
7 General Assembly Document A/1498, 22 November 1960.
8 Security Council Resolution S/RES/161 (1961), 21 February 1961.
9 Security Council Resolution S/RES/169 (1961), 24 November 1961.
10 Article 2 paragraph 7 of the Charter states that: '(n)othing contained in the present Charter shall authorize the United Nations to intervene in matters which are essentially within the domestic jurisdiction of any state . . .'.
11 Two years later, in 1966, France withdrew from the 'unified command' of NATO and henceforward was not generally regarded as a full member of the alliance.
12 Security Council Resolution S/RES/186 (1964), 4 March 1964.
13 'Certain expenses of the United Nations (Article 17, paragraph 2 of the Charter), Advisory Opinion of 20 July 1962', *ICJ Reports* 1962. The opinion was reached by a nine to five majority of the judgment panel.
14 Article 19 of the Charter states that a 'Member of the United Nations which is in arrears in the payment of its financial contributions to the Organization shall have no vote in the General Assembly if the amount of its arrears equals or exceeds the amount of the contributions due from it for the preceding two full years. The General Assembly may, nevertheless, permit such a Member to vote if it is satisfied that the failure to pay is due to conditions beyond the control of the Member.'
15 Security Council Resolution S/RES/359 (1964), 15 August 1964.
16 Security Council Resolution S/RES/128 (1958), 11 June 1958.
17 Security Council Document S/4055/Rev.1, 22 July 1958.
18 Security Council Resolution S/RES/179 (1963), 11 June 1963.
19 Article 40 states that in 'order to prevent an aggravation of [a] situation, the Security Council may . . . call upon the parties concerned to comply with such provisional measures as it deems necessary or desirable. Such provisional measures shall be without prejudice to the rights, claims, or position of the parties concerned. The Security Council shall duly take account of failure to comply with such provisional measures.'
20 Security Council Resolution S/RES/211(1965), 20 September 1965.
21 'West New Guinea' is one of a number of names given to the territory. It has also been known by thc Bahasa Indonesia names: 'Irian Barat' and more commonly, 'Irian Jaya'. It has recently been officially named 'Papua' by Indonesia in acknowledgement of local sentiments. 'West New Guinea' was however the name used most commonly in the United Nations in the 1960s.
22 The settlement was embodied in General Assembly Resolution A/RES/1752(XVII), 20 September 1962.

6 Peacekeeping and détente

1 Security Council Resolution S/RES/242 (1967), 22 November 1967.
2 Security Council Resolution S/RES/338 (1973), 22 October 1973.
3 Security Council Resolution S/RES/340 (1973), 25 October 1973. Interestingly, this resolution stated explicitly that the composition of the force should 'except the Permanent Members of the Security Council' thus making specific one of the characteristics of peacekeeping first set out by Hammarskjöld in the Summary Study.
4 Anthony Verrier, *International Peacekeeping: United Nations Forces in a Troubled World* (Harmondsworth Middlesex: Penguin, 1981), p. 106.
5 The Polish contribution balanced that of NATO member Canada. The contribution of both was primarily to the logistical side of the operation.
6 Security Council Resolution S/RES/350 (1974), 31 May 1974.
7 Security Council Resolution S/RES/425 (1978), 19 March 1978.
8 Security Council Document S/2000/460, 22 May 2000.

7 New horizons

1 General Assembly Resolution A/RES/ES-6/2, 14 January 1980.
2 This did not come until the end of October 1980 with the adoption of Security Council Resolution S/RES/622 (1988), 31 October 1988.
3 Security Council Resolution S/RES/479 (1980), 28 September 1980.
4 Security Council Resolution S/RES/598 (1988), 20 July 1988.
5 Security Council Resolution S/RES/619 (1988), 9 August 1988.
6 Security Council Resolution S/RES/660 (1990), 2 August 1990.
7 Security Council Resolution S/RES/678 (1990), 29 November 1990.
8 Security Council Resolution S/RES/689 (1991), 9 April 1991.
9 Security Council Resolution S/RES/806 (1993), 5 February 1993.
10 ONUCA was established by Security Council Resolution S/RES/644 (1989), 7 November 1989.
11 The joint undertaking was known as the Esquipulas II Agreement.
12 Security Council Resolution S/RES/650 (1990), 27 March 1990.
13 Security Council Resolution S/RES/693 (1991), 20 May 1991.
14 Security Council Resolution S/RES/717 (1991), 16 October 1991.
15 UNTAC had been formally established by Security Council Resolution S/RES/745 (1992), 28 February 1992.
16 *An Agenda for Peace: Preventive Diplomacy, Peacemaking and Peacekeeping*. Issued as United Nations Documents S/24111 (Security Council) and A/47/277 (General Assembly), 17 June 1992, paragraph 8.
17 Ibid., paragraph 43.
18 Ibid., paragraphs 44–5.
19 Ibid., paragraph 64.
20 Ibid., paragraph 69.
21 Ibid., paragraph 71.
22 Ibid., paragraph 51.
23 *Supplement to An Agenda for Peace: Position Paper of the Secretary-General on the Fiftieth Anniversary of the United Nations*. Issued as United Nations Documents S/1995/1 (Security Council) and A/50/60 (General Assembly), 3 January 1992, paragraph 103.
24 The force was legitimized by Security Council Resolution S/RES/1264 (1999), 15 September 1999.
25 Security Council Resolution S/RES/1272 (1999), 25 October 1999.
26 UNTAET website found at www.un.org/peace/etimor/UntaetB.htm.
27 Security Council Resolution S/RES/1410 (2002), 17 May 2002.

8 The break-up of Yugoslavia and the Soviet Union

1 Security Council Resolution S/RES/743 (1992), 21 February 1992.
2 Three UNPAs were established in Eastern Slavonia, Western Slavonia and Krajina.
3 Security Council Resolution S/RES/776 (1992), 14 September 1992.
4 Security Council Resolution S/RES/770 (1992), 13 August 1992.
5 The flight ban was imposed by Security Council Resolution S/RES/781 (1992), 9 October 1992.
6 Security Council Resolution S/RES/816 (1993), 31 March 1993.
7 Spiros Economides and Paul Taylor, 'Former Yugoslavia', in Mayall, J. (ed.), *The New Interventionism 1991–1994: United Nations Experience in Cambodia, Former Yugoslavia and Somalia* (Cambridge: Cambridge University Press, 1996), p. 80.
8 Quoted in Shashi Tharoor, 'United Nations peacekeeping in Europe', *Survival*, vol. 37 no. 2, 1995, p. 125.
9 UN member states were authorized 'acting through or in cooperation with [NATO] to establish a multinational force under unified command in order to fulfil . . . the Peace Agreement'. Security Council Resolution S/RES/1031 (1995), 15 December 1995.
10 The social and political chaos that came with the end of Albania's particularly extreme Communist state in fact led to one of the more unusual 'peacekeeping' interventions in the region. In 1997 Italy, which was in the front line of waves of Albanian refugees, sought and received Security Council approval to create a 'Multinational Protection Force' in Albania. See Security Council Resolution S/RES/1101 (1997), 28 March 1997.
11 The background to the unwieldy title of 'Former Yugoslav Republic of Macedonia' gives an indication of the persistence of historical sensitivities in the Balkan region. Greece insisted on this formulation, objecting to the new state being known simply as 'Macedonia' on the grounds that this would give the impression that it constituted the ancient territory of that name rather than a portion of it.
12 Security Council Resolution S/RES/795 (1992), 11 December 1992.
13 In December 1991, as the Soviet Union broke up, the CIS was formed by the former Soviet republics of: Armenia, Azerbaijan, Belarus, Georgia, Kazakhstan, Kyrgyzstan, Moldova, Russia, Tajikistan, Turkmenistan, Ukraine and Uzbekistan. The three Baltic republics of the USSR – Estonia, Latvia and Lithuania – also became independent but declined to participate in the CIS, looking instead towards western Europe for their new international identity.
14 Security Council Resolution S/RES/858 (1993), 24 August 1993.
15 Security Council Resolution S/RES/937 (1994), 21 July 1994.
16 See the secretary-general's report on the situation in Security Council Document S/2001/59, 18 January 2001.
17 Security Council Resolution S/RES/1138 (1997), 14 November 1997.

9 Africa I

1 UNASOG was established by Security Council Resolution S/RES/915 (1994), 4 May 1994.
2 Kofi Annan of Ghana had succeeded Boutros Boutros-Ghali as secretary-general in 1997. The United States had refused to support the customary second five-year term for Boutros-Ghali.
3 Security Council Resolution S/RES/1320 (2000), 15 September 2000.
4 The other former German colonies in Africa that were mandated to the allies and effectively attached to their own empires were: Tanganyika (modern-day

Tanzania) to Britain; Rwanda and Burundi to Belgium; Togoland and Cameroon, which were divided between Britain and France.

5 Security Council Resolution S/RES/276 (1970), 30 January 1970. Britain and France abstained on the resolution but did not veto it.

6 'Legal Consequences for States of the Continued Presence of South Africa in Namibia (South West Africa) Notwithstanding Security Council Resolution 276 (1970)', International Court of Justice Advisory Opinion, 21 June 1971. Found at www.icj-cij.org/icjwww/idecisions/isummaries/inamsummary710621.htm.

7 Security Council Resolution S/RES/435 (1978), 29 September 1978.

8 Security Council Resolution S/RES/629 (1989), 16 January 1989.

9 SWAPO took 57.32% of the vote against the DTA's 28.55%. This translated into 41 and 21 seats respectively in the 72-seat new national parliament.

10 Security Council resolution S/RES/626 (1988), 20 December 1988.

11 The name 'Polisario' is derived from the movement's full Spanish title Frente Popular para a Liberación de Saguia el-Hamra y Río de Oro.

12 Security Council Resolution S/RES/690 (1991), 29 April 1991.

13 Secretary-General's Report on the Situation in Western Sahara, Security Council Document S/2004/827, 20 October 2004.

14 The Bicesse 'Acordos de Paz' were issued as United Nations Document S/22609, 17 May 1991.

15 Security Council Resolution S/RES/696 (1991), 30 May 1991. The 'first' UNAVEM had just completed its task of overseeing the Cuban withdrawal.

16 The UN electoral team had registered five million voters in a few frantic months, and in September 1992 the elections for the 220-seat National Assembly were held with a turnout of 91 per cent. The MPLA was the clear winner with 129 seats against UNITA's 70. In the first round of the presidential contest dos Santos took almost 50 per cent of the vote against Savimbi's 40 per cent.

17 Security Council Resolution S/RES/864 (1993), 15 September 1993.

18 Security Council Resolution S/RES/976 (1995), 8 February 1995.

19 Security Council Resolution S/RES/1118 (1997), 30 June 1997.

20 Security Council Resolution S/RES/782 (1992), 13 October 1992 appointed a special representative for Mozambique and authorized the despatch of an advance party of military observers to the country. The operation in its entirety was established by Security Council Resolution S/RES/797 (1992), 16 December 1992.

21 Frelimo won 149 seats against Renamo's 112 in the 250-seat National Assembly. Chissano won the presidential poll more convincingly with 53 per cent of the vote against Dhlakama's 33 per cent.

22 Security Council Resolution S/RES/872 (1993), 8 October 1993.

23 See Boutros Boutros-Ghali, *Unvanquished: A US-UN Saga* (New York: Random House, 1991), pp. 129–40.

24 Security Council Resolution S/RES/1545 (2004), 21 May 2004.

25 Security Council Resolution S/RES/1125 (1997), 6 August 1997.

26 Security Council Resolution S/RES/1159 (1998), 27 March 1998.

27 *Africa Confidential*, vol. 44 no. 3, February 2003.

28 Security Council Resolution S/RES/1528 (2004), 27 February 2004.

10 Africa II

1 R. H. Jackson, *Quasi-States: Sovereignty, International Relations and the Third World* (Cambridge: Cambridge University Press, 1993).

2 William Reno, *Warlord Politics and African States* (London: Lynne Rienner, 1998).

3 William Shawcross, *Deliver Us from Evil: Warlords and Peacekeepers in a World of Endless Conflict* (London: Bloomsbury, 2000), p. 167.

4 The crisis also brought the secession of the northern part of the country, which had originally formed British Somaliland and which sought to separate itself from the chaos in the south.

5 Boutros Boutros-Ghali, *Unvanquished: A US-UN Saga* (New York: Random House, 1991), pp. 54–5.

6 Security Council Resolution S/RES/775 (1992), 28 August 1992.

7 Security Council Resolution S/RES/794 (1992), 3 December 1992.

8 Security Council Resolution S/RES/837 (1993), 6 June 1993.

9 The text of Presidential Decision Directive No. 25 along with the US state department's official commentary, which was issued with it, can be found in Michael G. MacKinnon, *The Evolution of US Peacekeeping Policy under Clinton: A Fairweather Friend?* (London: Frank Cass, 1999), pp. 125–39.

10 An alternative meaning for the acronym 'ECOMOG' became current in the region at this time: 'Every Car and Moving Object Gone'.

11 Security Council Resolution S/RES/866 (1993), 22 September 1993.

12 Security Council Resolution S/RES/1509 (2003), 19 September 2003.

13 *Africa Confidential*, vol. 45 no. 3, 4 February 2004.

14 Security Council Resolution S/RES/1181 (1998), 13 July 1998.

15 Security Council Resolution S/RES/1270 (1999), 22 October 1999.

16 UN Press Release SC/6789, 24 January 2000.

17 Security Council Document S/1999/790, 15 July 1999.

18 Security Council Resolution S/RES/1258 (1999), 6 August 1999.

19 Security Council Document S/2001/128, 12 February 2001.

20 Security Council Resolution S/RES/1445 (2002), 4 December 2002.

21 Security Council Resolutions S/RES/1493 (2003), 28 July 2003; S/RES/1565 (2004), 1 October 2004. In addition to its military contingents MONUC also included 475 civilian police.

22 Luttwak argued the case for 'positive' non-intervention in local conflicts in an influential article in 1999. Edward N. Luttwak, 'Give war a chance', *Foreign Affairs*, vol. 78 no. 4, 1999, pp. 36–51.

11 Peacekeeping and the international system in the twenty-first century

1 Details of the AU's involvement in Darfur can be found on the AU website at http://www.africa-union.org/DARFUR/homedar.htm.

2 The Sudan mission was established by Security Council Resolution S/RES/1590 (2005), 24 March 2005. The deployment of troops took place only very slowly thereafter, however.

3 'Report of the Panel on United Nations Peace Operations' issued as United Nations Documents A/55/305 (General Assembly); S/2000/809 (Security Council), 21 August 2000.

4 Ibid., paragraph 20.

5 Ibid., paragraph 29.

6 Ibid., paragraph 34.

7 Ibid., paragraph 48.

8 Ibid., paragraph 50.

9 Ibid., paragraph 52.

10 Ibid., paragraph 58.

11 Ibid., paragraph 59.

12 Ibid., paragraph 63.

13 Ibid., paragraph 54.

Bibliography

Abi-Saab, G. *The United Nations Operation in the Congo, 1960–1964* (London: Oxford University Press, 1978).

Aburish, S. K. *Nasser: the Last Arab* (New York: Thomas Dunne Books, 2004).

Acheson, D. *Present at the Creation: My Years in the State Department* (New York: Norton, 1969).

Adebajo, A. *Building Peace in West Africa: Liberia, Sierra Leone, and Guinea-Bissau* (London: Lynne Rienner, 2002).

Adebajo, A. *Liberia's Civil War: Nigeria, ECOMOG, and Regional Security in West Africa* (London: Lynne Rienner, 2002).

Adebajo, A. and Landsberg, C. 'Back to the future: UN peacekeeping in Africa', *International Peacekeeping*, vol. 7 no. 4, 2000, pp. 161–88.

Alaolmoki, N. *Life After the Soviet Union: The Newly Independent Republics of the Transcaucasus and Central Asia* (New York: SUNY Press, 2001).

Alden, C. 'The UN and the resolution of conflict in Mozambique', *Journal of Modern African Studies*, vol. 31 no. 1, 1995, pp. 103–28.

Alden, C. 'Swords into ploughshares? The United Nations and demilitarization in Mozambique', *International Peacekeeping*, vol. 2 no. 2, 1995, pp. 175–93.

Ali, T. M. and Mathews, R. O. *Civil Wars in Africa* (Montreal: McGill-Queen's University Press, 1999).

Allan, J. H. and English, J. A. *Peacekeeping* (New York: Praeger, 1996).

Andersson, H. *Mozambique: A War Against the People* (London: Macmillan, 1992).

Anstee, M. *Orphan of the Cold War: The Inside Story of the Collapse of the Angolan Peace Process, 1992–93* (London: Macmillan, 1996).

Anstee, M. 'Angola: a tragedy not to be forgotten', *The World Today*, vol. 52 no. 7, July 1996, pp. 190–1.

Archer, C. *International Organizations* (3rd edition, London: Routledge, 2001).

Arend, A. C. and Beck, R. J. *International Law and the Use of Force: Beyond the UN Charter Paradigm* (London: Routledge, 1993).

Armstrong, D., Lloyd, L. and Redmond, J. *International Organization in World Politics* (London: Palgrave, 2004).

Ashton, S. R. *In Search of Détente: The Politics of East-West Relations since 1945* (London: Macmillan, 1989).

Baehr, P. R. and Gordenker, L. *The United Nations in the 1990s* (New York: St Martin's Press, 1994).

Bailey, S. D. *The General Assembly of the United Nations* (London: Pall Mall, 1964).

Bailey, S. D. *How Wars End: the United Nations and the Termination of Armed Conflict, 1946–1964* (2 vols) (Oxford: Clarendon Press, 1982).
Bailey, S. D. *The Procedure of the UN Security Council* (2nd edition, Oxford: Clarendon Press, 1988).
Bailey, S. D. *The United Nations: A Concise Political Guide* (London: Macmillan, 1994).
Barnett, M. 'Partners in peace? The UN, regional organizations and peace-keeping', *Review of International Studies*, vol. 21 no. 4, 1995, pp. 411–33.
Barnett, M. *Eyewitness to Genocide: the United Nations and Rwanda* (Ithaca NY: Cornell University Press, 2002).
Baros, M. 'The UN's response to the Yugoslav crisis: turning the UN Charter on its head', *International Peacekeeping*, vol. 8 no. 1, 2001, pp. 44–63.
Bell, C. *The Diplomacy of Détente: The Kissinger Era* (London: Martin Robertson, 1977).
Bell, C. (ed.) *The United Nations and Crisis Management: Six Studies* (Canberra: Australian National University, 1994).
Bellamy, A., Griffin, S. and Williams, P. *Understanding Peacekeeping* (London: Polity, 2004).
Bendiner, E. *A Time for Angels: The Tragicomic History of the League of Nations* (New York: Knopf, 1975).
Bennett, A. L. *International Organization: Principles and Issues* (7th edition, Englewood Cliffs NJ: Prentice Hall, 2001).
Berdal, M. *Whither Peacekeeping* (London: International Institute for Strategic Studies, Adelphi Paper 81, 1993).
Berdal, M. 'Fateful encounter: the United States and UN peacekeeping', *Survival*, vol. 36 no. 1, 1994, pp. 30–50.
Berdal, M. and Leifer, M. 'Cambodia', in Mayall, J. (ed.) *The New Interventionism 1991–1994: United Nations Experience in Cambodia, Former Yugoslavia and Somalia* (Cambridge: Cambridge University Press, 1996), pp. 25–58.
Berman, E. *Managing Arms in Peace Processes: Mozambique* (Geneva: United Nations Institute for Disarmament Research, 1996).
Berman, E. G. and Sams, K. E. *Peacekeeping in Africa, Capabilities and Culpabilities* (Geneva: United Nations Institute for Disarmament Research, 2000).
Berridge, G. R., 'Diplomacy and the Angola-Namibia accords', *International Affairs*, vol. 65 no. 3, 1989, pp. 463–79.
Berridge, G. R. *Return to the UN: UN Diplomacy in Regional Conflicts* (London: Macmillan, 1990).
Beschloss, M. *Kennedy and Khrushchev: the Crisis Years, 1960–1963* (London: Faber & Faber, 1991).
Biermann, W. '"Old" UN peacekeeping and "new" conflicts: some ideas to reduce the troubles of post cold-war peace missions', *European Security*, vol. 4 no. 1, 1995, pp. 39–55.
Bingham, J. *U Thant: the Search for Peace* (New York: Knopf, 1966).
Bloomfield, L. with Bowman, E. H. *International Military Forces: the Question of Peacekeeping in an Armed and Disarming World* (Boston MA: Little Brown, 1964).
Bolton, J. R. 'Wrong turn in Somalia', *Foreign Affairs*, vol. 73 no. 1, 1994, pp. 56–66.
Bourantonis, D. (ed.) *The United Nations in the New World Order: The World Organization at Fifty* (London: Macmillan, 1995).
Boutros-Ghali, B. *An Agenda for Peace* (New York: UN, 1982).
Boutros-Ghali, B. *Unvanquished: a US-UN Saga* (New York: Random House, 1999).
Bowett, D. *United Nations Forces: a Legal Study* (London: Stevens & Sons, 1964).

Boyd, A. *Fifteen Men on a Powder Keg: a History of the UN Security Council* (London: Methuen, 1971).

Boyd, J. M. *Cyprus: Episode in Peacekeeping* (New York: Columbia University Press, 1966).

Boyd, J. *United Nations Peacekeeping Operations: a Military and Political Appraisal* (New York: Praeger, 1971).

Bull, H. (ed.) *Intervention in World Politics* (Oxford: Clarendon Press, 1984).

Bull, O. *War and Peace in the Middle East: the Experiences and Views of a UN Observer* (London: Leo Cooper, 1976).

Burns, A. L. and Heathcote, N. *Peacekeeping by UN Forces from Suez to the Congo* (London: Pall Mall, 1963).

Burns, E. L. M. *Between Arab and Israeli* (London: Harrap, 1962).

Bury, J. 'The UN Iraq-Kuwait Observation Mission', *International Peacekeeping*, vol. 10 no. 2, 2003, pp. 71–88.

Castellino, J. 'Territory and identity in international law: the struggle for self-determination in the Western Sahara', *Millennium: Journal of International Studies*, vol. 28 no. 3, 1999, pp. 523–51.

Clapham, C. 'Ethiopia and Eritrea: the politics of post-insurgency', in Wiseman, J. (ed.) *Democracy and Political Change in Sub-Saharan Africa* (London: Routledge, 1995), pp. 116–36.

Clapham, C. 'Rwanda: the perils of peacemaking', *Journal of Peace Research*, vol. 35 no. 2, 1998, pp. 75–92.

Clarke, W. and Herbst, J. 'Somalia and the future of humanitarian intervention', *Foreign Affairs*, vol. 75 no. 2, 1996. pp. 70–85.

Clarke, W. and Herbst, J. *Learning from Somalia: the Lessons of Armed Humanitarian Intervention* (Boulder CO: Westview, 1997).

Claude, I. L. *The Changing United Nations* (New York: Random House, 1967).

Claude, I. L. *Swords into Plowshares* (London: McGraw Hill, 1984).

Cliffe, L. *The Transition to Independence in Namibia* (London: Lynne Reinner, 1994).

Cohen, H. J. *Intervening in Africa: Superpower Peacemaking in a Troubled Continent* (London: Macmillan, 2000).

Comay, M. *UN Peace-Keeping in the Arab-Israeli Conflict, 1948–1975* (Jerusalem: Hebrew University, 1976).

Cooper, J. M. *Breaking the Heart of the World: Woodrow Wilson and the Fight over the League of Nations* (Cambridge: Cambridge University Press, 2001).

Cortwright, D. and Lopez, G. A. *The Sanctions Decade: Assessing UN Strategies in the 1990s* (London: Lynne Rienner, 2000).

Coulson, J. *Soldiers of Diplomacy: the United Nations, Peacekeeping and the New World Order* (Toronto: University of Toronto Press, 1998).

Cox, A. M. *Prospects for Peacekeeping* (Washington DC: Brookings Institution, 1967).

Crockatt, R. *The Fifty Years War: The United States and the Soviet Union in World Politics 1941–1991* (London: Routledge, 1994).

Crocker, C. *High Noon in South Africa: Making Peace in a Rough Neighbourhood* (New York: Norton, 1993).

Dallaire, R. *Shake Hands with the Devil: the Failure of Humanity in Rwanda* (London: Arrow Books, 2005).

Daniel, D. C. F and Hayes, B. C. (eds) *Beyond Traditional Peacekeeping* (London: Macmillan, 1995).

Dawson, P. *The Peacekeepers of Kashmir: the UN Military Observer Group in India and Pakistan* (London: Hurst, 1994).

Dayal, R. *Mission for Hammarskjold: the Congo Crises* (London: Oxford University Press, 1976).

Dee, M. '"Coalitions of the willing" and humanitarian intervention: Australia's involvement with INTERFET', *International Peacekeeping*, vol. 8 no. 3, 2001, pp. 1–20.

DeLong, K. and Tuckey, S. *Mogadishu!: Heroism and Tragedy* (Westport CT: Praeger, 1994).

Deng, F. M. and Zartman, I. W. *Conflict Resolution in Africa* (Washington DC: Brookings Institution, 1991).

Destexhe, A. and Shawcross, W. *Rwanda and Genocide in the Twentieth Century* (London: Pluto, 1995).

Diehl, P. F. *International Peacekeeping* (Baltimore MD: Johns Hopkins University Press, 1993).

Dobrynin, A. F. *In Confidence: Moscow's Ambassador to America's Six Cold War Presidents* (New York: Times Books, 1995).

Donald, R. *The Polish Corridor and its Consequences* (London: Butterworth, 1991).

Dorn, A. W. and Bell, D. J. H. 'Intelligence and peacekeeping: the UN operation in the Congo, 1960–64', *International Peacekeeping*, vol. 2 no. 1, 1995, pp. 11–33.

Doyle, M. W. *UN Peacekeeping in Cambodia: UNTAC's Civil Mandate* (London: Lynne Rienner, 1995).

Durch, W. 'Building on sand: UN peacekeeping in the Western Sahara', *International Security*, vol. 17 no. 4, 1993, pp. 151–71.

Durch, W. (ed.) *The Evolution of UN Peacekeeping: Case Studies and Comparative Analysis* (New York: St Martin's Press, 1993).

Durch, W. (ed.) *UN Peacekeeping, American Politics and the Uncivil Wars of the 1990s* (New York: St Martin's Press, 1996).

Economides, S. and Taylor, P. 'Former Yugoslavia', in Mayall, J. (ed.) *The New Interventionism 1991–1994: United Nations Experience in Cambodia, Former Yugoslavia and Somalia* (Cambridge: Cambridge University Press, 1996) pp. 59–93.

Erskine, E. A. *Mission with UNIFIL: An African Soldier's Reflections* (London: Hurst, 1989).

Evans, G. *Responding to Crises in the African Great Lakes* (London: Oxford University Press, 1997).

Fabian, L. L. *Soldiers without Enemies: Preparing the UN for Peacekeeping* (Washington DC: Brookings Institution, 1973).

Falk, R. 'The new interventionism and the Third World', *Current History*, November 1999, pp. 370–5.

Farrell, T. 'Sliding into war: the Somalia imbroglio and US army peace operations doctrine', *International Peacekeeping*, vol. 2 no. 2, 1995, pp. 194–215.

Fehrenbach, T. R. *The United Nations in War and Peace* (New York: Random House, 1968).

Fetherston, A. B. *Towards a Theory of United Nations Peacekeeping* (London: Macmillan, 1994).

Findlay, T. *Cambodia: the Legacy and Lessons of UNTAC* (London: Oxford University Press, 1995).

Findlay, T. (ed.) *Challenges for the New Peacekeepers* (London: Oxford University Press, 1996).

Fisas, V. *Blue Geopolitics: United Nations Reform and the Future of the Blue Helmets* (London: Pluto, 1995).

Fleitz, F. H. *Peacekeeping Fiascos of the 1990s: Causes, Solutions, and U.S. Interests* (Westport CT: Praeger, 2002).
Francis, D. J. 'Mercenary intervention in Sierra Leone: providing national security or international exploitation?', *Third World Quarterly*, vol. 20 no. 2, 1999, pp. 319–38.
Freedman, L. (ed.) *Military Intervention in European Conflicts* (Oxford: Blackwell, 1994).
Freeman, C. W. 'The Angola/Namibia Accords', *Foreign Affairs*, vol. 68 no. 3, 1989, pp. 126–41.
Freire, M. R. *Conflict and Security in the Former Soviet Union: the Role of the OSCE* (Aldershot: Ashgate, 2003).
Furley, O. (ed.) *Conflict in Africa* (London: I.B. Tauris, 1995).
Furley. O and May, R. (eds) *Peacekeeping in Africa* (Aldershot: Ashgate, 1998).
Gaddis, J. L. *We Know Now: Rethinking Cold War History* (Oxford: Clarendon Press, 1997).
Gaffen, F. *In the Eye of the Storm: A History of Canadian Peacekeeping* (Toronto: Deneau and Wayne, 1987).
Gardner, A-M. 'Self-determination in the Western Sahara: legal opportunities and political roadblocks', *International Peacekeeping*, vol. 7 no. 2, 2000, pp. 115–38.
Garthoff, R. *Détente and Confrontation: American-Soviet Relations, Nixon to Reagan* (Washington DC: Brookings Institution, 1985).
Gibbs, D. N. 'The United Nations, international peacekeeping and the question of "impartiality": revisiting the Congo operation of 1960', *Journal of Modern African Studies*, vol. 38 no. 3, 2000, pp. 359–82.
Glenny, M. *The Fall of Yugoslavia* (Harmondsworth Middlesex: Penguin, 1996).
Goodrich, L. M., Hambro, E. and Simmons, A. P. *Charter of the United Nations: Commentary and Documents* (New York: Columbia University Press, 1969).
Goodrich, L. M. *The United Nations in a Changing World* (New York: Columbia University Press, 1974).
Goodrich, L. M. and Simmons, A. *The United Nations and the Maintenance of International Peace and Security* (Washington DC: Brookings Institution, 1955).
Gordenker, L. *The UN Secretary-General and the Maintenance of Peace* (New York: Columbia University Press, 1967).
Gordenker, L. and Weiss, T. G. (eds) *Soldiers, Peacekeepers and Disasters* (London: Macmillan, 1991).
Goulding, M. *Peacemonger* (London: John Murray, 2002).
Goulding, M. 'The United Nations and conflict in Africa since the cold war', *African Affairs*, vol. 98 no. 391, 1999, pp. 155–66.
Gourevitch, P. *We Wish to Inform You that Tomorrow we will be Killed with our Families* (London: Picador, 1999).
Gromyko, A. A. *Memories* (London, Hutchinson, 1989).
Halim, O. 'A peacekeeper's perspective of peacebuilding in Somalia', *International Peacekeeping*, vol. 3 no. 2, 1996, pp. 70–86.
Halliday, F. *The Making of the Second Cold War* (London: Verso, 1987).
Hammarskjöld, D. *Markings* (London: Faber & Faber, 1964).
Harbottle, M. *The Impartial Soldier: A Study of the UN Operation in Cyprus* (London: Oxford University Press, 1970).
Harbottle, M. *The Blue Berets: the Story of the United Nations Peacekeeping Forces* (London: Leo Cooper, 1971).
Harbottle, M. and Rikhye, I. J. *The Thin Blue Line: International Peacekeeping and its Future* (New Haven CT: Yale University Press, 1974).

Harrelson, M. *Fires All Around the Horizon: the U.N.'s Uphill Battle to Preserve the Peace* (New York: Praeger, 1989).
Harris, G. *Recovering from Armed Conflicts in Developing Countries* (London: Routledge, 1998).
Hastings, M. *The Korean War* (London: Pan, 2000).
Heininger, J. E. *Peacekeeping in Transition: the United Nations in Cambodia* (New York: Twentieth Century Fund Press, 1994).
Henig, R. *Versailles and After, 1919–1933* (2nd edition, London: Routledge, 1995).
Higgins, R. *United Nations Peacekeeping, 1946–1979: Documents and Commentary (vol. 1: The Middle East; vol. 2: Asia; vol. 3: Africa; vol. 4: The Middle East)* (London: Oxford University Press, 1969–1981).
Hill, S. M. and Malik, S. P. *Peacekeeping and the United Nations* (Aldershot: Dartmouth, 1996).
Hillen, J. *Blue Helmets: the Strategy of UN Military Operations* (London: Brassey's, 1998).
Hirsch, J. L. and Oakley, R. B. *Somalia and Operation Restore Hope: Reflections of Peacemaking and Peacekeeping* (Washington DC: United States Institute for Peace, 1995).
Hiscocks, R. *The Security Council: A Study in Adolescence* (London: Longman, 1973).
Horn, C. von *Soldiering for Peace* (London: Cassell, 1966).
Hoskyns, C. *The Congo since Independence, January 1960–December 1961* (Oxford: Oxford University Press, 1965).
House, A. H. *The U.N. in the Congo: the Political and Civilian Efforts* (Washington DC: University Press of America, 1978).
Howard, M. 'The historical development of the UN's role in international security' in Roberts, A. and Kingsbury, B. (eds) *United Nations, Divided World: the UN's Role in International Relations* (2nd edition, Oxford: Clarendon Press, 1993), pp. 63–80.
Howe, H. 'Lessons of Liberia: ECOMOG and regional peacekeeping', *International Security*, vol. 21 no. 3, 1996/97, pp. 145–76.
Howe, H. M. 'Private security firms and African stability: the case of Executive Outcomes', *Journal of Modern African Studies*, vol. 36 no. 2, 1998, pp. 307–31.
Huband, M. *The Liberian Civil War* (London: Frank Cass, 1998).
Hughes, A. '"Impartiality" and the UN Observation Group in Lebanon, 1958', *International Peacekeeping*, vol. 9 no. 4, 2002, pp. 1–20.
Human Rights Watch, *Angola Unravels: the Rise and Fall of the Lusaka Peace Process* (New York: Human Rights Watch, 1999).
Hume, C. R. *The United Nations, Iran and Iraq: How Peacemaking Changed* (Bloomington IN: Indiana University Press, 1994).
Hutchful, E. *The ECOMOG Experience with Peacekeeping in West Africa* (South African Institute of Strategic Studies Monograph – no date). At www.iss.co.za/Pubs/Monographs/No36/ECOMOG.html.
International Crisis Group Report *Africa's Seven-Nation War*, May 1999. At www.crisisgroup.org/library/documents/report_archive/A400038_21051999.pdf.
International Peacekeeping, vol. 11 no. 1, 2004. Special issue on Peace Operations and Global Order.
Isaacson, W. *Kissinger: A Biography* (London: Faber & Faber, 1992).
Iyob, R. 'The Ethiopian-Eritrean conflict: diasporic vs. hegemonic states in the Horn of Africa, 1991–2000', *Journal of Modern African Studies,* vol. 38 no. 4, 2000, pp. 659–82.

Jackson, R. H. *Quasi-States: Sovereignty, International Relations and the Third World* (Cambridge: Cambridge University Press, 1993).

James, A. *The Politics of Peacekeeping* (London: Chatto & Windus, 1969).

James, A. 'The UN force in Cyprus', *International Affairs*, vol. 65 no. 3, 1989, pp. 481–500.

James, A. 'The United Nations', in Armstrong, D. and Goldstein, E. (eds), *The End of the Cold War* (London: Frank Cass, 1990), pp. 182–95.

James, A. *Peacekeeping in International Politics* (London: Macmillan, 1990).

James, A. *Britain and the Congo Crisis, 1960–63* (London: Macmillan 1996).

Jett, D. C. *Why Peacekeeping Fails* (London: Macmillan, 2000).

Johnstone, D. *Fools' Crusade: Yugoslavia, NATO and Western Delusions* (London: Pluto Press, 2002).

Jones, B. D. *Peacemaking in Rwanda: the Dynamics of Failure* (London: Lynne Rienner, 2001).

Jonson, L. and Archer, C. (eds) *Peacekeeping and the Role of Russia in Euroasia* (Boulder CO: Westview Press, 1996).

Keane, F. *Season of Blood: a Rwandan Journey* (Harmondsworth Middlesex: Penguin, 1996).

Kedourie, E. *Politics in the Middle East* (London: Oxford University Press, 1992).

Keller, E. J. and Rothchild, D. (eds) *Africa in the New International Order: Rethinking State Sovereignty and Regional Security* (London: Lynne Rienner, 1996).

Khrushchev, N. (ed. Strobe Talbott) *Khrushchev Remembers: The Last Testament* (London: André Deutsch, 1974).

Kissinger, H. *Years of Upheaval* (London: Weidenfeld & Nicolson, 1982).

Klinghoffer, A. J. *The International Dimensions of Genocide in Rwanda* (London: Macmillan, 1998).

Kumar, K. (ed.) *Postconflict Elections, Democratization and International Assistance* (London: Lynne Rienner, 1998).

Kuperman, A. J. 'Rwanda in retrospect', *Foreign Affairs* vol. 79 no. 1, 2000, pp. 94–118.

Kyle, K. *The Suez Crisis: Britain's End of Empire* (London: I.B. Tauris, 2002).

Lall, A. *The UN in the Middle East Crisis, 1967* (New York: Columbia University Press, 1968).

Laremont, R. R. (ed.) *The Causes of War and the Consequences of Peacekeeping in Africa* (Westport CT: Greenwood, 2001).

Larus, J. (ed.) *From Collective Security to Preventive Diplomacy: Readings in International Organization and the Maintenance of Peace* (New York: Wiley, 1965).

Lash, J. P. *Dag Hammarskjöld: Custodian of the Brushfire Peace* (London: Cassell, 1962).

Lefever, E. W. *Crisis in the Congo: A United Nations Force in Action* (Washington DC: Brookings Institution, 1965).

Lefever, E. W. *Uncertain Mandate: The Politics of the UN Congo Operation* (Baltimore MD: Johns Hopkins University Press, 1967).

Leffler, M. P. and Painter, D. S. *The Origins of the Cold War: An International History* (London: Routledge, 1994).

Lewis, I. and Mayall, J. 'Somalia', in Mayall, J. (ed.) *The New Interventionism 1991–1994: United Nations Experience in Cambodia, Former Yugoslavia and Somalia,* (Cambridge: Cambridge University Press, 1996), pp. 94–124.

Lie, T. *In the Cause of Peace: Seven Years with the United Nations* (New York: Macmillan, 1954).

Little, A. and Silber, L. *The Death of Yugoslavia* (Harmondsworth: Penguin, 1996).

Litwak, R. *Détente and the Nixon Doctrine: American Foreign Policy and the Pursuit of Stability, 1969–1976* (Cambridge: Cambridge University Press, 1986).
Louis, W. R. and Owen, R. *Suez 1956: The Crisis and its Consequences* (Oxford: Clarendon Press, 1989).
Louis, W. R., Stooky, R. W. and Wilson, R. (eds) *The End of the Palestine Mandate* (London: I. B. Tauris, 1986).
Luard, E. *A History of the United Nations: Vol. I: The Years of Western Domination, 1945–55* (London: Macmillan, 1982).
Luard, E. *A History of the United Nations: Vol. II: The Age of Decolonization, 1955–65* (London: Macmillan, 1989).
Luttwak, E. 'Give war a chance', *Foreign Affairs*, vol. 78 no. 4, 1999, pp. 36–51.
McCoubrey, H. and White, N. D. *International Organizations and Civil Wars* (Aldershot: Dartmouth, 1995).
MacKenzie, L. *Peacekeeper: The Road to Sarajevo* (Toronto: HarperCollins, 1994).
Mackinlay, J. *The Peacekeepers: an Assessment of Peacekeeping Operations at the Arab–Israel Interface* (Boston MA: Unwin Hyman, 1989).
Mackinlay, J. and Alao, A. *Liberia 1994: ECOMOG and UNOMIL Response to a Complex Emergency* (New York: United Nations University Occasional Paper Series 2, 1994).
MacKinnon, M. G. *The Evolution of US Peacekeeping Policy under Clinton* (London: Frank Cass, 1999).
McNulty, M. 'A double discrediting: France, Rwanda and military intervention', *International Peacekeeping*, vol. 4 no. 3, 1997, pp. 24–44.
MacQueen, N. 'National politics and the peacekeeping role: Ireland and the United Nations operations in the Congo', *War & Society*, vol. 6 no. 1, 1988, pp. 93–111.
MacQueen, N. 'Peacekeeping by attrition: the UN in Angola', *Journal of Modern African Studies*, vol. 36 no. 3, 1998, pp. 399–422.
MacQueen, N. *The United Nations since 1945: Peacekeeping and the Cold War* (London: Longman, 1999).
MacQueen, N. *United Nations Peacekeeping in Africa since 1960* (London: Longman, 2002)
Magyar, K. P. and Conteh-Morgan, E. (eds) *Peacekeeping in Africa: ECOMOG in Liberia* (New York: St Martin's Press, 1998).
Malan, M. *Peacekeeping in Africa: Trends and Responses* (South African Institute of Strategic Studies Occasional Paper No. 31, June 1998). At www.iss.co.za/Pubs/PAPERS/31/Paper31.html.
Malaquias, A. 'The UN in Mozambique and Angola: lessons learned', *International Peacekeeping*, vol. 3 no. 2, 1996, pp. 87–103.
Malcolm, N. *Bosnia* (London: Pan, 2002).
Malcolm, N. *Kosovo: A Short History* (London: Pan, 2002).
Martin, I. *Self-determination in East Timor: the United Nations, the Ballot, and the International Intervention* (London: Lynne Rienner, 2001).
Martin, I. and Mayer-Rieckh, A. 'The United Nations and East Timor: from self-determination to state-building', *International Peacekeeping*, vol. 12 no. 1, 2005, pp. 125–45.
May, R. and Cleaver, G. 'African peacekeeping: still dependent?', *International Peacekeeping*, vol. 4 no. 2, 1997, pp. 1–21.
Mayall, J. (ed.) *The New Interventionism 1991–1994: United Nations Experience in Cambodia, Former Yugoslavia and Somalia* (Cambridge: Cambridge University Press, 1996).
Mayall, J. 'Introduction', in Mayall, J. (ed.) *The New Interventionism 1991–1994: United Nations Experience in Cambodia, Former Yugoslavia and Somalia* (Cambridge: Cambridge University Press, 1996) pp. 1–24.

Mays, T. M. *Historical Dictionary of Multinational Peacekeeping* (Lanham MD: Scarecrow Press, 1996).

Mbadinga, M. I. 'The Inter-African mission to monitor the implementation of the Bangui Agreements (MISAB)', *International Peacekeeping*, vol. 8 no. 4, 2001, pp. 21–37.

Melvern, L. *A People Betrayed: the Role of the West in Rwanda's Genocide* (London: Zed Books, 2000).

Miller, L. B. *World Order and Local Disorder: the United Nations and Internal Conflicts* (Princeton NJ: Princeton University Press, 1967).

Miller, R. I. *Dag Hammarskjold and Crisis Diplomacy* (New York: Oceana Publications, 1961).

Moore, J. N. and Morrison, A. *Strengthening the United Nations and Enhancing War Prevention* (Durham NC: Carolina Academic Press, 2000).

Mortimer, R. A. 'Senegal's role in ECOMOG: the Francophone dimension in the Liberian crisis', *Journal of Modern African Studies*, vol. 34 no. 2, 1996, pp. 293–306.

Moskos, C. C. *Peace Soldiers: the Sociology of a United Nations Military Force* (Chicago: University of Chicago Press, 1976).

Murphy, J. F. *The United Nations and the Control of International Violence* (Manchester: Manchester University Press, 1983).

Nassif, R. *U Thant in New York, 1961–1971: a Portrait of the Third UN Secretary-General* (London: Hurst, 1988).

Nicholas, H. G. *The United Nations as a Political Institution* (London: Oxford University Press, 1971).

Nimer, B. *The United Nations Force in the Congo: a Political Analysis* (Washington DC: George Washington University, 1966).

Northedge, F. S. *The League of Nations: its Life and Times, 1920–1946* (Leicester: Leicester University Press, 1985).

O'Ballance, E. *The Congo-Zaire Experience, 1960–1998* (London: Macmillan, 1999).

O'Brien, C. C. *To Katanga and Back: a UN Case History* (London: Hutchinson, 1962).

O'Brien, K. A. 'Military-advisory groups and African security: privatized peacekeeping?', *International Peacekeeping*, vol. 5 no. 3, 1998, pp. 78–105.

Ofuatey-Kodjoe, W. 'Regional organizations and the resolution of internal conflict: the ECOWAS intervention in Liberia', *International Peacekeeping*, vol. 1 no. 3, 1994, pp. 261–302.

Olonisakin, F. 'UN co-operation with regional organizations in peacekeeping: the experience of ECOMOG and UNOMIL in Liberia', *International Peacekeeping*, vol. 3 no. 3, 1996, pp. 33–51.

Olonisakin, F. '"Home-made" African peacekeeping initiatives', *Armed Forces and Society*, vol. 23 no. 3, 1997, pp. 349–72.

Olonisakin, F. *Reinventing Peacekeeping in Africa: Conceptual and Legal Issues in ECOMOG Operations* (The Hague: Kluwer, 2000).

Ostrower, G. *The League of Nations from 1919–1929* (New York: Avery, 1996).

Ovendale, R. *Britain, the United States and the End of the Palestine Mandate 1942–48* (London: Royal Historical Society, 1989).

Ovendale, R. *The Origins of the Arab-Israeli Wars* (London: Longman, 1992).

Padelford, N. *The Financing of Future Peace and Security Operations under the United Nations* (Washington DC: Brookings Institution, 1962).

Paige, G. D. *The Korean Decision* (New York: Collier Macmillan, 1968).

Palin, R.H. *Multinational Military Forces: Problems and Prospects* (London: Oxford University Press, 1995).

Parsons, A. *From Cold War to Hot Peace: UN Interventions 1975–1995* (Harmondsworth Middlesex: Penguin, 1995).

Pearson, L. *Memoirs Vol. 2: 1948–1957* (Toronto: University of Toronto Press, 1973).

Pelcovits, N. A. *The Long Armistice: UN Peacekeeping and the Arab-Israeli Conflict, 1948–1960* (Boulder CO: Westview Press, 1993).

Pereira, Anthony, W. 'The neglected tragedy: the return to war in Angola, 1992–3', *Journal of Modern African Studies*, vol. 32. no. 1, 1994, pp. 1–28.

Peterson, M. J. *The General Assembly in World Politics* (Boston MA: Unwin Hyman, 1986).

Pipes, R. *US-Soviet Relations in the Era of Détente* (Boulder CO: Westview, 1981).

Powaski, R. E. *The Cold War: The United States and the Soviet Union, 1917–1991* (London: Oxford University Press, 1997).

Prendergast, J. *Frontline Diplomacy: Humanitarian Aid and Conflict in Africa* (London: Lynne Rienner, 1996).

Prunier, G. *The Rwanda Crisis, 1954–94* (London: Hurst, 1995).

Prunier, G. *Rwanda in Zaire: From Genocide to Continental War* (London: Hurst, 2000).

Pugh, M. (cd.) *Maritime Security and Peacekeeping: a Framework for United Nations Operations* (Manchester: Manchester University Press, 1994).

Pugh, M. (ed.) *The UN, Peace and Force* (London: Frank Cass, 1997).

Quandt, W. R. *Camp David: Peacemaking and Politics* (Washington DC: Brookings Institution, 1986).

Ratner, S. R. *The New UN Peacekeeping: Building Peace in Lands of Conflict after the Cold War* (London: Macmillan, 1995).

Reno, W. 'Privatizing the war in Sierra Leone', *Current History*, May 1997, pp. 227–30.

Reno, W. *Warlord Politics and African States* (London: Lynne Rienner, 1998).

Rikhye, I. J. *The Theory and Practice of Peacekeeping* (London: Hurst, 1984).

Rikhye, I. J. *Military Advisor to the Secretary-General: U.N. Peacekeeping and the Congo Crisis* (London: Hurst, 1993).

Rikhye, I. J., Harbottle, M. and Egge, B. *The Thin Blue Line: International Peace-Keeping and its Future* (New Haven CT: Yale University Press, 1974).

Roberts, A. 'The crisis in UN peacekeeping', *Survival*, vol. 36 no. 3, 1994, pp. 93–120.

Roberts, A. 'Communal conflict as a challenge to international organization: the case of the former Yugoslavia', *Review of International Studies*, vol. 21 no. 4, 1995, pp. 389–410.

Roberts, A. 'The United Nations: variants of collective security', in Woods, N. (ed.) *Explaining International Relations since 1945* (London: Oxford University Press, 1996), pp. 309–36.

Roberts, A. and Kingsbury, B. (eds) *United Nations, Divided World: the UN's Role in International Relations* (2nd edition, Oxford: Clarendon Press, 1993).

Rogel, C. *The Break-Up of Yugoslavia and its Aftermath* (Westport CT: Greenwood Press, 2004).

Roper, J., Nishihara, M., Otunno, O. and Schoettle, E. *Keeping the Peace in the Post-Cold War Era: Strengthening Multilateral Peacekeeping* (Washington DC: Brookings Institution, 1994).

Rosner, G. *The United Nations Emergency Force* (New York: Columbia University Press, 1963).

Rovine, A. *The First Fifty Years of the Secretary-General in World Politics, 1920–1970* (Leiden: Sijthoff, 1970).

Rumer, B. Z. *Central Asia at the End of the Transition* (London: M. E. Sharp, 2005).
Russell, R. B. *A History of the United Nations Charter* (Washington DC: Brookings Institution, 1958).
Russell, R. B. *United Nations Experience with Military Forces: Political and Legal Aspects* (Washington DC: Brookings Institution, 1964).
Ryan, S. *The United Nations in International Politics* (London: Palgrave, 2000).
Schmidl, E. A. (ed.) *Peace Operations between War and Peace* (London: Frank Cass, 2000).
Schofield, V. *Kashmir in Conflict: India, Pakistan and the Unending War* (London: I. B. Tauris, 2003).
Scott, G. E. *The Rise and Fall of the League of Nations* (London: Macmillan, 1973).
Seyersted, F. *United Nations Forces in the Law of Peace and War* (Leiden: Sijthoff, 1966).
Shawcross, W. *Deliver Us from Evil: Warlords and Peacekeepers in a World of Endless Conflict* (London: Bloomsbury, 2000).
Siekmann, R. C. R. *National Contingents in United Nations Peace-Keeping Forces* (Boston MA: Nijhoff, 1991).
Siilasvuo, E. *In the Service of Peace in the Middle East, 1967–1979* (London: Hurst, 1992).
Simmonds, R. *Legal Problems Arising from the United Nations Military Operations in the Congo* (The Hague: Nijhoff, 1968).
Simons, G. *The United Nations: A Chronology of Conflict* (London: Macmillan, 1994).
Simons, G. *UN Malaise: Power, Problems and Realpolitik* (London: Macmillan, 1995).
Skogmo, B. *UNIFIL: International Peacekeeping in Lebanon, 1978–1988* (London: Lynne Rienner, 1989).
Skold, N. *United Nations Peacekeeping after Suez: the Swedish Involvement* (New York: St Martin's Press, 1996).
Smock, D. R. (ed.) *Making War and Waging Peace: Foreign Intervention in Africa* (Washington DC: US Institute of Peace Press, 1993).
Snow, D. M. *Uncivil Wars: International Security and the New Internal Conflicts* (London: Lynne Rienner, 1996).
Somerville, K. *Foreign Military Intervention in Africa* (London: Pinter, 1990).
Sparks, D. L. *Namibia* (Boulder CO: Westview, 1992).
Staley, R. S. *The Wave of the Future: the United Nations and Naval Peacekeeping* (London: Lynne Rienner, 1992).
Stegenga, J. A. *The United Nations Force in Cyprus* (Columbus OH: Ohio State University Press, 1968).
Stevenson, R. W. *The Rise and Fall of Détente: Relaxations of Tension in US-Soviet Relations, 1953–84* (London: Macmillan, 1985).
Stjernfelt, B. *The Sinai Peace Front: U.N. Peacekeeping Operations in the Middle East, 1973–1980* (London: Hurst, 1992).
Stoessinger, J. G. *The United Nations and the Superpowers* (New York: Random House, 1977).
Stoessinger, J. G. with Rosner, G. *Financing the United Nations System* (Washington DC: Brookings Institution, 1964).
Tabory, M. *The Multinational Force and Observers in the Sinai: Organization, Structure and Function* (Boulder CO: Westview Press, 1986).
Tasier, A. and Mathews, R. O. (eds) *Civil Wars in Africa: Roots and Resolution* (London: McGill-Queen's University Press, 1999).
Thakur, R. C. *International Peacekeeping in Lebanon: United Nations Authority and Multinational Force* (Boulder CO: Westview Press, 1987).
Thakur, R. C. and Thayer, C. A. (eds) *A Crisis of Expectations: UN Peacekeeping in the 1990s* (Boulder CO: Westview Press, 1995).

Tharoor, S. 'United Nations peacekeeping in Europe', *Survival*, vol. 37 no. 2, 1992, pp. 121–34.

Thomas, H. *The Suez Affair* (London: Weidenfeld & Nicolson, 1967).

Tow, W. T. *Subregional Security Co-operation in the Third World* (London: Lynne Rienner, 1990).

Truman, H. *The Years of Decision* (New York: Doubleday, 1956).

Tuck, C. '"Every car or moving object gone". The ECOMOG intervention in Liberia', *African Studies Quarterly*, vol. 4 no. 1, 2000. At web.africa.ufl.edu/asq/v4/v4i1a1.htm.

U Thant *View from the UN: the Memoirs of U Thant* (New York: Doubleday, 1978).

United Nations *The Blue Helmets: A Review of UN Peacekeeping* (3rd edition, New York: United Nations, 1996).

United Nations *The League of Nations 1920–1946: Organization and Accomplishments* (New York: United Nations, 1996).

United Nations *The Report of the Independent Enquiry into the Actions of the United Nations during the 1994 Genocide in Rwanda* (December 1999). At www.ess.uwe.ac.uk/documents/RwandaReport1.htm.

Urquhart, B. *Hammarskjöld* (London: Bodley Head, 1973).

Urquhart, B. *A Life in Peace and War* (London: Weidenfeld & Nicolson, 1987).

Urquhart, B. 'Beyond the "sheriff's posse"', *Survival*, vol. 32 no. 3, 1990, pp. 196–205.

Verrier, A. *International Peacekeeping: United Nations Forces in a Troubled World* (Harmondsworth Middlesex: Penguin, 1981).

Vogt, M. A. 'Co-operation between the UN and the OAU in the Management of African Conflicts', in Malan, M. (ed.) *Whither Peacekeeping in Africa?* (Pretoria: ISS Monograph Series No. 36, 1999) pp. 45–60.

Wainhouse, D. W. (ed.) *International Peace Observation: a History and Forecast* (Baltimore MD: Johns Hopkins University Press, 1966).

Wainhouse, D. W. *International Peacekeeping at the Crossroads: National Support, Experience and Prospects* (Baltimore MD: Johns Hopkins University Press, 1973).

Waldheim, K. *In the Eye of the Storm: A Memoir* (London: Weidenfeld & Nicolson, 1985).

Walker, M. *The Cold War and the Making of the Modern World* (London: Fourth Estate, 1993).

Walters, B. F. and Snyder, J. *Civil Wars, Insecurity and Intervention* (New York: Columbia University Press, 1999).

Walters, F. P. *A History of the League of Nations* (London: Oxford University Press, 1960).

Wambaugh, S. *The Saar Plebiscite* (Cambridge MA: Harvard University Press, 1940).

Warner, D. *New Dimensions of Peacekeeping* (The Hague: Nijhoff, 1995).

Weiss, T. G. *Collective Security in a Changing World* (London: Lynne Rienner, 1993).

Weiss, T. G. *The United Nations and Civil Wars* (London: Lynne Rienner, 1995).

Weissman, S. R. *American Foreign Policy in the Congo, 1960–64* (Ithica NY: Cornell University Press).

Weller, M. and Lauterpacht, E. (eds) *Regional Peacekeeping and International Enforcement: the Liberian Crisis* (Cambridge: Cambridge University Press, 1994).

Wesley, M. *Casualties of the New World Order: The Causes of Failure of UN Missions to Civil Wars* (London: Macmillan, 1997).

Wheeler, N. J. *Saving Strangers: Humanitarian Intervention in International Society* (London: Oxford University Press, 2003).

Whelan, R. *Drawing the Line: the Korean War, 1950–1953* (Boston MA: Little Brown, 1990).
White, N. D. 'The UN Charter and peacekeeping forces: constitutional issues', *International Peacekeeping*, vol. 3 no. 4, 1996, pp. 43–63.
White, N. D. *Keeping the Peace: the United Nations and the Maintenance of International Peace and Security* (2nd edition, Manchester: Manchester University Press, 1997).
Whitman, J. *Peacekeeping and the UN Agencies* (London: Frank Cass, 1999).
Whitman, J. and Pocock, D. *After Rwanda* (London: Macmillan, 1996).
Whittaker, D. J. *The United Nations in Action* (London: UCL Press, 1995).
Whittaker, D. J. *United Nations in the Contemporary World* (London: Routledge, 1997).
Williams, M. *Civil-Military Relations and Peacekeeping* (London: Oxford University Press, 1998).
Woodhouse, T., Bruce, M. and Dando, M. (eds) *Peacekeeping and Peacemaking: Towards Effective Intervention in Post-Cold War Conflicts* (London: Macmillan, 1997).
Woodhouse, T. and Ramsbottom, O. 'Cosmopolitan peacekeeping and the globalization of security', *International Peacekeeping*, vol. 12 no. 2, 2005, pp. 139–56.
Woodward, S. L. *Balkan Tragedy: Chaos and Dissolution after the Cold War* (Washington DC: Brookings Institution, 1995).
Yoder, A. *The Evolution of the United Nations System* (3rd edition, London: Taylor & Francis, 1997).
Zacarias, A. and Chissano, J. A. *The United Nations and International Peacekeeping* (London: I.B. Tauris, 1996).
Zacher, M. W. *Dag Hammarskjöld's United Nations* (New York: Columbia University Press, 1969).
Zacher, M. W. *International Conflict and Collective Security 1946–77: The United Nations, the Organization of American States, the Organization of African Unity and the Arab League* (New York: Praeger, 1979).
Zartman, W. I. (ed.) *Collapsed States: The Disintegration and Restoration of Legitimate Authority* (London: Lynne Rienner, 1995).

Index